Story of the Sharifs and Ibn Saud

by

Ali al-Wardi, Ph.D.

لمحات اجتماعية من
تاريخ العراق الحديث

Translated from Arabic *by* Yasin T. al-Jibouri

Copyrights © 2024 by Yasin T. al-Jibouri

All rights reserved. No part of this publication may be reproduced, distributed, or transmitted in any form or by any means, including photocopying, recording, or other electronic or mechanical methods, without the prior written permission of the publisher, except in the case of brief quotations embodied in critical reviews and certain other non-commercial uses permitted by copyright law. For permission requests, write to the publisher, addressed "Attention: - Permissions (Story of the Sharifs and of Ibn Saud)," at the email address below.

Lantern Publications

info@lanternpublications.com

www.lanternpublications.com

Ordering Information:

Quantity sales. Special discounts are available on quantity purchases by corporations, associations, and others. For details, contact the distributor at the address below.

Shia Books Australia

www.shiabooks.com.au

info@shiabooks.com.au

ISBN: 978-1-922583-65-9

First Edition

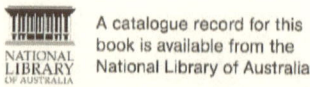

A catalogue record for this book is available from the National Library of Australia

*In the Name of Allāh,
the Most Compassionate, the Most Merciful*

Front cover of Supplement to Vol. Six
(Now Volume Seven)

Translator's Preface

Lantern has already published my English translation of Volume 6 of the eight-Volume book series by Dr. Ali al-Wardi titled لمحات اجتماعية من تاريخ العراق الحديث *Social Glimpses of Iraq's Modern History* and started marketing it through various platfoms, as you can see above, on September 25, 2022.

In 2014, Dar al-Ma'moon publishing house of the Iraqi Ministry of Culture decided to translate the then eight Volumes of this book series to more than one language, starting with English. I was then a member of this Dar's Advisory Committee while Dr. Alaa Abul-Hassan al-Allaq was its able and competent Director, so I attended all meetings relevant to this project which could not go beyond the completion of its first step: A five-member translation committee was formed to undertake the task of translating these Volumes to English, and this was done. The names of these translators selected for this undertaking were as follows: 1) Sawsan Salih Sirriyya, 2) Nadia Fayidh, 3) Yasin al-Jibouri, 4) Mustafa Nassir and 5) the late Kādhim Sa`d ad-Deen. It was also decided to name the Supplement to Volume 6 as Volume 7 due to its large size, and what you are reading is my translation of it. I was assigned the task of translating both Volumes 6 and 7, and this is exactly what I did.

The reader most likely asks about what happened to the English translations of the other Volumes of this series. The answer is available with the author's family. I feel honored and privileged to be able to make these two Volumes available to readers worldwide, and Lantern surely deserves the credit for making this possible.

Yasin T. al-Jibouri

Preface

The rise of the government of Al Saud [the Kingdom of Saudi Arabia] and the collapse of the Sharifs' government in Hijaz [then the Kingdom of Hijaz][1] were accompanied by serious changes that impacted the Islamic world in general and the Arab area in particular.

The effects of those serious changes have remained standing out up to now despite the passage of time and the multitude of storms through which this region has passed.

Due to the significance of this book from the historic and social standpoint, and due to the interest of the Arab reader in the Gulf in al-Wardi's works, particularly in this Volume, we have decided to issue this book independently so the reader, who is interested in this geographical area—the Arabian Peninsula—rather than any other, may acquire this book without the need to buy the entire [eight-Volume] book series of the *Social Glimpses of Iraq's Modern History*.

---

1 I, the Translator of this work, have added many statements to the text of my translation in order to clarify its meaning. I hope you will find them useful.

Contents

Translator's Preface	ix
Preface	xi
Introduction	1
The Feud Between Al-Husain and Ibn Saud	1
Syria's Events	2
Sharifs and the Society	3
The Green Turban	6
Dreams' Pillar	8
Chapter One: Mecca's Sharifs	12
Mecca's Sharifs	13
Mecca's Sharifdom Established	14
Abul-Futooh	15
The Hashemites	18
Qatadah	19
Hummaydhah Ibn Abu Nami	23
Abu Nami II	26
Sectarianism In Hijaz	28
From the Sequels to the Najaf Conference	31
War Against Wahhabis	33
Egyptian Campaign	38
Between Awn and Zaid	41
Awn Al-Rafeeq	45
Chapter Two: Al-Husain Ibn Ali	52
Al-Husain Ibn Ali	53
Early Life	53
Al-Husain Appointed Sharif	56
His Arrival at Mecca	58
Al-Husain's Activity	61

With Ibn Saud	62
The Aseer Campaign	66
The Beginning of Dispute With the Turks	68
The Start of Communication With the British	71
Cloth Merchant Ali Azghar	73
Faisal's Delegation	76
Mcmahon's Correspondence	79
Between What Is Hidden and What Is Apparent	81
Faisal the Actor	83
Another Theatrical Play	85
Revolution Declared	87

Chapter Three: Sharifi Rule In Syria ... 90
Sharifi Rule In Syria ... 91

The First Events	92
The Looting In Damascus	96
Between Faisal and Allenby	98
An Incident In Aleppo	100
Faisal In France	102
Faisal In England	105
The Weizmann-Faisal Agreement	107
His Return to Paris	117
What Happened During the Conference?	119
Investigation Committee Appointed	122
Between Faisal and [Felix] Frankfurter	124
Faisal's Return	127
Syrian [National] Congress	130
Propaganda Warfare	132
France-Britain Agreement	135
A Plan For a Treaty	137
Enthusiasm In Syria	139
Gen. Gouraud	141
Exciting News	143
Faisal's Return	144
Another Attempt	148

Contents

Faisal's Coronation 150
A Noise In Beirut 152
The Rikabi Administration 154
The Atassi Administration 156
Massacre at the Amil Mountain 158
Gouraud's Warning 161
The Uprising of the Masses 166
The Uprising Escalates 169
The Shift to War 172
The Battle of Maysalun 176
The Expulsion of the King 178
After the Expulsion 181
Strange Opinion 184
The Gap Between People and Government 186
Evaluating Faisal 189

Chapter Four: Al-Husain as King 194
Al-Husain as King 195
Al-Husain's Character 195
From the Family's Heritage 198
Bedouins' Mutiny 200
The Turba Incident 204
A Crisis In London 209
Al-Husain's Complex 211
Lawrence's Negotiations 212
Dr. Naji Al-Aseel 217
Al-Husain and Sons 222
Al-Husain In Trans-Jordan 224
Al-Husain As Caliph 227

Chapter Five: Abdul-Aziz ibn Saud 230
Abdul-Aziz ibn Saud 231
Early Life 231
Success Factors 233
The Rise of the Ikhwan 235

Story of the Sharifs and Ibn Saud

Conducive Opportunity	240
Invasion Postponed	241
The Riyadh Conference	242
The Jordan Raid	244
The Taif Incident	246
Al-Husain Abdicates	248
The Fall of Mecca	253
Ibn Saud Hesitates	256
Mecca's Scholars Consent	257

Chapter Six: Ali's Days as King 260

Ali's Days as King 261

The Defense Line	261
Persistent Al-Aseel	265
Philby Mediates	268
Sayyid Talib's Mediation	271
Al-Rayhani's Mediation	273
Activity of the Soviet Union's Consul	274
Story of the Planes	278
Story of the Armored Vehicles	281
The March 14 Battle	282
Residents' Condition	284
Jidda's Notables	285
The Soldiers' Story	287
How the Surrender Took Place	290
Ibn Saud Enters Jidda	294

Chapter Seven: Al-Husain's Last Years 296

Al-Husain's Last Years 297

Where He Stayed	297
Aid Sent	301
The Aqaba Problem	303
Al-Husain In Cyprus	308
The Complaint to the League of Nations	310
What Storrs Says	314

His Last Days 316
Poets Wander 318

Chapter Eight: Ibn Saud Suffers From Problems 324
Ibn Saud Suffers From Problems 325
Allegiance For Ibn Saud 325
The New Society 329
Al-Baqee` Graves Demolished 332
Incident's Echo In Iraq 335
During the Pilgrimage Season 340
Islamic Conference Held 344
Egyptian Delegation's Conference Activity 345
Ibn Saud's Dilemma 351
Faisal Al-Duweesh: 355
The Ikhwan Attack Iraq 358
The Riyadh Conference 361
The Revolt of the Ikhwan 364
The Ikhwan Crushed 366
Problem of the Sheikhs 368
Lobbin Meeting 373
Yemen's War 375
War's Echo In Iraq 379
An Attempt to Assassinate Ibn Saud 380
From Hardship to Prosperity 382
His Wives and Children 385
Philby 388

Conclusion 396
History Lessons 397
Between the Past and the Present 398
The Human Nature: 400

Introduction

This research I have written as an Appendix for Volume Six of my book series titled *Social Glimpses of Iraq's Modern History*, but it in reality fits to be an Appendix for all Volumes of this book series, the previous ones and the ones to follow. It discusses events that took place in Hijaz, Najd and Syria. They all are strongly linked to the Iraqi society and to its events, starting from the Safavid-Ottoman conflict up to the July 14 Revolution (1958). It may be right if I say that those events shed a significant light on Iraq's events and help understand them. They may also help the reader understand some hidden aspects of the human nature, its complexes and overall problems.

The Feud Between Al-Husain and Ibn Saud

This Appendix [now Volume 7] includes details of the feud between al-Husain ibn Ali and Abdul-Aziz ibn Saud. It is a feud which can be regarded as a model for what takes place among humans, a struggle for survival where each party thinks that right is only on his side and that falsehood is on his opponent's side. As we now study it in a subjective and neutral way, we find each of the two parties taking from the truth the side which it likes, renouncing the other.

I realized, during my youthful days, the period during which the feud was intense between al-Husain and Ibn Saud, and I saw people in Iraq divided into two groups: One of them inclined towards the Hashemites, and the other towards the Al Saud. Like other people, I was impulsive, due to the dictates of my social environment, so I used to be fanatical about whatever excited them, and I spoke and acted as they did. But after I passed through life's experiences and became acquainted with the secrets of history, I realized that I was looking at the truth from one angle, and that there was another side which I should also look at.

The conflict between al-Husain and Ibn Saud represents a struggle between two antitheses as depicted by Bernard Shaw in his plays: One of them is idealistic, full of dreams and principles, while the other is realistic, not inclining to dreams and principles but wants to succedd in life, not bothering about anything else. This life's problem is that the first character quite often fails in it and suffers, whereas the other quite often succeeds and flourishes. It can be said that each of these characters has its role in history's march, and history has to have two elements that interact with it, one of them is idealistic and the other is realistic.

Syria's Events

The part relevant to Syria is the most extensive in this Appendix[1]. I do not hide the truth from the reader that this part exhausted me a great deal, and it may be the most exhausting to me of all parts of the books I have written.

This part discusses the period during which Faisal ibn al-Husain ruled Syria, and it is a period that extended for about two years, from October of 1918 to July of 1920. It was a ruckus period filled with moral lessons, and every Arab reader ought to become familiar with its events from which he may derive admonishment.

Syria was during that short period the first Arab state in modern times to win its independence and to rule itself according to the Western democratic way. Faisal at the time was yet to learn the art of politics well, and he tried to be a popular ruler; so, he did not issue a final decision about a matter before consulting the people. But the harsh experiences which he lived during that period taught him lessons which he could not forget

---

1   It is no longer an Appendix, it is Volume 7. How can it be an Appendix when it is larger in size than the text to which it is appended?! – Tr.

as long as he lived. When he became king in Iraq thereafter, the lessons which he learned in Syria were always before his eyes. For this reason, we saw him following a double policy in Iraq: He once would look after the public and once after the British, suffering as a result a great deal, and this was one of the reasons for his early demise.

Many Iraqis occupied high government posts in Syria during that period. When they returned to Iraq thereafter, they had the lion's share of the high posts in it as well. But the lessons which they had learned in Syria left varying impacts on them. Some of them learned a great deal, whereas others learned a little, while still others learned nothing. Faisal tried to be like an orchestra maestro organizing the fiddling. He succeeded in so doing to a good extent, but hardly after his death in 1933 when they started fighting for power in an amazing way. A period of eight years passed that was the ugliest in Iraq's contemporary history. Prince Zaid says, "After Faisal I, Iraq's rulers distanced themselves from the public, becoming ignorant of what the latter wanted. I warned and brought attention, but nobody heard me."[1]

Sharifs and the Society

In the first and second chapters of this book, I attempted to study an aspect of the history of Mecca's Sharifs. Perhaps it is useful to tackle in this Introduction a study of the Sharifs phenomenon in general due to its social and historic significance which is strongly linked to the Iraqi society.

Actually, the Sharifs represent a social phenomenon which we notice in all Islamic lands. It is the phenomenon of sanctifying the individuals whose lineage is traced to the Prophet and their being regarded as a high class distinctive from other people.[2]

---

[1] Sulayman Mousa, *Memoirs of Prince Zaid* (Amman: 1976), p. 204.
[2] Regarding the status of Sayyids in the Iraqi society, refer to the ninth chapter of the author's book titled "A Study in the Nature of the Iraqi Society." – Tr.

An individual from this class is awarded various titles in various lands: In Iraq, Iran, Yemen, Hadramaut, Malaysia and Indonesia, such an individual is awarded the title of "Sayyid". In Egypt and Morocco, he is awarded the title of "Sharif". In some parts of India and Turkey, he is awarded the title of "Mir". In eastern and southern Africa, he is called "Mawla". As for Hijaz, one who descends from [Imam] al-Hassan [ibn Ali ibn Abu Talib] is given the title of "Sharif", whereas the one who descends from [Imam] al-Husain [ibn Ali ibn Abu Talib] is given the title of "Sayyid".

The beginning of the rise of a distinctive class in the Islamic society during the Umayyad era was under the "Quraysh" name. Before that, the Muslims were all one class with no distinctions among them. Quraysh remained distinct from the rest of people until the advent of the Abbasid era. It was then that the scope of that class shrunk, becoming restricted to only the descendants of Hashim, and they are two groups: the Abbasids and the Talibis. Each group had a league of its own that looked after its members and into their affairs. When the Abbasid state was in full swing, the class became restricted to only the Talibis. It, too, shrunk, becoming inclusive of the Alawids from among only the children of Fatima. It has remained so up to our time.

It is noteworthy that this class has rulings of its own relevant to the Islamic *fiqh* (jurisprudence). In his book titled *Al-Ashraf* (the Sharifs), Hassan al-Najjar says the following:

"`Allama al-Ajhuri mentions in his work *Mashariq al-Anwar* a narrative from Malik saying that the Sharifs were permitted to receive the *sadaqat al-fardh* (obligatory charity), which is the annual *zakat*..., and they are prohibited from accepting voluntary charity because the second implies demeaning, unlike the case with the first. But what is well known among most followers of Abu Hanifah, al-Shafi`i and Ahmed [ibn Hanbal] is that they permit taking voluntary charity rather than obligatory charity... Some researchers have stated, with regard to the wisdom in such

Introduction

a legislation, that the reason why they are prohibited from receiving charity is that it is people's filth, for they are too lofty and occupy a greater status to let their hand be the lower one. Some have said that the reason for the prohibition is that they used in the past to receive a fifth of the *khums* of the booty and of the *fay`* [booty taken without fighting] from the enemies while waging *jihad*. Since they were deprived of this right, they now are allowed to accept charity, be it obligatory or optional. The former reason makes sense and is acceptable, and on it are *fatwas* (edicts) now based. But whoever gives them charity has to be polite to them when giving it, so he must not do so intending it as an act of charity; rather, he should intend it as a gift and a means to earning nearness to the Messenger of Allāh through them...."[1]

Such is the viewpoint of Sunni *fiqh* about the Sharifs. As for the Shi`i *fiqh*, it has set up a loftier status for the Sharifs and a share greater than the *khums*, setting aside for them half the *khums* rather than its fifth. There is another difference between both types of *fiqh* in this regard which is: The Sunni *fiqh* has imposed the *khums* on the *fay'* and war spoils only, whereas the Shi`i *fiqh* imposes the *khums* on all gains and profits in addition to the *fay'* and war spoils.

It is worth mentioning in this regard that some *faqihs* did not recognize this class distinction for the Sharifs. They argue saying that Islam came to fight class distinctions and pride in lineage, and it is not reasonable that a new class should replace the classes that disappeared. These *faqihs* interpret "Muhammed's Progeny" as being Muhammed's nation, not family members, and they have many evidences in this regard for which there is no room here.[2] But this opinion is not advocated except by few Muslims. As for the masses, most of them see otherwise,

---

1 Hassan al-Najjar, *Al-Ashraf* (the Sharifs) (Cairo: 1938), pp. 30-31.
2 Look into this subject in the book titled "Al-Islam al-Sahih" (the sound Islam) by Muhammed Is`af al-Nashashibi. Look into its rebuttal in the book titled "Al-Iman al-Sahih" (the sound *iman* [conviction]) by Muhammed al-Kazimi al-Qazwini.

narrating in this regard many traditions of the Prophet. Ibn Hajar al-Haithami [al-Asqalani] has collected these traditions in his book *Al-Sawa`iq al-Muhriqa fil Radd `ala Ahl Bida` wal Zandaqa* (the burning thunderbolts in response to the folks of innovation and disbelief).

The Green Turban

The green turban has in late centuries become the mark that distinguishes the Sharifs from others. Its beginning is attributed to Abbasid caliph al-Ma'moon. When he appointed the Alawid Imam, Ali ibn Mousa al-Ridha, as his crown prince in 201 A.H./816 A.D., he took off the black garb which was the Abbasids' color and put on the green one instead. But this did not last long. Soon, al-Ma'moon returned to the black one after the death of Ali al-Ridha. It was after that forgotten till it was restored in Egypt by King al-Ashraf Sha`ban in 773 A.D./1371 A.D. who ordered the Sharifs to put a green mark in their turbans that distinguished them. Al-Maqrizi says, "This sultan obligated the Sharifs to distinguish themselves from others with a green mark in the men's turbans and in the women's outer garments, so they did it and have continued to do it..."[1]

The Sharifs kept distinguishing themselves with the green mark in their turbans until the year 1004 A.H./1595 A.D. when the ruler of Egypt ordered the Sharifs' turbans to be all green.[2] Since then, the green turban spread in many Islamic lands as a mark distinguishing the Sharifs from others.

In fact, the Sharifs did not all commit themselves to the green turban. Some of them kept the white turban as is the case with the Sharifs of Hijaz and Yemen. Some of them did not like to distinguish themselves from others through any mark whatsoever. What is noticed about the Shi`as of Iraq and Iran is

---

1 Taqi ad-Din al-Maqrizi, *Kitab al-Sulook* (book of conduct), Cairo, 1970, Vol. 3, Part 1, p. 199.
2 Art Sharif, *Encyclopedia of Islam*.

Introduction

that a Sayyid among them, if he belongs to the clergy or is a Mousawi, i.e. belonging to the lineage of [Imam] Mousa al-Kazim, puts on the black turban. It is believed that this turban is among the legacies of the Abbasid period, and al-Sharif al-Radhi may have been the first to start it, for it is known that when he took charge of the Talibis' league in 403 A.H./1012 A.D., he took the black color as his slogan in preference over the Abbasids' outfit.[1]

At any rate, some Sharifs used the green turban as means for covert begging. Also, some non-Sharifs used it as a means to raise their social status and also to beg. Hassan al-Najjar tells us about some of the tricks to which charlatans in Egypt resorted in the 20th Century saying the following:

"Some of those who have nothing to do with Ahl al-Bayt put on a green turban in the pretext they are *naqeebs* (chiefs) of one of the Sayyids, or to sit next to one of them claiming that he is an unlucky Sharif, a destitute in need of such-and-such if the giver would seek the acceptance of his grandfather, [Imam] al-Husain, and that of the Lady [Fatima], although he is not connected to them with any kinship. This, in my opinion, is contemptible trickery in addition to being a sin for wearing the green turban which the scholars had issued *fatwas* saying that it specifically belonged to the Sharifs. Moreover, it is the trickery of a cheater who extorts people's money with tricks and consumes it with falsehood. Applying trickery to the green turban was done by a man from the furthermost part of the Delta [of Egypt] who became engaged to a Sharif lady through the claim that he, too, was a Sharif. When they noticed the Sharifs' mark on his head, they believed him. He hardly engaged the girl when her father came to know, through one of his relatives, that they really did not belong to the Sharifs…"[2]

---

1 Adam Mitz, *Islamic Civilization* (tr. By Abu Reeda), Beirut: 1967, Vol. 1, p. 290.
2 Hassan al-Najjar, *Ibid.*, pp. 47-48.

Dreams' Pillar

The lofty status enjoyed by the Sharifs in the Islamic society found two pillars for it to support: The first was the abundance of traditions which are attributed to the Prophet and which urge looking after and respecting his offspring, and the other was the Muslims seeing the Prophet or his daughter, Fatima, in their dreams urging them to look after their offspring.

One of the beliefs that spread among the Muslims was that if they saw the Prophet in their dreams, they would think that they saw him truly because Satan, according to their belief, cannot take the Prophet's form in one's dream. This belief led to many myths and wrong traditions rising in the Muslim society, as I explained in detail in my book titled *Al-Ahlam bayna al-'Ilm wal 'Aqida* (dreams between science and belief).

Many dreams which urge respect for the Sharifs were narrated in Hijaz. The reason is that the Sharifs ruled Hijaz for a very long period of time and, like other rulers of past periods, they oppressed and assaulted people. Also, some Sharifs were Bedouins who intercepted the path of pilgrims; therefore, people were grumbling about them and, of course, cursing them. It is then that the Prophet or his daughter Fatima would appear to them in visions to reprimand them for their grumbling and cursing.

Ibn Hajar al-Haithami and others have narrated many such dreams, using them as evidences that they [Sharifs] must be looked after and their wrongdoings must be overlooked as the Shari'a [Islam's legislative system] rules. Following we quote a group of these dreams which we have selected from various sources:

1. A Sharif named Mateer was in Medina playing with pigeons (i.e. he was pigeon trainer) according to our expression in Iraq. When he died, a *faqih* refused to perform the funeral prayer service for him. But this *faqih* saw the Prophet in his

vision accompanied by Fatima al-Zahraa. Fatima turned her face away from him, so the *faqih* kept pleading for her sympathy till she went to him and remonstrated with him saying, "Does our status not include Mateer?" Since then, Mateer kept going to extremes in honoring the Sharifs.[1]

2. The adoring sheikh, Muhammed al-Farisi, used to hold in contempt Medina's Sharifs who descended from al-Husain for their pretense of rejection [of accepting charity]. Then one day he slept in the direction of the Prophet's grave. He saw the Prophet in his vision saying to him, "O so-and-so, why do I see you hating my children?" The sheikh said to him, "Far away it is that I hate them, I only hated their fanaticism against the Ahl al-Sunnah." The Prophet thereupon asked him, "Is not a disobedient son still is attached to his lineage?" The sheikh answered saying, "Yes, O Messenger of Allāh!" The Prophet then asked him, "This is [an example of] a disobedient son." When the sheikh woke up from his sleep, he started leaving none from among the descendants of al-Husain without going to extremes in being generous to him.[2]

3. A man from among the people of Yemen performed the pilgrimage in the company of his family via the sea route. When tax collectors searched him and searched under the women's clothes, the man suffered because of that and kept pleading to Allāh to condemn the Sharif who was then ruling Mecca, namely Muhammed ibn Barakat. Then he saw in his vision the Prophet shunning him. The man asked the Prophet why he was avoiding him, so the Prophet said, "Have you not seen among the unjust people one who is more unjust than this son of mine?!" The man woke up feeling terrified. He repented to Allāh, pledging that he would never, from then on, harm any Sharif with a word no matter what he did.[3]

---

[1] Ibn Hajar al-Haithami, *Al-Sawa'iq al-Muhriqa*, Cairo, p. 240.
[2] *Ibid.*, p. 240.
[3] *Ibid.*, p. 243.

Story of the Sharifs and Ibn Saud

4. When Abu Nami I, Mecca's Sharif, passed away, Sheikh Afeef ad-Din al-Dulasi refused to perform the funeral prayer service for him. But the sheikh saw in a vision that same night Fatima al-Zahraa standing at the Ka`ba as people were greeting her. When the sheikh went to greet her, she turned her face away from him three times. With a great deal of difficulty did the sheikh ask her why she shunned him, so she said, "Why did you not perform the prayers for my dead son?" He apologized to her and repented from doing any such a thing in the future, admitting his wrongdoing.[1]

5. Poet Ibn Abbas al-Dimashqi went to Mecca to perform the pilgrimage when some Sharifs intercepted him, looting everything he had and even wounding him. He, therefore, wrote a poem in which he spoke ill of the Sharifs in the worst manner. When he slept that night, he saw in his vision Fatima al-Zahraa performing the *tawaf* (circling) of the House (Ka`ba), so he greeted her but she did not respond to his greeting. He, therefore, kept pleading to and beseeching her, asking her what sin he had committed. She responded to him with a poem which she composed, similarly to the way he had composed his, in its scansion and rhyme scheme, in which she stated that her children are distant from doing the deeds which he described in his poem. Rather, times have turned treacherous against them, abusing them, and that he had to repent to Allāh. The poet woke up from his sleep terrified. Allāh healed his wounds. He, therefore, composed a new poem in which he expressed his repentance to Allāh on account of his first poem, pledging that he would regard whatever the Sharifs did as being good even if they cut him to pieces with the sword or the spear.

6. The famous Sufi Muhyi ad-Din ibn `Arabi narrates saying that a man from among the people of Hijaz talked to him saying, "I used to hate what the Sharifs in Mecca were doing to people, thereupon I saw in a vision Fatima daughter of the

---

1 Abdul-Malik al-`Isami, *Simt al-Nujoom al-`Awali*, Cairo, Vol. 4 p. 227.

Introduction

Messenger of Allāh turning her face away from me. I, therefore, greeted her and asked her why she was turning her face away from me. She said, 'You speak ill of the Sharifs.' I said to her, 'My Lady! Do not you see what they are doing to people?' She said, 'Are they not my descendants?' I said to her, 'From this moment on, I declare my repentance,' whereupon she became pleased with me, and I woke up."[1]

The anecdotes we have stated above are a drop in the bucket, and it is easy to find their likes in various Islamic lands. We do not have to say that Mecca's Sharifs benefitted from them a great deal in supporting their rule which lasted for about ten centuries as we will discuss later.

---

1 Muhammed Is`af al-Nashasheebi, *Al-Islam al-Saheeh*, Jerusalem (1354 A.H./1935-6), p. 164.

Chapter One
Mecca's Sharifs

Mecca's Sharifs

The Sharifs of Hijaz, especially during late times, were quite few in number. Perhaps the ratio of their number to the total population is close to that of the Sayyids to the total population of Iraq. In their social status, they varied in degrees. There were primarily Sharifs who belonged to the ruling family. These had a status close to that of the emirs from among the king's relatives in monarchies, and every one of them had his mansions, entourage and slaves. As for the rest of Sharifs, they varied in status according to the personal capabilities or their families' fanaticism. Among them were Bedouins who intercepted the pilgrims' routes just like other Bedouins. And there were among them those who worked in lowly jobs. Ibn Jubayr, who visited Hijaz in the 6th Hijri Century (12th Century A.D.), tells us about the miserable conditions in which some Sharifs lived saying,

"Most of the town's residents, the town of Jidda, including its deserts and mountains, are Sharifs, Alawids, Hassanis, Husainis and Ja`faris, may Allāh be pleased with their honorable ancestors, and their hardship of living would cause the stones to crack out of pity for them. They involve themselves in any profession such as leasing camels if they had any, selling milk, water or fruits which they pick or firewood which they gather. This may have been handled by their Sharif women themselves; so, praise belongs to Allāh Who decrees whatever He wills. There is no doubt that they are members of a Household for whom Allāh chose the Hereafter and has not chosen life in this world; may Allāh count us among those who follow the love for Ahl al-Bayt from whom He removed all abomination and perfected them with a perfect purification."[1]

Mecca's Sharifdom[2] Established

The Sharifs of Hijaz remained up to the 4th Hijri Century without power, and they did not have anything to distinguish them from the rest of the population other than a high status which stemmed from lineage to the Prophet. In the year 358 A.H., which coincided with 969 A.D., a Husaini Sharif, namely Ja`far ibn al-Husain from the lineage of Mousa al-Joon, was able to establish a sort of emriate in Mecca which he called "Mecca's Sharifdom". It is the Sharifdom that lasted for them up to the year 1925 A.D. when it was crushed by Ibn Saud as we will come to discuss in a forthcoming chapter.

Circumstances helped Ja`far ibn al-Hassan to establish this Sharifdom. Hijaz was at the time under the authority of the Akhshidi government in Egypt, and that State was living its last days; soon it fell in the hands of the Fatimids. When Fatimid al-Mu`izz established himself in power in Egypt, he wrote Ja`far ibn al-Husain appointing him as *wali* (provincial governor) over Hijaz in the name of the Fatimid State. It was then that Ja`far stopped the supplication for the Abbasid caliphs which used to be recited during the Akhshidi period, and he started supplicating for the Fatimids instead. He also introduced the statement of *"Hayya `ala Khayril-`Amal"* (come to the best of deeds) which distinguishes the Shi`a *adhan* from that of Ahl al-Sunnah.

The Husaini Sharifs used to reside in Medina and its outskirts, and they enjoyed influence in it. They, in turn, seized the opportunity to declare their independence in Medina in the year 360 A.H./970 A.D., two years after their cousins, the Hassanis,

---

1 Muhammed ibn Jubayr, *Rihlat Ibn Jubayr* (journey of Ibn Jubayr), Baghdad: 1937, p. 42.

2 Do not try to look the word "Sharifdom" in the dictionary because you will not find it. As a Translator, I have had to coin this word which may be harmonious with "kingdom," "sheikhdom," and the like. – Tr.

had established Mecca's Sharifdom, and they started supplicating for the Fatimids as they (Hassanis) were doing. They also introduced the statement of "Hayya `ala Khayril-`Amal".

When reports about the above reached the Abbasids in Baghdad, they sent to Mecca the Talibis' *naqeeb*, namely al-Husain ibn Mousa al-Mousawi, father of al-Sharif al-Radhi, whom they placed in charge of Iraq's *hajj*-related matters. This *naqeeb* was able to convince Ja`far ibn al-Hassan to stop the supplication for the Fatimids and to restore it for the Abbasids. Apparently, Ja`far did not continue to do that for long; rather, he resumed the supplication for the Fatimids, and he may have returned again to supplicate for the Abbaids...[1]

Abul-Futooh

Founder Ja`far ibn al-Hassan passed away in 370 A.H./981 A.D., so he was succeeded as Sharif of Mecca by his son, Eisa. When Eisa died in 384 A.H./995 A.D., he was succeeded by his brother al-Hassan who is given the title "Abul-Futooh" (father of conquests). He was one of the greatest Sharifs in his personality and the strongest physically. It has been said that if he held a [silver minted] dirham, he could deface it with his hand, blotting out its inscription.[2] Moreover, he was an articulate poet.[3]

Abul-Futooh spent his first ruling years busy with wars, fighting his cousins, the Husainis, in Medina, and also his other cousins, the Hassanis, in Yemen.[4] It seems that he was very ambitious, desiring the caliphate for himself: He saw the Islamic world as having three contending caliphs: the Abbasid caliph in Baghdad, the Fatimid caliph in Egypt and the Omayyad caliph in

---

1 Ahmed al-Siba`i, *Tarikh Mecca* (history of Mecca), Mecca: 1372 A.H./1953 A.D., p. 29.
2 *Ibid.*, p. 133.
3 Ahmed al-Dawoodi, *`Umdat al-Talib*, Beirut, p. 109.
4 Fuad Hamzah, *Qalb Jazeerat al-Arab* (heart of the Arab Peninsula), Riyadh: 1988, p. 314.

Andalusia, and he might have regarded himself as the most worthy among them as the caliph.

Like other Hassani Sharifs, Abul-Futooh was a Shi`a who followed the Zaidi sect. It is known that the Zaidi sect is distinguished from the other Shi`a sects by being pleased with both sheikhs [Abu Bakr and Omar ibn al-Khattab], considering them as just imams, whereas the other sects cast doubts about them and dissociate themselves from them. In 401 A.H./1011 A.D., Abul-Futooh received an order from Fatimid caliph al-Hakim bi Amrillah to dissociate himself from both sheikhs and to make an announcement in this regard during the Ka`ba sermon. Abul-Futooh resented this order and wanted to take it as an opportunity to cede from the Fatimids and to declare himself as the caliph.

Abul-Futooh issued instructions to announce al-Hakim's order to the public from the pulpit in the Ka`ba. This led to a tumult and agitation among the pilgrims and the residents of Hijaz, and people assembled desiring to break the pulpit on the head of the announcer. It was then that Abul-Futooh declared his mutiny against the Fatimids. He followed it by declaring himself caliph, using the name "al-Rashid Billah". He started receiving the oath of allegiance from the people of Mecca and Medina. After that, Bedouin tribes swore it to him, such as Banu Saleem, Banu Hilal, Banu Awf and Banu Amir. Abul-Futooh seized the money and precious items found in the Ka`ba and the wealth of some merchants in Jidda. He put on a sword which he claimed to be Thul-Fiqar and carried a rod which he claimed it belonged to the Messenger of Allāh.[1]

Abul-Futooh headed thereafter towards Sham (the Levant) as head of a huge force comprised of Bedouin tribes that followed him, as well as others. Whenever he passed by a place, its residents went to him to declare their obedience and to swear

---

1 Abdul-Malik al-`Isami, *Simt al-Nujoom al-`Awali* (thread of the lofty stars), Cairo, Vol. 4, p. 196.

the oath of allegiance to him, as was people's tradition when someone attained the world's riches.

Al-Hakim bi Amrillah did not remain a spectator towards all of this; rather, he started distributing funds in order to get people away from Abul-Futooh. He encouraged one of the Sharifs from among Abul-Futooh's relatives to occupy Mecca and to declare himself the Sharif over it. He also blocked rations from reaching Hijaz, causing hardship to the Hijazis and prompting their grumbling. Abul-Futooh realized the need to reconcile with al-Hakim, so he sent him a message that he sought to repent to him, restoring the supplication for him in the Ka`ba. Al-Hakim, therefore, forgave him and kept him as Sharif over Mecca.

It is worth mentioning that a strange incident took place during the time of Abul-Futooh in 413 A.H./1023 A.D. Its summary is that a man from among the Egyptian pilgrims approached the Black Stone carrying a pin in his hand with which he hit the stone three times, causing three small pieces to fall off it. Shaking with emotion, he said, "Till when should this stone be worshipped and kissed?! Neither Muhammed nor Ali can prevent me, for I am this day demolishing this House!" The man was tall and big and he had helpers who stood at the Mosque's gate to defend him. People feared him and kept their distance from him, but a man from among the people of Yemen rushed towards him with his dagger. It was then that people crowded around him, killing him and cutting him to pieces then burning him. After that, they went after his helpers, killing some of them. The people of Mecca fell on the Egyptian pilgrims, looting them. The looting mania spread to others. When calm reigned, the custodians of the Ka`ba from the Banu Shayba came, took the pieces of the Black Stone that had fallen, kneaded them with musk, rockrose and gum then returned them to their places. The cracks around them are still visible.[1]

---

1 *Ibid.*, Vol. 4, pp. 197-198.

The Hashemites

Abul-Futooh died in 430 A.H./1039 A.D. and was succeeded as Sharif by his son, Shukr, who was strong like him. Wars went on between him and the Husainis in Medina which ended by his victory over them. Since then, Medina was subjected to the Sharif of Mecca after it used to be independent.

Shukr died in 452 A.H./1061 A.D. without leaving behind a son; rather, he had only one daughter. This was the reason for a dispute and a war between two Sharif families: the Sulaymanis and the Hashimis (or Hashemites). Wars went on between them for a long period of time until the Hashemites were able to subdue their opponents. It was then that their chief, Muhammed, seized the post of Sharif of Mecca. He was famous for his surname "Abu Hashim".

The Hashemite family kept ruling Mecca up to 598 A.H./1202 A.D. It is known for alternating its political loyalty between the Abbasids and the Fatimids. It used to once supplicate for these and once for those, according to whoever paid it more.[1]

This alternating was started by Abu Hashim himself; he used in the first years of his term to supplicate for the Fatimids in his sermon and recite the *athan* according to their way. But the Saljuke sultan, Alp Arsalan, sent him Iraq's *naqeeb* (chief) of the Talibis, namely Nour al-Huda al-Zayni. In 458 A.H./1066 A.D., the *naqeeb* was able to convince Abu Hashim to terminate the supplication in his sermons for the Fatimids and to supplicate for the Abbasids instead. When the report reached the Fatimids, they were very angry with him and blocked the rations from reaching Hijaz as an act of revenge; therefore, Abu Hashim was forced to restore the supplication for the Fatimids. In 463 A.H./1071 A.D., Alp Arsalan sent him the *naqeeb* again carrying precious gifts and thirty thousand dinars plus a pledge of an annual salary of ten thousand dinars. A huge army was in the

---

1 *Shorter Encyclopedia of Islam*, Art., Mecca.

naqeeb's company. Abu Hashim, therefore, terminated the supplications for the Fatimids and started praying for the Abbasids. In his sermon, he said, "Praise is due to Allāh Who has guided us, we people of His House, to the sound opinion, compensating His sons with the attire of youth after that of old age and inclined our hearts to obey and follow the imam of the group."[1]

What is odd is that Abu Hashim kept the Shi`a *athan* despite his supplication for the Abbasids; therefore, the latter sent him Sharif Abu Talib to convince him to abandon the Shi`i *athan*. Abu Talib debated with him a great deal, so Abu Hashim said to him, "This is not something right which he advocates; rather, it was done by [Abdullah] ibn Omar [ibn al-Khattab] in some of his trips; so, what do you have to do with Ibn Omar?!" Abu Hashim was now convinced. He dropped the Shi`i *athan* and restored that of the Sunnis.[2]

Abu Hashim did not continue to supplicate for the Abbasids for long. In fact, he kept shifting from the Abbasids to the Fatimids and vice versa according to the pressure of circumstances or to the money temptation. The Abbasids had in 484 A.H./1092 A.D. to deal with him forcefully, sending him a force of Turks, and a fierce fighting took place between him and the Turks. This was the beginning of the sectarian seditions in Mecca: Pilgrimage seasons became in the ensuing years a time for competition and feud among the followers of the Abbaids and Fatimids, each group desiring the supplication and the *athan* in the Ka`ba for itself.

Qatadah

In early 598 A.H./1201-2 A.D., the Hashemites' authority came to an end at the hands of one of their Sharif opponents named Qatadah ibn Idris. This man was first living with his folks

---

[1] Abdul-Malik al-`Isami, *Ibid*., Vol. 4, p. 200.
[2] Ahmed al-Siba`i, *Ibid*., p. 135.

near Yanbu' in a quasi-Bedouin way. He aspired to get the position of Mecca's Sharif. On Rajab 27, 598 A.H./April 22, 1202 A.D., while Mecca's people were busy celebrating, Qatadah took them by surprise with a stunning attack. He was easily able to seize Mecca and to kick the Hashemites out.

Qatadah started supplicating for Abbasid caliph al-Nasir li Dinillah. In 600 A.H./1204 A.D., caliph al-Nasir summoned Qatadah to Baghdad. He gave him promises and let him hear what he desired. Qatadah responded to him and left for Iraq. When he reached near al-Najaf, where a large crowd of people came out to welcome him, he saw among them a darvish driving a lion with an iron chain. Qatadah, therefore, took that as a bad omen, returning immediately to Hijaz where he wrote caliph al-Nasir five lines of poetry of which we would like to quote the first and the last:

و لــو أنني أعــرى بهــا و أجــوعُ   بلادي و ان جــارَت عليَّ عزيــزةٌ
و مــا أنــا الا المِسكُ في غَيرِ أرضِكُـم   أضــوعُ، و أمّــا عندَكُــم فأضيــعُ

*My homeland, though it may be unfair to me, is precious
Even if I may be without clothes in it and without food,
I am in lands other than yours like musk,
Fragrant, but among you, I am lost.*[1]

Al-Nasir was very angry because of these verses, so he wrote Qatadah a letter in which he threatened him saying, "When winter takes off its garb and spring puts on its outfits, we shall fight you with soldiers the like of whom you never saw, and we shall get you out of it [Mecca] humiliated, abased." Al-Nasir then prepared a battalion of soldiers which he dispatched to Mecca in order to discipline Qatadah.

---

[1] Ahmed al-Dawoodi, *Ibid.*, pp. 115-116.

Chapter One: Mecca's Sharifs

Qatadah prepared himself to fight al-Nasir's battalion and sent to his cousins, the Husainis, in Medina seeking their aid. He wrote them these lines of poetry:

وَآلَ حُسَيْنٍ كَيْفَ صَبْرُكُمْ عَنَّا؟ بني عمنـا مــن آل مــوسى و جعفـرٍ
فلا تتركونـا يَتَّخذُنـا الفَنـا فَنـا بني عَمِّنـا، إنّـا كأفنـانِ دَوحَـةٍ
بــدا بأخيـهِ الأكلُ ثُـمَّ ثَنى إذا مــا أخٌ خَلّى أخـاهُ لآكلٍ

O cousins from the offspring of Mousa and Ja'far,
And offspring of al-Husain: How do you forget about us?
Cousins! We are like tree branches, so
Do not leave us to destiny to play havoc with us.
If one leaves his brother to be devoured by one,
The devourer will finish him next after finishing the first.

The Husainis responded to Qatadah's call for help, so they went collectively to Mecca. When the Nasiri battalion reached it, the Hassanis and Husainis both encountered it, defeating it and causing it to go helter skelter.[1]

About one year after this incident, war broke out between the Hassanis and Husainis. A fierce fighting took place at Thul-Halifah where Qatadah won victory, so he composed one line of poetry on the occasion:

بَـدأتِ ولكـن صِرتِ بَينَ الأقـاربِ مَصـارعُ آلِ المُصطفى عُـدتِ مِثلَمـا

O killings of the Family of the Chosen one: You returned
As you started, but this time you are among the relatives.

After his victory, Qatadah headed towards Medina which he besieged. In Medina, the Husainis were under the leadership of one of their men named Salim ibn Qasim. This man was able to end the siege on the city, then he started chasing Qatadah until he reached Mecca which he placed under siege. He sent a

---

[1] Abdul-Malik al-'Isami (above reference), Vol. 4, p. 209.

message to Qatadah saying, "One siege for one siege, cousin." Salim could not continue the siege because some of his fellows dispersed from around him through enticements from Qatadah, so he returned to Medina.[1]

Qatadah's rule continued for about twenty years most of which he spent waging wars and looting pilgrims. The author of ʿOmdat al-Talib described him saying, "Qatadah was tyrannical[2], ruthless, harsh, strict and decisive."[3]

An eyewitness described him saying, "I found him circumambulating the House (Kaʿba), supplicating, pleading in a somber way. He is like the lion in his courage, the ascetic in reverence and the moon in perfection and radiance."[4]

Qatadah used to say, "I am more worthy of the caliphate than the Abbasid al-Nasir [li Din-Illah]." He brought back the statement of حَيَّ على خَيْرِ العَمَلِ "Come along for the best action [performing the prayers]." In 618, his son, Hassan, killed him, and it is said that he strangled him then appointed himself Sharif after him. Abdul-Malik al-ʿIsami, one of the people of Mecca, commented on the above saying, "Then Qatadah's oppression of the people intensified and so was his harming the pilgrims, Iraqis and others, demonstrating infringement, so much so that there was a public uproar. He harbored ill intentions against the Abbasid al-Nasir caliph, so hands were raised invoking the Almighty's curse on him; therefore, Allāh killed him at the hands of his son, Hassan ibn Qatadah."[5]

---

1 *Ibid.*, Vol. 4, pp. 209-210.
2 The original Arabic word is حبّازا which means "falconer," but I think it is a typographical error and should read جبّازا instead, and this is how I have translated it. – Tr.
3 Ahmed al-Dawudi (*Ibid.*), p. 115.
4 Abdul-Malik al-ʿIsami (*Ibid.*), Vol. 4, p. 212.
5 *Ibid.*, Vol. 4, p. 213.

Chapter One: Mecca's Sharifs

Hummaydhah Ibn Abu Nami

In 651 A.H./1253 A.D., a man from among Mecca's famous Sharifs and men of righteousness, namely Abu Nami I, who descended from Qatadah's lineage, became the Sharif of Mecca, a position which he maintained for fifty years. Al-Maqrizi says the following about him: "It was said that had he not been a Zaidi, he would have been regarded as being fit to be a caliph on account of his good attributes."[1]

Abu Nami died in 701 A.H./1302 A.D., leaving thirty male offspring and twelve females. A tough competition took place among his offspring over who would be the Sharif of Mecca. This lasted for several years, resulting in calamities and horrific incidents.

The competition was the toughest among four brothers: Hummaydhah, Abul-Ghaith, Rumaithah and Utayfa. They were receiving assistance in their competition from either Iraq or Egypt. In 715 A.H./1315 A.D., Hummaydhah sent one of his slaves to his brother, Abul-Ghaith, who was competing with him for the post of Sharif, who slaughtered him as people looked on. Then Hummaydhah invited his other brothers for a banquet and presented to them the head of their killed brother cooked in a pot. He also posted near each of them two black slaves with unsheathed swords so they might swear the oath of allegiance to him. They, therefore, had to surrender to him against their will.[2]

Rumaithah fled to Egypt to plead to King al-Nasir ibn Qalawoon for help. He narrated to him how Hummaydhah removed his name from the sermon in the Ka`ba, lauding instead the ruler of Yemen. Al-Nasir, therefore, supplied Rumaithah with a large force with which Rumaithah returned to Mecca where he over-powered and arrested Hummaytha. But Hummaytha was

---

1 Taqi ad-Din al-Maqrizi, *Kitab al-Sulook* (the book of conduct), Cairo, 1976, Vol. 1, Ch. 3, p. 927.
2 Abdul-Malik al-`Isami (*Ibid.*), Vol. 4, pp. 227-228.

able to flee and to seek help in Iraq of the Mogul sultan, [Muhammad] Khudabandah son of Argon son of Abaqa son of Holagu [Khan]. Khudabandah welcomed him and was generous to him, and Hummaytha stayed with him for a good while.

It is worth mentioning that Khudabandah had just embraced the Shi`a Ithna-`Asheri sect due to being influenced by the famous Shi`ite scholar, `allama al-Hilli. Humayydha was able to have an impact on Khudabandah through his fanaticism for the new sect, urging him to send with him a Mogul army to occupy Mecca where his name would be mentioned in the sermon from its pulpits.[1] It is said that Hummaydhah also enticed Khudabandah to get the army to reach Medina following the occupation of Mecca in order to inter the graves of both Sheikhs and to move their remains outside the sacred precincts of the Prophet's Mosque.[2]

Khudabandah responded to the enticement of Hummaydhah and supplied the latter with a large Mogul army. Hummaydhah marched with this army towards Hijaz via the desert route. Many tribes, especially Khafaja headed by Muhammed ibn Isa ibn Muhanna, joined it. When Hummaydhah and his hosts reached a place in the desert between Basra and Qateef near the present location of Kuwait, a report reached them about the death of Khudabandah in the Heeza هيضة. This report caused the army to disperse. The tribes, especially Khafaja, took the opportunity and fell on the army to loot and kill. The head of Khafaja was shouting the name of King al-Nasir, the sultan of Egypt.[3] Hummaydhah demonstrated in that incident rare courage, fighting in a way never heard of before. One of those who witnessed him fighting described him saying, "I kept hearing about the military campaigns of Ali ibn Abu Talib until

---

1 Taqi ad-Din al-Maqrizi (Ibid.), Cairo, 1971, Vol. 2, Ch. 1, pp. 147-148.
2 Abbas al-Azzawi, *Al-Iraq Bayna Ihtilalayn* (Iraq between two occupations), Baghdad, 1935, Vol. 1, pp. 441-442, 445.
3 Taqi ad-Din al-Maqrizi (Op. Cited), vol. 2, Ch. 1, p. 148.

Chapter One: Mecca's Sharifs

I witnessed them [their likes] from Sayyid Hummaydhah with my own eyes."[1]

This incident took place in late Thul-Hijjah of 716 A.H./ March 1317 A.D. Hummaydhah suffered in it heavy losses, losing most of his men. Also, everything he had had, the women, wealth and steed, were looted. When the report about the incident reached King al-Nasir in Egypt, he was greatly pleased by it, and he summoned the head of Khafaja, Muhammed ibn Isa, whom he gifted a great reward.[2]

Commenting on that incident, al-Nuwairi says, "*Khara*banda— meaning derogatively Khudabandah—had, seven days before his death, disseminated an order not to make any reference to Abu Bakr and Omar, may Allāh be pleased with them, and that he was determined to raise a detachment of three thousand cavaliers to go to Medina to inter the graves of Abu Bakr and Omar, may Allāh be pleased with them, and to move their corpses, so Allāh hastened his death."[3]

Hummaydhah and those who survived were all able to reach Mecca. After efforts and various attempts, Hummaydhah was also able to restore his Sharif post and to expel his brother, Rumaithah, from the city. He stopped referring to King al-Nasir in sermons and, instead, supplications were made for Sultan Abu Sa`eed son of Khudabandah. Rumaithah went to Egypt. King al-Nasir supplied him with a force that took him to Mecca. Hummaydhah had hardly heard about Rumaithah's approach when he fled Mecca and sought refuge in Yemen from which he returned with an army to restore his power over Mecca, but fate did not give him time to do so when one of his slaves leaped on him and killed him as he was sleeping.[4] This took place in 720 A.H./1320 A.D., so he rested and let people rest!

---

1 Ahmed al-Dawoodi (*Ibid.*), p. 118.
2 Taqi ad-Din al-Maqrizi (Op. Cit.), Vol. 2, Ch. 1, p. 148.
3 As cited from Abbas al-Azzawi (Op. Cit.), Vol. 1, p. 445.
4 Abdul-Malik al-`Isami (Op. Cit.), Vol. 4, pp. 230-231.

It is worth mentioning in this regard that when Hummaydhah was in Iraq, he married an Iraqi woman who gave birth to his son Muhammed. This son remained in Iraq with his maternal uncles, and he had a large number of offspring. One of his descendants, namely `Utayfah عُطَيفه, became quite famous; he died in 934 A.H./1528 A.D. This man earned a prestigious status with Safavid Shah Isma`eel when the latter conquered Baghdad in 914 A.H./1508 A.D. This Shah granted him the plot of land named after him (al-`Utayfiyya العُطَيفيّة) located on the right flank of the Tigris River between Baghdad and al-Kadhimiyya. He also placed him in charge of hajj-related matters and as the *naqeeb* (chief) of the Kadhimiyya Shrine and its caretakers. Many presently famous Iraqi families have descended from this `Utayfah, such as the al-Habboobis, al-Zainis, al-Radhis, al-Hadis in Baghdad, and al-`Utayfis, Sarkashiks[1] and al-Haidaris in al-Kadhimiyya. Also, many caretakers of the Grand al-Kadhimiyya Shrine belong to `Utayfah.

Abu Nami II

In 931 A.H./1525 A.D., a man nicknamed "Abu Nami" II (the Second), in order to be distinguished from the first Abu Nami, assumed the post of Sharif. This man earned a high status with Sulayman the Law-Giver, the Ottoman sultan to whom Abu Nami sent his son, Ahmad, to Istanbul (Constantinople) carrying many gifts from the Arabian Peninsula such as steed, falcons, fabrics and perfumes. Ahmad was handsome, and when he entered the sultan's meeting place, the latter stood up to him as

---

1 Being a resident of al-Kadhimiyya, I could not identify these "Sarkashiks" سركشيك. For one thing, this word does not sound Arabic. When I looked it up via Google, I could not find any Arabic text about it; instead, I found numerous references to it in Persian (Farsi); therefore, I conclude that this word is most likely a Persian adjective denoting the Arab founder of this dynasty. Unfortunately, I do not know Farsi! Another possibility is that it is one of many typographical errors I found in this book as I have been translating it. In order to underscore my point, I checked this word in Ibn Manzour's *Lisan al-Arab* (Arabs' Tongue) lexicon and could not find any root word close to it. Had there been such a word, it should have been indicated on p. 428, Vol. 3, of this extensive lexicon. – Tr.

a sign of respect, something which he never did to anyone else. The sultan showered Ahmad with many gifts of outfits, and so did the sultan's wife who announced to people that she regarded "Sharif Ahmad" to be like her own son.[1]

Abu Nami II thereafter earned glory and influence, becoming quite famous in Hijaz and was praised by poets in great poems. He maintained his post of Sharif for more than sixty years; he died in 992 A.H./1584 A.D., and he may have remained a Sharif longer than anyone else.

Abu Nami II is regarded as the true founder of the Sharifdom (institution). He is grandson of the dynasty that maintained the post of Sharif until it was crushed by Ibn Saud in 1925. Abu Nami was known to be very strict about lineage. Throughout his life, he used to make distinctions among people based on their lineage and family, relying in so doing on a tradition of the Prophet in which he said, "I have been ordered to treat people according to each person's [social] status." He held the view that one's roots identified him, that if one's lineage was honorable, so was his conduct. As for commoners, they, according to Abu Nami, were mean, and if one of them earned a lofty station in the society, harm could result.[2]

It seems that the Ottoman State used to support Abu Nami's viewpoint. It was, in fact, quite prevalent among people; many people believed in it and many still do even in our days. This attitude prompted Abu Nami to establish principles which came to be known collectively as the "Abu Nami Law" intended to officially distinguish the Sharifs from others. Only a limited number of Sharifs knew those principles. The Sharifs would circulate them among themselves and not permit anyone else to become familiar with them. The author of the book titled *Tarikh al-Hijaz* (history of Hijaz) claims that he became familiar with

---

1   *Ibid.*, Vol. 4, p. 326.
2   *Ibid.*, Vol. 4, pp. 334-335.

some of those principles which he mentioned in his book as follows:

1. Sharifdom is hereditary within the Hashemite dynasty.
2. A Sharif must not engage in any profession or trade except in lumber and coal, cameleering and agriculture.
3. If a Sharif is killed, four men should be taken from the family or village of the killer to be killed in retribution.
4. If one slaps a Sharif, his hand must be severed.
5. If one verbally abuses a Sharif, his tongue must be cut off.
6. A Sharif must not be tried in his opponent's meeting place.
7. If a Sharif attempts to kill another Sharif, or if he raises a weapon in his face, he must be banished from the land.
8. If a Sharif kills a non-Sharif, he (the first) must not be killed.
9. A ruling Sharif receives a third of the killed person's blood money (*diyya*).[1]

It seems that this law was not carried out to the letter due to its excessive harshness and violation of the Shari`a, but it somehow helped safeguard the status of the Sharifs, turning them into a sort of closed-in class in Hijaz.

Sectarianism In Hijaz

The Safavid-Ottoman feud, which erupted in Iraq in the 10th Hijri Century/the 16th Century A.D., had its impact on Hijaz: During the season of pilgrimage in the year 1042 A.H./1633 A.D., an order from the Ottoman sultan in Istanbul reached Mecca prohibiting the Iranians from performing the hajj and *ziyara*. It was announced at Mecca's markets in order to notify the Iranians of it so they would in turn convey it to their brethren upon returning to their homeland.[2]

The Sharif of Mecca at the time was a man named Zaid ibn Muhsin. This man declared his shift of allegiance from the Zaidi

---

[1] Husain Muhammed Naseef, *Tarikh al-Hijaz*, Cairo: 1349 A.H./1930 A.D., Vol. 1, pp. 17-18.
[2] Ahmed al-Siba'i (Op. Cit.), p. 257.

Chapter One: Mecca's Sharifs

sect to the Hanafi one, the sect adopted by the Ottoman State. The author of *Tarikh Mecca* (history of Mecca) says the following about this man: "This man used to follow the Zaidi sect of his kinsfolk, then he differed from them and reverted to the belief of the Sunnis, embracing the sect of Imam Abu Hanifah. His folks used to suffer a great deal at the hands of the Sunnis who prevented them from practicing their beliefs."[1]

A rumor spread among the residents of Mecca during that time saying that the performance by the Shi`ites of the pilgrimage was not regarded as complete unless they besmirched the Ka`ba with filth. Many people believed this rumor as is usually the case when some people are carried away with their sectarian fanaticism. On Shawwal 8, 1088 A.H./December 4, 1677 A.D., a sectarian sedition took place in Mecca as a result of this rumor. Below is a description of that incident as narrated by a man from among the people of Mecca who witnessed it with his own eyes; he said,

"On a Thursday, the 8th of Shawwal of the year 1088 A.H./November 24 (according to the Julian calendar/December 4 according to the Gregorian calendar), 1677 A.D., a strange incident and an amazing catastrophe took place. That night, the Black Stone, the door of the Ka`ba, the Friday prayers area and the covering sheets of the Venerable House were dirtied with something which looked like feces in its stink and badness; so, anyone who wanted to kiss the Stone had his face and hands dirtied, too. People were horrified as a result, and the Turks were quite agitated. They met, so the Stone, the door and covering sheets were washed with water, and the Turks, pilgrims and those in the neighborhood, were quite agitated. A virtuous man who was given the title "Dars Aam" and who used to look at a group of Rafidhis at the Haram Mosque, observing how they prayed, prostrated, moved, etc., was at the House and the Standing Place [Maqam Ibrahim], and he used to burn and sigh.

---
1 *Ibid.*, p. 258.

When this incident took place, he said, 'This is the doing of nobody other than these mean Rafidhis who stick around in the Haram Mosque.' At that time, destiny had it that the renowned scholar, Sayyid Muhammed Mu'min al-Radhawi, was sitting behind the Maqam reciting the Book of Allāh, the most Great, the most Honored. They went to him, snatched the Qur'an from his hands and beat him on the head. He was pulled and taken out of the Mosque's gate known as Bab al-Ziyada and thrown out. He was then subjected to a barrage of rocks thrown at him until he was killed. When they grabbed him at the Mosque, they were approached by a Sharif from among the Rifa`i Sayyids named Sayyid Shams ad-Din, so they returned to Shams ad-Din to give him the same treatment. He was beaten until he died and his corpse was dragged. They went to another man, beat him, took him out and killed him, throwing him on those who were killed before him. Then they did the same to a fourth then a fifth man. I saw them all thrown, corpses remaining on top of each other as passers-by kept cursing and kicking their corpses. I saw the stinking thing and pondered on it. I found it not to be feces (as rumored) but a type of vegetable, a dough kneaded with lentils left to simmer in vinegar and rotted oils. Due to its stench, one could classify it among filthy objects. This action took place when the moon disappeared that Thursday night, the 8th of the said month. The culprit was not found, and most likely it was committed deliberately as means to kill those folks, and Allāh knows what the hearts hide; He knows what is innermost and what is manifest."[1]

What is noteworthy is that another such incident took place in the year 1143 A.H./1731 A.D. It is summed up thus: A caravan of Shi`a pilgrims reached Mecca too late for the pilgrimage season, so the Shi`ites resided in Mecca in order to perform the pilgrimage the next season. It was then that a rumor spread in Mecca among the commoners that the Shi`as had placed some

---

[1] Abdul-Malik al-`Isami (Op. Cit.), Vol. 4, p. 529.

filth in the Ka`ba, causing a public uproar, and the men in uniform, too, were furious. They all went to the judge, but the latter fled away from them fearing their seditions, so they went to the *mufti*. They took the *mufti* out of his house, taking with him a number of *faqihs*. They took them all to the Sharif's vizier and were able to extract from the latter an order to keep the Shi`ites away from Mecca. Then they went out to the markets calling for the expulsion of the Shi`as from Mecca and for looting their homes.

Mecca's Sharif at the time was Muhammed ibn Abdullah, and he was not pleased with what had taken place. The masses went the next day to the judge to ask him to mediate with the Sharif to endorse the vizier's decision to expel the Shi`as. First, the Sharif refused to endorse the said decision, then he felt obligated to go along with the masses in order to avoid the public sedition. The Shi`as, therefore, went out of Mecca, and some of them went to Taif whereas others went to Jidda. When the sedition was allayed, the Sharif was able to arrest its proponents, then he sent a message to the Shi`as asking them to return to Mecca, whereupon they returned.[1]

It is noteworthy in this regard that the allegation of defiling the Ka`ba with filth was stirred later in 1942 when an Iranian man named Sayyid Abu Talib Yazdi was thus charged. An order was issued to hang him, and the order was carried out, as many people looked on, in the area between the Safa and the Marwa. His execution stirred a huge uproar in Iran, and it is said that King Abdul-Aziz ibn Saud paid one hundred thousand riyals as reparation to the man's family.

From the Sequels to the Najaf Conference

In 1156 A.H./1743 A.D., Nadir Shah held his famous conference in Najaf to unite the Shi`ites and the Sunnis. A large

---

1 Ahmed al-Siba`i (Op. Cit.), p. 296.

number of scholars from both sides attended it from Iran, Afghanistan and Turkstan (Turkey). It was also attended from Baghdad by Sheikh Abdullah al-Suweedi who was then the most senior Sunni scholar in Iraq. From Kerbala, it was attended by Sayyid Nasr-Alah al-Haeri who was the senior Shi`a scholar in it. After lengthy discussions between both groups, it was agreed to endorse terms the most important of which were two: The first was that the Shi`ites should stop condemning the *sahaba*. The second was the Sunnis must recognize Shi`ism as a fifth sect called the "Ja`fari sect" after Imam Ja`far al-Sadiq D. Also, among the terms was that the Shi`ites must be permitted to pray and to deliver the sermon in the Shami (Syrian) corner of the Ka`ba during the pilgrimage season once the appointed imam has finished his prayer.[1]

After the commencement of the conference, Nadir Shah sent Sayyid Nasr-Allāh al-Haeri to Mecca to pray in the Shami corner according to the conference's resolution. He sent with him a copy of the conference's minutes. He also sent letters to Mecca's Sharif, Mas`ud ibn Sa`eed, and also to its judge and mufti telling them that he was sending them the imam of the Ja`fari sect to carry out the resolutions of the conference.

When al-Haeri reached Mecca, Sharif Mas`ud welcomed him and was nice to him. He was permitted to pray and to deliver his sermon at the Shami corner, but the commoners did not relish it, so they raised their voices in protest in an uproar. Keep in mind that only thirteen years had passed after the second incident of defiling the Ka`ba. Evidences point out that Sheikh Abdullah al-Suweedi, who had gone to perform the pilgrimage that year, had a hand in instigating the public uproar.

The Turkish minister in Jidda sent Sharif Mas`ud a letter asking him to hand over al-Haeri to him so he would kill him, but the Sharif refused to hand him over and said, "I shall protect

---

[1] Look up the details and resolutions of this conference in the fifth chapter of the first part of this book.

him until I write the Caliphate house and get its answer to see what it orders me to do."[1] The Turkish minister did not accept this answer and charged the Sharif of inclining towards the Ja`fari sect.

The Sharif quickly wrote the sultan in Istanbul telling him of the matter and asking for his opinion. He received the answer from the sultan during a short period ordering him to arrest al-Haeiri and to hand him over to the Shami man in charge of the pilgrimage affairs, namely As`ad Pasha the Great. The Sharif carried out the sultan's order. Al-Haeri was transported and escorted by As`ad Pasha to Sham (the Levant) where he was jailed in the Damascus Fortress. A short period thereafter, al-Haeri was summoned to Istanbul, so he was transported there under custody. It is narrated that he died of poison, but he received an official mourning and was buried in a grave that suited his status, one which still stands.[2]

It seems that Sharif Mas`ud realized his critical situation following this incident, and he may have heard the rumors circulated about his inclining towards the Ja`fari sect, so he ordered the "Rafidhis" to be cursed from the pulpits[3] in order to avoid such rumors.

War Against Wahhabis

In the mid-18th Century A.D., the Wahhabi call started surfacing in Najd. Few years after its inception, the Wahhabis sent thirty of their scholars to Mecca to debate its scholars. Dahlan, author of the book titled *Khulasat al-Kalam fi Umara' al-Balad al-Haram* (a summary of what is said about the rulers of the Sacred Land), says that Sharif Mas`ud ordered the scholars of both Harams (Mecca and Medina) to debate with the Wahhabi scholars, so they debated with them and found their beliefs to be

---

1 Ahmed al-Siba`i (Op. Cit.), p. 300.
2 Ali al-Wardi, *Lamahat Ijtima`iyya* (Social Glimpses), Vol. 1, p. 141, Baghdad: 1969.
3 Ahmed al-Siba`i (Op. Cit.), p. 300.

corrupt. The judge of the Shari`a wrote the evidence of their apostasy, ordering them jailed, so Sharif Mas`ud jailed some of them whereas the rest ran away.¹

Sharif Mas`ud ordered to prohibit the Wahhabis from performing the pilgrimage, and this prohibition remained in effect during the time of his successors. In 1788, Ghalib ibn Musa`id became the Sharif of Mecca, and he was a cunning and tyrannical man. The Wahhabi call had grown in his time and many tribes joined it, so Sharif Ghalib decided to fight and crush them.

Ghalib sent several military campaigns to Najd in which he did not succeed. In 1798, he was forced to reconcile with the Wahhabis, permitting them to perform the pilgrimage. The Wahhabis took the ceasefire opportunity with Ghalib to direct their raids against Iraq, and in 1802, they committed their famous foul deed in Kerbala which they raided suddenly, killing many of its residents and looting its residents. They also looted the coffers of the Shrine of Imam al-Husain D as we described in detail in the first part of this book.

The Wahhabis breached their agreement with Sharif Ghalib in 1802. Othman al-Mudha'ifi, the vizier of Sharif Ghalib and the husband of his sister, joined the Wahhabis, so the latter felt strengthened through him. Al-Mudha'ifi returned at the head of a large army of Wahhabi tribes to lay a siege and eventually overrun Taif. The Wahhabis committed in Taif a horrible massacre, looting everything in the city, as was their habit in every town they conquered, since they regard its residents as polytheists whose blood should be shed and wealth looted.

When Taif was overrun, prince Saud ibn Abdul-Aziz was on his way to invade Iraq. When the news of the conquest of Taif at the hands of the forces of Othman al-Mudha'ifi reached him, he was greatly elated, so he abandoned the plan to invade Iraq and

---

1 Muhsin al-Ameen, Kashf al-Irtiyab (uncovering the doubts), 3rd ed., p. 7.

went to Hijaz. Prince Saud was able to conquer Mecca without a fight because the Sharif had already withdrawn from it by then and gone to Jidda where he fortified himself.

On the 8th of Muharram of 1218 A.H./April 30, 1803 A.D., prince Saud entered Mecca wearing the *ihram* garbs (of the pilgrims), so he circumambulated, performed the *sa`i* and slaughtered about one hundred camels. On the next day, his caller called ordering people to assemble in the morning of the next day. When people were all present at the set time, Prince Saud ascended the steps of the Safa with the *mufti* on his right side and the judge on his left and delivered a conventional sermon imitating the Prophet 7 upon his conquest of Mecca. He said the following:

"Allāh is Great! Allāh is Great! There is no god but Allāh alone; He was truthful to His promise; He supported His servant, carried out His promise and granted His hosts the upper hand. There is no god but Allāh; we worship none but Him, being sincere to Him in our creed though the unbelievers detest it. Praise be to the One Who is true to His promise to us. O people of Mecca! You are the neighbors of His House, feeling secure through His security, residing the areas of His Haram, and you are in the best area. Be informed that everything in Mecca is prohibited; besides it, no other place is without population; its game is never scared, its trees are never uprooted, yet it was made lawful for one hour of the day. We used to be the weakest of the Arabs. When Allāh deemed this religion to gain the upper hand, we propagated it while everyone was ridiculing us, fighting us over it, looting our cattle then we would buy them from him. We kept inviting people to Islam, and all the tribes whom your eyes see and whom you hear accepted Islam through this sword—raising his sword in the direction of the Ka`ba—and I was this year on a campaign in the direction of Iraq. But when I heard what happened to the Muslims during the invasion of Taif, how they were confronting you with their invasion, I feared for you because of the Bedouins and the desert dwellers. So, you should praise Allāh Who guided you to Islam and saved you from polytheism, and I call on you to worship only Allāh and to abandon the polytheism which you used to uphold. And I ask you to swear the oath of allegiance to me according to the religion of Allāh and His Messenger, that you should accept as master the one whom He appoints as the master and to be the enemies of whomsoever he brands as his enemy, during the time of ease and during hardships, to listen and to obey."

Once Prince Saud finished his sermon, he sat down and people rushed to swear the oath of allegiance to him in the vanguard of whom were: the *mufti*, the judge and Sharif Abdul-Mu`een, brother of Sharif Ghalib. Then Prince Saud ordered the people of Mecca to demolish all domes and graves under them so there would be none to worship save Allāh.

The next morning, the Wahhabis, together with many residents of Mecca, rushed to carry shovels to demolish the domes in the prayer area, then they demolished the dome over the birthplaces of the Prophet 7, of that of Abu Bakr, Ali ibn Abu Talib and Lady Khadija. They kept doing so until there was no sign of a dome. During their demolition, they were reciting martial poetry, beating drums and cursing the graves as they were saying, "They are only names which you called." It is said that one of them urinated on the grave of Sayyid Mahjoob.[1]

Prince Saud ordered to burn the hookahs (hubble-bubbles) and all amusement instruments, prohibiting smoking and the use of tobacco. He also prohibited praying for aid from creatures, the building of domes over graves and the kissing of thresholds. He also banned any statement added to the *athan*, such as blessing the Prophet 7, or the caller to prayers saying, "O most Merciful of all those who have mercy," or seeking the pleasure of the *sahaba* which he regarded as a form of polytheism. Then he ordered the book written by Muhammed ibn Abdul-Wahhab,

---

1 Op. Cit., pp. 21-23.

which is titled *Kashf al-Shubuhat* (unveiling what is doubtful), to be taught at the Mosque in a public circle attended by scholars and residents, which they did.

After Prince Saud had remained in Mecca for about twenty-four days, he went with his armies to Jidda to conquer it. Sharif Ghalib had already fortified himself behind Jidda's bulwarks in preparation to fight him. The fighting between both sides went on for eight days without Saud being able to conquer Jidda. Saud was forced to return to Najd following a disturbing report which reached him. Sharif Ghalib was able to return to Mecca.

The wars went on between Sharif Ghalib and the Wahhabis who were able in 1804 to tighten the siege of Mecca, preventing rations from reaching it, causing famine to spread throughout it. This condition went on up to the next year. Some people had to eat hides, date stones, poppy seeds, cats and dogs[1] or any animal, and they drank blood and ate a plant called ochrit which caused them to develop swellings. Children were seen lying dead in the alleys.[2]

Sharif Ghalib was forced in February of 1806 to sign a treaty of reconciliation with the Wahhabis. They reconciled on the condition Hijaz would be under the control of the Wahhabis and that Sharif Ghalif would remain in charge of his emirate as their vassal.

When the pilgrimage season approached the next year, prince Saud said to both Syrian and Egyptian men in charge of it, "What are these small sticks which you bring and which you glorify?!," pointing out to the loaders. They answered him that those loaders were to signal people to assemble, and it was an ancient tradition. He, therefore, said to them, "Do not do that after this year, and if you bring them, I shall break them." He also

---

1 Ahmed al-Siba'i (Op. Cit.), p. 351.
2 Muhsin al-Ameen (Op. Cit.), p. 32.

preconditioned that they should not bring with them any drums or flutes.

In the next pilgrimage season, when the Syrian man in charge of the pilgrimage approached Medina, Prince Saud sent him a message saying, "Do not enter Hijaz unless you adhere to the term which we imposed on you the past year." The man in charge of the pilgrimage caravan returned together with the pilgrims in his company to their homeland. It is said that Saud ordered to burn the Egyptian loader that year. He also ordered his caller to call on people saying: "Nobody reaches both Harams (Medina and Mecca) after this year if he has shaven his beard." Since then, the Egyptians and Syrians stopped performing the pilgrimage[1], and the Iraqis, too, stopped[2].

Saud ordered the demolition of all domes which used to be in the Baqee` area and in Medina with the exception of that of the Prophet's Mosque. He also seized all the precious items and jewels stored in the Prophetic Chamber which included four emerald chandeliers in each of which there was a diamond giving out light instead of a wax candle.[3]

Egyptian Campaign

Ottoman sultan Mahmud [Khan] II instructed Muhammed Ali Pasha, provincial governor of Egypt, to send armies to Hijaz to expel the Wahhabis from it. Muhammed Ali prepared a strong campaign under the leadership of his oldest son, Toson Pasha. In 1811, the campaign crossed the Red Sea in boats to Yanbu` and occupied that town after a fierce fighting. The soldiers looted the town and took its women captive, according to Jabarti[4]. But when the campaign advanced towards Medina, reaching near

---

1 Hafiz Wahba, *Jazeerat al-Arab fil Qarn al-`Ishreen* (Arabian Peninsula in the Twentieth Century), p. 226, Cairo: 1967.
2 Muhsin al-Ameen (Op. Cit.), p. 35.
3 *Ibid.*, p. 35.
4 According to the previous source, p. 37.

Badr, it was suddenly attacked by the Wahhabis who inflicted a terrible defeat on it, forcing it to withdraw to Yanbu`.

Muhammed Ali Pasha prepared another campaign which was able to attract the tribes to it with the huge money it doled out and was finally able to conquer Medina, Jidda and Mecca. Sharif Ghalib supported and cooperated with it. The Sharif advanced at the head of a large force towards Taif which he conquered. Othman al-Mudha'ifi fell captive, so the Sharif ordered him to put an iron chain round his neck, then he sent him to Egypt.

When Muhammed Ali Pasha heard the reports of the victories which his armies in Hijaz scored, he went in person to them. Upon his arrival at Jidda, Sharif Ghalib was present to meet him. Then a delegation from Prince Saud went to him, too, seeking a peace treaty and also asking for the release of Othman al-Mudha'ifi, offering a ransom of one hundred thousand French riyals. Muhammed Ali said to the delegation, "As regarding al-Mudha'ifi, he has already been sent to Islambul (Istanbul). As for the reconciliation, we do not oppose it provided all what we have spent on the armies, from the beginning of the war up to this day, be paid and all what was taken away from the treasures of the Prophet's Chamber must be returned..." The delegation returned disappointed. Al-Mudha'ifi was sent to Istanbul where he was put on a display at its markets together with his fellow, Ibn Madyan, then they both were executed.[1]

Muhammed Ali Pasha left Jidda for Mecca. When he reached it, Sharif Ghalib surrounded him with great signs of welcome, exaggerating his hospitality for him. On his part, Muhammed Ali exaggerated his signs of respect for the Sharif, kissing his hands in front of people. Both of these men pledged inside the cubic structure of the Ka`ba to be loyal to each other and that they would never betray each other.

---

1 *Ibid.*, p. 41.

Story of the Sharifs and Ibn Saud

The Ottoman sultan was angry with Sharif Ghalib because of his past reconciliation with the Wahhabis, so he wrote Muhammed Ali ordering him to arrest the Sharif and to send him to Istanbul. Muhammed Ali felt embarrassed about carrying this order which had come from the sultan after his pledge to the Sharif while being in the interior of the Ka`ba to always be loyal and to never betray him. Muhammed Ali finally found a legitimate trick that enabled him to carry out the order: He commissioned his son Toson Pasha, to carry it out and did not do so by himself in order to avoid violating his covenant. Toson Pasha carried out the command, ordering the arrest of Sharif Ghalib after kissing his hands.

Sharif Ghalib was sent to Egypt with both his sons, Abdullah and Husain, and with four of his slaves. His wealth and possessions were confiscated, and everything in his house was seized. His women and bondmaids were taken out of the house after searching them in the most shameful way. But when he reached Egypt, he was received with a great celebration: Cannons were fired and his women were permitted to join him, then he was sent to Salonic [or Thessaloniki (Greek: Θεσσαλονίκη [θesalo'nici]), which is often referred to internationally as Thessalonica or Salonica – Tr.] with his women and both his sons as well as slaves. The sultan ordered to return to them everything which had been confiscated from them and to grant them sufficient salaries. Sharif Ghalib spent most of his life in Salonica and died of the plague in 1816.[1]

Wars continued between the Egyptian campaign and the Wahhabis. Muhammed Ali Pasha had to return to Egypt in 1815, leaving behind the command of the campaign to his son, Toson. In late 1816, Toson died of fever, so Muhammed Ali appointed his second son, Ibrahim Pasha, as commander of the campaign. Ibrahim was able to score victory over the Wahhabis and to

---

1 Abdullah Philby, *Tarikh Najd* (History of Najd), p. 139, tr. By Omar al-Dirawi, Beirut, Lebanon.

pursue them until he reached in 1818 their capital, al-Dar`iyya. After laying a siege on al-Dar`iyya for six months, it surrendered to him, so Ibrahim killed its clergymen then sent Abdullah ibn Saud, who had succeeded his father in commanding the Wahhabis, to Istanbul where he was executed as ordered by the sultan. In June of 1819, Ibrahim Pasha received an order from his father, Muhammed Ali, to destroy al-Dar`iyya completely, so Ibrahim carried out the order, and al-Dar`iyya was turned into ruins.[1]

Between Awn and Zaid

Egypt's control over Hijaz lasted almost thirty years. The Egyptian army did not withdraw from Hijaz except in 1840. That period had a great impact on the Sharifdom post: The Sharif of Mecca before then used to be the absolute ruler of Hijaz, and the authority of the Ottoman government over him was almost nominal.[2] But after that, the Sharif became partner in authority with a Turkish governor, and he had with him regular forces under his command. Since then, a feud started between the governor and the Sharif which sometimes intensified and other times eased. The governor wanted to impose the authority of the state in Hijaz, whereas the Sharif wanted to restore the glory of his ancestors' absolute rule.

It can be said that the struggle among the Sharifs themselves, as a result, suffered a new element which never existed before: the influence of the state and the orders of the sultan. After the struggle among the competing families used to be confined to Hijaz and depended only on force, it now started, moreover, to be circulated in the lobbies of Istanbul where each family tried to win favor with the sultan and distort the image of its contender.

The period of the Egyptian rule in Hijaz witnessed the beginning of the famous struggle between two Sharif families:

---

1   *Ibid.*, p. 161.
2   Sulayman Mousa, *Al-Haraka al-Arabiyya* (The Arab Movement), p. 44, Beirut, 1970.

the family of the offspring of Zaid and the family of the offspring of Awn. This is the struggle that went on even after World War I and had its impact on the near history of the Sharifs.

Abdul-Muttalib son of Ghalib was the leader of the offspring of Zaid, and he assumed the post of Sharif in 1827, but his term did not last long because he had a contender for the post: Muhammed son of Abdul-Mu`een, leader of the offspring of Awn. The offspring of Zaid claimed that Muhammed ibn Abdul-Mu`een was not a Sharif but a man whose lineage was unknown, that he used to work as a servant of the lady Sharif Hazima daughter of Abdul-Muttalib. But Muhammed Ali Pasha wanted to make of him an opponent of Abdul-Muttalib out of personal vendetta and in order to harm and weaken the Sharifs.

In early 1828, a fierce battle took place in Taif between forces of Abdul-Muttalib and those of Muhammed ibn Abdul-Mu`een. The Egyptian forces supported Muhammed, so he scored victory over his opponent. Abdul-Muttalib, therefore, sought his security, and he left Hijaz for Istanbul where Sultan Mahmud warmly welcomed him upon his arrival, surrounding him with his generosity and keeping him in his company in Istanbul.

The period during which Muhammed continued to be the Sharif went on until 1851 when the sultan ordered to depose him for an unknown reason. The government appointed Abdul-Muttalib as the Sharif in his place. Muhammed went to Istanbul where he and his sons lived as protégés of the sultan a life of prestige just as his opponent, Abdul-Muttalib, had before then lived.

This time, Abdul-Muttalib did not continue to be the Sharif for more than four years. In 1854, an incident took place that led to his ousting. The sum-up of the incident is that the Turkish governor, Kamil Pasha, had received an order from the sultan to prevent the public sale of slaves in the markets in order to cope with a treaty signed between the Ottoman government and

Chapter One: Mecca's Sharifs

Britain. Kamil Pasha summoned the slave traders and notified them of the order. Hardly the report spread in Mecca when a public uproar took place and people called for *jihad*. Students of theology met at the house of their chief to request him not to surrender to this order which, according to their opinion, violated the Islamic Shari`a. They also asked him to go with them to the judge's house to prevent the issuing of the order. The chief scholar responded to their request and accompanied them to the judge's house. The masses joined them on the way as they were shouting to revolt, and they clashed with the Turkish protection force in a fierce fighting that extended to the Haram Mosque. Many persons from both parties were killed.

Sharif Abdul-Muttalib was at the time in Taif. When he heard about the matter, he decided to stand beside the residents against the Turkish force. He gathered his followers and went with them to Mecca. The Turkish force quickly withdrew to Jidda where it fortified itself. The governor declared that the sultan's order had reached him to depose Abdul-Muttalib from the Sharif post and to reinstate Muhammed ibn Abdul-Mu`een in his place.

On April 26, 1855, a ship arrived at Jidda carrying Muhammed ibn Abdul-Mu`een, so festivities were held in Jidda celebrating his coming. Muhammed marched at the head of large forces towards Taif where Abdul-Muttalib was fortifying himself. He launched a fierce attack on Taif, forcing his way through it and arresting Abdul-Muttalib whom he sent escorted to Istanbul. The sultan forgave him and housed him in a mansion with prestige.[1]

On March 29, 1858, Muhammed ibn Abdul-Mu`een died of sickness which let him live for only few days, so his son, Abdullah, assumed the post of Sharif. Abdullah kept his Sharif post up to the time of the first constitution in the Ottoman state at the hands of Madhat Pasha in 1877, so Abdullah was deposed and his brother, al-Husain ibn Muhammed, who was a supporter

---

1 Ahmed al-Siba`i (Op. Cit.), pp. 375-376.

of Madhat Pasha and of the constitution, was appointed in his place.

Al-Husain ibn Muhammed remained in his post as the Sharif for two years and few months. In 1880, al-Husain was killed in Jidda by an Afghani darvish who stabbed him with a poisoned dagger. Tales have varied about the reason why he was killed, and it is said that Sultan Abdul-Hamid was the one who masterminded his assassination after the abolition of the constitution and the banishment of Madhat Pasha.

Abdul-Muttalib was reinstated in his post as the Sharif, and he was transported from Istanbul to Hijaz by a special ship affiliated with the sultan. He reached Mecca on May 28, 1880 and was awarded a huge welcome. He was then advanced in age, yet he kept treating the relatives of Awn and the supporters of the constitution with cruelty. In 1881, when Madhat Pasha and his supporters went to Mecca on their way to the Taif Prison, Abdul-Muttalib overlooked them from the window of his mansion as he kept saying, "I advised you, Madhat, but you did not listen."[1]

Awn's family could not remain silent about how Abdul-Muttalib ruled, so a delegation from it went to Istanbul to present to Sultan Abdul-Hamid documents proving the communications which Abdul-Muttalib was carrying out with the British. Zaid's relatives claimed that those documents were forged.[2] Apparently, those documents influenced the sultan who issued his order in 1882 to depose Abdul-Muttalib from his post as the Sharif and to appoint in his place a man from among Awn's relatives, namely Awn ibn Muhammed ibn Abdul-Mu`een, who is famous by the name *Awn al-Rafeeq*, "Awn the fellow". Abdul-Muttalib was thereafter arrested and remained in jail till his death in early 1886; he was more than a hundred years old.

---

1 *Ibid.*, p. 384.
2 Anis Saigh, *Al-Hashimiyyoon al Thawra al-Arabiyya al-Kubra* (the Hashemites and the Great Arab Revolution), pp. 35, Beirut: 1966.

Chapter One: Mecca's Sharifs

Awn Al-Rafeeq

Awn al-Rafeeq was Sharif of Mecca for 23 years, from 1882 to 1905. In fact, an entire book deserves to be written about him due to his strange character and the various tales and myths circulated about him.

One historian described him saying that the Sharifdom of Mecca reached during his time "its ultimate end of weakness and decline,"[1] whereas another historian described him as "the Ma'moon of his time and the al-Rashid of his country"[2]. The author of *Tarikh Mecca* (history of Mecca) provides us with a portrait of him which may be closer than others to reality; he says the following:

"It seems that Sharif Awn was... weird, self-contradictory in his actions, some of his contemporaries sanctify the depth of his knowledge, love for the public good, simplicity in private meeting places and affection towards peace-loving people. Others criticize him for misbehaving when in the company of close friends, cruelty in treating pilgrims, going to extremes in punishing those who oppose him and inventing the 'Khaznawis' who were persecuting the public." The author of *Tarikh Mecca* describes the "Khaznawis" as men whom Sharif Awn used as his private bodyguards to serve him, so they started behaving in a tyrannical way towards the public, taking advantage of their clout to persecute or even covet others' wealth. Nobody dared to complain against them. It is said that Sharif Awn used to hand pick them from among the public classes, vesting on them powers with which they were able to humiliate certain individuals out of vendetta."[3]

---

[1] Fuad Hamzah (Op. Cit.), p. 323.
[2] Quoting the manuscript of a book by Sayyid Hibat-ad-Din al-Shahristani titled *Thikra Jalalat al-Husain* (in Memoriam of His Majesty al-Husain). I thank Sayyid Jawad al-Shahristani for lending me this book.
[3] Ahmed al-Siba'i (Op. Cit), p. 390.

Story of the Sharifs and Ibn Saud

One of the matters because of which Sharif Awn al-Rafeeq became famous is his close association of a mentally unbalanced man named Ali Bu. This man used before that to wander about the streets in the nude, lowering his gaze and not speaking to anyone. If a passerby talked to him and insisted on speaking to him, this man would answer him with one and only statement to which he was accustomed: "It shall be done; it shall be done by the will of Allāh." It is said that the reason why Sharif Awn associated himself with this man is that the latter made a prediction for the Sharif which proved later to be true, so Awn believed that that man was holy. Sharif Awn, therefore, built the man an opulent mansion and vested on him luxurious clothes, bringing him close to him and requiring Mecca's dignitaries to kiss his hands and to respect him. This man maintained this high status until Awn al-Rafeeq died in 1905, so the man returned to roaming the streets anew.[1]

Another thing which was well known about Awn is that he used to love justice, or at least he wanted to be famous for so inclining to an amazing degree. It is said that he sometimes would order the jailing of animals and even of inanimate objects if they were behind a crime against someone. So, if a rock fell on someone and wounded him, he would order to beat that rock or execute it so people would understand that he would not neglect to affect retribution against a criminal even if it were an inanimate object that could bear no responsibility. It happened once that a rooster fell on logs belonging to a woman from the Levant, causing the logs to fall and wound the woman, so the Sharif ordered to jail the logs and did not release them except after that woman had submitted a petition to him in this regard.[2]

Among the accusations leveled against Sharif Awn is that he used to incline to the Wahhabi faith. The reason behind this accusation is that he ordered the demolition of sacred graves

---

1 *Ibid.*, pp. 390-391.
2 This is stated in the manuscript belonging to al-Shahristani.

such as that of Abdullah ibn al-Zubayr in Mecca and that of Eve in Jidda. Amin al-Rayhani narrates saying that the consulates of foreign countries (in Jidda) objected to Sharif Awn when he ordered the demotion of Eve's grave. They said to him, "It is up to you to do so to the graves of men of piety, but Eve is the mother of all people, and we protest against demolishing her gravesite." Sharif Awn was convinced of their statement, so he abandoned the idea of demolishing that grave.[1]

What is amazing is that at the time when his opponents used to accuse him of Wahhabism, the Shi`ites used to think that he was one of them. Sheikh Baqir al-Tasatturi, a Shi`ite scholar, was close to Sharif Awn. He used to go to visit him and spend years in his company. This sheikh was sure about Sharif Awn being Shi`ite.

The Shi`ites produced an evidence testifying to Sharif Awn being a Shi`ite through a number of matters which include the following: He stopped the merry celebrations which the people of Hijaz used to hold on the Ashura day thinking that it was the day when the ark of Noah settled on the Judi (Mountain). Sharif Awn, therefore, said to them, "We belong to Muhammed's nation, and the Ark of the Progeny of the Prophet was afflicted with its famous affliction on this very day," referring to the way al-Husain D was killed in Kerbala, "so the Prophet 7 must surely feel sad, and his nation must grieve, too."[2]

Also among those evidences is that he composed a lengthy poem eulogizing the death of Fatima al-Zahraa J and faulting those who harmed her. He delivered the poem in person to the pilgrims in the Ka`ba in 1904. The reality is that this poem gained fame among the Shi`ites of Iraq, and those who recite commemorative poems still recite it in their *majalis* commemorating the martyrdom of Imam al-Husain D, and they recite from it this line in particular:

1　Amin al-Rayhani, *Mulook al-Arab* (Arab kings), Vol. 1, p. 63, Beirut: 1951.
2　This is quoted from the handwritten manuscript of al-Shahristani.

Whose daughter is she? Whose mother is she?
Whose consort is she?
Woe unto whoever started the tradition of oppressing and harming her, whoever he may be.

It can be said, anyhow, that Sharif Awn was neither a Wahhabi nor a Shi`ite but a sect standing all by itself. One of those who socialized with him and came to know him describes him saying, "He used to get along with every sect through the best of what they had in order to sift their minds. He would then affect in them his policy and will and thus gather from all of this the hearts of the Islamic sects, the near and the far... Sharif Awn knew the arts fully well and was familiar with many sciences. Whenever a scholar met him, he would not leave him without believing that his knowledge is less than that of the Sharif... Every Islamic sect used to perform the pilgrimage believing that the ruler of both Harams (Mecca and Medina) was a member of its sect..."[1]

This strange policy followed by Sharif Awn must have pleased some people while making others angry. Apparently, the commoners were mostly pleased with it and admired it. As for the elite groups, they were angry because of it. In the vanguard of those who were critics of Sharif Awn was the governor, Nouri Pasha. Mecca's dignitaries and scholars wrote letters against Nouri to Sultan Abdul-Hamid complaining about him and speaking ill of him. The sultan sent a committee to Mecca to investigate. It was headed by Ratib Pasha. When the committee reached Jidda, it was welcomed by a messenger sent by Sharif Awn carrying a purse in which there were six thousand gold liras as a gift to Ratib Pasha.[2] When the committee investigated the complaints, it found out that they were baseless, clearing

---

1 This is quoted from al-Shahristani's manuscript.
2 Sulayman Mousa (Op. Cit.), p. 45.

Chapter One: Mecca's Sharifs

Sharif Awn of the charges leveled against him, labeling them as "fraud and false." A short while thereafter, the sultan ordered to oust Nouri Pasha from his post as governor and to appoint Ratib Pasha in his place.

In 1904, the famous poet Ahmed Shawqi composed a lengthy poem vehemently condemning Sharif Awn and urging the sultan to depose him. He submitted the poem to the sultan. Below is a sample of its verses:

وَاسْتَصْرَخَتْ رَبَّها في مَكَّةَ الأُمَمُ   ضَجَّ الحِجازُ و ضَجَّ البَيتُ والحَرَمُ
خليفةَ اللهِ أنتَ السَيِّدُ الحَكَمُ   قَد مَسَّها في حِماكَ الضُّرُّ فاقضِ لها
أللشَريفِ عليها أم لَكَ العَلَمُ؟   لكَ الرُبوعُ التي ريعَ الحَجيجُ بها
ان أنتَ لم تَنتَقِم، فاللهُ مُنتَقِمُ   أُهينَ بها ضيوفُ اللهِ واضطُهِدوا
تُسبى النِساءُ و يُؤذى الأهلُ و الحَشَمُ ؟   أفي الضُحى و عيونُ الجُندِ ناظِرةُ

وتُستَباحُ بها الأعراضُ والحُرُمُ؟   و يُسفَكُ الدَمُ في أرضٍ مُقَدَّسةٍ
ونَعلُهُ دونَ رُكنِ البَيتِ تُستَلَمُ   يَدُ الشَريفِ على أيدي الوُلاةِ عَلَتْ
مُبالَغٌ فيهِ والحَجّاجُ مُتَّهَمُ   نيرونُ ان قيسَ في بابِ الطُغاةِ بهِ
في العَفوِ عَن فاسِقٍ فَضلٌ ولا كَرَمُ   أدَّبَهُ أدَبَ أميرِ المؤمنينَ فما
بينَ البُغاةِ و بينَ المُصطَفى رَحِمُ   لا تَرْجُ فيهِ وَقاراً للرَسولِ فما
وفيهِ نَخوَتُهُ والعَهدُ والشَمَمُ   ابنُ الرَسولِ فتىً فيهِ شَمائِلُهُ
آلُ النَبيِّ بِأعلامِ الهُدى خُتِموا   ما كانَ طه لِرَهطِ الفاسِقينَ أباً
وباتَ مُستَأمناً في قومِهِ الصَنَمُ   مُحَمَّدٌ رُوعِيَت في القبرِ أعظُمُهُ
مِنهُ العُهودُ أتَت للناسِ واللِمَمُ¹   وخانَ عَونُ الرَفيقُ العَهدَ في بَلَدٍ

---

1 Ahmed Shawqi, *Al-Shawqiyyat*, Beirut, Vol. 1, pp. 211-213.

Story of the Sharifs and Ibn Saud

Here is a rough translation of these verses:
Hijaz, the House and the Haram have roared,
And nations loudly cried pleading to their Lord:
Though under your protection, harm afflicted them, so
Judge for them, O Allāh's viceregent, you are the judge we know.
To you belong the lands where pilgrims have tarried:
Does their flag belong to you or to the Sharif?
In them, Allāh's guests have been insulted and persecuted,
If you do not seek revenge, surely Allāh will.
Does it happen in daytime under eyes of guards armed?
Women taken, families and their retinues harmed?
The Sharif's hand is now over that of the governors,
And his sandals are received at the corner of the House,
Nero is now compared with other tyrants,
And even al-Hajjaj is now among defendants,
So discipline him, commander of the faithful, for
There is no honor or pride in forgiving a sinner,
Do not expect to see in him reverence for the Prophet,
No kinship is there between the Chosen One and aggressors.
The son of the Prophet is the one who has his greatness,
One who has his manliness, trustworthiness and loftiness,
Taha is never a father of the open sinners' offspring,
The Prophet's Progeny are sealed with renown men of guidance.
Muhammed's remains are in the grave revered,
Whereas an idol is now safe among his folks.
Awn al-Rafeeq has betrayed the promise in a land
Where people learned respect for promises and covenants.

This poem, despite its eloquence, did not have any effect on the sultan. Perhaps the money purses which the *wali* used to receive from the Sharif were more eloquent than this poem.

Anyhow, Awn died the next year, so his nephew, Ali ibn Abdullah, became the Sharif, but he was desposed in 1908 and al-Husain ibn Ali ascended to the Sharifdom after him.

Chapter Two
Al-Husain Ibn Ali

Al-Husain Ibn Ali

Al-Husain ibn Ali is the most famous Sharif of Mecca of all times. He drove the Sharifdom to the peak, but it quickly collapsed at his own hands. He, above all, enjoys a great significance in the history of contemporary Arabs and in that of Arab nationalism. We will try in this chapter to say something about his life up to his leading a revolution against the Turks, and we will in later chapters return to study the rest of the chapters of his life.

Early Life

His name is: al-Husain ibn Ali ibn Muhammed ibn Abdul-Mu`een, a descendant of Awn. He was born in Istanbul in 1853 to a Circassian mother named Waseela Khanum. His grandfather, father and uncles used to live at the time in Istanbul when their opponent, Abdul-Muttalib, one of Zaid's offspring, was the Sharif [of Mecca].

In 1855, when Muhammed ibn Abdul-Mu`een became Sharif, following the ousting of Abdul-Muttalib, he left Istanbul for Mecca with his sons and family, including his little grandson, al-Husain. In 1858, when Muhammed died, the Sharif who succeeded him was his son, Abdullah. Ali, al-Husain's father, returned to Istanbul where he died in 1870. As for his son, al-Husain, he stayed under the care of his uncle, Abdullah, in Mecca. In 1875, al-Husain married Abidiyya Khanum, daughter of his uncle Abdullah, who gave birth to four sons: al-Hassan, Ali, Abdullah and Faisal. The first died young, then the mother also died in 1889.

The early indications of his political activity surfaced in 1880 when Abdul-Muttalib, an offspring of Zaid, became Sharif for the second time. Al-Husain was among the members of the delegation sent by Awn to Istanbul to urge the sultan to depose Abdul-Muttalib. The offspring of Zaid claim that al-Husain was one of the most active members of the delegation and that he was the one who forged documents against Abdul-Muttalib. They also accused him of contacting the British Ambassador in Istanbul to ask for help against the offspring of Zaid and to urge him to rely on the relatives of Awn in preference over all others.[1]

When Abdul-Muttalib was ousted in 1882 from his post as the Sharif, Awn al-Rafeeq assumed this post after him. The relationship between al-Husain and his uncle, Awn, was very good: Awn quite often visited al-Husain at his house and was nice to his family, playing with his sons, so much so that he used to put the bridle in the mouth of Abdullah son of al-Husain and order him to run as a horse in order to have fun.[2]

In his *Memoirs*, Abdullah narrates an interesting incident that took place to him in those days. Its summary is that he and his sons had a teacher teaching them calligraphy. His name was Sheikh Othman al-Yamani. This teacher's gums were bleeding, so his mouth smelled very bad. He used to put the pencil in his mouth before dipping it in the inkpot, getting the ink mixed with his blood. Abdullah wanted to play a trick on him, so he brought some strong pepper and put it in the inkpot of his brother, Faisal. When the Sheikh put the pencil in his mouth after dipping it in the inkpot, he felt the sting of the pepper, then pain intensified and his mouth became sore. He decided to punish Faisal, thinking that he was behind it. He put both Faisal's feet in the spanking tool. Faisal kept screaming while swearing that he was innocent. The incident ended by releasing the teacher after apologizing to him, giving him cash and an outfit. When the report reached Sharif Awn al-Rafeeq, he summoned Abdullah and kept laughing, wondering about what he had done

---

1 Anees Saigh, *Al-Hashimiyyoon wal Thawra al-Arabiyya al-Kubra* (the Hashemites and the Great Arab Revolution), pp. 34-35, Beirut: 1966.
2 This is quoted from the handwritten manuscript of Hibat-ad-Din al-Shahristani.

Chapter Two: Al-Husain ibn Ali

and saying, "This is a strange and unusual shrewdness," then he ordered to summon the teacher and also to bring a dentist. He said to the teacher, "Othman! You wanted to teach our sons calligraphy, and they have taught you how cleanness should be." Then he summoned the dentist and ordered him to pull the teacher's teeth. The teacher kept screaming and pleading for help, so Sharif Awn ordered to leave him alone, giving him one thousand and five hundred riyals with a piece of advice to seek medical care.[1]

The good ties between al-Husain and his uncle, Sharif Awn, did not last long but started gradually worsening as time passed by. Sharif Awn kept charging al-Husain of instigating people against him, urging them to complain about him. He asked Sultan Abdul-Hameed to summon him to Istanbul in order to get rid of him, so an order came from the sultan that al-Husain should go to meet him. Al-Husain went to Istanbul in 1893 and the sultan welcomed him nicely, appointing him as a member in the state's consultative council. He ordered a furnished house on the Bosphorus to be prepared for him.

When al-Husain settled in his Istanbul home, he summoned his sons and other family members to him, so they arrived in early March of 1894. Fifteen days after their arrival, Safwat Afandi al-Awwa, a Syrian military officer, was appointed to teach al-Husain's sons some lessons, such as mathematics, history, geography and the Turkish language. Amin al-Rayhani narrates saying that Abdullah was diligent in his studies, but Faisal was lazy, always late in his lessons. Safwat al-Awwa went to al-Husain to complain to him about Faisal's laziness and about his being late, so al-Husain said to him, "Beat him, son, and have no fear..."[2]

In Istanbul, al-Husain married a Circassian girl who gave birth to his daughter Saliha. Shortly thereafter, the wife died, so

---

[1] Ubaydullah ibn al-Husain, *Muthakkarati* (My Memoirs), pp. 11-13, Jerusalem: 1945.
[2] Amin al-Rayhani, *Faysal al-Awwal* (Faysal I), p. 12, Beirut: 1958.

al-Husain married after her Aadila Hanum, granddaughter of Rasheed Pasha, the famous Turkish politician, who gave birth to his son Zaid as well as two daughters, Fatima and Sarah.[1]

Citing Nouri al-Sa`eed, Ms. Bell narrates in one of her letters saying, "He [Nouri al-Sa`eed] told me lots of gossip about the Sharif's family: the three sons by one mother, Ali, Abdullah and Faisal, of whom Abdullah was the favourite and Faisal always kept at a distance and was sent off to do far-away jobs. When their mother died, the Sharif married a Circassian. She quarreled with Ali over the management of the household, and Ali hated her son, Zaid, whom Faisal loved. Both Ali and Abdullah were terribly jealous of Faisal now."[2]

Al-Husain's stay in Istanbul went on for about seventeen years, and his life in it was not opulent to the degree that suited his status. Mrs. Ericson quotes Faisal, who described their life in Istanbul, as saying the following: "It was narrow and hard; meat was provided for us only once a week."[3] In his Memoirs, Abdullah says, "As regarding our stay in Istanbul, it was one of imposition, one of learning and of moral lessons..."[4]

Al-Husain Appointed Sharif

When the Ottoman constitution was made public on July 24, 1908, Mecca's Sharifdom was in the hands of Ali son of Abdullah, cousin of al-Husain and brother of his first wife. He was very slow in supporting the constitution, so an order was issued to oust him and to appoint his uncle, Abdullah son of Muhammed, instead of him. Abdullah used to reside in Istanbul, and he was old and sick. He died suddenly two days after the nomination

---

1 Sulayman Mousa, *Muthakkat al-Ameer Zaid* (Memoirs of Prince Zaid), pp. 14-213, Amman: 1976.
2 Elizabeth Burgoyne, *Gertrude Bell: From Her Personal Papers 1914-1926*, London: Ernest Benn Limited, 1961, p. 245.
3 Ericson, *Faisal King of Iraq* (translated by Oemr Abul Nasr), Beirut, 1934, p. 33.
4 Abdullah ibn al-Husain (Op. Cit.), pp. 36-37.

Chapter Two: Al-Husain ibn Ali

order. It is said that he died of elation[1], and it is also said that he died of poison[2].

While still in power, al-Husain submitted a petition to Sultan Abdul-Hamid requesting him to appoint him as the Sharif because he was "the most senior of the Hashemite family and the most worthy of the status of the fathers." The petition was carried by his son, Abdullah, who took it to Grand Vizier Kamil Pasha. On November 1, Sultan Abdul-Hamid summoned al-Husain and appointed him as Sharif of Mecca, also vesting on him the status of a cabinet minister.

Reports have varied about what prompted the Ottoman government to appoint al-Husain as the Sharif of Mecca. Some of those reports said that the Unionists were the ones who chose al-Husain to be the Sharif, whereas the sultan opposed that choice.[3] Others said that the Unionists desired to appoint Ali Haidar, grandson of Abdul-Muttalib from the offspring of Zaid, but the British ambassador pressured them to appoint al-Husain.[4] It was also said that the British ambassador used to enjoy influence with the Grand Vizier, Kamil Pasha, and this man insisted on appointing al-Husain contrarily to the opinion of the sultan who used to think that al-Husain was a dangerous man and that he would not be satisfied with partnership but would covet more, and he might threaten the throne of the Ottoman sultanate.[5]

Abdullah narrates in his *Memoirs* a tale that reflects the opposite of what we have stated. He says that when his father, al-Husain, wanted to leave Istanbul to go to Mecca, he met Sultan Abdul-Hamid to bid him farewell, and he was in seclusion with

---

1 Anees Saigh (Op. Cit.), pp. 36-37.
2 Ahmed al-Siba'i, *Tarikh Mecca* (history of Mecca), Cairo: 1372 A.H./1952 A.D., p. 396.
3 George Antonius, *Yqdhat al-Arab* يقظة العرب (Arabs' Awakening), translated by Nasir ad-Din al-Assad and Ihsan Abbas, Beirut: 1962, p. 178.
4 Anees Saigh (Op. Cit.), p. 37.
5 Muhammed Tahir al-Omari, *Muqaddarat al-Iraq al-Siyasiyya* مُقَدَّرات العراق السياسية (Iraq's Political Allotments), Baghdad: 1925, Vol. 1, p. 177.

him for more than one hour and a half. The sultan, therefore, said to him, "I plead to Allāh to deal with those who prevented me from benefitting from your Hashemite talents. I fear for this State from this quarrelsome group." Al-Husain said to him, "If you face hardship, let us be your safe haven, and we shall collect wealth for you and force the rebels to bow down to you." The sultan's eyes then overflowed with tears and said, "Thank you, Thank you, Allāh bless you, but such time is not opportune yet..."[1]

His Arrival at Mecca

Al-Husain and his family left Istanbul in November of 1908 in one of the Khedive company ships, and many bade him farewell in the vanguard of whom was Kamil Pasha. On December 3, the ship reached Jidda, and the welcome he received there was huge as we are told by one of the city's residents who says the following:

"The port's pier was over-crowded with welcoming people at the top of whom was a large number of Sharifs. They greeted him with the best of greeting, demonstrating to him their great pleasure at his assuming the post of governor of Mecca. This was the way with all people, especially those of Hijaz, in expressing their pleasure with every governor or ruler even if their hearts were not pleased. He settled in Jidda as guest of my father, Sheikh Muhammed Naseef. He was greeted by Hajj Muhammed Ali Zainul... in a detailed sermon which included a great deal of jewels of praise and compliments. Al-Husain responded to him with emotion that caused his eyes to shed tears..."[2]

Many delegations from various cities and tribes of Hijaz were present to welcome al-Husain. Among those delegations was

---

1　Abdullah ibn al-Husain (Op. Cit.), p. 27.
2　Husain Muhammed Naseeb, *Tarikh al-Hijaz* (history of Hijaz), Cairo: 1349 A.H./1929 A.D., Vol. 1, p. 7.

Chapter Two: Al-Husain ibn Ali

one representing the Advancement and Unification Party. The head of the delegation stood up to deliver a speech to welcome al-Husain. He described him as the "constitutional ruler," expressing his hope that he would act according to the spirit of the time and renewal. Al-Husain responded to this speech violently, pointing out that he did not know those 'new' matters, that Hijaz was the land of Allāh where there is only the Shari`a of Allāh which includes enjoining what is right and forbidding what is wrong. "So, let each of you go to his job: the government official to his job, the merchant to his trade, the craftsman to his profession..., and beware of what has been said, what is being said and what will be said, for these lands of Allāh are not anyone's property. The sultan, who ordered to have a constitution, and his predecessors are all proud of being servants of both Harams. The constitution of Allāh's land is the Shari`a of Allāh and the Sunnah of His Prophet." The members of the delegation, therefore, went out from the presence of al-Husain stumbling and wrote to Istanbul saying that Abdul-Hamid had sent them a man who did not pay attention to anyone, nor did he recognize the constitution nor any renewal.[1]

Al-Husain remained in Jidda for three days then left for Mecca which he reached on December 7. Welcoming him there was his brother, Sharif Nasir, the advisor Kadhim Pasha, Mecca's judge and Abdul-Qadir al-Sheebi, caretaker of the Ka`ba, as well as many others.

On the third day after his arrival at Mecca, he sent his son, Abdullah, to Taif to bring his maternal uncle, the deposed Sharif Ali ibn Abdullah, who was there. In his *Memoirs*, Abdullah narrates saying that when he reached Taif and met the deposed Sharif, he spoke to him in private. The following dialogue went on between them:

ALI: "What will you do to me?"

---

[1] Abdullah ibn al-Husain (Op. Cit.), pp. 24-25.

ABDULLAH: "Everything that is good, by the will of Allāh."

ALI: "Do you accept, O Abdullah, that I should travel to Istanbul so the petty-minded promoters of the Advancement and Unification Party would do to me what they have done to their ministers?"

ABDULLAH: "By the will of Allāh, this will not happen."

ALI: "How so?"

ABDULLAH: "Do whatever pleases you: If you wish to stay, you are in your homeland, after you come to a common agreement with your cousin. And if you want to leave, remain in Egypt and do not travel to Istanbul except after you feel comfortable."

ALI: "Do you guarantee this for me?"

ABDULLAH: "I will try, by the will of Allāh."

ALI: "Am I not your paternal uncle?"

ABDULLAH: "Yes, by Allāh."

ALI: "Do you accept that I should be insulted?"

ABDULLAH: "God forbid! But I have a pledge to you witnessed by Allāh that if I am unable to carry out your wish, I shall not part with you wherever you go."

ALI: "I now am pleased." Then his eyes watered, and he kissed Abdullah.[1]

When Ali reached Mecca in the company of his maternal nephew, Abdullah, he went to meet al-Husain. Al-Husain welcomed him from the hall's door then seated him on his own chair and remained in seclusion with him for a good while. On the next day, al-Husain held a special council to decide the fate of the deposed Sharif. They, therefore, disputed in his regard, and Abdullah insisted on permitting him to go to Egypt saying,

---

1 *Ibid.*, p. 38.

Chapter Two: Al-Husain ibn Ali

"I have pledged to him that if he is taken to Istanbul, I shall travel with him; whatever happens to him will happen to me, too." It was finally decided to allow him to travel to Egypt.[1] It is said that at the time of his departure for Egypt, he carried with him a great deal of money with which he bought real estates and a beautiful mansion in the Dome Gardens neighborhood which at the time was one of Cairo's luxurious areas. He lived there a life of ease and opulence.[2]

Al-Husain's Activity

The customary tradition in Hijaz since the end of the Egyptian campaign in 1840 was that the Sharif would handle the affairs of the Bedouins and tribes, while the Turkish governor would look after the administrative affairs in the cities. Al-Husain did not submit to this tradition but tried to get out of it, so he kept disputing with the governor regarding his powers. He did not let any resident seek a judgment except from him, be it with regard to personal status or civilian liberties. Al-Husain kept firming his relationships with the dignitaries of Hijaz by being humble and kind to them, urging them to submit complaints to Istanbul against the governor. Through this way was he able to oust five governors in eight years.

In the fall of 1908, there were delegate elections in which two men won as delegates representing Mecca: Abdullah ibn al-Husain and Sheikh Hassan al-Sheebi, son of the Ka`ba's caretaker. Both men travelled to Istanbul via the sea route in order to attend the sessions of the delegates' council. But upon their arrival, they were both notified by the council's head that telegrams from Mecca had arrived protesting their election, saying that Abdullah was not suitable to be a delegate because he did not meet the legal age requirement, and that Sheikh Hassan al-Sheebi was an illiterate who could neither read nor write. When

---

1 *Ibid.*, p. 39.
2 Husain Muhammed Naseef (Op. Cit.), p. 5.

those telegrams were submitted to the council, one of the MPs protested saying, "Whom do you want? Should Mecca send you one who is better than the son of the Sharif and the son of the one who opens the House of Allāh?!" All council members shouted, "No objection; no objection." It was then that Abdullah and his fellow were brought to the council's hall.[1]

When the delegate elections were held for the second time in the spring of 1912, Abdullah was reelected to represent Mecca, while his brother, Faisal, was elected to represent Jidda. Abdullah and his brother were accustomed to spending the time, while the council was in session, in Istanbul then returning to Hijaz in the summer.

What is known about Abdullah is that he was quite articulate, wearing a merry face; his personality was attractive and he was abile to win friends; therefore, he was actually the true representative of his father in Istanbul's political circles. As for his brother, Faisal, he was his opposite: He spoke very little, inclining to be serious and having a nervous temper. It is not known about him that he undertook any noticeable activity in Istanbul inside the council or outside it.

With Ibn Saud

In 1910, the first signs of the dispute between al-Husain and Ibn Saud surfaced. It is the struggle that lasted almost fifteen years: Sometimes it intensified, and some other times it died down. It ended up in Ibn Saud being victorious and in the disappearance of the Sharifs' rule in Hijaz as we will discuss in the forthcoming chapters.

Bad circumstances surrounded Ibn Saud in 1910 as well as an acute financial crisis because of drought. Apparently, the Ottoman state wanted to use that opportunity to impose its hegemony over him, so it instructed al-Husain to march against

---

1 *Ibid.*, Vol. 1, p. 8.

Chapter Two: Al-Husain ibn Ali

him. In July, al-Husain led his forces towards Najd. When he reached the Shi`ra, the first Najd village from the Hijaz direction, he arrested Sa`d, brother of Ibn Saud. Al-Husain wrote Ibn Saud saying, "If you attack us, we will leave the camp and tents for you and return with your brother, Sa`d, to Mecca, and he will remain with us until you seek a reconciliation."

Khalid ibn Luay, ruler of al-Kharma, undertook the task of reconciling both sides. He was one of the Sharifs, but he inclined to Ibn Saud and to Wahhabism. He went to Ibn Saud and said to him in his Bedouin jargon, "Listen, Abdul-Aziz, I am going to teach you something. The Sharif has no ill intention towards you, No, by Allāh. But he wants to improve his image with the Turks; so, write him something that will benefit him with the Turks while not harming you. I guarantee the return of Sa`d and that the Sharif will not interfere in Najd's affairs, that is, if you do not go beyond your limits. But if he transgresses against you, I, Khalid ibn Luay, grant you a pledge witnessed by Allāh to be with you, by Allāh, just as my fathers used to be with your fathers, and just as my grandfathers used to be with your grandfathers." Ibn Saud was convinced of what Khalid had said, so he wrote him a pledge to pay the state six thousand pounds every year.[1]

Al-Husain released Sa`d. On September 23, Ibn Saud sent one of his cousins, namely Abdul-Aziz ibn Abdullah, to al-Husain accompanied by three thorough-bred mares as a gift with a letter full of flattery and compliments. Its text was as follows:

> *Your most great and conscientious emir of Venerable Mecca, our master Sharif Husain Pasha son of Sayyid Ali, may Allāh prolong his glory and loftiness, Aameen.*
>
> *After sending you more greetings, the continuous mercy of Allāh and His blessings, while inquiring about your honorable fragrant mood, may you remain in perfect health and happiness,*

---

[1] Ameen al-Rayhani, *Tarikh Najd al-Hadith* (modern history of Najd) and Appendices, Beirut, 1954, pp. 192-193.

achieving the praiseworthy merits, our conditions, due to Allāh's generosity, are beautifu. We have already sent Your Excellency a letter which we hope reached you at your pleasure. We submit to Your Excellency that according to your kindness, the loftiness of your resolve and high vision, we presented our brother, Abdul-Aziz Abdullah Al Saud, according to our service of yourself. We would like to further send you a gift in order to seek a blessing from your feet: We sent with him [the horses named] al-Saqlawiyya, al-Hamdani and Khailan, not, by Allāh, because you need them, and there is no doubt about our objective, we simply wish to bring ourselves closer to you. We here consider ourselves as your servants, and the favor belongs to Allāh then to you. Our gift to you is: our heads and whatever is at our disposal. But it [gift] is a gift for the respectful sons. We wrote this letter to underscore our serving you and what seems to be obligatory; otherwise, your command over us is at any rate complete. However you fare with us and cast your eyes over us, you, by the will of Allāh, will find it doubled with services, hearing and obeying. This much you must know. The son is at your service, and please do convey our greeting to the honorable masters, Ali, Faisal and Zaid. From our end, our sons, Muhammed and Saud and all the Al Saud, greet you, may God always protect you.

Servant of the state, creed and homeland,

The Prince of Najd and of the heads of its tribes,

Abdul-Aziz Al Saud

Month of Ramadhan 18, 1328 A.H./September 10, 1910 A.D.[1]

Thereafter, al-Husain wrote Ibn Saud reminding him of what he had notified him, i.e. that he was making preparations to attack Hijaz, and that some tribes residing at the borders complain about his assaults on them. Ibn Saud responded to him

---

1 Hafiz Wahba, *Jazeerat al-Arab fil Qarn al-'Ishreen* (the Arabian Peninsula in the 20th century), Cairo: 1967, pp. 337-338. See also: Ameen Sa'eed, *Tarikh al-Dawla al-Saudia* (history of the Saudi state), Beirut, Vol. 2, pp. 51-52.

with a letter of flattery and endearment more than what he had included in the first letter. It is a lengthy letter from which we would like to excerpt the following:

"... Now, your son, servant and slave of your favor—referring to himself—listens and obeys Allāh then your own self..., as you command, so shall I submit to the command of Allāh then to yours. Had I been the criminal, I am at your command: As you order, so shall I do, being patient regarding your discipline... I, by Allāh, by Allāh and by Allāh, do swear that your pleasure and serving you are dearer to me than the pleasure of Abdul-Rahman—meaning his father—and his service. Then I have already granted you a pledge witnessed by Allāh, the security of Allāh, that I am your son, listening to you and obeying you, never disobeying your advice in any matter. I am at your service if you wish to hold a meeting between myself and the forgers at any time you wish, I shall attend it. If you wish to do so from a distance, we can remain in communication with each other, and we fall under the faring of Allāh then of your own self. Yet they cannot forge and pass it on to Your Excellency. They claim I am mobilizing the people of Najd in order to fight you or rebel against you; No by Allāh, No by Allāh, No by Allāh. I never sought their aid to invade you because our relationship is chilled and because of some corruption which is not hidden from you. Do not ever imagine that my coming here is to fight you or for any reason that incurs your anger. Rather, it is seeking nearness to you... Our duty is to expedite the messenger to you in order to answer your dear query, and we are waiting for the management of Allāh then yours, remaining at your service. This is our obligation. Please convey our Salam to the honorable gentlemen, and from our end, your sons Muhammed, Saud and all the Al Saud family kiss your hands, and may the Almighty always protect you.

"Shawwal 15, 1328/October 7, 1910 A.D."[1]

---
1 Hafiz Wahba (Op. Cit.), pp. 338-339.

We do not have to say that this throwing into one's hands expressed by Ibn Saud towards al-Husain was only one manifestation of the cunning whereby Ibn Saud was famous. During that period, he was busy with his internal problems, and he did not see his interest lying in being involved in another problem with al-Husain, so he preferred to appease him and to try to be liked by him temporarily until he finished solving his domestic problems. Apparently, al-Husain did not understand that, and he might have become conceited due to the flattery and subjugation expressed to him by Ibn Saud, so he thought that the latter was weak and would always remain weak. Al-Husain kept looking at Ibn Saud during the next years with this attitude, dealing with him thereupon, and this was al-Husain's mistake; it was one of the most important factors that finally led to his pitiful end.

The Aseer Campaign

The Aseer region is part of Yemen and lies to the south of Hijaz. In those days, it used to be a governorate under the authority of the Ottoman state with the town of Abha as its metropolis. Its governor was Sulayman Shafeeq Pasha. In 1910, Sayyid Muhammed al-Idrisi revolted against the state. He used to enjoy influence and sanctity in that region, so he was successful in his revolution. The Italians used to help him. Late that year, al-Idrisi was able to lay a siege to Abha where there were large Turkish forces, and the siege lasted about ten months during which the residents suffered so much. They had to eat cats and dogs, and more than a thousand of them starved to death.[1]

The Ottoman state sought assistance from al-Husain to quell al-Idrisi's revolution, so al-Husain prepared a campaign for it and summoned his son, Abdullah, from Istanbul, to be with him in the campaign. He also brought with him his other son, Faisal.

---

1 Sulayman Mousa, *Al-Haraka al-Arabiyya*, Beirut: 1970, p. 54.

Chapter Two: Al-Husain ibn Ali

On April 16, 1911, the campaign moved from Mecca comprised, in addition to the local forces, of three Turkish regiments numbering three thousand men.

When the campaign entered Aseer's lands, the Idrisi forces kept launching raids on it time and over again, inflicting serious losses on it.[1] On July 16, the campaign reached Abha and was able to lift the siege and to enter it.

The Constitution Day coincided on the 24th of July, few days after al-Husain had reached Aseer. That day coincided with the anniversary of the commencement of the mission of Prophet Muhammed 7 according to the lunar calendar, so a celebration was held in Abha on this occasion in which al-Husain delivered a speech praising in it the Ottoman state and condemning al-Husain in the ugliest way, charging him with serving foreign states for his own personal gains. Below is the text of the speech:

"Brothers! Be informed with full conviction that had it not been for the existence of this Ottoman state, had it not been for its caliphs' extreme care about the Islamic nation, especially our Mawlana, the present commander of the faithful—meaning Sultan Rashad—the hands of foreign states would have snatched you as the wolves snatch lone cattle. This is so because all states have for long been involved in the decline of Muhammed's Shari`a through these conceited men who serve them for their own personal gains. Brothers! Are you pleased with the actions of these folks who endeavor to ruin your lands in the name of righteousness? I do not know how you were fooled by these folks and their likes while you have sound reason and genuine Arab manliness. Your early forefathers were the most dignified of all Arabs. From them did you inherit lofty determination. Are you not the offspring of Tubba` people?! Are you not the ones about whom my grandfather, the Messenger of Allāh 7, had said: 'Knowledge comes from Yemen; wisdom comes from Yemen'?! Are your honored predecessors not the ones who were famous

---
[1] Abdullah ibn al-Husain (Op. Cit.), p. 61.

for instinctive brilliance and crowned glory?! O Allāh, O Allāh, O custodians of the Arab nation with regard to your religion: Do not lose it; rather, safeguard it and shade yourselves with the shade of the Ottoman flag which is the slogan of Islam. Do not be impressed by the statements of those who cause corruption, who try to carry out the purposes of those who mobilize for their own sake the enemies of the Islamic religion. Due to the goodness of your substance and your lack of experience in foreign politics, you think that they serve the religion, while they, by Allāh, are isolated from it, serving none but their own personal objectives, shielding themselves with the name of the religion. So, I warn you against being impressed by such villains who have swiftly abandoned the creed; rather, you should obey the commander of the faithful. You should know that anyone who opposes him in fact opposes Allāh and His Messenger, and anyone who opposes him will incur the wrath of Allāh, losing the [goodness of] life in this world as well as the Hereafter, and such is the manifest loss."[1]

The Beginning of Dispute With the Turks

Al-Husain's speech in Abha represented the peak of harmony between himself and the Turks, but this harmony did not last long. It quickly started to vanish, and hostility gradually replaced it.

The dispute between al-Husain and the Turks started in Abha after the delivering of the said speech. The governor of Aseer noticed that al-Husain was not sincere in his intention regarding his Aseer campaign; rather, he intended it to strengthen his own influence. The governor was convinced that al-Husain was no less hostile towards the Ottoman state than al-Idrisi. He described him saying, "He is an Idrisi equipped with rifles and cannons."[2]

---

1   Husain Muhammed Naseef (Op. Cit.), Vol. 1, p. 21.
2   Ali Fuad, *Kaifa Ghazawna Misr?* (How we invaded Egypt), translated by Najeeb al-

Chapter Two: Al-Husain ibn Ali

What intensified the dispute between al-Husain and the Turks, according to Abdullah's narrative in his *Memoirs*, is that al-Husain saw some horrific atrocities committed by the Turkish soldiers against al-Idrisi's followers: Bodies grilled on fire, with tent rods inserted into their mouths and taken out of their rectums, were displayed before him four times... Also, six severed heads were displayed before him the penis of each of which had been stuck into its [severed head's] own mouth... When al-Husain witnessed all of that, he said to Nazeef Beg, a Turkish commander, "This is not appropriate!" Nazeef Beg answered him saying, "Did they not burn our hearts?!"[1]

Al-Husain decided to return to Hijaz with his forces before ending the war with al-Idrisi, so he left Abha on July 31, 1911. Abdullah narrates in his *Memoirs* a story that has its own implications in this regard: When al-Husain reached Taif, the governor of Hijaz, Hazim Beg, was waiting to welcome him in the company of Sharif Nasir ibn Muhsin, one of the offspring of Zaid. Al-Husain had known before his arrival that Sharif Nasir had spread bad rumors about the Aseer campaign and that he had rumored that al-Husain himself was killed in it. As soon as al-Husain saw him among the welcoming party next to the governor, he ordered to get him out violently, so the governor protested saying, "Excuse me, Sir, he came with me." Al-Husain said, "So what he came with you?!" The governor said, "I represent the sultan, and this treatment insults the sultan himself." Al-Husain answered saying, "Have you yet left any aspect from the side of the sultan which you have not insulted yet?! I, not you, am the representative of the sultan."[2]

The provincial governor (*wali*) sent a telegram to Istanbul describing what happened, so the following telegram was sent to al-Husain by Ibrahim Haqqi Pasha, the Grand Vizier: "The

---

Armanazi, Beirut: 1962, p. 87.
1 Abdullah ibn al-Husain (Op. Cit.), p. 66.
2 *Ibid.*, p. 68.

people in high positions have come to know about the rough treatment from your Hashemite self against Sharif Nasir son of Muhsin who rushed to welcome you with His Excellency Hazim Beg, the governor of Hijaz. The sultan wishes that you should summon the Sharif referred to above to appease and please him."

Al-Husain responded with the following telegram: "Since the reasons that necessitated what Sharif Nasir ibn Muhsin has received of reprimanding and expulsion are not related to me personally, I see no reason to demonstrate regret for what I have done. What was rumored by the person referred to, i.e. the weakness of the forces that were with me, and that we all were decimated, were not intended by him except to create a revolutionary movement here, too, for he deserves what has happened to him. Reports reached me from the scribes of the governorate, yet the governor brought him while knowing it; collusion and corruption are not among my characteristics."

The answer came immediately from the Grand Vizier saying, "The Sublime Porte cannot overlook the implications of going against the wish of the high authorities here and which was conveyed to you in the previous telegram and which we underscore in this one. We add that the sultan is awaiting the outcome."

Al-Husain answered thus: "I, being aware of my own dignity, the man who is regarded as the second base following in status the Vice Regent, do not think that the sublime wish is intended to demean this high status. The Sublime Porte, which cannot overlook the desire of the men in high position there, is asked: How can this shameful accusation be leveled against a man who hardly rubbed the dust of travel from his endeavor for the glory of the sultan?! The Sublime Porte is free to do whatever he likes."

The Sublime Porte did not answer this telegram. Apparently, the Turkish government was busy with a new matter that distracted it from the problem with al-Husain which was: A war was about to erupt between Turkey and Italy, and it might have desired to reconcile with him as a result of it. On the eve of Eidul-Fitr, which coincided with September 25, 1911, Othman Beg, commander of the Gendarmerie, went to al-Husain and told him that a telegram had arrived from the Sublime Porte to the governor asking him to visit al-Husain to apologize to him. He also said, "Does our master accept his apology?" Al-Husain expressed his readiness to welcome him. The visit took place in the morning of the next day during the Eid prayers.[1]

Only four days had passed since this reconciliation when the war with Italy broke out. Al-Idrisi was encouraged by that war, so he repeated the attack on the Turkish forces in Aseer. Italy supplied him with weapons, and an Italian destroyer shelled the Turkish garrisons on the Red Sea coast.

The Ottoman state sought al-Husain's help again. Al-Husain sent his forces to Aseer in the spring of 1912 led by his son, Faisal, who could not do anything of significance because the hot weather and malaria had exhausted his forces, and Faisal himself was sick with the malaria virus. It was rumored in Mecca that Faisal died of fever. It was said that one of Faisal's daughters was terrified upon hearing the news that her father had died, so she fell headlong and became, as a result, paralyzed. Faisal finally returned transported on a carrier due to his extreme weakness.[2]

The Start of Communication With the British

During the first week of February of 1914, Abdullah son of al-Husain was on his way from Mecca to Istanbul. He was hosted in Cairo by Khedive Abbas Hilmi in the Abidin Mansion. Abdullah took the opportunity to meet [Lord] Kitchener [then British Secretary of State of War] [1868 – 1947], the British Attaché in Egypt, in the presence of his East secretary, [Sir] Ronald Storrs [1881 – 1955]. He kept talking to him about the

---

1 *Ibid.*, p. 70.
2 Ameen al-Rayhani, *Faisal al-Awwal* (Faisal I), pp. 13-14.

tense relations between the Turks and his father, al-Husain, hinting that the Turks might oust his father from his Sharif post. He asked him indirectly about the position of the British government in this regard and whether it was possible Britain would assist his father if he declared revolution against the Turks. Kitchener gave him an ambiguous and flexible answer which pointed out to the conventional friendship then standing between Britain and Turkey and that it was not probable Britain would interfere in the domestic affairs of the Ottoman state. After that, Abdullah met Storrs alone, and the latter was nice in his talk to him regarding the same subject, but Storrs' answer was not different from that of his boss, Kitchener.[1]

On Abdullah's return from Istanbul in April of 1914, he passed by Cairo and was also accommodated at the Abidin Mansion where Storrs met him. A lengthy dialogue went on between them. In his *Memoirs*, Storrs says the following about that dialogue:

"... I visited him at Abidin Mansion and sat for two hours under the magic of his talk... He kept reciting for me the Seven Hung Poems, the magnificent Jahili poems, narrating for me the glories and lamentations of Antar ibn Shaddad, and we must have drunk during that large quantities of the excellent Khedive coffee. Then he asked me in an absolute way: 'Can Great Britain supply my father, the Sharif, with twelve or at least six machineguns?' When I asked him about the purpose behind these machineguns, he gave me the same answer weapons buyers give: for defense. Then he added, 'They are for defense against the Turks' attack.' I felt that I did not need instructions from my superiors to tell him this: 'It never occured to us to think of providing a weapon to be used against a friendly state— meaning the Ottoman State—and Abdullah should not have

---

1 George Antonius (Op. Cit.), p. 206.

expected any other answer from me, but we parted on as good terms as friendship and affinity could be."¹

Abdullah felt disappointed with the Storrs meeting, but he drew one benefit from that meeting: the birth of a strong friendship between himself and Storrs, for both were fond of chess and ancient Arab literature. It became a habit of Abdullah whenever he passed by Cairo to meet his friend, Storrs, and they would usually meet in a back room in the building housing the *Muqattam* newspaper.² In his *Memoirs*, Storrs says that the relationship between himself and Abdullah kept growing as time went by.³

Cloth Merchant Ali Azghar

When World War I was declared in Europe in August of 1914, Kitchener was on a vacation in Britain, so he was appointed minister of war. Storrs wrote him from Cairo saying, "Could you authorize me to make sure from Abdullah about the path the Arabs will undertake if Turkey joined the war? Obviously, their bias to us, in addition to other considerations, will strengthen our military position."⁴ The answer arrived on September 24 to the attaché at the British Accreditation House in Cairo as follows:

"I have asked Storrs to send on my behalf a confidential messenger to be chosen with caution to Sharif Abdullah to ascertain whether he and his father, as well as the Hijaz Arabs, will stand by our side, or if he will be against us, if the armed German influence in Istanbul is able to force the sultan, against his will, and to force the Sublime Porte, to carry out hostile and military acts inimical to Great Britain."⁵

---

1 Sir Ronald Storrs, *Orientations*, London: Readers Union Ltd., 1939, pp. 129-130.
2 Zain Noor ad-Din Zain, *Al-Sira` al-Dawli fil Sharq al-Awsat* الصراع الدولي في الشرق الأوسط (International Dispute in the Middle East), Beirut: 1971, p. 205.
3 Storrs (Op. Cit.), p. 120.
4 George Antonius (Op. Cit.), pp. 209-210.
5 Storrs (Op. Cit.), p. 157.

Based on these orders which he received, Storrs kept looking for a trusted messenger to send to Mecca. He finally chose a Baha'i man working as a cloth merchant in the Jamaliyya Quarter of Cairo named Ali Asghar. The reason behind choosing this man was that he was the father of the wife of Husain Rohi Afandi, the translator at the Accrditation House. As soon as Storrs started mentioning the name of this man in his Memoirs, the "X" mark was used for him in order to hide his identity.

Ali Asghar left Cairo carrying a gift from Storrs to Abdullah with a letter in which Storrs stated that the Turkish government was determined to declare war on Britain; therefore, the British government was ready to provide the needed aid to al-Husain to defend the rights of the Arabs. He reached Jidda on October 8 and from there he hired a donkey to carry him to Mecca. Upon his arrival at Mecca, he did not find al-Husain or his sons there, for they were hunting in Taif as it was their custom every year. One of al-Husain's relatives in Mecca, Sharif Sharaf, was acting as his representative. About Sharif Sharaf, Ali Asghar says that he was like the Egyptians in their belief that the Germans would win the war.

Ali Asghar sent to Taif a special messenger informing al-Husain of his mission and of seizing the opportunity, so he circumambulated the Ka`ba, describing doing so as being very silly but a sort of good physical exercise.[1]

Few days later, al-Husain and his sons arrived at Mecca. When al-Husain read Storrs' letter, he consulted with his sons, Abdullah and Faisal, about how he should answer Storrs. The brothers differed in their views. Abdullah was of the opinion to declare a revolution against the Turks in cooperation with Britain. As for Faisal, his opinion was: The Arabs were not fully ready for the revolution, and he feared the revolution might fail. He was of the view that it would be better for the Arabs to stand

---

1 *Ibid.*

Chapter Two: Al-Husain ibn Ali

beside Turkey during its hour of need and will thus win favor with it.

Each of Abdullah and Faisal insisted on his opinion adamantly. After serious considerations, al-Husain reached a compromise: Abdullah would write Storrs telling him of his desire to reach an understanding with Britain, but his religious status prevented him from changing his current stance of neutrality, that despite all of that, he might declare the revolution against the Turks if they forced him to do so provided Britain pledges to provide effective assistance.[1]

Ali Asghar returned with the answer to Cairo which he reached on October 31. The war between Britain and Turkey was declared that day. The Accreditation House sent a telegram to Kitchener about Abdullah's answer, so an answer from him arrived on the same day; this is how it read:

"Greetings to Sharif Abdullah. Germany is now able to buy the Turkish government with gold although Britain, France and Russia had ensured the safety of the Ottoman Empire if Turkey maintained neutrality in this war. The Turkish government, contrarily to the desire of the sultan and because of the German pressure, has undertaken military actions, invading the borders of Egypt with armed gangs followed by Turkish soldiers who are now assembling in the Aqaba to invade Egypt. So, if the Arab nation supports Britain in this war, Britain will ensure that there will be no interference in the domestic affairs of the Arabian Peninsula, and it will provide for the Arabs every kind of assistance against any outside foreign aggression. Someone from the staunch Arab race may assume the caliphate in Mecca or Medina, and good things may happen, God willing, from these evil things that are now taking place."[2]

---

1 George Antonius (Op. Cit.), pp. 211-212.
2 Public Records Office, London, FO 371/2139. [Arabic text indicates: 2139-371, but I looked it up via the Internet and found numerous references to 371/2139 instead, so I have used it here. –Tr.]

Storrs prepared a letter to Abdullah according to this telegram which reached him from Kitchener, and Ali Asghar carried the letter to Mecca from which he returned to Cairo on October 10. The Accreditation House in Cairo, therefore, wrote the foreign ministry in London the following telegram:

"The messenger returned from his second trip carrying a second letter from Sharif Abdullah. The letter is written in cordial statements and stresses once more his kind sentiments towards Great Britain. It frankly indicates that his father does not intend to adopt a policy hostile to our interests. The Sharif of Mecca repeatedly stressed orally that his friendship is much stronger than what his letter expressed, but he pointed out to his position in the Islamic world and the current political situation in Hijaz made it impossible for him to presently sever his ties with Turkey, but he is waiting for the suitable opportunity. He informed the messenger that the Turks were taking advantage of our alleged blockade of rations from reaching the holy places."[1]

Faisal's Delegation

The Turks were ignorant of the covert communication between al-Husain and the British. When they declared the call for "jihad", they sent al-Husain a message asking him to support this call, so he answered them saying that he supported the call from the depth of his heart, and that he supplicated to Allāh to crown it with success, but he was afraid his participation in the *jihad* would prompt the British to seek revenge against him by shelling his sea ports and cutting off the rations routes from al-Hijaz, so famine would then take place and the tribes would revolt.

The Turks realized that the Sharif was making excuses in order to lag behind rather than support them, so they decided to get rid of him. On a February 1915 day, when the Turkish

---

1   *Ibid.*

governor, Waheeb Pasha, was travelling from Mecca to Medina, the suitcase of one of his entourage fell, so a Bedouin found and delivered it to Sharif Ali who, in turn, sent it to his father. It was found out that the suitcase contained documents in which there was evidence that the Turks were plotting against al-Husain.

Al-Husain decided to send his son, Faisal, to Istanbul. The outward reason for it was to present to the sultan and to the grand vizier a complaint against Waheeb Pasha. But the real cause was to contact the Arab leaders in Damascus and to get to know their stance vis-à-vis Kitchener's offers, the extent of their enthusiasm for them and readiness to carry them out.

Faisal reached Damascus on March 26, 1915, so Jamal Pasha received him with a warm welcome and invited him to reside at the general command's quarters, but Faisal asked to be excused in the pretext he had promised the Bakris to be their guest. Faisal remained a guest of the Bakris for four weeks during which he met secretly with the prominent *al-Fatat*, The Young Arab Society, members. He joined their society after swearing the oath. He also met with Arab military officers from among the members of the *Ahd* (Covenant) Society and some Damascus leaders, such as Ridha Pasha al-Rikabi, head of the municipality, Sheikh Badr ad-Din al-Husain, senior scholar of theology of the Levant. Faisal's talks with them went on with extreme caution and secrecy. They used to go to the house of the Bakris about midnight for fear of watchful eyes and spies. Faisal informed them of Kitchener's offer to his father and that his father hesitated about it. He asked them to express to him their own opinion in this regard, giving them time to think until his return from Istanbul.

Faisal left Damascus for Istanbul which he reached on April 23. He was received there with a great welcome, and he met the sultan and senior state officials. He submitted to them the documents which contained the plot against his father, so they appeased him and issued an order to transfer Waheeb Pasha from Hijaz, appointing in his place Ghalib Pasha, a peaceful and good-hearted man, whom they told to maintain a good relationship with al-Husain.[1] The reason of this leniency, which the state officials expressed towards al-Husain, is rendered to the intensification of the Dardanelles campaign at that time. The Ottoman state was then in its most critical times, and Istanbul almost fell to the allies; therefore, the statesmen found out that it was beneficial to mitigate al-Husain until the Dardanelles anguish dissipated.

Faisal returned to Damascus which he reached on May 23. He found its leaders determined to support the revolution at its inception, writing a covenant in this regard which included a map of the Arab lands whose independence Britain had to recognize in exchange for the Arabs supporting it during the war. Faisal remained in seclusion with Yasin al-Hashimi for a good while. This man used to enjoy prominence in the Levant at the time due to being the chief of staffs of the 12th legion headquartered in Damascus. Most of its soldiers were Arabs. Faisal asked him about the type of assistance which Hijaz could offer Syria in order to participate in the revolution. Al-Hashimi answered him saying, "We do not ask for anything, and we do not need anything; all you have to do is to lead us and march in the vanguard."[2]

Six Damascus leaders swore the oath of loyalty, pledging to regard Sharif Husain as the representative of the Arab people provided the Arab division stationed in the Levant should rise like one man in case Britain assented to the conditions stated in the covenant. In order to underscore this covenant, Sheikh Badr al-Din al-Husaini gave his ring to Faisal to deliver it to his father as a symbol of the trust of the people of the Levant in him.[3]

---

[1] Ameen Sa'eed, *Al-Thawra al-Arabiyya al-Kubra* (the Great Arab Revolution), Cairo, Vol. 1, p. 106.
[2] *Ibid.*, Vol. 1, p. 109.
[3] George Antonius (Op. Cit.), p. 245.

Faisal donated to the al-Fatat Society the sum of one thousand gold liras to assist it in carrying out its functions, and he ordered a copy of the covenant written in very small type size which he gave to one of his followers who put it in his shoe, sewing on it the shoe's lining in order to get it to reach al-Husain in Mecca secretly.

Faisal found out that he could not return to Hijaz before meeting Jamal Pasha whose permission he would seek to travel. Jamal Pasha was at the time in Damascus, so Faisal travelled to it by train. At his arrival, he took the opportunity to visit the camp of the army raised for the second Sinai campaign, so a party was held in his honor. He delivered a speech to the party saying, "The Arab nation must participate in the *jihad*, and I am going to Hijaz in order to return at the head of a large army of volunteers to participate in the second campaign."[1]

Faisal returned to Mecca, reaching it on June 20, 1915. He provided his father with a detailed report of his mission and explained to him how he personally changed his opinion: After having opposed the revolution against the Turks, he now was a supporter of it.

Mcmahon's Correspondence

Al-Husain's mind finally settled on negotiating with the British as a prelude for declaring the revolution, so he sent in mid-July a man whom he trusted to the British Attaché in Cairo, Sir Henry McMahon. Since then, the famous correspondence between both men started, and it is known as the "al-Husain-McMahon Correspondence".

The exchange of letters went on in Arabic, and their number reached ten. Five of them were sent by al-Husain to McMahon and the others were their answers. What is noticed is that al-Husain wrote on his letters, by way of prose literature to which

---

1 Ameen Sa'eed (Op. Cit.), Vol. 1, p. 107.

ancient Arabs were used, interjected sentences filled with implications, digressions, axioms, wise adages and empty resonating statements. Apparently, McMahon took advantage of it, so he used to respond to those letters with flexible statements whose reader would imagine that they promise something, whereas in reality they do not. McMahon did not forget to start his letters with the conventional greeting statements that are full of praise and excessive compliments, such as his saying, as he addressed the Sharif, "To the master with coveted lineage, the dynasty of the Sharifs, the crown of pride, the branch of Muhammed's tree, the Ahmedi Qarashi garden, owner of the lofty station and sublime status, the Sayyid and the son of a Sayyid, the Sharif and the son of the Sharif, the revered great Sayyid, His Excellency Sharif Husain, master of everyone, emir of Venerable Mecca, the *qibla* of all the world, the focal point of all obedient believers, may his blessings encompass all people..."[1]

Al-Husain's problem is that instead of signing a clearly stated and precise treaty with the British, he depended on such letters which could be understood according to the differences in viewpoints. When some of his advisors advised him to ask the British to draw an agreement ratified by the British parliament, he answered them saying that those who agreed with him were the government itself, then he pointed to his pocket and said, "And their promises are right here."[2]

Some British writers believe that the ambiguity in McMahon's correspondence was deliberate, rendering it to his secretary, Storrs, who knew Arabic very well. The British at the time were negotiating with France about Syria, and the direction of the negotiations contradicted the promises which they had made to al-Husain. So that the British could get rid of this predicament,

---

[1] See an image for it on p. 283 of the previously quoted source by Zaid Noor ad-Din Zain.
[2] Khairiyya Qasmiyya, *Al-Hukooma al-Arabiyya fi Dimashq* (the Arab government in Damascus), Cairo: 1971, p. 29.

they filled all their letters to al-Husain with ambiguity and resonant statements.[1]

Between What Is Hidden and What Is Apparent

Early in 1916, al-Husain decided to send his son, Faisal, to Damascus again to study the situation in it and the extent of the Syrians' readiness to support the revolution at its eruption. Faisal travelled to Damascus accompanied by fifty cavaliers in the claim they formed the vanguard of the *mujahidins*' forces being prepared in Hijaz to participate in the second Sinai campaign.

As usual, Faisal was hosted by the Bakris whereas his cavaliers were accommodated at a farm belonging to the Bakris located in the Qabun, five miles from Damascus. After studying the situation, Faisal found out that Damascus was different from the way it used to be during his first visit: Jamal Pasha had started, since the past summer, to launch a campaign of terror on the advocates of Arab nationalism in the Levant, hanging a number of them on August 21, 1915, while some others were being tried at courts in Alia with cruelty. The Arab officers were transported together with their soldiers to distant places, and genuine Turkish forces were brought to replace them in the Levant. Also, many dignitaries were banished with their families to Anatolian lands. Add to this, famine started appearing in the Levant. Famine intensified particularly in Lebanon, so people were distracted by it from the revolution and nationalist issues.

In February, Anwar Pasha, the Turkish minister of war, went to Damascus and from it he took the train to Medina accompanied by Jamal Pasha and Faisal. Al-Husain was summoned to Medina to meet both ministers, but he asked to be excused, sending each of them a sword studded with precious stones.

---

1 Elizabeth Monroe, *Britain's Moment in the Middle East*, London: 1963, pp. 31-32.

In Medina, a show was made of the force which al-Husain was covertly preparing for the revolution while pretending it was prepared for participation in the Sinai campaign. Anwar Pasha directed this question to Faisal: "Has all of this force been prepared to fight the enemies of Islam?" Faisal answered, "Yes."[1]

Anwar and Jamal returned to Damascus in the company of Faisal. In early March, when Anwar Pasha returned to Istanbul, he sent a telegram to al-Husain repeating his request to declare holy *jihad*. Al-Husain had by then run out of patience and wanted to reveal some of his intention towards the Turks, so he sent on March 16 a telegram to the grand vizier and to Anwar Pasha saying that he would not declare *jihad* except according to these terms: a declaration of general amnesty for political prisoners of conscience, granting Syria and Iraq the non-central rule they demand, and making the governing of Mecca hereditary among his sons. "If these demands are not met, please do not expect me to participate in a war which I had advised you not to join, and I shall contend myself with supplicating for the state to win victory," he added.

This telegram had a heavy impact on the grand vizier and on Anwar Pasha, so they both sent a telegram to al-Husain violently reprimanding him. In it, they pointed out to Faisal staying in Damascus as a guest of the fourth army until the end of the war. "If you do not send the *mujahidin* you promised to send to Damascus, the outcome against you will not be pleasant," they said. Al-Husain answered them saying that when he sent Faisal to Damascus, he thought that he would never see him again, "So, do whatever you want."

It seems that the grand vizier found that this violence towards al-Husain could involve them in a problem which they did not need, so two days later he sent him a telegram containing almost an apology. Al-Husain, therefore, responded by thanking him

---

1   Arskin (Op. Cit.), pp. 49-50.

and promising that he would send the mujahidin as soon as Faisal reached Medina.[1]

Faisal the Actor

Faisal remained in Damascus with his fifty cavaliers for about five months during which his political skills became visible. He was skillful in sweet talking Jamal Pasha and thus removing the doubt from his heart at the time when his father was making preparations to revolt against the Turks.

In his *Memoirs*, Jamal Pasha says that he summoned Faisal in early April of 1916 in the presence of the chief of his war staffs, Ali Fuad Beg. He kept remonstrating with him strongly about his father's conduct in Mecca and that of his brother, Ali, in Medina. He said to him, "I want you to realize that if you want to remain our friends, you must adhere to the laws of friendship. But if you have other goals, it is better you resort to weapons and start your revolution immediately, thus ending this farce and each of us becomes the enemy of the other, declaring his enmity, and the matter will then belong to Allāh..." Faisal's face turned yellow as a result of those words, according to Jamal Pasha, then he stood up and turned to Jamal Pasha as he was putting his hand on his chest and said, "Pardon me, Your Excellency! How can it occur to you to attribute to us such accusations? And how can it fit us to be traitors while we belong to the lineage of the Prophet which you can see that the greatest sign of honor for it is that it is among the sincere subjects who are loyal to the caliph?! My father, brother and I are not traitors of the people or of the government; rather, we are loyal and trusted servants of our most respectful sultan who for so long overwhelmed us with his boons. Rest assured that I will mend the dispute that stands between my brother and governor Basri Pasha, and I will commission him to be present to kiss your hands!" Jamal Pasha says that after Faisal had left, he went to the

---

1 Abdullah ibn al-Husain (Op. Cit.), pp. 105-107.

house of Ali Fuad Beg while being in an agitated status and wept bitterly. He comments saying, "Yes, by Allāh, had I come to know about the correspondence then going on between McMahon and Sharif Husain, I would have immediately ordered Faisal arrested in Damascus and his brother, Ali, in Medina, and I would have sent a Turkish division hastily to Mecca to arrest Sharif Husain in Mecca and thus abort the ominous revolution in its cradle."[1]

Faisal was then trying to get from Jamal Pasha an amnesty for defendants being tried in Alia. He interceded on their behalf with him, urging the dignitaries of Damascus to intercede for them, too. On Friday, Faisal threw a banquet for Jamal Pasha and his officers at the Bakris' farm in the Qabun. Having finished eating, he tried to steer the discussion to the defendants' issue and that it would be good to pardon them. Jamal Pasha, therefore, said to him, "Had you known the details, you would have been very sorry for interceding for them to be pardoned."

At the dawn of May 6, seven defendants were hanged at the Marja Square in Damascus and fourteen at the Burj Square in Beirut. Faisal was then staying at the Qabun farm. While he was eating breakfast with his hosts from among the Bakris, a messenger from Damascus arrived carrying to them the special issue of the *Sharq* newspaper which contained the hanging report and the names of those who were hanged. Grimness overshadowed all those present, and some of them recited the Fatiha, but Faisal jumped as if he was suddenly touched by Satan. He pulled the *kaffiyeh* from his head and threw it on the ground, violently stepping on it as he shouted, "O Arabs! Death now is good!"[2]

Faisal rushed to Damascus where he met Jamal Pasha who talked to him about the reasons that prompted him to hang the defendants, explaining their "treason" and how they contacted

---

1   Jamal Pasha, *Muthakkarat Jamal Pasha* (Memoirs of Jamal Pasha), translated by Ali Ahmed Shukri, Baghdad: 1963, pp. 243-244.
2   George Antonius (Op. Cit.), p. 242.

Chapter Two: Al-Husain ibn Ali

foreign countries. In his *Memoirs*, Jamal Pasha narrates saying that Faisal said to him, "I swear by the sanctity of the forefather, had I known that the criminals' crime is that horrible, not only would I have declined to seek intercession for them, but I would have asked their limbs to be torn so their torment may be prolonged. The curse of Allāh be on them."[1]

Another Theatrical Play

In mid-May, a confidential letter reached Faisal from his father informing him of the approaching eruption of the revolution, so Faisal kept looking for a trick whereby he could leave Damascus for Mecca without stirring Jamal Pasha's suspicion.

Faisal went to meet Jamal Pasha to whom he said, "The *mujahidin* have been assembled in Medina and are ready to go to Damascus to participate in the Sinai campaign." Faisal rhetorically asked, "Does the Pasha not see that in order to enhance the awe of their arrival that my father should send one of his sons to be in their vanguards?" The trick was swallowed by Jamal Pasha who suggested to Faisal to be the one who should be in the vanguard of the *mujahidin*. Faisal pretended to be hesitated, saying that both his brothers were older than him and had the right to be ahead of him. The Pasha answered him saying, "Nevertheless, I request you to go, and let one of your brothers come, too, if he can, but it is necessary for you to go to Medina in order to expedite the preparations, and let your private entourage accompany you."[2]

Jamal Pasha claims in his *Memoirs* that he was aware of Faisal's trick, that he permitted him to leave Damascus because he had prepared a plan to strike at al-Husain's revolution at the time of its inception. Below is the text of what Jamal Pasha stated in his *Memoirs* in this regard:

---

[1] Jamal Pasha (Op. Cit.), p. 242.
[2] George Antonius (Op. Cit.), p. 288.

"One day, about mid-May, Sharif Faisal came to me and informed me that his brother had received orders from his father to join the Sinai army, and that he—meaning Faisal—desired to seek my permission to go to Medina to bring his brother to Jerusalem, emphasizing to me that his departure would have a good impact on the hearts of the *mujahidin*. Since I had by then become used to the tricks of Sharif Husain and his sons, I preferred to be the winner, so I thought for a short while then said, 'Very well, I have granted you permission; so, go in the morning to the volunteers in Medina and welcome them on my behalf then bring them all here. I shall issue an order to the railroads authority to transport the soldiers and shall send some scholars from Damascus to accompany you; thus, you will form a special delegation to welcome the *mujahidin*.' I hardly finished these sentences when his face shone and he almost flew in ecstasy. The truth thus became obvious to me; it was no longer covered. Ali Fuad Beg, chief of my war staffs, even turned to me and said, 'I am convinced that the revolution will be started in the Hijaz very soon, for I saw how Sharif Husain was so glad due to my trick to the extent he could not hide his feelings.' Ali Fuad Beg shared my views and endorsed the plan which I carried out since another plan had already been adopted..."[1]

Jamal Pasha says that Faisal had hardly left Damascus via train when he [Jamal] sent behind him a leader known for his patriotism and firmness, namely Fakhri Pasha, in order to assume the leadership in Hijaz as soon as the revolution started. There was a Turkish force of two or three thousand soldiers dispatched from Istanbul to Yemen, so Jamal Pasha ordered it to stay in Medina, and that it should be armed with rifles which were (originally) intended to be sent to the Sharif's men. Apparently, Jamal Pasha was sure that those measures were sufficient to crush the revolution in its cradle.[2]

---

1   Jamal Pasha (Op. Cit.), pp. 244-245.
2   *Ibid.*, pp. 246-247.

Chapter Two: Al-Husain ibn Ali

Revolution Declared

In the summer of 1916, Ghalib Pasha was in command of the army in Hijaz in addition to occupying the post of provincial governor (*wali*). He, as we have already pointed out, is a peaceful and good-hearted man. He used to complain of a kidney ailment, so he left Mecca with the largest portion of his soldiers to Taif to spend the summer season there, unaware of what destiny was hiding for him.

No more than one thousand and two hundred soldiers had remained in Mecca of the army. In the morning of June 10, 1916—which coincided with Sha`ban 9, 1334 A.H.—as the soldiers were training outside their barracks without weapons, they suddenly found themselves under a rain of bullets, so their leader, Darvish Beg, rushed to the telephone and asked al-Husain about the reason behind those bullets. Al-Husain gave him this answer: "The Arabs do not accept you all as their rulers while you are in their lands. You have insulted them and are hostile to them." It was then that Darvish Beg resorted to trickery. He pretended that he and his soldiers were all ready to surrender, but as soon as he entered the barracks, he ordered his soldiers to arm themselves. Thus, a fierce fighting started between them and the Bedouins who surrounded them.[1]

The Turks had an advantage which the Arabs did not have at the inception of the revolution: cannons (primitive artillery). They had in Mecca two garrisons: Ajyad, three hundred meters from al-Husain's mansion, and Jarool, which lied at the distance of two hundred meters from it. The cannons of both of these garrisons kept shooting their bombs at the mansion, shelling it day after day. Al-Husain demonstrated an exceptional courage during that time. He persisted on sitting in his office every day firmly without changing his place. A bomb entered his room and passed one span from him, piercing the foundation of the room,

---

[1] Muhammed Tahir al-Omari (Op. Cit.), Vol. 1, pp. 243-244.

yet he did not pay it any attention. His musical band kept playing music before the mansion as was its habit every day. It so happened that a bomb fell near the players, so they dispersed frightened, but al-Husain ordered them to continue to play even if they all died, so they returned to play under the danger of the bombs.[1]

There is no room here to talk about the Arab Revolution, for it is a lengthy and divergent talk. Suffices to mention here that the first Turkish garrison that surrendered to the revolution was the Jidda one, doing so on June 16, i.e. six days after the declaration of the revolution, and the British fleet assisted in overpowering it. On July 6, both Ajyad and Jarool garrisons were seized. On September 22, the Taif garrison capitulated. Nobody remained firm in the fighting other than Fakhri Pasha, commander of the Medina garrison. This man was quite tough, firm, believing in being an Ottoman and a Sufi from among the followers of the Baktashi *tareeqa* (Sufi method). He kept ascending the pulpit of the Prophet's Haram (mausoleum) time and over again to curse the Arabs, condemning [Sharif] al-Husain and all Sharifs and describing them as having conspired with the infidels against the Islamic caliphate.

The revolution could not overrun Medina and finally contended itself with surrounding it with some of its forces while directing the other part to the north. The forces that went northward were led by Faisal ibn al-Husain assisted by a number of Iraqi and Syrian officers. With them was the renown British officer, Lawrence. These forces occupied Al-Wajh Port on January 24, 1917 and the Aqaba on June 6, then they reached Damascus on October 1, 1918.

It is worth mentioning in this regard that al-Husain was sworn as the King of Mecca on October 29, 1916. Abdullah says the following in his *Memoirs*: "Al-Husain did not desire it, insisting on refusing the allegiance, but the men of the state and

---

[1] Salman Mousa (Op. Cit.), p. 76.

the leaders of the revolution, as well as senior pilgrims from Iraq and the Levant, all pressured him to accept. They said to him, "We all are not ready to serve the revolution except on the condition that you accept what we have offered...," so al-Husain consented.[1]

---

1   Abdullah ibn al-Husain (Op. Cit.), pp. 129-130.

Chapter Three
Sharifi Rule In Syria

Sharifi Rule In Syria

In the summer of 1918, forces of Prince Faisal ibn al-Husain, which were camping on the Eastern bank of the Jordan River, represented the right wing of the British forces assembled in Palestine under the command of General [Edmund] Allenby [1861 – 1936]. On September 19, General Allenby started his major attack on the Turkish forces. In three days, he was able, through a brilliant plan, to inflict crushing blows on the Turkish forces that tore them to pieces. At that juncture, the Arab forces kept racing with the British forces to reach Damascus. On the 30th of September, the vanguard of both groups reached close to it, so the Turks were forced to withdraw from Damascus hastily, blowing up before their withdrawal munition depots as they had done in Baghdad when they withdrew from it.

At 6 o'clock the next morning of October 1, 1918, the Australian cavaliers entered Damascus from the western side, whereas the Arab forces entered it from the south. It is said that Gen. Allenby desired the Arabs would enter Damascus side by side his forces in order to vest on his army, in the minds of the residents, the characteristic of an ally rather than that of a conqueror.

Sharif Nasir was at the head of the Arab forces that entered Damascus as a representative of Prince Faisal. With him, there was Oudah Abu Tayih, sheikh of the Huwaytat tribe, Nouri al-Sha`lan, sheikh of the Rola tribe, and Sultan al-Atrash, sheikh of the Druze. With him there were also Lawrence and Nouri al-Sa`eed. The people of Damascus received the Arab and British forces with unprecedented enthusiasm: The streets were over-crowded with people to the extent it was impossible to pass through them, and shouts rose sky high. Subhi al-Omari described what he saw in Damascus when he entered it; he was a regular officer in the Arab forces. He said,

"... At the entrance of the Maydan Quarter, we saw thousands of people who came to welcome us. We marched along the Maydan route and found people assembled on the way from the Alia Gate to the Marja by the thousands, on the streets and on rooftops, men, youths and old men. Everyone was welcoming us in various ways: with clapping, shouts, martial songs, ululations and the throwing of flowers. In the hands of some men there were bottles of rose and flower water which they were sprinkling on us, a Damascus greeting way..."[1]

This heralded the start of the Sharifi rule in Syria, the rule that lasted sixty years and was full of exciting events and social lessons, and we will try in this chapter to briefly study those events and lessons.

The First Events

The first exciting event which Damascus witnessed in the Sharifi era was that of Algerian princes Sa'eed and Abdul-Qadir. These princes are grandsons of the famous Algerian revolutionary Abdul Qadir al-Jaza'iri [also spelled Abdelkader El Djezairi], and they were residing in Damascus where they had a large number of followers known as the "Maghribis المَغاربة ". Actually, they saved Damascus from looting and chaos when the Turks withdrew from it on September 30. They posted their Maghribi followers at various quarters of the city, and those followers kept patrolling the quarters on horseback, especially the quarters of the Jews and Christians, and they played an effective role in spreading security and comfort among their residents.

The last Turk who withdrew was the deputy provincial governor, Miralay Bahjat Beg. Shortly before his withdrawal, he

---

1 Subhi al-Omari, *Lawrence Kama Araftuh* (Lawrence as I knew him), Beirut: 1969, p. 227.

Chapter Three: Sharifi Rule In Syria

met with Shukri Pasha al-Ayyubi and handed him over the city's administration, but al-Ayyubi found out that Prince Sa`eed al-Jaza'iri had actually taken charge of administering the city, so he did not want to quarrel with him over it. Prince Sa`eed had hoisted the Arab flag on the Sarai building and declared the setting up of an interim government over which he presided in the name of King Husain, sending telegrams in this regard to various parts of Syria.

On the morning of the next day, when the Arab forces entered Damascus, princes Sa`eed and Abdul-Qadir were in a meeting with Shukri al-Ayyubi and Sharif Nasir at the Sarai, so Lawrence entered their meeting place accompanied by Nouri al-Sa`eed. Lawrence had a prior knowledge of Prince Abdul-Qadir and harbored a great deal of grudge against him, charging him with inclining to the Turks and betraying the Arabs. As soon as Prince Sa`eed cast a look at Lawrence as the latter entered the place, he stood in his face and kept addressing him in a defiant language. He said to him, "Yesterday, I and my brother, Abdul-Qadir, we grandsons of Abdul-Qadir al-Jaza'iri, formed with Shukri Pasha al-Ayyubi, the offspring of Salah ad-Din, a national government and called out the name of al-Husain as King over all the Arabs as the defeated Turks and Germans saw and heard."[1]

This statement angered Lawrence very much, and he was about to answer him, but he heard the sound of a quarrel in the adjacent hall, so he rushed to see what was going on. There, he found each of Oudah Abu Tayih and Sultan al-Atrash raising his weapon in the face of the other and so did their followers, and bullets were almost fired had some of those present not thrown themselves between the disputants, thus preventing them from shooting.[2]

---

1 T.E. Lawrence, *Seven Pillars of Wisdom* [translated into Arabic as A'midat al-Hikma al-Sab`a أعمدة الحكمة السبعة], Beirut: 1963, p. 437.
2 Sulayman Mousa, *Muthakkarat al-Ameer Zaid* (Memoirs of Prince Zaid), Amman: 1976, p. 166.

Story of the Sharifs and Ibn Saud

When Lawrence returned to the first hall, he found out that both Algerian princes had gone home, so he summoned them to his presence. Shortly after that, both princes arrived at the Sarai in the company of their bodyguards. Sparks of anger could be seen flying from their eyes. Before all those present, Lawrence announced that in his capacity as a deputy of Prince Faisal, he ousted the local government founded by Prince Sa`eed al-Jaza'iri and his brother and appointed in their place a new government over which Ridha Pasha al-Rikabi presided provided Shukri Pasha al-Ayyubi would represent him until his return, and that Nouri al-Sa`eed would be a general commander of the armed forces.

This statement weighed very heavily on both princes, and Sa`eed kept cursing Lawrence and describing him as a Christian Briton, seeking the aid of Sharif Nasir against him in his capacity as a follower of his religion and race. Then Abdul-Qadir, unsheathing his dagger, stood up and swiftly assaulted Lawrence with a barrage of taunts, with his mouth shivering on account of his extreme ire. But Oudah Abu Tayih was swift to assist Lawrence, falling over Abdul-Qadir and preventing him from reaching Lawrence. Nouri al-Sha`lan interfered to declare that the mighty Rola tribe stood on the side of Lawrence[1]. Both princes, therefore, withdrew from the Sarai as they were threatening to seek revenge against Lawrence because of being an unbelieving Christian[2].

Lawrence decided to kill Abdul-Qadir and commissioned Nouri al-Sa`eed to do it, whereas Nouri in turn commissioned Subhi al-Omari. Subhi al-Omari says the following in this regard:

"On the first or second day of the Damascus entry, while I was in charge of the security of the city's central area, with my

---

1 Lawrence (Op. Cit.), pp. 439-440.
2 Phillip Knightley and Colin Simpson, *The Secret Lives of Lawrence of Arabia*, New York: McGraw-Hill, 1970, translated into Arabic as المخفي من حياة لورنس العرب by Lawand and al-Abid, Beirut: 1971, p. 96.

Chapter Three: Sharifi Rule In Syria

headquarters near the quarters of the command which was at Victoria Hotel, Nouri al-Sa`eed asked to meet me at the said quarters. Lawrence was sitting near him, so he said to me, 'Prince Abdul-Qadir is working with the French against the Arab rule, and he is trying to undermine security; so, I want you to take a number of your brigade to kill him.' I was surprised about this matter, and after thinking for a while, I said to him, 'I understand from your order, Sir, that you are requiring me to bring him; so, if he disobeys and resists, we must bring him alive or dead.' Nouri drowned himself in his thoughts for a short while and kept exchanging looks with Lawrence then said, 'Alright, do it.' Then he said, 'Go to the police commissioner and ask him personally and confidentially to give you someone who would lead you to Abdul-Qadir's house.' I went to the police commissioner and conveyed the order to him, so he brought me such a person. As soon as I reached my headquarters, a messenger came to me to convey Nouri al-Sa`eed's request that I should see him. When I entered, I found out that Lawrence was still with him. He said to me, 'We changed our mind,' so I got out."[1]

Abdul-Qadir remained at large up to November 9, 1918. In the morning of that day, policemen went to his house to arrest him with his brother, Sa`eed. The police were able to arrest his brother. As for him, he resisted the police and kept cursing the head of the government, Ridha al-Rikabi, then rushed to his mare and set out towards the Salhiyya route. When he reached the Salhiyya Bridge, the police fired at him and killed him.

Sa`eed was jailed at the Mazza Prison for ten days then transported to Haifa where he was placed under surveillance. In mid-1919, he was released and permitted to reside in Beirut. There, he joined the party that supported France and was hostile to the Arab government of Damascus. He kept spending money seeking to promote himself and France. Many Lebanese people supported him, and the newspapers that were biased to France

---

1 Subhi al-Omari (Op. Cit.), p. 233.

started praising him and publishing reports about him in a way that drew attention to him and raised his status.

The Looting In Damascus

On the next day, following the Arab forces entering Damascus, looting incidents took place which Lawrence attributed to Prince Abdul-Qadir al-Jaza'iri. He says, "In the morning of the next day, a citizen came to wake me up as he was shivering of fear. He informed me that Abdul-Qadir had declared revolution against the rule which we had set up yesterday. I, therefore, summoned Nouri al-Sa`eed quickly being convinced that that Algerian fool was digging his own grave. This man had mobilized his men and delivered a speech to them announcing that the men of the government were nothing but stooges of Britain. He called for crushing their rule in its cradle in order to serve the religion and caliphate. Since his supporters were used to obeying him without discussion, they regarded his statement as God-sent and rushed to fight us. A number of the Druze, for whom I refused awards given for late services which they had rendered to us, joined Abdul-Qadir not because they loved him or due to zeal for the religion or the caliphate, or due to loyalty to the defeated Turks, but out of their love for plundering and looting, so long as the opportunity was there. What proves the soundness of this view is that they fell on open shops to loot their contents instead of going to fight us..."[1]

Subhi al-Omari does not agree with this statement of Lawrence. He mentions the incident as follows: "Security prevailed and nothing disturbed it except one incident which was the last of simple individual incidents which had to take place under such circumstances. This incident is that members from the Sha`lan Bedouins and the Druze wanted to benefit from this situation to loot whatever their hands could reach, so some of them went to homes north of the Mazza from the

---

1   Lawrence (Op. Cit.), p. 441.

direction of al-Zakhr alley, others went near the plateau. They looted some homes and headed from there to Damascus, so I was notified of it, and an order was issued by me to strike at them and to arrest anyone who could be caught."

Al-Omari describes how the looters were hit with machineguns saying, "We set up the machineguns in the place over which today's Samiramis Hotel stands, and we waited for them to arrive. Few minutes later, we saw them coming from the plateau areas, and they were about one hundred cavaliers and cameleers. There was only one building on the street facing the present bridge besides the almshouse. They were carrying on their mounts whatever they could loot from the homes, and they were chanting as they were advancing. I let them reach close to the bridge which faced us. It was then that I ordered fire to be opened on them starting from their rear and up to their vanguard at the same time. They started falling from their mounts. Those who had advanced and were near us rushed fleeing from over the bridge in the direction of the Hijaz [railroad] station, so the soldiers hunted them with the bullets of their rifles. The others fled away via the route leading to the Salhiyya Gate. Among them were those who fled via the plateau route. The whole issue ended in ten minutes. The street facing the almshouse became full up to the Hijaz station with twenty-two killed men and about thirty wounded. After that, I sent the soldiers towards them, so they gathered those who survived. They also gathered the weapons, camels and steed in the police stables and kept them under guard. As for those killed and wounded, they were all left in their places as a moral lesson for others. One hour later, an order came to me to release them and to hand over to them their animals, the wounded and rifles provided they would leave the city. Thus it was, and nothing important took place other than this incident."[1]

---

1 Subhi al-Omari (Op. Cit.), p. 229.

Between Faisal and Allenby

At one o'clock in the afternoon of October 3, General Allenby entered Damascus in a convertible car and was accommodated at the Victoria Hotel. It was said that at the time of his arrival, he was worried because shortly before then, he had received a telegram ordering him to act in accordance with the Sykes-Picot Agreement upon seizing Damascus[1]. It is the agreement that placed Syria under France's authority. It is also said that other telegrams had reached him from British and French offices the gist of which was: "Strangulate the movement of Faisal and Lawrence in its cradle; stop the Arab torrent; remember the Sykes-Picot Agreement."[2] Allenby, therefore, rushed to summon the Australian commander of the cavalry, Gen. Shovell, and to ask him to send a car to fetch Faisal to the Victoria Hotel immediately.

Upon the arrival of Allenby's order, Faisal had arrived by train near Damascus, and the city's crowds had gathered on street sidewalks and house balconies ready to welcome him. It seems that Faisal found himself in a critical situation from which he did not know how to get out: Was he going to respond to the commander's order and thus disappoint the masses, or will he respond to the crowds and thus disobey the commander's order?!

Faisal decided to respond to the crowds provided he would go to meet the commander thereafter; therefore, he left the car which Shovell had brought him, mounted an Arabian horse and paraded himself in the streets of Damascus in a crowded cortege surrounded by one thousand and five hundred Bedouin horsemen carrying swords and spears. The residents welcomed him with deafening shouts and threw on him flowers and roses, so much so that Faisal could not help crying.[3]

---

1 Knightley and Simpson (Op. Cit.), p. 91.
2 Zain Nur ad-Din Zain, *Al-Sira'al-Dawli fil Sharq al-Awsat* الصراع الدولي في الشرق الأوسط (International Conflict in the Middle East), Beirut: 1971, p. 79.
3 Arksin, *Faisal: King of Iraq*, translated by Omar Abu al-Nasr, Beirut: 1934, p. 112.

Chapter Three: Sharifi Rule In Syria

In his march, Faisal headed towards Victoria Hotel. When he entered the reception hall, he found Allenby standing waiting for him in the company of his entourage. This was their first meeting. Wavell says, "Both men were at odds with each other: Allenby was the self-confident Briton with the huge body, a man who was used to issuing orders, whereas Faisal represented the simple, ascetic and slim Arab, but marks of authority could be seen on him..."[1]

Shovell narrates in a recently published report saying, "Allenby started speaking, directing his talk at Faisal as Lawrence translated for them. He said that Faisal would assume the government of Syria on behalf of his father under France's protection, supervision and financial support, that this rule would include only interior Syria and has nothing to do with Lebanon and Palestine. Faisal responded to this statement by saying that he did not recognize anything for France, that he was ready to receive only British assistance and would not agree to rule any country that has no sea outlet. Here, Allenby turned to Lawrence to ask him, 'Did you not inform him that Syria would be under France's mandate?' Lawrence answered, 'No, Sir. I did not know that.' Allenby then said to him, 'But you knew fully well that Faisal would have nothing to do with Lebanon.' Lawrence answered, 'No, Sir, I did not know that, either.'

"Finally, Allenby concluded the dialogue by making this statement: 'I am Sir. Edmund Allenby, the general commander, and you are Faisal, a general under my command, and you have to obey my order and accept the status quo until the matters are settled once the war had been concluded.' Faisal surrendered to this decision and went with his entourage out."[2]

Following Faisal's exit, Lawrence requested Allenby to release him from service, telling him that the time for his vacation was opportune and that he desired to go to England. Allenby

---

[1] Zain Noor ad-Din Zain (Op. Cit.), pp. 79-80.
[2] Nightley and Simpson (Op. Cit.), pp. 101-102.

answered, "Yes, it is better you travelled." Lawrence, therefore, left. On October 4, he left Damascus for London. On the 30th of the same month, Lawrence met King George V in order to receive from him the medal which was awarded him in appreciation of his great efforts in [quelling] the Arab Revolution. One of those who attended the meeting narrates saying that Lawrence refused to accept the medal from the king in the excuse he was tied by a pledge to Faisal whereas he now saw the British government betraying the Arabs according to the Sykes-Picot Agreement. Lawrence added saying that he was a prince among the Arabs and that he now intended to adhere to their side during the times of ease and of hardship, and that he might fight France if needed in order to save Syria. Then Lawrence ended his talk with the king asking him to excuse him for having refused to accept the medal from him.[1]

An Incident In Aleppo

The French were exerting their utmost effort to enhance their influence in Lebanon, bringing a huge amount of Egyptian pounds estimated at five and a half million to distribute to the supporters and advocates, using Beirut as the center of their propaganda campaign. Iskendar al-Riyashi narrates saying that French officer Cullender summoned the Lebanese leader Habib al-Saad and said to him in the presence of al-Riyashi, "The story after the entry of the large British army has become one of competition between us and themselves over these lands. They now forget about the Sykes-Picot Agreement and stick to the right of conquest due to the consideration that their army is the one that conquered it." Al-Riyashi says that Cullender said to him, "If the British have filled Syria and Lebanon with their troops, France still has other means to compete with them."[2]

---

1 Desmond Stewart, *TE Lawrence: A Biographical Review*, London: 1977, p. 216.
2 Iskendar al-Riyashi, *Ru'saa' Lubnan Kama Araftuhum* (Heads of Lebanon as I Knew them), Beirut: 1961, p. 216.

Chapter Three: Sharifi Rule In Syria

At the time when Lebanon was robust with propaganda for France, Syria was to the contrary, robust with propaganda against France. The propaganda in both countries assumed a religious tone, harping on the cord of sectarianism, leading to a regrettable incident in Aleppo.

The reason behind the incident was a rumor that spread in Aleppo in late February of 1919 claiming that the volunteer Armenian soldiers in the French forces assaulted the Arabs residing in Adana and surrounding areas, so the Muslims in Aleppo were agitated and decided to hold a protest demonstration on February 28 which happened to be a Friday.

Shukri al-Ayyubi was then the military governor of Aleppo, while Ali Jawdat al-Ayyubi was its military governor[1]. In his *Memoirs*, Ali Jawdat says that when he came to know about the decision to carry out the demonstration, he suggested to Shukri Pasha to prevent it due to undesired outcomes that could be expected from it, but Shukri Pasha did not agree with his suggestion. While Ali Jawdat was at home receiving his visitors as usual, the phone rang, and it was Shukri Pasha telling him that a massacre took place between the Muslims and the Armenians at the Friday Market. Ali Jawdat, therefore, rushed to ride his horse and to go to the headquarters of his soldiers to direct them to the location of the incident. In almost one hour, the incident came to an end after many people had been killed or wounded whose number was estimated by some to exceed a hundred.[2]

The French made so much fuss about the incident, regarding it as evidence for the soundness of their claim that the Arabs are not fit for self-rule, and they kept disseminating bad propaganda about it in Europe.[3] The American Red Cross Society provided

---

1 This is what the original Arabic text reads on p. 102. Quite obviously, there is an error here. Most likely, the first Ayyubi was Aleppo's military governor while the other Ayyubi was the military governor of Damascus, not Aleppo. – Tr.
2 Ali Jawdat, *Thikrayat* (Memories), Beirut: 1967, pp. 75-76.
3 Muhammed Tahir al-Omari, *Muqaddarat al-Iraq al-Siyasiyya* مُقَدَّرات العراق السياسية

aid to any Armenian individual willing to migrate from Aleppo, getting them to reach Beirut and securing their sea travel to the countries of their choice.[1]

Shukri al-Ayyubi was recalled to Damascus and was replaced by Ja`far al-`Askari. Also, Naji al-Suweedi was appointed as his aide.[2] Naji al-Suweedi invited the Armenian and Muslim dignitaries to a general meeting in order to remove hostilities. Following that, Armenian dignitaries threw a tea party at the Armenian orphanage to which they invited Aleppo dignitaries from all sects. They exchanged sentiments of affection and brotherhood. Armenian dignitaries sent a telegram to the office of the Supreme French Commission in Beirut asking it not to use Armenian volunteers against Syria and the Syrians.[3]

Faisal In France

On November 8, Lawrence sent al-Husain in Mecca the following telegram:

"I think that talks will be held among the allies in Paris within fifteen days about the Arabs issue. General Allenby has sent a telegram that you wish to have someone to represent you there. So, if the matter is as such, I hope you will send Faisal because his dazzling victories have created a personal reputation for him in Europe... So, if you consent to send him, please send him a telegram to get ready to leave Syria immediately, and [to remain abroad] for almost one month. I also wish you ask General Allenby to prepare a ship to transport him to France. You must send a telegram to the governments of Great Britain, France, the United States and Italy telling them that your son will be going to Paris to represent you."[4]

(Iraq's political destinies), Baghdad: 1925, Vol. 3, p. 142.
1   Yousuf al-Hakim, *Soorya wal `Ahd al-Faisali* (Syria and Faisal's Era), Beirut: 1966, p. 61.
2   Ali Jawdat (Op. Cit.), p. 78.
3   Yousuf al-Hakim (Op. Cit.), p. 61.
4   Mousa, *T.E. Lawrence*, London: 1967, p. 216.

Chapter Three: Sharifi Rule In Syria

As soon as al-Husain received this telegram, he sent a telegram to his son, Faisal, the text of which is as follows:

"Our ally, Great Britain, wishes you attend [the Paris Peace Conference] to represent the Arabs' interests and everything that will be essential for their life, be it relevant to the borders or the administering of what is known to you, in an assembly that will be held in Paris on the 24th of this month of November. So, in order to oblige the opinion of Her Greatness [Britain], go as fast as you can to Paris... Since our only link is the British Greatness, and we have no connection, nor is there any occasion to be connected to anyone else in our political principles, all your remarks and whatever you see in this subject you must express to its Greatness and honorable representatives, be they your fellows in the assembly or political attachés. Whatever they vest on you by way of a statement or an action, be it at the assembly or somewhere else, you should do. Avoid everything else. This is the degree (extent) of your assignment regarding the assembly. Choose what is good for the people, in your intentions, and Allāh will then be your Master."[1]

On the 16th of the same month, Lawrence sent Faisal a telegram via the British foreign ministry asking him to go to Europe in his Arabian outfits and to be accompanied by only one Iraqi officer, namely Nouri al-Sa`eed, if possible, and that he could also be accompanied by two of his main Syrian aides.[2]

When the telegram reached his father, Faisal was in Aleppo, so he rushed to Beirut via the Homs and Tripoli route. When he reached Beirut, the Muslims in it awarded him a great enthusiastic welcome. Some youths stopped Faisal's carriage, untied its horses and kept pulling the horses themselves along the streets of Beirut as they were shouting, "We accept no sultan other than

---

1 Hafiz Wahba, *Jazeerat al-Arab fil Qarn al-Ishreen* (The Arabian Peninsula in the 20th Century), Cairo: 1967, p. 174.
2 Mousa (Op. Cit.), p. 217.

you! And we accept none other than the Arabs!"¹ Apparently, they intended by so doing to defy the French and their Maronite ܡܰܪܽܘܢܳܝܶܐ supporters.

The French were upset by this visit, so much so that they almost ignored it, regarding it as part of the British plan aiming at encouraging the Lebanese factions loyal to Britain and to Faisal. They also regarded it as part of Faisal's efforts to annex Lebanon to the government of Damascus.²

Faisal departed Beirut on the 20th of November aboard a British cruiser accompanied by his entourage comprised of Nouri al-Sa`eed, Rustam Haidar, Faiz al-Ghaseen, Tahsin Qadri and the latter's doctor brother, Ahmed Qadri. He reached Marseille on the 25th of the month. There, he found Lawrence welcoming him in his military uniform, but he was putting the *iqal* on his head instead of the military beret.

From the French side, Faisal was welcomed by Col. [Edouard] Brémond, the officer who lived in Morocco for several years and mastered Arabic. Faisal was welcomed by a mixture of courtesy and cold shoulders. Brémond informed Faisal that the French government welcomed him as a guest of honor, but it did not recognize any diplomatic status for him; i.e. it did not regard him as a representative of King Husain at the peace conference. Brémond then turned to Lawrence to say that the French government welcomed him as a British officer who wears the outfits that suit his military rank, but it would not welcome him if he remained disguised in the Arabs' outfits. Lawrence became very angry and said, "You are dismissing me, and I shall leave this evening." Lawrence actually left after having returned to the French the medal which they had awarded him during the war.

The French thought that Lawrence worked against their interests, and that he was urging Faisal to resist their ambitions

---

1 Sulayman Mousa, *Al-Haraka al-Arabiyya* (the Arab Movement), Beirut: 1970, p. 417.
2 Zain Nur ad-Din Zain (Op. Cit.), p. 92.

in Syria. They also believed that King Husain's call to send a deputy representing him at the Peace conference was masterminded by Lawrence.[1]

The French government arranged for Faisal a lengthy program whereby it intended him to visit the sites where the battles had taken place during the war, surrounding him with all respect and regards in order to bear a psychological impact on him. Faisal realized that it wanted to distance him from Paris and from participating in the Peace conference when it opened.[2]

Faisal could not tolerate these French schemes, so he held Brémond's hand, took him aside and said, "We have fought side by side; this means that we are brothers in arms. Tell me frankly: What is the truth? Also tell me, without beating behind the bush, does the French government desire my presence in Paris or not? I left my brother, Zaid, representing me in Damascus, and he is young. Since the matters are not stable there, it is better I left for Damascus instead of wasting my time here."[3]

This statement weighed heavily on Brémond, so he contacted his government and suggested it ought to invite Faisal to meet the President of the Republic. The government adopted this suggestion. On December 7, Faisal met Henry Poincaré, President of the French Republic. The interpreter between them was Si Kaddour Benghabrit. The meeting lasted only few minutes, and the discussion in it did not go beyond common courtesy statements.[4]

Faisal In England

On December 9, Faisal left Paris with his entourage for London. There, he was welcomed warmly and became a guest of

---

1 Mousa (Op. Cit.), p. 218.
2 Ahmed Qadri, *Muthakkarati anil Thawra al-Arabiyya al-Kubra* (My Memories about the Great Arab Revolution), Damascus: 1956, p. 94.
3 Mousa (Op. Cit.), p. 219.
4 Khairiyya Qasmiyya, *'Awni Abdul-Hadi*, Beirut: 1974, p. 21.

the British government at the Carlton Hotel which, at the time, was one of the most plush. Faisal remained in England for one month, and Lawrence remained with him like his shadow, exerting himself as he responded to his requests and always addressed him with "Sir".

On the 12th of the month, Faisal met King George V, and Lawrence was with him as his interpreter. Lawrence was wearing the full Arabian outfit. These outfits caused one of the men of the king's entourage angry, so he kept reprimanding Lawrence saying, "Is it wise, Col. Lawrence, that a subject of the king, who is also a military officer, should come wearing foreign clothes?" Lawrence calmly answered him, "If a man serves two masters, and if he has to make one of them angry, it is better to make the stronger one angry... I have come to be an interpreter for Prince Faisal, and this is his outfit."[1]

King George V awarded Faisal the Victoria necklace and said that he was awarding it in memory of the joint bloods, the Arabs' and the Britons', having been spilled on the fighting fields side by side, that he hoped there would be love between them always and forever. Faisal spoke saying that he came as a representative of his father to offer thanks to the assistance he had received from King George and his government, that his father hoped such love would always endure. King George responded saying, "We do not abandon assisting your father and all Arabs, and I assure you that you will find Britain supporting you."[2]

During his stay in London, Faisal was the object of respect and honoring; senior British personalities raced to meet him and throw sumptuous banquets for him at their mansions. Awni Abdul-Hadi, who was a member of his entourage, says, "The few days which Prince Faisal spent in London were sufficient to develop His Highness a great deal, transforming him from an

---

1   Hart, *T.E. Lawrence*, London: 1965, p. 386.
2   Sulayman Mousa (Op. Cit.), p. 425.

Arab prince staunchly rooted in the Bedouin culture to a civilized Prince."[1]

The Weizmann-Faisal Agreement

[Chaim] Weizmann, the famous Zionist leader, seized the opportunity of Faisal's presence in London to ask for an appointment to meet him in order to convince him to endorse the Balfour Declaration. On December 11, the first meeting between them took place at the Carlton Hotel, and it was attended by Lawrence in his capacity as the interpreter.

It is believed that Weizmann utilized the concern that took control of Faisal about the ambitions of the French in Syria and the inclination of the British to bargain with them at the expense of the Arabs, so he started explaining to Faisal how the Jews could be the only support for the Arabs in this predicament: The Jews have a great deal of wealth and experience in economy, and they have a great deal of influence in various superpowers, especially the United States. So, if the Arabs agree with them, after all they are cousins, there will be no force on earth that can harm them. Weizmann told Faisal that *the Jews **did not** have any political ambitions in Palestine,* for they are business people with money, and they have no weapons with which they can fight or seize any country. All their objective is to improve the Arab lands with their money and minds, for the Arab lands are vast and are not [all] inhabited, whereas the Jews are ready to provide assistance to the Arabs as sincere friends...[2]

Weizmann kept repeating these statements and the like to Faisal. It is worth mentioning that these statements were not new, for the Zionists used to keep repeating them to Arab leaders even before the war, and some of them believed these statements, especially the pillars of the non-centralism party in Egypt.[3] They

---
1 Khairiyya Qasmiyya (Op. Cit.), p. 23.
2 Sulayman Mousa (Op. Cit.), pp. 435-436.
3 Abdul-Aziz Muhammed Awadh, *Al-Shakhsiyya al-Filistiniyya wal Isti'an al-Yahudi*

were also believed by al-Husain himself.[1] Moreover, Lawrence shared this same opinion of the Jews and exerted *his* efforts to convince Faisal of its truth.

It can be said, anyhow, that Weizmann was able, with help from Lawrence, to have a serious impact on Faisal and to convince him of the truth of what he had told him regarding the Jews' sincerity to the Arabs and the extent of benefit the Arabs would reap from the Jews. When Weizmann finished talking to Faisal, the latter spoke saying, "The Arabs will accept the Jews' request if they sense their sincerity and realize its benefit, for the Arabs need money for land reformation, and they ask you for political assistance with the nations, especially America." It was then that Weizmann stretched his hand and said to Faisal that he pledged to him on behalf of the Jews "to die together and live together," whereupon Faisal said, "If you are loyal to your statement, I will be loyal to my statement that the Arab Kingdom shall not be partitioned."[2]

[Below are pages extracted from English sources handwritten by Faisal and the typed agreement between him and Chaim Weizmann. They are included here for the reader by the translator of this book who obtained them from the Internet, making sure there are no copyright infringements. Some pages have been enlarged so they would be easier to read.]

الشخصية الفلسطينية و الاستيطان اليهودي (The Palestinian Personality and the Jewish Settlement) in Palestinian Affairs شؤون فلسطينية magazine of August 1974.

1 Sulayman Mousa (Op. Cit.), p. 428.
2 *Ibid.*, p. 41.

Chapter Three: Sharifi Rule In Syria

> If the Arabs are established as I
> have asked in my manifesto of January addressed
> to the British Secretary of State for Foreign
> Affairs, I will carry out what is
> written in this agreement. ~~If you~~
> ~~demands or changed so~~.
> If changes are made, I can
> not be answerable for failing
> to carry out this agreement.
>
>   Feisal ibn
>   Hussein

His Royal Highness the Emir FEISAL, representing and acting on behalf of the Arab Kingdom of Hedjaz, and Dr. CHAIM WEIZMANN, representing and acting on behalf of the Zionist Organisation,

mindful of the racial kinship and ancient bonds existing between the Arabs and the Jewish people, and realising that the surest means of working out the consummation of their national aspirations, is through the closest possible collaboration in the development of the Arab State and Palestine, and being desirous further of confirming the good understanding which exists between them,

have agreed upon the following Articles:-

ARTICLE I.

The Arab State and Palestine in all their relations and undertakings shall be controlled by the most cordial goodwill and understanding and to this end Arab and Jewish duly accredited agents shall be established and maintained in the respective territories.

ARTICLE II.

Immediately following the completion of the deliberations of the Peace Conference, the definite boundaries between the Arab State and Palestine shall be determined by a Commission to be agreed upon by the parties hereto.

ARTICLE III.

In the establishment of the Constitution and Administration of Palestine all such measures shall be adopted as will afford the fullest guarantees for carrying into effect the British Government's Declaration of the 2nd of November, 1917.

ARTICLE IV.

All necessary measures shall be taken to encourage and stimulate immigration of Jews into Palestine on a large scale, and as quickly as possible to settle Jewish immigrants upon the land through closer settlement and intensive cultivation of the soil. In taking such measures the Arab peasant and tenant farmers shall be protected in their rights, and shall be assisted in forwarding their economic development.

ARTICLE V.

No regulation nor law shall be made prohibiting or interfering in any way with the free exercise of religion; and further the free exercise and enjoyment of religious profession and worship without discrimination or preference shall forever be allowed. No religious test shall ever be required for the exercise of civil or political rights.

ARTICLE VI.

The Mohammedan Holy Places shall be under Mohammedan control.

ARTICLE VII.

The Zionist Organisation proposes to send to Palestine a Commission of experts to make a survey of the economic possibilities of the country, and to report upon the best means for its development. The Zionist Organisation will place the aforementioned Commission

Chapter Three: Sharifi Rule In Syria

at the disposal of the Arab State for the purpose of a survey of the economic possibilities of the Arab State and to report upon the best means for its development. The Zionist Organisation will use its best efforts to assist the Arab State in providing the means for developing the natural resources and economic possibilities thereof.

ARTICLE VIII.

The parties hereto agree to act in complete accord and harmony on all matters embraced herein before the Peace Congress.

ARTICLE IX.

Any matters of dispute which may arise between the contracting parties shall be referred to the British Government for arbitration.

Given under our hand at LONDON, ENGLAND, the THIRD day of JANUARY, ONE THOUSAND NINE HUNDRED AND NINETEEN.

Chaim Weizmann

Article IX, dated January 3, 1919, is reproduced and enlarged below:

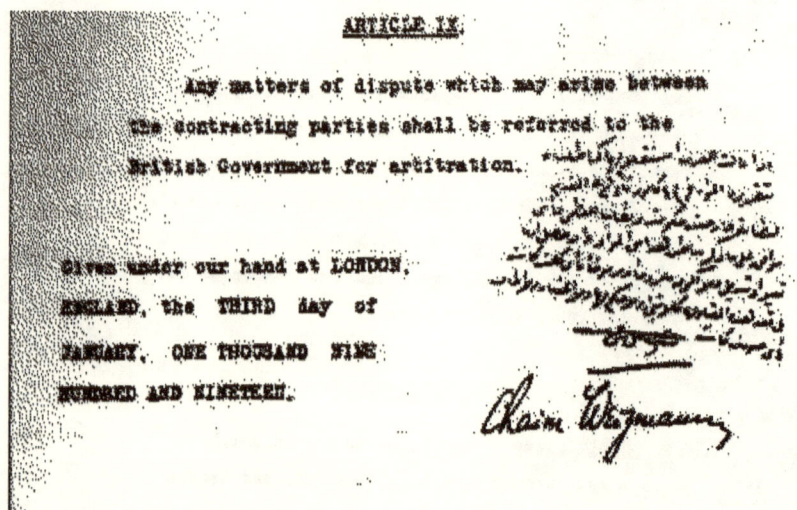

Faisal's Arabic text reads:

اذا نالت العرب استقلالها كما طلبناه بتقريرنا المؤرخ ٤ كانون الثاني ١٩١٩ المقدم لنظارة خارجية بريطانيا العظمى، فانني موافق على ما ذُكِر بنطاق هذه المواد، وان حصل أدنى تغيير أو تبديل، فلا أكون ملزوما و مربوطا بأي كلمة كانت، بل تُعَدّ هذه المقاولة لا شيء و لا حُكم لها و لا اعتبار و لا أُطالَب بأي صورة كانت»

It was finally agreed on by Faisal and Weizmann to sign an agreement [above] comprised of nine articles indicating the racial kinship and the ancient ties between the Arabs and the Jews, the necessity of cooperation between them, the providing of guarantees for implementing the Balfour Declaration, the encouraging of a Jewish immigration to Palestine and of religious freedom.

It seems that when Faisal saw the final form of the agreement typed and prepared to be signed, he realized the dire consequences

Chapter Three: Sharifi Rule In Syria

of what he had done; therefore, we find him holding a pen and writing on its margin the following reservation:

"If the Arabs win their independence, as we demanded it in our report dated January 4, 1919 submitted to the attention of the foreign [ministry] of Great Britain, I will then agree to what is stated in these articles. And if the slightest change or substitution takes place, I will not be obligated or tied to any word whatever; rather, this contract will be nil, non-binding, having no value and I will not be held to any demand in any way whatever it may be."[1]

Undoubtedly, this statement, which Faisal wrote, was a skillful political blow that rendered the agreement worthless from the practical standpoint. Yet we, despite that, notice that when Lawrence translated the statement into English, he made some alteration in it that distorted its gist, for its translation [provided by Lawrence] was as follows:

"If the Arabs are established as I have asked in my manifesto of January 4 presented to the British Secretary of Foreign Affairs, I will carry out what is written in this agreement. [A line and a half is written then scratched] If changes are made, I cannot be answerable for failing to carry out this agreement. – Faisal ibn Husain"[2]

This question confronts us: "In his support for Zionism, was Lawrence its hired agent, or was he carrying out instructions of Balfour, the British foreign minister [or "Secretary of Foreign Affairs," as Lawrence worded it][3], or was it something else?

According to the viewpoint of the famous British historian, Toynbee endeavored to bring the Arabs and the Jews closer to

---

1   Look at the reservation's graphic image as it is written in Faisal's hand in the magazine *Afaq Arabiyya* آفاق عربية in its June 1977 issue, p. 117.
2   *Ibid.*, p. 119.
3   The reader can notice that the translation provided by Lawrence is shorter than the one I have provided: The number of words of my translation is 82, whereas that of Lawrence is 61... This suggests that Lawrence did, indeed, overlook or deliberately ignore some text, failing to translate it. – Tr.

each other. Lawrence was acting as prompted by his own personal discretion. Toynbee says the following in this regard: "... Lawrence was independent in his thinking. As I know, Lawrence advised Faisal not to fight on two fronts at the same time: France and Zionism, and that the danger posed by France was visible, and it wanted to crush Syria, whereas the Zionist plans were still within the scope of theories, that wisdom dictated that he should now seek help from the Jews to resist France. Thereafter, whatever will be will be."[1]

Awni Abdul-Hadi, who was among Faisal's entourage in London, has another opinion about Lawrence. He says, "Lawrence was jumping on two ropes. He pretended to the Arabs that he was an Arab at heart and a bosom friend, whereas he was once working for the interest of the Arabs and once for the interest of the Jews. Lawrence is British, neither an Arab nor a Jew, and nobody is ignorant of the role he played in convincing His Highness the Prince to sign the agreement known as the Weizmann-Faisal Agreement."[2]

We have on this occasion to cite the impression Weizmann himself had of Lawrence. He says the following about him in his *Memoirs*: "I have at this point to express my appreciation of the services rendered by Lawrence to *our cause* and to add something in describing his *magnificent* character... His relationship with the Zionist movement was quite positive despite his great inclination towards the Arabs, and describing him as an enemy of Zionism is wrong. Lawrence, as is the case with Faisal, was of the opinion that the Jews could provide a great assistance to the Arabs, and that the Arab world would reap a great deal of benefit from the establishment of a homeland for the Jews in Palestine..."[3]

---

1 Sulayman Mousa (Op. Cit.), footnote on p. 434.
2 Khairiyya Qasmiyya (Op. Cit.), p. 25.
3 Chaim Weizmann, *Trial and Error*, New York: 1949, p. 236.

Chapter Three: Sharifi Rule In Syria

His Return to Paris

Faisal returned with his entourage to Paris on January 9, 1919 and was accommodated at the mansion of Countess Tonnier[1] [Tonnelier] as a guest of the French government. Faisal wrote the French government asking for permission to attend the peace conference as a representative of the Arab countries. He received an answer from it indicating that the French government regretted its inability to book a seat for him at the conference. This answer came as a violent shock to Faisal. Lawrence rushed to meet Lloyd George and Lord Curzon who were staying at the Astoria Hotel. At two o'clock after midnight, Lawrence returned to Faisal who was still sleepless, pacing in his room, falling prey to puzzlement and concern, so Lawrence started talking to him saying, "Sir, Lloyd George sends you his greeting and says that two seats have been assigned for you at the conference instead of one."[2] Faisal was quite pleased, and his regard for Lawrence grew even greater.[3]

The peace conference was inaugurated in the Versailles suburb on the 18th of the month. Faisal and Rustam Haidar represented the Arabs assisted by Nouri al-Sa`eed, Awni Abdul-Hadi and Lawrence. Lawrence was putting the *iqal* on his head, and this annoyed the French.

It can generally be said that Faisal, during the peace conference, gained some good reputation for the Arabs and increased the number of their supporters. He dazzled the eyes, especially those of women, due to being handsome and to his flowing white cloak and gilt *iqal*. Newspapers consistently

---

[1] I could not trace this name. Neither Elizabeth Burgoyne, in her book about Gerturde bell, which covers the period from 1914 – 1926, nor Ms. Bell herself in her book titled *The Desert and the Sown* makes any reference to this lady. But I found one that seems to be quite close to it: Gabrielle Émilie Le Tonnelier de Breteuil, marquise du Châtelet. It is likely this Countess descended from the above lady who lived from 1706 – 1749. – Tr.

[2] Khairiyya Qasmiyya, *Al-Hukooma al-Arabiyya fi Dimashq* (The Arab Government in Damnascus), Cairo: 1971, p. 95.

[3] Sulayman Mousa (Op. Cit.), p. 465.

published his photograph and talked about him. The Europeans up to then were not used to seeing Arab sheikhs as they are used to them nowadays.

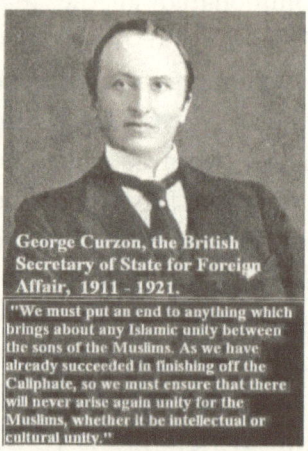

George Curzon, the British Secretary of State for Foreign Affair, 1911 - 1921.

"We must put an end to anything which brings about any Islamic unity between the sons of the Muslims. As we have already succeeded in finishing off the Caliphate, so we must ensure that there will never arise again unity for the Muslims, whether it be intellectual or cultural unity."

Upon seeing him, they remembered the merriments of "One Thousand and One Nights". An American who attended the conference, namely attorney Robert Lansing, said this about him, "His voice seemed as if it was puffing the fragrance of incense and implying the presence of luxurious carpets and green turbans glittering with gold and jewels." This attorney describes Faisal's character saying, "Despite being young, he demonstrated maturity in thinking rarely seen in youths, and he seemed in his appearance and clothing like an ancient prophet weighed down by heavy knowledge."[1]

Among those who were attracted to Faisal was the French scholar Anatole France. This scholar used to live on the Shanzelize Street near the mansion where Faisal was accommodated, and he used to quite often visit Faisal and eat food at his table[2]. He also used to invite Faisal to eat with him in the company of editors-in-chief of French newspapers.[3]

---

1 Lansing, The Big Four and Others of the Peace Conference, London: 1922.
2 Ibrahim Saleem Najjar, *Al-Malik Faisal al-Awwal* (King Faisal I), Beirut, footnote on p. 67.
3 Khairiyya Qasmiyya, *Awni Abdul-Hadi*, p. 27.

Chapter Three: Sharifi Rule In Syria

Also, the wife of American President [Woodrow] Wilson described Faisal saying that his face looked like a picture of Christ. She later wrote him many letters, and it is believed that she had an impact on her husband in favor of the Arabs.[1]

It is worth mentioning that the British had a role in promoting the propaganda for Faisal in the conference's lobbies and on newspaper columns. It is believed that they wanted to turn Faisal into a winning card in their hands when they bargained with the French in some disputed issues, especially the Mosul issue, as we will later discuss.

The French realized the secret behind this British game and kept looking at Faisal as they would at a British agent, and the newspapers kept after that harping on this chord, trying to downgrade Faisal and promote bad publicity against him.

What Happened During the Conference?

It was decided to let the 6th of February be the date for Faisal to deliver his address at the Peace Conference. Faisal spent the night before preparing the speech with help from Rustam Haidar and Awni Abdul-Hadi, and Lawrence prepared the translation of the address into English also with their help.

When Faisal delivered his speech at the set date, his style was calm, firm and contained frankness mixed with politeness. He nicely censured the Sykes-Picot agreement and simplified the Arabs' demands for unity and independence. He mentioned how the Arabs joined the allies in the war at the most critical times, and their losses reached twenty thousand killed. When one of those who were then present interrupted him, pointing out to the Arabs being among the nations that are not advanced in civilization, Faisal answered him in a clear and sharp voice saying, "I belong to a nation that enjoyed civilization when all other lands whose representatives are sitting in this hall were

---

1 Mousa (Op. Cit.), p. 226.

inhabited by barbarians." Orlando, representative of Italy, tried to respond to him by pointing out to Rome's seniority of civilization, so Faisal strongly interrupted him by saying, "Yes, this was the case before Rome was founded."[1]

One man stood during the conference strongly in support of Faisal, and another man stood strongly opposing him. The supporter was Dr. Howard Bliss, head of the Syrian Protestant College which is now called the "American University-Beirut". Iskandar al-Riyashi explains the support expressed by Dr. Bliss towards the Arabs by saying that it was the result of the tough competition which existed in Beirut between the American Protestant College and the French Jesuit College: When the French entered Beirut in October of 1918, they started filling the government offices with graduates of the Jesuit College and other Catholic institutes, so Dr. Bliss was angry because of that. He carried his briefcase and went to Paris to meet President [Woodrow] Wilson. A strong friendship tied both men. Wilson treated him as a fellow and kept listening to him.[2]

Anyhow, Dr. Bliss delivered on February 13 a speech at the conference in which he demanded a neutral committee sent to Syria to sift the population's desire according to the principle of self-determination advocated by President Wilson. Wilson was impressed by this speech to a great extent.

As regarding the man who stood to oppose Faisal during the conference, he was Shukri Ghanem, a Lebanese by origin, but he was residing in France for 35 years, and he was famous as a playwright and was editing *Al-Mustaqbal* (the future) newspaper which was published in Paris during the war.

This man entered the conference's hall after Dr. Bliss had finished delivering his speech. He was head of a delegation calling itself the "Syrian delegation". [Georges] Clemenceau

---

1   Lloyd George, *The Truth about the Peace Treaties*, London: 1938, Vol. 2, p. 1039.
2   Iskandar al-Riyashi (Op. Cit.), pp. 218-221.

introduced the delegation to the conference then asked Shukri Ghanem to deliver his speech. Shukri delivered a lengthy speech decorated with pharases in which he challenged Faisal in a provocative way. He said something like Faisal represented Hijaz and had no right to speak in the name of all Arabs, especially the Syrians, for Damascus is no less than one thousand and five hundred kilometers distant from Mecca; so, what spiritual ties and intellectual proximity linked a Hijazi and a Syrian, or the Bedouins and the civilized people? Annexing Syria to the Arabian Peninsula was a stark violation of the sanctity of the land where the Syrian people and their history are rooted. Then Shukri spoke about the topic of the Syrian people participating in a referendum. He said that he did not recommend it at present, that it would be better logically for the superpowers to assign a state from among them to help this small country stand on its feet. Then Shukri pleaded to the states to let France be the one to which this "noble mission" would be assigned, since it is the only state qualified to achieve what the Syrians aspire. Then Shukri concluded his speech with one line of ancient Arab poetry:

صرتُ في غَيرِهِ بَكيتُ عليهِ   رُبَّ يَومٍ بَكَيتُ مِنهُ، فلمّا

Perchance there is a day that caused me to cry,
But when living another, shedding tears on it did I.

Then he said, "Gentlemen! Are you going to leave us weep over our painful past while you are our only hope, the ones whom we consider as the representatives of justice, righteousness and human mercy?"[1]

As soon as Shukri Ghanem started delivering his speech, it was noticed that one of the members of the American delegation passed a sheet of paper to President Wilson stating that Shukri had spent most of his life in France, prompting Wilson not to pay attention to his speech. Then Wilson stood up shortly after

---
1 Zain nur ad-Din Zain (Op. Cit.), pp. 104-105.

that and started walking towards the other side of the hall until he reached the window. He kept looking through it to the outside as he was putting his hands in his coat's pockets. This led to confusing and annoying the French. Clemenceau turned to his foreign minister, Pichon, to reprimand him for bringing Shukri Ghanem to the conference, whispering roughly in his ears saying, "Why did you bring this man here?" Pichon stretched his hand in a hopeless protest and said, "I did not know that he would deal with the matter like this!"[1]

Investigation Committee Appointed

In the morning of March 20, a secret meeting was held at the apartment of Lloyd George in Paris for heads of the four superpowers. A tense discussion went on during it about the Arabs and the Syrian issue. French minister Pichon opened the discussion, pointing out to the preliminary agreement between Clemenceau and Lloyd George in London before the conference. Lloyd George answered him saying that he did not swerve from the context of the Sykes-Picot agreement except with regard to Mosul and Palestine, and if France intended to occupy Damascus with French armies, he would regard that as a stark violation of their [Britons'] treaty with the Arabs. Pichon responded to him saying that there was no agreement between France and the Arabs. Lloyd George then said, "The Sykes-Picot in its entirety was based on a letter sent by McMahon to King Husain, and it is dated October 24, 1915." Lloyd read excerpts of it supporting his viewpoint then kept praising the assistance provided by King Husain and the Arabs to the allies during the war. He said that Britain had recruited about one million soldiers against the Turks, and that their soldiers were the ones who occupied Syria with assistance from the Arabs whose help was "essential", that King Husain placed all his resources on the fighting field, thus

---

1 *Ibid.*, pp. 104-106.

Chapter Three: Sharifi Rule In Syria

providing extreme material help to win the war. General Allenby supported his statement saying, "The Arabs' help is priceless."

It was then that President Wilson joined the argument saying, "The United States is not concerned about the claims of Britain and France with regard to any nation except if the residents wanted them both; therefore, the only way to treat the issue is to find out the desire of the residents of those areas." Everyone present endorsed Wilson's suggestion, but Clemenceau said that the investigation must include Palestine, Iraq and Armenia, so Lloyd George answered saying that he had no objection.

Anyhow, the meeting ended as the hearts were in discord, so much so that Wilson left the meeting hall cursing everyone and everything. He said that he never did anything during the past 48 hours except talking, and that he was disgusted of the whole subject.[1]

In another meeting held by the four superpowers on March 25, an official agreement was reached to appoint a committee of French, British, Italian and American members to send it to Syria and neighboring areas should a need for it arise for a fact finding mission and that a report should be written and submitted to the Peace Conference about its findings.

This decision was the source of a great deal of happiness for Faisal. It is said that when he heard about it, he kept drinking Champaign—for the first time—in a gulp as if he was drinking water, then he rode in his carriage passing by the quarters of the American and British delegations. He kept pelting the Creaon Building, the Majestic Hotel and the French foreign ministry with stuffings and pillows saying that he could not express his feelings except through that way since he did not have bombs.[2]

---

1   Sulayman Mousa (Op. Cit.), pp. 472-473.
2   George Antonius, *Yaqdhat al-Arab* (Arab Awakening), translated by Nasir ad-Din al-Assad and Ihsan Abbas, Beirut: 1962, p. 400.

Between Faisal and [Felix] Frankfurter

On March 1, 1919, the French newspaper *Le Matin* published a statement by Faisal in which he said, "We are glad, due to our sense of humanity and manliness, to see indigent Jews migrating to Palestine and their settlement is welcome. We act according to the national obligations provided they remain under an Islamic authority, or under a Christian authority receiving its mandate from the League of Nations."

In his *Memoirs*, Weizmann says, "This statement which the *Le Matin* newspaper published for Faisal was clear in its hostility towards us, and the prince's secretary was swift in denying it[1]. As for Awni Abdul-Hadi, who was then Faisal's secretary, he denied that the said statement was denied."[2]

Whatever the case may be, the Zionists were interested in this statement, so they contacted their friend, Lawrence, to work to minimize its impact or to cancel it, so Lawrence arranged for a meeting between Faisal and Mr. Felix Frankfurter, a member of the American Zionist Delegation to the Peace Conference. An agreement was reached by both men to exchange two letters containing the gist of the discussion that went on between them. It is said that Lawrence and Frankfurter met after that, so Frankfurter wrote the letter which he would direct in his name to Faisal, and Lawrence wrote the letter in which Faisal would include his answer to it.[3] Then Lawrence went to Faisal and returned carrying the letter signed by Faisal. Below is the text of the letter translated from Weizmann's *Memoirs*:

---

1 Weizmann (Op. Cit.), p. 245.
2 Khairiyya Qasmiyya, *Awni Abdul-Hadi*, p. 25.
3 Sulayman Mousa, *Al-Haraka al-Arabiyya* (the Arab Movement), p. 444.

Chapter Three: Sharifi Rule In Syria

Hijaz Delegation – Paris
March 3, 1919

Dear Mr. Frankfurter,

I would like to seize this opportunity of my first communication with the American Zionists to inform you of what I was saying to Dr. Weizmann in [the subject of] the Arabian Peninsula and Europe. We feel that the Arabs and the Jews are cousins, and they suffered the same persecution from countries stronger than them. It is a good coincident that they have been able to make the first step for cooperation so they may together achieve their national goals. We, Arabs, especially those of us who are educated, look at the Zionist Movement with a very deep sympathy. Our delegation in Paris is fully familiar with the proposals submitted by the Zionist Organization to the Peace Conference, and we regard these proposals to be moderate and appropriate. We shall exert our utmost effort, in as much as is relevant to us, to work towards their achievement. We also welcome the Jews who come to the homeland from the depth of the heart. We have maintained the strongest ties with the leaders of your Movement, especially Dr. Weizmann, and they continue. He has been the greatest supporter of our cause, and I hope the Arabs will soon be able to reward the Jews for their good deeds. We work together in order to reform and nourish the Middle East, and our Movement and yours complement each other. The Jewish movement is nationalistic and not imperialist. So is our movement: nationalist and not imperialist, and there is room in Syria for both of them. I think that in reality, any of these movements cannot win real success without the other. Those who are less informed and responsible than our leaders try to forget the necessity of cooperation between the Arabs and the Jews, and they have taken advantage of the local disputes which have to rise in Palestine in the early stages of the movement. I am afraid some of these folks have distorted your goals to the Arab farmers, *and they have also distorted our goals to the Jewish farmers, and the result is that interest-seekers have benefitted from these artificial differences. I would like to express to you my firm belief that these differences are not in principle; rather, they are matters related to the details, as is the case with disputes that rise among neighboring nations which can be resolved through mutual good intentions. Actually, almost all these differences will disappear when the facts become clearer. I and my people look forward to the day when we help you and you help us, so the lands whose matters concern us and your own selves may restore their suitable place among the civilized nations of the world.*

Sincerely,

Faisal[1]

The Zionists were interested in this letter and depended on it more than they did on the Weizmann-Faisal Agreement, for the note which Faisal wrote on his agreement with Weizmann caused it to lose its value. As for this letter, they regarded it as an important document in their hands on which they would rely in their disputes with the Arabs. Weizmann says the following in his *Memoirs*: "This great letter ought to be taken into consideration by the critics who accuse us of having started our Zionist work in Palestine without paying attention to the wishes of the Arab world or its prosperity. Nobody should forget that the views expressed in this letter come from a recognized Arab leader, one who bears their hopes, and they came as a result of many deliberations..."[2]

In [October of] 1929, when the British Shaw Commission went to Palestine, the Zionists presented this letter to the Commission, relying on it. Awni Abdul-Hadi, who was then in Palestine, felt obligated to send a telegram to Faisal in Baghdad asking him for an explanation for it. The head of the royal *diwan*

---

1 Weizmann (Op. Cit.), pp. 245-246.
2 *Ibid.*, p. 246.

(office), Rustam Haidar, answered him saying, "His Majesty does not remember that he wrote anything like this by himself."[1] Awni Abdul-Hadi comments on this saying, "I can emphasize that Faisal did not write that letter at all. Had this letter been true, why did the Zionists fail to produce its original copy bearing Faisal's signature? All they presented of it was a second typed copy with the word 'Faisal' in a corner of it. When I examined it, I immediately realized that it was forged. It is likely Lawrence was the one who sent the letter without Faisal's knowledge."[2]

Faisal's Return

When the four superpowers decided on March 25, 1919 to send a committee to Syria to investigate, Faisal decided to return to Syria in order to work towards preparing the public opinion in it to receive the committee. He was, hence, represented at the [Paris] Peace Conference by Awni Abdul-Hadi and Rustam Haidar. He left Paris for Syria.

Faisal reached Beirut on April 30 where he received a huge welcome in which delegations from various Syrian areas participated. Faisal left Beirut accompanied by those delegations heading to Damascus which he reached on May 3. There, he was welcomed in a way which nobody else was welcomed: Triumph arches were installed for him, and he rode in a carriage pulled by eight horses according to the way of the kings of Britain.

At the time of his arrival, Faisal was exhilarated with optimism, thinking that the world was in his grip. He placed all his hopes on the coming investigation committee, and he was confident that the said committee would become familiar with the population's desire for independence, and that the states would have to favorably respond to this desire and everything would come to a happy ending!

---

[1] The reader remembers that it was actually Lawrence who wrote that letter, not Faisal. – Tr.
[2] Mousa (Op. Cit.), p. 230.

Story of the Sharifs and Ibn Saud

Two days after he had reached Damascus, he summoned the delegations that had come with him from Beirut to a general evening meeting at the hall of the government house. When everyone was present, Faisal delivered a lengthy speech in which he reviewed the revolution which his father had carried out in Hijaz and his efforts when he was in Europe, during the Peace Conference, the difficulties which he faced there and the extent of his success in removing those difficulties. What is noticed is that Faisal kept in his speech harping on a new chord which was not known before: He shifted from demanding the Arab unity, which incorporates all Arab countries, to demanding the independence of each Arab country on its own. He justified this by saying that the Arab countries differed from each other according to the levels of education and culture; therefore, the present circumstances were not sufficient to comprise of the Arabs a single nation. Then Faisal concluded his speech by saying, "The situation nowadays, therefore, is in your hands. The foreign settlements have been completed due to the favor of the Creator, Praise and Exaltation belong to Him, and through the good intentions of those in the superpowers who became our allies. I cannot distinguish between one and the other with regard to the good intentions. They accepted the statements I threw before their hands."

Faisal implied in his above statement Syria's independence from Hijaz, so it would not be under its authority. He turned to those present to ask them if they agreed with him in this trend, if they relied on him, and if he could continue along this path while they were pleased with it. They answered with, "Yes, Yes, Yes; we are fully pleased," and they kept shouting for him and applauding time and over again.

In the end, Faisal asked each of those present to express his opinion freely and frankly. They stood up one after the other to speak as follows:

Chapter Three: Sharifi Rule In Syria

Sa'd ad-Din al-Khalil: "Horan provides His Highness whatever he asks for."

A member of the Palestinian delegation: "The Palestinians' blood and wealth are at the service of the prince!"

A member of the Amiri delegation: "We have put on for the war its attire, we and all the Arabs; whoever is not killed, let him die!"

Nouri al-Sha'lan: "We all, Rola Arabs, are more obedient to you than your right hand, and anyone who is not like us does not belong to the Islamic creed!"

Naseeb al-Atrash: "We, all tribes of Syria, the Arabs and the Druze, sacrifice our lives towards serving you and the Arab nation, and anyone who swerves from this path betrays his conscience, honor and the Arabs!"

Abdul-Husain Sadiq: "I, on behalf of the Amil Mountain [residents] swear the oath of allegiance to you till death!"

Muhammed Fawzi al-Azm, Muhammed Abidin and As'ad al-Sahib: "We are at your command, we sacrifice ourselves for your sake and endorse you!"

Patriarch of the Roman Catholics: "[We stand] as Your Highness orders; so, order whatever you please!"

A Roman Orthodox patriarch: "An agreement between us and Your Highness exists in this hall according to terms which do not depart from your transparent memory, so we are firm on it!"

Old Syriacs' bishop: "I speak on behalf of the Syriac nation in Syria indicating that they all obey your command; we swear the oath of allegiance to you with our hearts and we depend on you!"

Chief Jewish Rabbi: "Our wealth and lives are before your hands, Your Highness the prince!"

Sa'eed Sulayman: "All the people of Baal-Bek County are at your command, hundreds and thousands, all await your signal!"

Omar al-Atassi: "I have come from Homs, and I did not bid the people of Homs farewell except after they had commissioned me thus: They hand over to you their blood and lives!"

Ibrahim al-Khateeb: "We have commissioned you to be the sultan, the Lebanon Mountain is an inseparable part of Syria!"

Armenian Bishop (speaking in the Turkish language): "I thank the Arabs' kindness and humanitarianism towards the Armenian immigrants during the four years of the war [World War I, 1914 – 1918]; our history will write the name of the Arabs in gold; I bless and thank you!"

Once they had finished their statements, Faisal resumed his speech, swearing by the honor of his fathers and grandfathers to look at the Syrians with the same eyes, without any distinction based on religion, family or class affiliation; personal competence is the basis, and a man may belong to a lofty family but is unable to manage a job. "So, let everyone be informed that I am not biased to anyone because he belongs to a family of prestige and power; rather, I look at his personal ability...," he said.[1]

Syrian [National] Congress

The most that occupied Faisal's mind at the time was how he could mobilize the Syrian public opinion to face the investigation committee with the desired opinion. After deliberating with his advisors, he set his mind on electing a parliamentary council in order to put the committee before the reality, since this council represented the Syrian people according to the democratic method known in civilized countries.

The common belief was that the committee would arrive shortly; therefore, Faisal instructed to hold the elections in a

---

1 Ameen Sa'eed (Op. Cit.), pp. 25-34.

Chapter Three: Sharifi Rule In Syria

hurry. The elections went on in Syria according to the Ottoman electoral law. As for Lebanon and Palestine, the election went on according to the dossiers method.

While Faisal was busy with the elections, a telegram reached him from Rustam Haidar in Paris saying that France opposed the participation in the committee, and that Britain followed suit, but President Wilson insisted on sending the committee provided it would be purely American, and the committee would soon reach Syria.

Faisal felt disappointed by this report, but he, nevertheless, kept working with his aides to prepare the public opinion to face the American committee on its arrival. Propagandists started spreading in various parts of the country admonishing people to hold a unified opinion demanding the unity of the Natural Levant which incorporated Lebanon and Palestine and for its independence, provided it be under the American mandate, or under a British mandate in case America refuses to accept the mandate. As for France, its mandate could never be accepted.

Once the elections had been completed, the council was inaugurated on June 3 under the label "the Syrian Congress". It was attended by one hundred and four members, while sixteen members were absent. There were no representatives from Lebanon because the French authority prevented them from attending. Hashim al-Atassi was unanimously elected as the president of the conference.

What is noteworthy is that a violent argument took place in the conference's second session when a petition was presented to thank Prince Faisal for his efforts to serve Syria. Muslim clerics noticed that the petition did not have the *basmala*, so they objected. Some young members of the parliament responded to them. Their view was that the nation was looking forward to a new dawn and government that coped with the spirit of the time; therefore, the religions must maintain their inviolability and sanctity distantly from politics as is the case in Europe and America. The clerics strongly rejected this opinion. The argument between both parties was heated and almost reached the degree of division and hostility. It was then that Christian member Yousuf al-Hakim stood up to propose a compromise between both parties which was: Two words only should be written at the top of the petition: "Bism Allāh" (in the Name of Allāh), so all MPs applauded this view and endorsed it.[1]

Propaganda Warfare

On June 10, the American investigation committee reached Jaffa (Yafa يافا) with Mr. Charles Crane presiding over it accompanied by Dr. Henry King. It kept touring the country, spending forty-two days during which it visited 36 cities, met 1,520 delegates and received 1,863 petitions.

The committee found out that in all areas—with the exception of Lebanon—most people agreed on the viewpoint advocated by Faisal, i.e. demanding independence for all Syrian lands with a mandate from America or Britain over them. As for Lebanon, especially in the Maronite circles, the matter was the opposite: People were demanding a French mandate.

There were two factors in Lebanon that had their effect in steering people in the direction of demanding the French mandate: They were: the efforts of the Maronite priests on the one hand, and the French money on the other.

The Maronite priests looked at the matter as a sectarian-religious one, regarding the American committee as having Protestant inclinations. They asked their followers to resist it and to unite against it.[2]

Lebanese journalist Iskandar al-Riyashi was among those whom the French commissioned to distribute money in those

---

1 Yousuf al-Hakim (Op. Cit.), pp. 95-96.
2 Ameen al-Rayhani, *Faisal al-Awwal* (Faisal I), Beirut: 1958, p. 48.

Chapter Three: Sharifi Rule In Syria

days. He describes this in two of his books in a facetious way. He says, "In their propaganda, the French used all means that fell in their hands and all the men whom they could use. Mr. Crane, head of the committee, had a headache since the first hour when thousands crowded his office singing a new song that filled the villages of Lebanon at the time which was: 'France is the mother of the world, all the world, so be proud, O Lebanese folks!' The bullies of Beirut were among those used by the French for this purpose: They kept roaming around carrying petitions demanding the French mandate, making people sign them by force. One of those bullies received such petitions which he returned three days later carrying ten thousand signatures, so he was rewarded with a gold lira for each signature."[1]

Mr. Crane knew beforehand that the Muslims and the Druze did not want France, but he was surprised with the piles of petitions demanding the French mandate, and they were filled with names such as Muhammed, Mahmud, Ali, Husain..., etc. Beirut, moreover, witnessed Druze horsemen wearing white and red burnouses and embroidered caftans and carrying bent swords, circling their eyes with a wide circle of desert kohl. They came every day in convoys, looking radiant, chanting and glorifying the Almighty. The expenses of those convoys exceeded one and a half million gold liras: Each Druze horseman had to get a compensation for going to Beirut from the Shawf or the Druze Mountain. A horseman would probably go there several times after changing his clothes and name, each time getting a compensation for his trouble.[2]

All Syrian lands became as if they were in the arena of a propaganda war and intense screams between Damascus and Beirut, one calling for the French mandate and the other for the American or British one. Everyone who called for the French mandate was regarded in Syria as a traitor of his homeland. As

---

1   Iskandar al-Riyash, *Qabl wa Ba'd* (Before and After), Beirut: 1953, p. 30.
2   *Ibid.*, p. 35.

for Lebanon, the stigma of treason was the lot of anyone who called for the American or British mandate.

Yousuf al-Hakim says the following in his *Memoirs*: "Syria included a small group of people calling for the French mandate, but it did not dare to make its voice heard for fear of the masses holding it in contempt, so it was silent against its will, not speaking except a whisper with those whom it trusted." Al-Hakim narrates the story of a Damascus leader who received an offer from a friend to take from the French one thousand gold liras in order to call for the French mandate, so that leader adamantly refused. The friend, therefore, directed this question to him: "Do you see the British mandate as being better than the French one?!" The leader's answer came thus: "I do not prefer either over the other, but I see it wise for the small minority to oppose the majority in its way of thinking."[1]

The American committee went to Paris after completing its mission. It submitted its report to the American delegation to the Peace Conference. The report contained setting the mandate for a limited period over Syria and Iraq provided the United States of America would place Syria under its mandate, while Britain should place Iraq under its mandate, that if the United States refused to accept the mandate over Syria, it should be awarded to Britain. But if Syria insisted on sticking to its interests in Syria, it can be granted a mandate over Lebanon Minor only. The report also included limiting the Jewish immigration and the abandonment of the idea of making Palestine a Jewish state.[2]

The report found nobody interested in it at the Peace Conference, for France and Britain joined ranks to kill it in its cradle. Destiny willed that President Wilson should be inflicted by a dangerous ailment during that period; therefore, the report was thrown in the corner of negligible things and was not published except in the last month of 1922 when it was too late!

---

1 Yousuf al-Hakim (Op. Cit.), p. 88.
2 George Antonius (Op. Cit.), p. 411.

Chapter Three: Sharifi Rule In Syria

It can be said, at any rate, that the referendum carried out by the committee in Syria had angered France without benefitting the Arabs. French newspapers kept attacking Britain violently, accusing it of enticing the Syrians to be hostile towards France in order to save itself from the commitments imposed by the Sykes-Picot Agreement, or to haggle on amending them. The British newspapers did not keep silent about this charge, so they started paying the French newspapers back in their own measure.[1]

France-Britain Agreement

According to the Sykes-Picot Agreement, it was decided to let all of Syria be under the supervision of France in addition to the oil-rich Mosul area. Apparently, Britain regretted having forfeited the Mosul area to France, so it started trying to reclaim it from France and annex it to Iraq.

Lloyd George says this in his *Memoirs*: "When [Georges] Clemenceau went to London after the war, I accompanied him to the French Embassy. When we reached the Embassy, he asked me what I wanted specifically from France. I immediately answered him that I wanted to annex Mosul to Iraq and that Palestine, from Dan to Bi'r Sab`, should be under the British control, so Clemenceau agreed to it without hesitation."[2]

It was only natural that Clemenceau's consent to forfeit the Mosul area should be for a compensation, and this compensation was that all of Syria should be under the French mandate.[3] The final agreement between Britain and France on it took place on September 15, 1919 when it was decided to withdraw the British garrisons from Syria and Klikya كيليكا (Cilicia), and that Syria and Lebanon be placed under the French mandate, all in exchange for putting Palestine and Iraq under the British mandate. It is

---

1 *Ibid.*
2 Lloyd George (Op. Cit.), Vol. 2, p. 1038.
3 Mousa (Op. Cit.), p. 220.

said that the agreement also included Britain abandoning Faisal and France given the free hand in dealing with him as it pleased.¹

Lloyd George had sent, before signing the agreement, a telegram to Faisal asking him to come quickly, so Faisal rushed to leave Damascus six hours after the arrival of the telegram. He took the train to Haifa and from it he boarded a British destroyer that transported him to Marseille on September 17. There, he read in the newspapers the details of the agreement concluded between Lloyd George and Clemenceau, so he was overcome with dismay.²

Faisal reached London on the eve of September 18, so he went to meet Lloyd George accompanied by Allenby. Lloyd George was courteous to him and tried to mitigate him, but he frankly explained to him that he had to agree with France.³ He said to him, "We cannot abandon our ally after it had promised to maintain Syria's independence; so, you have to come to an understanding with Monsieur Clemenceau."⁴ Lloyd George promised him to try to support his viewpoint with Clemenceau.

Faisal felt that the British, who were yesterday his allies, had now sold him to his French opponents, so he opposed and protested but to no avail. Before this, he had placed his hopes on America, but he felt disappointed, too. He realized that he was facing two paths for which there was no third: either come to an understanding with France or declare a boycott of both Britain and France together. He finally decided to go to France and to try to reach an agreement with it through the best means, surrendering his affair to Allāh.

---

1 Ameen Sa'eed, *Al-Watan Al-Arabi* (the Arab Homeland), Cairo, p. 30.
2 Sulayman Mousa (Op. Cit.), p. 506.
3 Ahmed Qadduri (Op. Cit.), p. 138.
4 Yousuf al-Hakim (Op. Cit.), p. 113.

Chapter Three: Sharifi Rule In Syria

A Plan For a Treaty

Faisal reached Paris on October 20, 1919. He stayed in it for more than two months which he spent negotiating with the officials in the French foreign ministry under the supervision of Clemenceau. Rustam Haidar and Awni Abdul-Hadi were assisting Faisal in the negotiations. The negotiations were tough and obstacles rose from time to time.

There was an agreement finally reached between both parties on a draft treaty about which Awni Abdul-Mahdi said that it was the best that could be reached under those circumstances, since a skillful politician must differentiate between what can and what cannot be.[1] It is worth mentioning in this regard that Clemenceau was different from the conventional politicians in his treatment of the colonial issues: He was flexible, lenient, and those politicians accused him of being progressive, fearing him. Swedish researcher Lönnroth says, "The financial and military circles in France accused Clemenceau of being lenient more than he should be towards the Syria issue."[2] Ahmed Najjar, who was at the time among Faisal's entourage, narrates saying, "Pointing to the hair on his head, Clemenceau said to Faisal, 'This hair you see on my head has turned gray due to suffering from politics in this land. I am not colonialist, and I do not believe in colonialism. I offer you a treaty which no other French politician dares to present to you to sign. So, think carefully and give me your answer."[3]

The treaty indicated that France respected, on its side, the independence of the Arab state in Damascus, that this state must respect France's occupation of Lebanon and the coast up to Iskandaroun and that it could derive every assistance it needed

---

1 Khairiyya Qasmiyya, *Al-Hukooma al-Arabiyya fi Dimashq* (the Arab Government in Damascus), p. 160.
2 [Johan] Lönnroth, *Lawrence of Arabia*, trans. by Ruth Lewis, p. 77.
3 Ibrahim Saleem Najjar (Op. Cit.), p. 68.

from France. The treaty pointed out to temporary measures until a final settlement would be reached at the Peace Conference.

Deep down, Faisal was inclined to endorse the treaty, and his advisors accepted it save Dr. Ahmed Qadri. Faisal wrote his father, al-Husain, a letter in which he pointed out to his critical situation and to having been forced to agree with France. In his letter, he said, "I am now fully convinced that Britain used us for its own benefit then left us, and that America abandoned us after harming us and was the cause of our falling into this critical situation. It is difficult for the Syrians to score a victory over the French due to the absence of the means, of the military equipment and to the absence of the culture that prompts the nation [to do so]. I, therefore, saw when I reached Paris to arrive at a sort of understanding with the French which I take out of the old path based on fully adhering to the side of the British."[1]

Al-Husain was during that period angry with his son, Faisal, for declaring the independence of Syria from Hijaz. When Faisal's letter reached him, he did not endorse its contents and sent his private physician, Dr. Thabit Nu`man, to Paris carrying a letter to Faisal ordering him not to sign any treaty that opposed the past British promises made to him. Dr. Thabit reached Paris before the signing of the treaty; therefore, Faisal had to ask to be excused from signing the treaty, promising Clemenceau to submit the treaty plan to the Syrians and to urge them to accept it.[2]

Faisal left Paris for Syria. Evidences point out that he intended to convince the Syrians to accept the treaty and thus put his father before the reality in the pretext the land's people were the ones who accepted the treaty, and he had nothing to do with it.

---

1 Sulayman Mousa (Op. Cit.), p. 68.
2 *Ibid.*, pp. 520-521.

Chapter Three: Sharifi Rule In Syria

Enthusiasm In Syria

The period during which Faisal was absent from Syria—which lasted almost four months—was distinguished by the rise of the public enthusiasm and its gaining momentum. Prince Zaid represented his brother, Faisal, in the government, and he was a youth with little experience, so he was carried away with the public enthusiasm and sometimes supported it publicly and other times discreetly.

Public enthusiasm started since Faisal's departure from Damascus to Europe on September 12. It is said that he is the one who sowed its first seed because he met shortly before his departure with the leaders and told them that he expected them to undertake a public movement to change the nation into an armed one and to turn the homeland into military barracks.[1] Perhaps Faisal intended it to enhance his stance in the upcoming negotiations with the politicians of Britain and France, not knowing that when public enthusiasm sets out thunderously, nobody would be able to stop it at a certain limit.

When reports reached Damascus about the agreement between Faisal and Clemenceau, people were agitated, and they kept declaring their frustration with Britain and saying that it sold Syria to the French in exchange for Mosul's oil. When the British forces started withdrawing from Syria according to the agreement, people's uproar intensified, and they decided to raise a Syrian army to fill the gap left by the withdrawal of the British forces. Residents of Damascus areas, therefore, contacted each other and agreed to choose four men from each quarter in order to meet and decide what they saw as needed to defend the homeland. The deputies kept meeting every evening at one of the quarters. Their meetings became like a local popular parliament where speeches and enthused poems were delivered.[2]

1　Khairiyya Qasmiyya (Op. Cit.), p. 144.
2　Ameen Sa'eed, *Al-Thawra al-Arabiyya al-Kubra*, Cairo, Vol. 2, p. 102.

On November 10, a large demonstration came out in Damascus and went to the government house where it submitted to Prince Zaid a telegram in order to send it to Faisal in Paris protesting the notion of fragmenting the country. On the next day, Zaid received from Faisal a telegram saying, "Communications continue with the allies. Tell the people to be patient and wise while maintaining security and calm as they wait for my answer."[1] This telegram did not have the slightest impact on the public, and it may have increased their enthusiasm and agitation.

During that period, the talents of a popular leader surfaced, one who could excite the masses with his enthusiastic speeches, namely Sheikh Kamil al-Qassab, a turbaned cleric. On November 27, a large meeting was held at the house of the Al [family of] al-Barudi in the Channels Quarter attended by Druze sheikhs. Sheikh Kamil stood up and delivered a speech in his exciting manner, lauding the national enthusiasm in the Arab nation and the sacrifices it offered for the sake of freedom and independence. He denounced the rumor that Prince Faisal desired to reach an understanding with the French, the enemies of yesterday, of today, and of tomorrow, he said. At the end of his speech, he asked a committee named "the Supreme National Committee" be formed to prepare the resistance against the French and to organize a thousand volunteers whom it would equip and dispatch to the fighting field. On December 10, Sheikh Kamil al-Qassam announced in a committee meeting that he met the government men and found them in agreement with the people regarding what he and they wanted. Then he said, "The nation has decided to take to defense; men from the Maydan Quarter have actually volunteered and will install their tents tomorrow at the Mazza."[2]

On the 21st of the month, Prince Zaid ratified a conscription draft law mandating the recruitment of men from twenty to

---

1 Yousuf al-Hakim (Op. Cit.).
2 Ameen Sa'eed (Op. Cit.), Vol. 2, pp. 102-103.

forty years old, making the service period six months and the monetary fine for exemption thirty pounds excluding one who is the only son in the family.

During that period, gangs rose to fight the French in the Alawide mountains and in the Kalkh Hill near Hama, as well as in the Biqaa, Aamil Mountain and the Golan Heights, and the government in Damascus encouraged those gangs secretly and provided them with money and weapons.

It is worth mentioning in this regard that the French forces were at the time busy fighting the Turkish forces in Klikya. The Syrians felt that they sympathized with the Turks due to vendetta towards the French. Turkish propaganda leaflets started spreading in Aleppo encouraged by some Syrian and Iraqi officers. Those leaflets were signed by Mustafa Kamal Pasha. Here below we quote a paragraph in one of them which was directed to the Syrian people:

"As a Muslim, I plead to you not to pay attention to the differences between us that led us to sever ties. We ought to remove all misunderstanding between us, and let us all direct our weapon towards the treacherous parties that wish to partition our homeland... The *mujahidin* who believe in what is right will soon visit their Arab brethren, and they shall tear the enemies apart; so, let us live as brothers-in-religion, and death to our enemies."[1]

Gen. Gouraud

France appointed Gen. [Henri] Gouraud [1867 – 1946] as its High Commissioner in Beirut. This general was one of the commanders of the Dardanelle where he became quite famous and where he lost one of his arms. Apparently, France meant, by appointing this man, to settle the Syria issue which had for so long disturbed it, via a military solution.

---

1   Zain Nur ad-Din Zain (Op. Cit.), pp. 140-146.

Gouraud reached Beirut on November 21, 1919 and was awarded the greatest reception. It is known that he was a proud man who loved flowers; therefore, he surrounded himself since his arrival with the appearances of opulence. Bisharah al-Khouri says about him the following in his *Memoirs*: "This general wanted to surround himself with awe since receiving the tasks of his post, and one of the manifestations of it was his forming a national guard to accompany him on an Arabian horse as he moved about the city. He imposed that all guard members should be from the Druze Mountain, and he thought they all were so, but some cavaliers were brought from various villages of Lebanon. Their eyes were marked with kohl so they would fool the authority that they were from the Druze Mountain. A politician received a handsome commission for their volunteering, and this guard cost a great deal of money [to put together]."[1]

The most serious problem which Gouraud faced after reaching Beirut was the spread of the war among the Turkish and French forces in the Klikya. When the British forces withdrew from that area, only the French forces had to face the Turks. Mustafa Kamal Pasha had prepared there a large regular army, arming gangs from among the farmers that kept forcing their way through the villages. The Armenians who lived in those country villages suffered a great deal.

Gouraud sent to Klikya two large divisions, but he faced a great difficulty in supplying them with rations and equipment because the government of Damascus prevented him from using the Syrian train to transport the rations. He, therefore, had to transport them via the sea route to Alexandria, and this took fifteen days, whereas the train route would have taken only four days.[2] There is no need to say that this action by the Damascus

---

[1] Bisharah Khalil al-Khouri, *Haqa'iq Lubnaniyya* (Lebanese facts), Beirut. [No page number provided. –Tr]

[2] Andriyao, *Tarikh al-Druze wa Tamarrud Dimashq* (History of the Druze and the Rebellion of Damascus) translated by Hafiz Abu Muslih, Beirut: 1971, p. 29.

government caused Gouraud to bear a great deal of grudge towards it, so he decided to crush it.

Exciting News

Before returning to Syria, Faisal had agreed with Clemenceau to keep the treaty secret so that on reaching Damascus, he would be able to convince the Syrians of it in a calm atmosphere free of excitements. What is strange is that as he left Marseilles on January 7, 1920, the French newspaper *Le Matin* published a report about the treaty saying, "Prince Faisal, being in harmony with France, has accepted its mandate over all Syria. In return, France accepted the setting up of an Arab area that incorporates four cities: Damascus, Homs, Hama and Aleppo, provided they would be under his rule assisted by French advisors and inspectors... Also, the Prince agreed to cooperate with France rather than with anyone else in economic and financial affairs." The French foreign ministry immediately denied the report, but the newspaper emphasized its authenticity, adding other details in articles that followed.[1]

Here, we have the right to ask: Was publishing that report as an exclusive, one which a newspaper's editor was able to obtain in his own efforts, or was it arranged by some French politicians for a certain purpose intended for it?!

Most likely, publishing this report was arranged and deliberate, for the conservative circles and conventional politicians from among the opponents of Clemenceau in France could not relish the signing of such a treaty which, in their view, harmed France's interests. They—as we have already seen—accused Clemenceau of being too lenient than he should have been towards the Syria issue. It is not unlikely that they were the ones who deliberately published that report that way in order to instigate the Syrians to reject the treaty. This is something which

---

1 Muhammed Jameel Bayham (Op. Cit.), pp. 160-161.

often takes place in the press world, and such events took place in Iraq in 1948 as we will discuss in a forthcoming chapter of this book by the will of Allāh!

Anyhow, publishing the report about the treaty in the *Le Matin* newspaper seriously influenced the Syrian public opinion. It was like the spark that ignites a fire: The masses set out to condemn the treaty and curse anyone who supported it, whoever he might be.

Faisal's Return

Faisal reached Beirut on January 14, 1920. Before his arrival, he had received a telegram from Clemenceau telling him that his government had ratified the treaty provided the prince undertook effective measures to let calm rain on the Syrian people, and that he would please them with his policy. Faisal presented this telegram to Gen. Gouraud when he met him in Beirut. It is said that Gouraud asked him, "Can you stop the disturbances in Syria?" Faisal answered him saying that it would be easy for him to stop the disturbances because he himself was the one who stirred them in order to create problems for France.[1]

Faisal left Beirut two days after he had arrived there. When he reached Damascus, the public welcome for him was relatively lukewarm.[2] Faisal felt that the atmosphere was charged against him and against the treaty, and he kept talking to his guests, explaining the situation, asking them to keep it secret from the public. On the next day that followed his arrival at Damascus, a huge demonstration came out and reached his mansion with shouts, so he came out from the balcony to greet it. Sheikh Kamil al-Qassab stood up to speak to the demonstrators. Directing his speech at Faisal, he said, "I am confident that you do not accept, far it is from you to accept, to be a prince over a land where you

---

1 Op. Cit., p. 162
2 George Antonius (Op. Cit.), p. 417.

are shadowed by a foreign flag."¹ Faisal spoke to thank the demonstrators for their sincerity and national awareness, assuring them that the issue of the country was yet to be settled and calling on them to be calm and to rely on the nation's declared right after relying on Him, the most Praised and Exalted One.[2]

In the eve of January 22, the Arab Club threw a big party in honor of Prince Faisal on the occasion of his return from Europe. It was attended by many dignitaries, government officials and public leaders. A number of speakers spoke from the podium, one after the other, and they were all trying to denounce the treaty through hinting and indirect references, demanding full independence not tainted by any protection or mandate, and that this independence must be defended by everything precious or cheap.

Physician Abdul-Rahman al-Shahbandar was one of the speakers and the most enthusiastic. He criticized the standing government and described himself as belonging to the people and, because of his profession, he entered people's homes and knew their mindsets.[3] Then he took out his stethoscope and said that it helped him every day to listen to the beats of the people's hearts that were concerned about the country's fate, complaining about the weakness of the political activity.[4]

Once the speakers finished their speeches, Faisal stood up and started delivering a lengthy speech which indicated the deep pain he felt. He started his speech by thanking the youths who threw the party. He pointed out that last year, he noticed in the club a sign written on it saying "Political talks are prohibited," but that he now did not notice it. He justified this by the present political conditions that ruled, that the new generation must

---

1 Khairiyya Qasmiyya (Op. Cit.), p. 159.
2 Yousuf al-Hakim (Op. Cit.), p. 127.
3 Ahmed Qadri (Op. Cit.), p. 167.
4 Yousuf al-Hakim (Op. Cit.), p. 83.

neglect its lessons and books and pay attention to politics, believing that defending the homeland was above everything and that knowledge came second. Then he said, "Perhaps you have noticed that I stutter, for I am not an orator, and I am not used to saying too much because I am used to silence. One who knows me from the past knows this to be the case; therefore, I wish this nation to be silent like me, working much and saying a little... For one and a half year, we have been saying, 'Enough speeches, enough talks, we are in the days of action, not in the days of talks. Talks do not bring any benefit, but actions benefit a great deal. I have been absent from the country for four months, and I do not doubt that history preserves what I have done in the West, be it good or bad, a little or a lot. I do not regard myself as being free of sins because I was saying what my conscience inspired me. When I returned here, I saw the nation quite enthusiastic, but it is an enthusiasm that does not go beyond words. It would have been better if this enthusiasm were accompanied by action. I invite the nation to do that; there is no life for it except if it does what I am saying." Then Faisal talked about the speech by Abdul-Rahman al-Shahbndar, defending the government and saying, "It stands according to the opinion of the one whom the nation endorsed: myself. The government is my own person, and I do not allow an individual or a group to say that the government is such and such or demand to replace one ruler with another. This is so because I am in charge until the nation's council is held, and I will then forfeit the responsibility." Then Faisal pointed to al-Shahbandar's stethoscope and how he knew the people's heart beats and said, "The first action Dr. al-Shahbandar should do is to raise the standard of the art in which he specializes; so, if each of us does what he must do in the field of his specialization, the movement of the entire nation will then be regulated: A soldier fights, a leader leads the soldiers, a politician manages the affairs as the circumstances dictate to him, and the doctor cures the sick. So, one must not trespass the limits of his specialization to the mission of someone else, nor should he interfere in anything outside the scope of his experience and commitments." Then Faisal returned to his basic subject and said, "I reiterate and emphasize to you, my brothers, that I am working to achieve what you demand of me, which is: full independence [for Syria]..., but, at the same time, I say that there are between you and the Western nations ties that connect you, ties which you cannot do without, because the modern means of transportation have caused Europe to be in the inside of Syria. If you say that you can do with her, I will know that you do not want life... We nowadays are in a critical situation. We must not, during this situation, look down at the nations because by looking down at one of them, we will have [actually] looked down at our own selves. Before us are big and great nations. We must respect every nation and every government so long as it respects our homeland, independence and interests."[1]

When Faisal finished his statement, he thought that those present were convinced of the truth of what he had said, and this is a delusion which quite often seizes politicians who do not know the nature of humans. The evidences which Faisal brought in his speech were, according to him, strong and convincing, and he thought that as long as they were so, they had to be strong and convincing according to others, too. He did not know that the enthusiasm that controlled the public opinion put people in a world different from the one in which he was. He was looking at matters in the light of the principle that says that "Politics is the art of what is possible," whereas they were looking at them in the light of "the will of the people" and "dying in the cause of the homeland," and there is a vast distance between both outlooks!

---

1 Look at p. 87 of the previous reference and also Ahmed Qadri (Op. Cit.), pp. 167-168.

Another Attempt

Faisal wanted to carry out another attempt to convince the people to accept the treaty, so he wanted to hold a secret meeting with the administrative board of the Young Arab Society which had a great impact on the Syrian public opinion at the time. The meeting was held at the house of Dr. Ahmed Qadri on February 6. Faisal presented to the attendants the treaty plan on which he agreed with Clemenceau. He defended it and said that it was the maximum that could be attained. He requested them to be realistic in their treatment of political matters. But they did not respond to his request, rejecting the treaty and insisting on rejecting it, so Faisal said to them, "Rejecting the treaty means declaring war on France." Their answer was: "We are ready to declare the war on both France and England."[1]

The next day, Faisal summoned the members of the administrative board separately, one after the other, in order to convince them, but he did not succeed, so Ali Ridha al-Rikabi suggested to him to oust the board and to replace it with another, so Faisal agreed. Fifty Society members met at al-Rikabi's house headed by Prince Zaid. Sheikh Kamil al-Qassab opened the session with one of his fiery speeches in which he assaulted the administrative board, charging it with sacrificing the interest of the country and demanding its ousting. Then each speaker repeated the same statement. A board member stood up and said, "We have done what we could, so you should try yourselves." Then an election went on. New members won, including al-Rikabi.[2]

Faisal was not satisfied with this but kept encouraging people to establish a new party to stand in the way of the Young Arab Society and thus limit its power. A party was, indeed, founded in the name of the "Syrian National Party." Conventional dignitaries

---

1   Ameen Sa'eed (Op. Cit.), Vol. 2, p. 125.
2   *Ibid.*, Vol. 2, p. 126.

Chapter Three: Sharifi Rule In Syria

joined it, and Muhammed Kurd Ali wrote the party's proclamation in a decorative way.[1]

We do not need to say that this attempt had to sooner or later fail, for any political party derives its strength from the masses rallying round it, and the masses by nature do not like moderation: a thing, anything, in its view, is either black or white, and there can be nothing in the middle. One who wants to earn a status among the masses has to walk with them and share their enthusiasm; otherwise, they would hold him in contempt and regard him as a traitor of the homeland.

The masses in Damascus became skeptical about the patriotism of any man rumored to be supportive of the treaty; therefore, people kept accusing Nouri al-Sa`eed of treason, shouting against him on the streets, and a secret leaflet directed against al-Rikabi spread among the public.[2]

Faisal finally realized that convincing the masses of accepting the treaty was extremely difficult or almost impossible. He, therefore, was puzzled, not knowing whether to be in harmony with the public and thus lose politics or with politics and thus lose the public. The masses cannot be a positive factor in politics except if they have a wise leadership that knows how to steer them. A political thinker says, "The leaders of the masses must walk before them, not behind them." He means that the leaders must be the ones who direct the masses, not the latter directing them.

It seems that the masses of Damascus at the time did not have such a wise leadership. Its leaders were of the type of Kamil al-Qassab who would walk behind the masses and shout with them without having their independent opinion towards which they could direct the masses; therefore, Faisal was in a

---

1 Ahmed Qadri (Op. Cit.), pp. 172-174.
2 Khairiyya Qasmiyya (Op. Cit.), p. 161.

psychological situation for which nobody could envy him: He was between both parts of the grindstone.

During that period, Percival Phillips, correspondent for the *British Daily Express* newspaper, met Faisal then wrote his newspaper describing Faisal's psychological condition. He said, "Prince Faisal gave me the impression, during my recent interview with him, that he is a man at the verge of total collapse as a result of the despair he felt. This is so because everyone here is skeptical about him. The French do not trust him. His father, the King of Hijaz, does not trust him, believing that Faisal had surrendered himself and his homeland to servitude through a treaty about which Mecca knew nothing."[1]

Faisal's Coronation

On January 20, 1920, Clemenceau's administration fell and was replaced by a new administration headed by [Alexandre] Millerand [1859 – 1943]. The new head of state was known to be the opposite of Clemenceau: inflexible with regard to the Syrian issue and wanted to solve it through military force.

Millerand declared before the French parliament, as soon as he ascended to power, that occupying Syria needed a large military force. He demanded the parliament to agree to earmark the money needed for it and said, "This is for the sake of France bringing the people of Syria, under its banner, the bliss of the good government as it had done in Morocco."[2]

This shift in the French policy made Faisal sense the need for going along with the public enthusiasm. He probably feared the loss of both ways. In other words, he feared he might lose both masses and politics. In early May of 1920, an agreement was reached between him and the leaders of the Syrian political parties to put France before the reality by declaring the

---

1 Daily Express, 24 February 1920.
2 *Afaq Arabiyya* magazine of May 1977, p. 119.

Chapter Three: Sharifi Rule In Syria

independence of Syria and swearing fealty to Faisal as the King over it, and it was decided to do it on the 8th of the month.

It is said that a family problem faced Faisal then: According to the traditions of the Hashemite family, he was not supposed to advance ahead of his brother, Abdullah, who was older than him. After deliberating with party leaders, a solution was reached: The Iraqis who were present in Syria should declare Iraq's independence and swear fealty to Abdullah as King over Iraq on the same day when Faisal receives the oath of allegiance.[1]

The Syrian [National] Congress was summoned to convene in a hurry, and the Iraqis who were present in Syria were summoned to elect a congress of their own. In the afternoon of March 6, the Syrian Congress convened. It decided that Syria was fully independent in its natural borders which included Lebanon and Palestine, and that Faisal was King over all of it. At the same time, the Iraqis met at the house of Nouri al-Sa`eed in the Martyrs Quarter (hayy al-shohada) and elected from among them the following individuals in order to declare the independence of Iraq: Ja`far al-`Askari, Sa`eed al-Sheikhli, Ali Jawdat al-Ayyubi, Abdullah al-Dulaimi, Jameel al-Midfa`i, Tahsin Ali, Isma`eel Namuq, Sami al-Orfali, Faraj `Imarah, Rasheed al-Hashimi, Ridha al-Shibibi, Sabeeh Najeeb, Mahmoud Adeeb, Naji al-Suweedi, Tawfiq al-Suweedi, Ibrahim Kamal, Younus Wahbi, Hamdi Sadr ad-Din, Ahmed Rafeeq, Nouri al-Qadhi, Makki al-Sharbati, Thabit Abdul-Nur, Ibrahim Tohalah, Izzat al-Karkhi, Abdul-Lateef al-Falahi, Tawfiq al-Hashimi, Muhammed al-Bassam, As`ad sahib and Muhammed Khairo.

On the appointed day, i.e. March 8 [1920], a huge celebration was prepared at the Municipality House in the Marja which was attended by heads of the religious sects, dignitaries and state representatives. It was noticed that the British did not attend the celebration, whereas the French did with signs of jubilation showing on their faces, something which drew attention. Among

---
1 Muhammed Tahir al-Omari (Op. Cit.), Vol. 3, p. 189.

the interesting things that took place at the beginning of the celebration was that Nouri al-Sha`lan, head of the Rolah tribe, came accompanied by ten of his armed followers and occupied the forefront of the hall. One of those in charge of welcoming the guests approached him and requested him in a nice way to order his followers to stand with the invited dignitaries, but the sheikh refused, unsheathed his sword and shouted at the man to return to his place, so he returned disappointed.

Faisal arrived at the site of the celebration riding a horse, so the masses crowding the Marja park shouted for him. Shortly thereafter, Muhammed Izzat Druzah, secretary of the Syrian Congress, went out to the balcony that overlooked the masses to recite the decision of the Congress announcing the independence of Syria and the choosing of Faisal as its King. He was followed by Tawfiq al-Suweedi who read the resolution of the Iraqi Congress declaring the independence of Iraq and the choosing of Abdullah as the King over it. Then the head of the Damascus municipality, Ghalib al-Zaliq, advanced carrying Syria's new flag which is the same Hijazi flag with the addition of another star to it. The escort of Fakhri al-Barudi received it and hoisted it over the mast, whereupon the masses shouted. A banner was raised on which this statement was written: "Long live King Faisal!" Cannons were then fired one hundred and one rounds.

A Noise In Beirut

The declaration of monarchy was met by France and Britain with anger. On May 9, Lord Curzon, the British foreign minister, sent a telegram to Faisal containing a violent protest. He said to him, "The Syrian Congress has no legitimacy, and Britain does not recognize the right of any group in Damascus that speaks on behalf of Palestine and Iraq."[1] On April 1, Lord Curzon sent a telegram to al-Husain and his son, Abdullah, saying this: "Britain does not consider the twenty-nine Iraqis who met in Damascus

---

1   Zain Nur ad-Din (Op. Cit.), p. 151.

Chapter Three: Sharifi Rule In Syria

as representatives of Iraq, and the Peace Conference alone is the one that will determine the future of Iraq after ascertaining the wishes of the [Iraqi] people." Al-Husain responded to him saying that he had nothing to do with the Peace Conference, and that his relationship was confined to Britain only, that he carried out the revolution and risked everything, facing perils and catastrophes, depending on that relationship and due to his trust in the honor of Great Britain which is famous for keeping its promises.[1]

In Beirut, protest petitions kept reaching the headquarters of the Maronite patriarch from everywhere in Lebanon expressing a rejection of those who signed them of annexing Lebanon to Faisal's new state without consulting the people of Lebanon. On March 12, the Administrative Council of [Mount] Lebanon prepared a resolution which it submitted to the Peace Conference through Gen. Gouraud protesting the resolution of the Syrian Congress and saying that the said Congress had no right to interfere in Lebanon's affairs and administration. On March 22, a crowded meeting was held in Baabda which was attended by members of the Administrative Council and a crowd of Lebanon's dignitaries and representatives of its Christian sects. During it, a declaration was made of the independence of Lebanon. Then the Lebanese flag was hoisted on the Baabda's Sarai, so Lebanese army battalions paraded in front of it to salute it.[2]

As a result, some sectarian tension took place between the Muslims and the Christians in Beirut. Mosque preachers started preaching in the name of King Faisal, so orders were issued to them from the French authority to mention in their sermons the name of the Ottoman caliph Muhammed Waheed ad-Din, but the speakers refused and denounced the interference of the [French] authority in religious affairs. The most outspoken of them in this regard was Sheikh Muhyi ad-Din al-Makkawi, al-

---

1 Sulayman Mousa (Op. Cit.), p. 544.
2 Zain Nur ad-Din Zaid (Op. Cit.), pp. 153-154.

Majeediyya Mosque speaker. The authority, therefore, arrested him on April 5 and banished him to Arwad Island, so the Muslims were furious, and a demonstration came out in Damascus protesting his banishment. King Faisal sent Gen. Gouraud and Gen. Allenby as well as the French government telegrams protesting their insulting the Islamic creed when the military authority interfered in the religious affairs and prevented the speakers at mosques from supplicating according to the wish of the population.[1]

The French authorities had to release Sheikh Muhyi ad-Din, and it issued a statement denying it interfered in the religious affairs. It also stated that France respected all religions equally; it did not accept the supplication for His Majesty King Faisal be used to stir political disputes.[2]

The Rikabi Administration

On March 9, that is, the day that followed the coronation of Faisal, the royal decree issued orders to form the first Syrian cabinet. It was comprised of: Ridha al-Rikabi as its head, Alaa ad-Din al-Darubi as head of the Consultative Council, Ridha al-Sulh for the interior ministry, Abdul-Hameed al-Qaltaqji as minister of war, Jalal ad-Din Zahdi for the ministry of treasury, Sa`eed al-Husaini as the foreign minister, Faris al-Khuri as the minister of finance, Sati` al-Husari as the minister of education and Yousuf al-Hakim as minister of [public] services.

Most of these ministers were middle-aged men who inclined towards moderation in politics; therefore, the enthusiastic nationalists started accusing them of weakness and of little interest in defending the homeland. Criticism of this cabinet intensified following the announcement of the resolutions of the San Remo Conference on April 25 which placed Syria under the French mandate and Iraq and Palestine under the British

---

1 Khairiyya Qasmiyya (Op. Cit.), p. 190.
2 Ameen Sa`eed (Op. Cit.), Vol. 2, p. 142.

Chapter Three: Sharifi Rule In Syria

mandate. The parties and masses were furious about those resolutions, and they started attacking the administration, accusing it of not sharing their resolve to fight France to the end.[1]

This opposition was led by a young 36-year old military officer named Yousuf al-Azmah who was at the time occupying the post of aide to the minister of war, and he was in the rank of major, but Faisal granted him an honorary major general rank in appreciation of his services. This officer was supported in his opposition by Ihsan al-Jabiri, head of the royal *diwan* (office) and by minister of information Sati` al-Husari.

The Turkish forces were at the time dealing heavy blows to the French in Klikya, reaching in their advance close to the Syrian borders which they started threatening. Al-Rikabi was of the opinion that he should cooperate with the French to defend Syria's northern borders.[2] But Yousuf al-Azmah opposed this view, for he used to incline to reaching an agreement with the Turks against the French. During those days, an altercation took place between al-Rikabi and Yousuf al-Azhah in the presence of the king. Yousuf, therefore, said to the king, "If Your Majesty allows, we would be able to throw the French into the sea with this foot." Al-Rikabi asked him about the extent of military force he had to fight France, so Yousuf al-Azmah answered: 4,000 soldiers, 12 cannons and 36 shells. Al-Rikabi then responded to him saying, "I am afraid your foot would have a hole in it before you throw the French into the sea."[3]

Opponents of the Rikabi administration finally held secret meetings at Ihsan al-Jabiri's house during which they decided to topple it. The king was biased to them. On May 2, 1920, al-Rikabi felt fed-up with the plot being woven against him, so he left his office and went home determined to resign. The king, therefore,

---

1 Khairiyya Qasmiyya (Op. Cit.), p. 178.
2 Sulayman Mousa (Op. Cit.), p. 553.
3 Khairiyya Qasmiyya (Op. Cit.), pp. 178-179.

sent him Ihsan al-Jabiri to mitigate him and to advise him to be patient, so al-Rikabi answered him saying, "I cannot be patient when I see what goes on in the capital, especially in the Syrian Congress, the recklessness and the excessive demands which may lead to the loss of order and to a disturbance at the borders, all forewarning of an ill fate."[1] Then al-Rikabi wrote down his resignation in which he said that he was resigning due to health reasons and handed it over to al-Jabiri.

The Atassi Administration

On the day that followed al-Rikabi's resignation, King Faisal commissioned Hashim al-Atassi to form a new cabinet. He did so as follows: Ridha al-Sulh as the head of the Consultative Council, Alaa ad-Din al-Darubi for the interior ministry, Abdul-Rahman al-Shahbandar for the foreign ministry, Yousuf al-Azmah for the ministry of war, Faris al-Khuri for the finance ministry, Jalal ad-Din Zahdi for the ministry of justice, Sati` al-Husari for the ministry of education and Yousuf al-Hakim for the ministry of [public] services [or public works].

What is noticed is that five members of the new administration had served in the resigning administration, and the new cabinet included only two new ministers: Yousuf al-Azmah and Abdul-Rahman al-Shahbandar, and they looked alike due to being young and among the most enthusiastic and self-motivated people. What is noteworthy is that the king before then used to hate al-Shahbandar and to regard him as his enemy. He said the following about him once: "When I came to know al-Shahbandar, I held all the people of the Levant in contempt..."[2] Apparently, the king permitted him into the cabinet in order to get close to him and to allay his enthusiasm.

---

1 Yousuf al-Hakim (Op. Cit.), p. 157.
2 Yousuf Abyash, *Rihlat al-Imam Muhammed Rasheed Ridha* (Travels of imam Muhammed Rasheed Ridha), Beirut: 1971, p. 300.

Chapter Three: Sharifi Rule In Syria

When the Atassi administration stood before the Syrian Congress and recited its statement, the Congress protested against it because the said statement did not include a clear reference to the defense and to its means, so the cabinet members went aside into a room. Al-Shahbandar came out after that and said to the Congress: "You ask us, Gentlemen, about the defense, and we tell you that we were not created save from defense and to defend," whereupon the Congress members applauded this statement and granted the cabinet their vote of confidence.[1]

The Atassi administration kept working as hard as it could to prepare means of defending the country. The first thing it did in this regard was rethinking the conscription law which was neglected by the former administration, making the service period one year instead of six months. It also issued national loan bonds in the amount of half a million dinars for a 6% interest in lieu of pawning one million donums[2] of state lands. Leaflets publicizing for this loan were distributed to people, and they contained the following statements: "Are you eastern...?" "Are you an Arab...?" "Do you want to live in freedom...?" "Do you want full independence...? If so, take part in the Syrian loan... There is no life save in independence, and there is no independence without funds."[3]

Yousuf al-Azmah exerted a great deal of effort to prepare and arm the Syrian army, then he went to Aleppo in the pretext of looking into strengthening the means for defending the northern borders, but he was actually after reaching an understanding with Mustafa Kamal Pasha. There, he contacted representatives of the Pasha with whom he discussed the establishment of military cooperation between the Arabs and the Turks. It seems that the British came to know about that contact. Churchill made this statement at the British House of Commons: "The Arabs

---

1   Muhammed Tahir al-Omari (Op. Cit.), Vol. 3, p. 215.
2   One donum (or dunam) is equivalent to one thousand square meters. – Tr.
3   Khairiyya Qasmiyya (Op. Cit.), p. 179.

now try, for the first time, to come to an understanding with the Turks in order to find a common issue between them after our policy had succeeded in keeping them apart."[1]

The French realized that under those circumstances, they were unable to keep both Syria and Klikya and had to forfeit either of them in order to keep the other. One of their political thinkers stated saying, "Had France, in order to make its decision based on the benefits and calculations alone, it would have tilted in favor of Klikya over Syria, but France had traditions and many moral links connecting it to Syria for several centuries. So, it has, then, to hold on to those ties and traditions and to forfeit Klikya in order to keep Syria if need be."[2]

Gen. Gouraud, therefore, signed a truce with Mustafa Kamal Pasha on May 30, 1920, then he kept withdrawing his forces from Klikya, massing them in the direction of the Damascus government.[3]

Massacre at the Amil Mountain

The Amil Moutnain is located in the south of Lebanon. It is bordered by the Mediterranean on the west and the Golan Heights on the east. Most of its residents are Twelver [Ithna-Asheri] Shi`ites who are called "Mutawla," which means those who follow [Commander of the Faithful] Ali. The mountain, in addition to the Shi`ites, used to house a Christian minority, mostly Maronite. During that period, sectarian frictions took place. Those frictions would erupt once and calm down another. Muhammed Izzat Darooza says, "The propaganda and incitement had led in the areas of the Golan and Amil Mountain, which are adjacent to each other, to some hostile frictions between the Muslims and the Christians. After the declaration of independence and monarchy, these frictions started expanding, and some

---

1 *Ibid.*, p. 186.
2 Sati` al-Husari, *Maysalun*, Beirut, p. 8.
3 Sulayman Mousa (Op. Cit.), p. 555.

Chapter Three: Sharifi Rule In Syria

images of gang wars from both sides appeared on their stage: The Christians were armed with French weapons and masterminded by French hands under the guise of self-defense and the repelling of aggression, and the Islamic forces were armed by Arab weapons and led by Arabs in order to foil the schemes and instigations of the French, and to hinder the latter from reaching their goals..."[1]

On April 24, 1920, the Shi`ites held a conference in the Valley Hujair at the distance of fifteen miles south of al-Nabatiyya. It was attended by Shi`ite scholars and dignitaries headed by Kamil Beg al-As`ad and the renown mujtahid Sayyid Abdul-Husain Sharafud-Din [al-Mousawi]. They unanimously decided to join Faisal's Arab government and refuse to succumb to the French rule.[2]

This conference intensified the sectarian tension in the area, and rumors started spreading among the population instigating each sect against the other. An elderly man from the Amil Mountain talked to me saying, "A rumor spread among the Shi`ites that the Christians burned the Qur'an and also deflowered seven Shi`ite girls." He rendered this rumor to French plots. The result was the Shi`ites became fiercely furious, so they attacked a Christian village near the Palestinian borders called "Ayn Ibil", killing a large number of its residents.

The Christians accused one of the Shi`ite scholars who attended the Hujair conference of being the one who was behind the massacre. According to them, he made *istikhara* with the rosary beads on slaughtering the Christians.[3] But the Shi`ites render the cause to the French. One of their authors says the following in this regard: "The French armed the Christians with rifles and tempted them to bully their neighbors, sparking in

---

[1] Muhammed Izzat Druza, *Al-Haraka al-Arabiyya al-Haditha* (Modern Arab Movement), Saida: 1950, Vol. 1, p. 124.
[2] Muhammed Jabir Al Safa, *Tarikh Jabal Amil* (History of the Amil Mountain), Beirut, p. 226.
[3] Ameen al-Rayhani (Op. Cit.), p. 53.

them the fire of fanaticism. Those Christians kept assaulting Shi`ite passersby and the poor, causing the Shi`ites to respond in a similar way, so the catastrophe took place that disturbed the friendship between the followers of both creeds, something which the men of wisdom regretted."[1]

When Gen. Gouraud came to know about the massacre, he decided to seek revenge against the Shi`ites. On May 5, 1920, a French campaign comprised of four thousand soldiers led by Col. Niager moved from Beirut, took the coastal route until it reached Sur. There, it burned the house of mujtahid Abdul-Husain Sharaf ad-Din which contained a precious library. Then it turned towards the interior and started burning many villages and ranches, executing about thirty men on the charge of participating in the Christians' massacre.

When the Amil Mountain was totally controlled, the French authority called a large number of Shi`ite dignitaries, Druze and Christians to a meeting in Saida. The meeting was held on June 5. Colonel Niager stood up to deliver a strongly worded speech directed at the Shi`ites and read the harsh sentences issued against them. Some of them were sentenced to be executed and some others were banished for good. Among those who were banished was Abdul-Husain Sharaf ad-Din, Kamil al-As`ad, Rashid Asiran and Muhammed Sa`eed al-Bazzi. At the conclusion of his speech, Niager said that the French government did not relish issuing such strict sentences against the Shi`ite dignitaries, but they were the ones who "brought it on themselves".

Then Niager mentioned terms. He said that the campaign would not leave the area except after fulfilling them. Those terms were: the payment of a fine in the amount of one hundred Egyptian pounds, the returning of looted items to their owners, the giving of a handwritten pledge to protect the Christians, the handing over of the weapons, the surrendering of the criminals and the bearing of the responsibility for every new incident. The

---

1 Muhammed Jabir Al Safa (Op. Cit.), p. 227.

Shi`ites accepted these terms with the exception of the last one. They said that they could not bear the responsibility for any new incident because they could not be in every place at the same time, but they pledged to exert their effort to prevent incidents from happening.

A committee was formed to collect the imposed fines. The committee members seized the opportunity to keep collecting for themselves more than what they had collected for those who suffered damages. Ameen al-Rayhani, who quotes some well-informed individuals, says, "The members of the committee collected, through their skill, 485,000 liras. They paid those who suffered damages 50,000 liras and put the rest in their pockets."[1]

Anyhow, misery and desolation reigned on Amil following that event, and many residents of Amil were forced to sell what they owned in order to pay the fine. King Faisal tried to alleviate their pain, so he sent a protest to Gen. Gouraud and also sent Lloyd George asking mediate in the name of humanity, pointing out that the French arming the Christians would lead to religious extremism and will crush his efforts to create a unified Islamic-Christian nationality.[2]

Gouraud's Warning

On July 10, 1920, an incident took place in Beirut that led to Gouraud being angry and to increasing his hatred of the Damascus government. It is summed up thus: Individuals came from Damascus and secretly contacted some members of the Lebanon Administration Council. They presented to them a large bribe which the French sources estimated at forty-two thousand pounds. With this bribe, they were able to convince seven of their members to sign a petition asking for the independence of Lebanon and the setting up of economic cooperation between Lebanon and the government of Damascus.

---

1   Ameen al-Rayhani (Op. Cit.), p. 28.
2   Khairiyya Qasmiyya (Op. Cit.), p. 28.

Those seven members decided to travel to Paris to submit the petition to those in charge of the Peace Conference, but the French authority had already come to know of their decision through a spy who had infiltrated their ranks, so they were arrested as they were leaving Beirut. They were sentenced to banishment and to the payment of a huge fine.

Faisal meanwhile intended to travel to France for a reconsideration of the treaty. He sent Nouri al-Sa`eed to Beirut to open discussions with Gouraud with regard to that trip. It so coincided that Nouri al-Sa`eed arrived at Beirut at the same time when the seven members were arrested. When Nouri started speaking with Gouraud, the latter said to him that he had some demands to submit to Faisal, and that he would not agree to Faisal travelling unless he accepted those demands. Then Gouraud submitted a summary of those demands as follows: 1) the Riyaq-Aleppo railroad must be put at the disposal of the French army, 2) the cancellation of the conscription and the releasing of the conscripts from service, 3) the acceptance of the French mandate without any term or condition, 4) the punishment of those accused of hostility towards France, and 5) the accepting of the paper money issued by the French.

Nouri al-Sa`eed returned to King Faisal to inform him of the matter. On July 14, Col. Niager reached Damascus carrying an official warning which contained those five demands with a respite of four days ending at the night of 18-19 July. If the demands were not accepted during that period, the French government would have the absolute power to fare with Faisal's government.

Gouraud's warning had a great deal of effect on Faisal and his cabinet ministers who all met to study the situation in order to see how they would resolve it and get out of it. Gloom prevailed over them all with the exception of Yousuf al-Azmah who was optimistic. Sati` al-Husari says, "Yousuf al-Azmah was working actively and demonstrating a great deal of optimism in all

Chapter Three: Sharifi Rule In Syria

actions, so much so that he wanted to start issuing official proclamations about the military movements, but we protested and advised him to wait so the world would not think that we were the ones who started the aggression..."[1]

Yasin al-Hashimi was summoned in order to benefit from his military expertise and was appointed as commander of the Majdal Anjar front which was the most important of all fronts due to its falling on the Damascus-Beirut highway. Al-Husari says that he visited al-Hashimi at his house and said to him in full frankness and in the tone of one who is certain and firm, "The available army cannot defend the country... It cannot withstand before the enemy for more than two hours at the highest estimation." Al-Hashimi added saying, "The cannons that have been paraded before you have a very small number of shells, and they are not enough for a war that continues for more than one hour. I can say that if the army is engaged in a regular war, it will run out of ammunition two hours later."[2]

Al-Husari got out of al-Hashimi's house feeling very disturbed and puzzled. He went to the ministers and told them what he had heard from al-Hashimi. The king came to know of al-Hashimi's opinion, so he summoned the ministers. A meeting convened with some of them in his presence, and they started studying the military situation in the light of the opinion expressed by al-Hashimi. When the ministers asked Yousuf al-Azmah about the weapons and ammunitions available to the army, he answered, "The army has enough ammunition to resist the French for a period of time and perhaps to defeat them and force them back if they turn their backs in the first epic." When the ministers asked him to submit a written statement in the same meaning, he answered them angrily, "Do you not trust

---

1 Sati` al-Husari (Op. Cit.), p. 121.
2 *Ibid.*, p. 122.

what I say while I am your fellow who is in charge of the army's affairs?"[1]

King Faisal summoned senior military commanders in order to express their opinion in the matter. At three o'clock in the afternoon of July 16, the commanders were present, and so was al-Hashimi, and they all kept expressing their viewpoints, each in his own style and according to his own knowledge. The king insisted on them to submit a single unified opinion, so the commanders withdrew to a side room where they remained in seclusion. Then they came out shortly thereafter carrying one unified opinion the summary of which was: "If the war is not serious, the army can resist for several hours. But if the fighting intensifies, the army's resistance will not last for more than five minutes."[2]

It was then that the king turned to al-Hashimi soliciting his opinion. Al-Hashimi spoke, directing his criticism to Yousuf al-Azmah and expressing his opinion that the war was not necessary. Then he asked, "If it is possible to repel the French on the Damascus line, what can be done if the French division falls on the Arab army from Aleppo?" A number of commanders protested against him and said, "The matter is one of honor, Pasha," so he responded to them by saying, "The honor is rendered to the ministers, not to the soldiers."[3]

The meeting ended without a decisive outcome. The king wanted to know what the British thought before deciding in the matter, so he sent Nouri al-Sa`eed and Adil Arsalan to Haifa to consult with Gen. Allenby. The two men returned from Haifa to say that Allenby advised them to accept the warning quickly without hesitation. Allenby wrote Faisal a letter in which he insisted on the need to accept the warning in order to let Gouraud

---

1 Yousuf al-Hakim (Op. Cit.), p. 181.
2 Ameen Sa`eed (Op. Cit.), Vol. 2, p. 180.
3 *Al-Iraq* newspaper of april 19, 1930.

Chapter Three: Sharifi Rule In Syria

miss his chance which he tried to seize, that is, entering Damascus as conquerors would.[1]

The king and his ministers settled their decision on accepting the warning, but another problem faced them: Gen. Gouraud hinted in his letter which supplemented the warning to the need to change the administration which he described as having exerted all its efforts to drag the country to war, and that its staying in power implied hostility towards France.

The king and some of his ministers thought of commissioning Ridha al-Rikabi to put together a new cabinet. But when al-Rikabi was present, he asked to be excused. Directing his statement at the king, he said, "I have for so long told you, Sir, that these boys will get us in a deep pit, and they have to bear the repercussions of what they have expressed." Al-Rikabi was pointing with his looks at Yousuf al-Azmah.[2]

When the king lost hope of al-Rikabi forming the cabinet, he turned to Yasin al-Hashimi, but the latter asked to be excused, too. A violent verbal altercation then took place between Yousuf al-Azmah and al-Hashimi. Yousuf al-Azmah explained al-Hashimi's stance as due to his [al-Azmah's] jealousy of him.[3] He kept directing harsh statements at al-Hashimi. He said to him, "You, Pasha, confused minds and revealed the army's secrets when you informed some ministers of its ammunition, although you are the one who is responsible for its supplies. So, it does not befit you to escape the judgment after your declarations got us to the present crisis." Al-Hashimi responded to him saying, "I acquainted the administration with the truth about the army's rations so we may not be deceived by your statements and the country is thus driven to a war which we do not have any hope of winning. As regarding the responsibility for the shortcoming, it falls on the shoulders of those who preceded me in heading

---

1 Ihsan al-Hindi, *Ma'rakat Maysalun* (the Battle of Maysalun), Damascus: 1967, p. 55.
2 Khairiyya Qasmiyya (Op. Cit.), p. 201.
3 Ahmed Qadri (Op. Cit.), p. 240.

the rations affairs and were in charge of the defense affairs." Here, the king interfered and said to al-Hashimi, "But you, Yasin, were head of the rations for ten months. Why did you not work to acquire the necessary weapons?!"[1]

Here, Yousuf al-Azmah advanced in his famous enthusiasm and performed the military salute of the king then said, "I am ready, Your Majesty, to defend the homeland with all my strength up to the last breath if you grant me your confidence." The king thanked him and pleaded to the Almighty to grant him success, appointing him deputy general commander of the armed forces, that is, a representative of the king who is the general commander.[2]

Yousuf al-Azmah resumed his talk. He addressed al-Hashimi saying, "Pasha, you want to make us a ladder on which you ascend, then you will be the prime minister." Al-Hashimi answered him strongly, "If I need a ladder, I will look for a strong one."[3]

The king and his ministers returned after this deliberation in the matter of the warning to decide unanimously to accept it. The king signed a telegram in this meaning and delivered it to Colonel Tola, assistant French liaison officer. Tola wired it to Gen. Gouraud.

The Uprising of the Masses

At the time when the officials were studying the situation as we explained above, the masses, together with the Syrian Congress, were in a status of a huge agitation. Demonstrations came out to the streets shouting, "To war! To war!" The king was left in the middle: between these and those in an amazing quagmire!

---

1 Yousuf al-Hakim (Op. Cit.), p. 192.
2 *Ibid.*, p. 193.
3 *Al-Iraq* newspaper of April 19, 1930.

Chapter Three: Sharifi Rule In Syria

On July 15, i.e. on the day that followed Gouraud's warning, the Syrian Congress held a session to look into the matter. The session was enthusiastic. Speakers followed one another, and they all called for war and directed censure to the Atassi administration, charging it with weakness and inclination to capitulation. The masses at that time had surrounded the quarters of the Congress shouting for it. Some members from among them broke the doors open and entered the hall screaming, demanding war. It was then that forty-five Congress members presented a proposal that the Syrian Congress, which represented the Syrian nation, did not recognize any treaty or agreement related to the country's destiny if it is not ratified by the Congress. The Congress accepted this suggestion, and they decided to disseminate it among the public.

King Faisal summoned the Congress members to a meeting in the garden of his mansion at 4:30 in the afternoon of July 17. A pavilion was erected in the garden for this purpose. When the members arrived, the king met them smiling and tried to explain to them how the Syrian army was not up to the task of defending the country against the French forces which were equipped with the most modern military equipment. He stated that the duty mandated on them to deal with the matters without being hasty, but with wisdom, through peaceful negotiations with Gen. Gouraud. There were among those present many people who inclined to the king's opinion to seek peace, but they did not dare to publicly express their opinion, remaining silent. The enthusiasts, therefore, held the reins of speaking, and they kept arguing with the king strongly. One of them addressed him in a very rude tone, but the king suppressed his anger and ignored him.

At the end of the meeting, when the king lost hope of convincing them, he presented to them a proposal which he thought was useful. It was this: Each of them must write, once he returns home, a private letter expressing in it his opinion as he believes in it before Allāh, then he must send it to the king. The king promised them to act according to the majority's viewpoint which reached him.[1] The king thought that the opinions expressed thus would be realistic, having no impacts of insinuation or intimidation.[2] But the members of the Congress realized the dangerous implications of the king's proposal, so they advised each other to reject it.

In the morning of the next day, July 18, the Syrian Congress held an emergency session. Demonstrations came to it. The demonstrators were carrying daggers and swords and chanting martial songs. Then they shouted for the fall of the cowards who had weak spirits. In the afternoon of that day, the Congress held another session in which it decided to summon the Atassi administration to ask it about the plan which it decided to follow in facing the warning the deadline of which was ending at midnight.[3]

In the morning of July 19, the administration's report accepting the said warning spread among the public, so Damascus rose because of this report, and thousands of its citizens crowded the Marja Square shouting. Sheikh Kamil al-Qassab stood up to deliver a speech in which he urged them to carry the sword to defend the threatened homeland, denouncing and threatening the men of the government. Speakers spoke one after the other to urge people to resist no matter what the cost would be.[4]

At the same time, the Syrian Congress held a session to face the administration and to ask it about its plan. But the head of the Congress, Sheikh Rasheed Ridha, announced that the prime minister had told him of the administration being unable to be present before the Congress because it is waiting for the return of the messenger who had gone to Beirut to negotiate. Here, a

---

1 Muhammed Tahir al-Omari (Op. Cit.), Vol. 3, p. 246.
2 Ameen Sa'eed (Op. Cit.), Vol. 2, p. 185.
3 Rafeeq al-Tameemi, *Al-Ayyam al-Sood* (the Black Days), Baghdad: 1933, p. 13.
4 *Ibid.*, p. 14.

member advanced to submit this proposal: The government becomes illegitimate in case it ratified a contract which went against the decision of the Congress, and the ministers had to bear the consequences of it towards the homeland. The Congress members unanimously accepted this proposal and issued instructions to print and publish it in the *Asima* (the capital) newspaper. They also chose from among themselves a delegation headed by Rasheed Ridha to meet the king and to submit the proposal to him.

The Uprising Escalates

As the masses and the Syrian Congress were at the peak of enthusiasm, a telegram arrived from Gouraud saying that accepting the warning was not sufficient; rather, he demanded the immediate implementation of its terms, and he extended the warning's deadline two more days to end at midnight of July 20-21.

This was a new shock to the king and his cabinet ministers. In the evening of that day, while the king was drowned in his dilemma, not knowing what to do if a request reached him from the delegation of the Congress asking to meet him. When he permitted them and they entered, a heated discussion went on between him and them. The king could not control his nerves, so he angrily said to them, "Who are you...? I am the one who created Syria...!" Rasheed Ridha, therefore, responded to him by saying, "Are you really the one who created Syria?! Syria was created before you yourself was!"[1]

The king decided to suspend the sessions of the Syrian Congress for two months. In the morning of the next day, minister of war Yousuf al-Azmah went to the Congress and recited the suspension decision, so some members tried to ascend

---

1 *Ibid.*, p. 14.

to the speakers' podium to protest, but the war minister shouted threats at them and signaled them to disperse, so they dispersed.[1]

In the afternoon of July 20, the ministers met in the presence of the king and decided to respond to the recent warning of Gouraud, that is, implementing its terms immediately, including the army's demobilization. Col. Tola received the decision then wired it to Gen. Gouraud at 7:30 pm.

The report hardly spread among the people in the morning of the next day when demonstrations set out on the streets shouting threats and warnings. They were headed by Sheikh Kamil al-Qassab. A group from among the demonstrators kept shouting for the toppling of the administration and for taking it to the Supreme Court charged with high treason.[2] Another group kept shouting against the king, demanding his fall with the administration.[3] A notion spread in some circles to depose King Faisal and to swear fealty to [his brother] Prince Zaid in his place.[4]

A massacre took place then near the Damascus Fortress because some soldiers who were relieved from their army duty set out, under enticement by some party leaders, intending to attack the Fortress and seize the weapons stored in it to use them to defend the homeland. In their vanguard, Othman Qasim, one of the members of the Young Arab society, was shooting bullets from his pistol in the air in order to encourage them.[5] They were joined by many commoners, so they broke the doors of the prison in the fortress and looting started spreading in the nearby markets. Prince Zaid, together with security commissioner Taha al-Hashimi, rushed to lead a force armed with machineguns to

---

1 Ihsan al-Hindi (Op. Cit.), pp. 58-59.
2 *Ibid.*, p. 59.
3 Sati` al-Husari (Op. Cit.), p. 127.
4 Yousuf al-Hakim (Op. Cit.), p. 193.
5 Ahmed Qadri (Op. Cit.), p. 248.

Chapter Three: Sharifi Rule In Syria

shoot at the demonstrators. A large number of them were killed and wounded.¹

Taha al-Hashimi tells us in his *Memoirs* about that incident saying, "... Several soldiers came out of the Baramika garrison raising their weapons in the claim the government had surrendered to the French. They passed by the Nasr (triumph) Street and passed by the site's guards. Instead of the latter pushing them back, they joined them. The mobsters were enthused, so their crowds grew larger, and they attacked the fortress. The guards defended it. They attacked the weapons depot which they confiscated, releasing the prisoners. Shooting started in the town and went on up to midnight. Some shops were looted. Twenty-five men were killed and thirty-five were wounded."²

As this bloody demonstration went on near the fortress, there was another demonstration was getting close to the king's mansion with shouts and rioting. A delegation from it representing the national parties requested to meet the king. The king at that hour was still meeting with his cabinet ministers after having finished accepting the recent warning of Gouraud. The king permitted the delegation to meet him, and the ministers withdrew to an adjacent room. The delegation's meeting with the king was not free of roughness and daring, angering the king to the extent that he could not control his nerves.

Narratives have differed describing that meeting and what went on during it. Yousuf al-Hakim, who was one of the ministers who withdrew to the adjacent room, says that one of the members of the delegation was prompted by his foolishness to address the king thus: "Your Majesty, the nation will not accept an understanding with the French, and it will hold those responsible for it severely accountable," so the king became

---

[1] Sulayman Mousa (Op. Cit.), p. 563.
[2] Khaldun Sati' al-Husari, *Muthakkarat Taha al-Hashimi* (Memoirs of Taha al-Hashimi), Beirut: 1967, Vol. 1, pp. 61-62.

angry about this statement and said in a loud voice which the ministers in the adjacent room heard: "Nobody threatens me! I am more capable than you in serving my homeland, which is your homeland! Do you wish to wage a war with a strong state while you do not have a force that can face it?"[1]

There is another narrative by Khairud-Din al-Zurakli: The delegation hinted to the king that he had to leave the country, so the king shouted in their faces saying, "I entered the country as a conqueror and shall not leave it save by force. If you have the sufficient force that can get me out, do it, and my blood and yours will be on the street."[2]

As soon as the delegation left the mansion, the king was notified that the demonstrators were approaching the mansion shouting for his stepping down. He made a covert signal to his senior doorman, a black Hijazi man, whereupon a group of Bedouin horsemen numbering two hundred quickly got out to the street and kept roaming up and down the main street from the mansion to the Marja Square, as they were chanting.[3]

Sati' al-Husari says, "We remained in the mansion until after midnight trying to calm the king's nerves on the one hand and to undertake the necessary measures to calm the agitation of the masses on the other. I did not return home except shortly before daybreak. I laid down on the bed feeling extremely tired."[4]

The Shift to War

Damascus dawned on July 21 calmly following that memorable night, but quickly a sudden report reached the king: The French forces were marching in the direction of Damascus. The king was stunned by that report and summoned to him the

---

1 Yousuf al-Hakim (Op. Cit.), p. 193.
2 This is quoted from Anis Sa'igh, *Al-Hashimiyyoon wal Thawara al-Arabiyya al-Kubra* (the Hashemites and the Great Arab Revolution), Beirut: 1966, p. 153.
3 Yousuf al-Hakim (Op. Cit.), pp. 193-194.
4 Sati' al-Husari (Op. Cit.), p. 127.

Chapter Three: Sharifi Rule In Syria

French liaison officer, Col. Cousse, to inquire about what was really happening. Cousse demonstrated a great puzzlement and promised to travel immediately to look into the matter. Then he set out. In the afternoon of that day, Cousse returned to say that the reason behind the marching of the French forces was the telegram accepting the warning, which the king had yesterday sent, not reaching Gen. Gouraud at the set time but was late half an hour because gangs had cut off telegraph lines. Cousse suggested sending one of the cabinet ministers to Gouraud to reach an understanding with him.

Sati` al-Husari was chosen to travel to Alia to seek an understanding with Gouraud. He rode in a convertible car accompanied by the king's bodyguard, Jameel al-Alshi, and Col. Tola. The street was crowded with cars and caravans of mules and camels and with military units. Al-Husari was able to reach Alia only in the morning of the next day, the 22nd of July. A lengthy dialogue went on between him and Gouraud, and it became clear to al-Husari that Gouraud was determined to occupy Syria under any pretext and at any cost. Gouraud said to al-Husari, "We no longer trust you… It is our obligation to ask you for new guarantees." Then he took out of a drawer in his desk a memorandum containing eight guarantees and started to read it to al-Husari. Al-Husari found out that he had no choice except to ask Gouraud to postpone his march for a short while so he could return to Damascus and discuss with the king the new guarantees. Gouraud did not accept this delay except after a great deal of hesitation.

Al-Husari faced difficulty in returning to Damascus in the desired speed. Perhaps the French obstructed his return for certain covert reasons. Al-Husari did not reach Damascus except at a late hour of the night. In the morning of the next day, the cabinet held a meeting in the presence of the king to look into the reports al-Husari had brought. As the ministers were meeting, Col. Cousse arrived with an urgent telegram from

Gouraud dated 10:00 o'clock in the morning of July 22 saying in it that the French forces, due to military considerations, had to continue their march until they reached Khan Maysalun. It was then that the king and his ministers realized that they had no option before them except to fight.

War shouts set out in the streets and squares of Damascus. The king summoned Sheikh Kamil al-Qassab and said to him, "We have decided to defend ourselves as you wanted, so show us your resolve and energy and bring us the patriotic forces that you say they are ready to fight." Al-Qassab answered saying, "Since you have decided to defend, I promise you to recruit ten thousand men carrying rifles up to the evening." Al-Qassab went out to roam the shops of Damascus calling for starting the war. A short period of time later, al-Qassab returned carrying rifle cartridges and various types of pistols in the pockets of his cloak. He gave them to the king saying, "I bought these bullets from a shop in the city. Who told you that there is no ammunition in the country?" Yasin al-Hashimi, who was present then, bitterly laughed and said, "Is it with such ammunition and these volunteers, who think that the war is like demonstrations and picnics, that we can repel the French army especially since guerilla warfare differs from the regular one?!"[1]

The king went to the Umayyad Mosque where he ascended the pulpit and delivered a speech to the people saying, "I wanted to spare you the marching of the enemy army by responding to their demands, but they did not budge. So, if you need your homeland, then come out and defend it."[2]

---

1   Ahmed Qadri (Op. Cit.), p. 252.
2   Khairiyya Qasmiyya (Op. Cit.), pp. 203-204.

Chapter Three: Sharifi Rule In Syria

The railroad administration prepared trains each of which moved on the hour to carry the volunteers to the front in Khan Maysalun. The volunteers crowded to the trains carrying whatever rifles, swords, pistols or even clubs they could carry. A number of women volunteered to tend to the wounded, and some of them put on military outfits. In their vanguard was Lady Nazik [or Naziq as some writers spell it] al-Abid who carried a president emeritus rank in the Arab army [right photo→].

Jameel Bayham says, "The volunteers joined the army prompted by enthusiasm and national duty, but most of them were unaware of the war and its woes. Each of them contended himself by carrying a rifle so that, relying on his courage, he would be counted among the heroes. They imagined as if they were on a military picnic, and this prompted some of them who are fond of the hookah to carry it with them to that picnic."[1]

Yousuf al-Azmah decided to go in person to the front. He went to bid the ministers farewell. He took Sati` al-Husari aside in a corner of the hall and spoke to him in Turkish saying, "I am going! I am leaving Layla—his daughter—as a trust with you,

---

1   Muhammed Jameel Bayham (Op. Cit.), p. 253.

please do not forget this." It was clear from his statement that he was determined not to return from the front alive.

Yousuf al-Azmah went to bid the king farewell. A dialogue went on between both of them the gist of which we cite for you verbally as Ahmed Qadri, who was present then and there, narrates it thus:

YOUSUF: "I have come to receive the orders of Your Majesty."

FAISAL: "Allāh bless you; so, are you travelling to Maysalun?"

YOUSUF: "Yes, master, if you do not wish to accept the most recent warning."

FAISAL: "Why did you so strongly insist on defense?"

YOUSUF: "It is because I thought that the French could trample with their feet on all international and human rights and come to occupy Damascus. I pretended through maneuvering that I was facing them likewise."

FAISAL: "Can the sublime honor be safe of harm if blood is not spilt on its sides?"

YOUSUF: "So, then, does His Majesty the King permit me to die?"

FAISAL: "After matters had reached this limit, we all must die an honorable death, thus also saving the country from a civil war."

YOUSUF: "Then I leave my only daughter, Layla, with Your Majesty."[1]

The Battle of Maysalun

The battle in Maysalun started about five o'clock in the morning of July 24 and went on up to noon. The number of the Arabs who participated in it is estimated at three thousand.

---

1 Ahmed Qadri (Op. Cit.), p. 253.

Chapter Three: Sharifi Rule In Syria

Some of them were regular soldiers and the rest were volunteers. It, in fact, was not a battle [in the full sense of the word], but was rather similar to a massacre. The French forces had ten planes, many tanks and artillery pieces, whereas the Arabs had only few cannons, and the ammunition distributed to them was not even suitable to the weapons in their hands.[1]

The Arabs demonstrated steadfastness which could not be taken lightly. Four hundred of their men were killed, not counting the injured, and this was a high percentage in a fighting army. Among those killed were quite few clerics who regarded fighting in Maysalun as *jihad* in the way of Allāh.

Yousuf al-Azmah, in his capacity as the minister of war, was supposed to be distant from the fighting field, but he preferred to actually participate in it because he wanted to die. At 10:30 am, he was hit by a machinegun bullet fired from a French tank, so he fell on the ground flopping in his blood.

Through his death, this man proved that he was different from some people who would be enthusiastic during the time of safety, but during the hour of danger, they would run away or surrender. It is worth mentioning here that later, Faisal set aside a monthly salary for the daughter of Yousuf al-Azmah, and the daughter kept receiving it continuously until Faisal died in 1933.[2]

When news of the killing of Yousuf al-Azmah spread among the soldiers, the spirit of defeat spread among them, so they started quickly withdrawing towards Damascus. What really hurts is that the people of the villages located between Maysalun and al-Mazza fell on the withdrawing soldiers, looting them.

The French army entered Damascus at five o'clock in the afternoon of July 25, and in its vanguard was the front's commander, Gen. [Mariano] Goybet on horseback. The shops in Damascus were then closed, and people stood on sidewalks

---

1 Zain Nur ad-Din Zain (Op. Cit.), p. 266.
2 Sati` al-Husari (Op. Cit.), p. 200.

watching the army's march with silence and gloom. On August 1, Gen. Gouraud reached Damascus which he entered in a great procession. It is said that he immediately headed to the grave of Salahuddin (Saladin) al-Ayyubi, stood on it and said, "Salahud-Din! You told us at the inception of your Crusades: 'You [Crusaders] went out of the East and will never return to it,' yet here we have returned; so, rise to see us here in Syria."[1]

Some Bedouin sheikhs demonstrated some meanness after the battle. One of them received from the treasury of the Arab army shortly before the battle of Maysalun five hundred pounds to fight the French, but as soon as he noticed the Arab army's defeat, he and his followers fell on the withdrawing soldiers to loot their weapons and luggage.[2] Nouri al-Sha'lan, chief sheikh of the Rola, had done the same: He received from Faisal in August of 1918 thirty thousand gold liras. But when Gouraud entered Damascus, he came out to welcome him, joined his procession with his men and was seen in the procession raising his sword.[3]

The Expulsion of the King

During the battle of Maysalun, King Faisal was at the headquarters of the military command in Hama. When he came to know about the result of the battle, he and his entourage withdrew to the Kiswa, a railroad station twelve miles to the southwest of Damascus.

Faisal summoned his ministers to meet with him at the Kiswa, so they all reached it with the exception of two: Alaa ad-Din al-Darubi and Faris al-Khuri. About fifteen leaders of the demonstrations, such as sheikh Kamil al-Qassab, Othman Qasim and Shukri al-Quwwatli, also reached it. Everyone used train carriages as their homes, but some of them could not bear to stay in the Kiswa, so they took a train which was about to travel to

---

1 Ihsan al-Hindi (Op. Cit.), p. 201.
2 *Ibid.*, p. 209.
3 Sulayman Mousa, *Al-Haraka al-Arabiyya* (Arab Movement), p. 658.

Chapter Three: Sharifi Rule In Syria

Dar`a (Darra) then Haifa. Among them were Abdul-Rahman al-Shahbandar and Kamil al-Qassab.

Faisal was expected under those circumstances to get out of Syria for good to declare to the world the injustice meted to him at the hands of France which claimed to be the mother of freedom and human rights, but Faisal did not do that. Rather, he preferred to return to Damascus to come to terms with the French and to surrender to their will. Describing the king's psychological state at the Kiswa, Sati` al-Husari says the following:

"King Faisal and his entourage arrived in cars in the evening shortly before sunset. He was in an unusual condition, vastly differently from his usual conditions. All his movements and stills indicated that he was in a status of a great hesitation and worry. It became clear to me from monitoring those movements that his mind was preoccupied with something which he inclined to hide from us. I told myself that perhaps he still hoped to reach an understanding with the French and is waiting for some reports that would help achieve such an understanding. It became clear to me shortly thereafter that my presumption was identical to the fact and reality. He had sent Nouri al-Sa`eed as his representative to meet the French, postponing all his decisions up to the time when the reports of that meeting reached him. He, therefore, was waiting for those reports impatiently, avoiding having to speak and express an opinion in any subject whatever it might be."[1]

In the eve of July 25, a telegram reached the king from Nouri al-Sa`eed carrying the glad tiding that a temporary agreement was reached with the French, so the king became optimistic and was carried away in his optimism in an unusual way.[2]

On the next day, oral reports came underscoring the context of the said telegram, so this increased his optimism and he

---

1 Sati` al-Husari (Op. Cit.), pp. 164-165.
2 Ibid., p. 165.

decided to dissolve the Atassi administration and form a new cabinet comprised of ministers known for their support for the French mandate. He actually instructed the forming of this administration, so it was comprised of Alaa ad-Din al-Darubi as the head (prime minister), Abdul-Rahman al-Yousuf as head of the Consultative Council, Ataa al-Ayyubi as minister of the interior, Badee` al-Mu'ayyid as the minister of education, Jameel al-Alshi as minister of war, Jalal ad-Din Zuhdi as minister of justice, Faris al-Khuri as minister of finance and Yousuf al-Hakim as minister of [public] services.

The king returned to Damascus which he reached shortly before midnight. He was still optimistic, thinking that the French would welcome him and accept to cooperate with him. But he was surprised in the morning by the fact that they did not want him and regarded him as the first person responsible for the bloody disturbances that had taken place. They asked him in the most rude way to leave Damascus within two days, placing at his disposal a special train to transport him to Dar`a. The king protested very strongly without finding any echo for his protest, so he found himself forced to ride the train. The train moved carrying him at five o'clock in the morning of July 28.

Nobody was there to bid the king farewell at the Damascus station other than few individuals. He was accompanied on the train by Sati` al-Husari, Awni Abdul-Hadi, Ihsan al-Jabiri, Tahsin Qadri and Ahmed Qadri. When they reached Dar`a, they used the train carriages for their accommodation as they had done in the Kiswa.

The heads of Horan tribes came to welcome the king, and he kept urging them to fight the French, so they answered him saying that they were ready to fight the French provided they would get the support of the British.[1]

---

1   Ahmed Qadri (Op. Cit.), pp. 274-275.

Chapter Three: Sharifi Rule In Syria

On the next day, i.e. July 29, a telegram reached the king from Alaa ad-Din al-Darubi pleading to him to leave Dar`a in order to safeguard the security of Horan from calamities and destruction. At the same time, a French plane dropped leaflets directed to the tribes of Horan warning them that they should ask Faisal to leave Dar`a in the next ten hours, and if he refused, the train must take him back to Damascus; otherwise, their land would be the target of bombs. The king, therefore, had to leave the country, going with his entourage to Haifa [in Palestine].

After the Expulsion

When he left Syria, Faisal was in a pathetic psychological and physical condition. Ibrahim Najjar says, "Faisal was physically weak since childhood, so much so that they used to say about him that he had a [chronic] chest problem[1], and they quite often were worried about him because of this ailment. When he was thus violently shocked in Damascus, it had its impacts on his psyche and on his lungs to a very serious extent, so much so that whoever saw Faisal after his departure from the Syrian capital thought that he was looking at a figure in a wax museum. Had a physician examined all his veins, he would not have found one drop of blood in them..."[2]

Faisal reached Haifa on August 1, 1920. The High Commissioner in Palestine, Sir Herbert Samuel, says the following in his *Memoirs*, "I decided to welcome Faisal on the Palestinian lands not as a helpless refugee but as a respectful friend. I, therefore, ordered a detachment of soldiers to salute him at the [train] station when he arrived, then I advanced with Sir Ronald Storrs to welcome him. It was said to me after that that King Faisal after those tough days through which he lived did not know if those soldiers had gone to arrest him or to honor

---

1 I think they mean he suffered from asthma or bronchitis which showed its effects on his grandson, Faisal II, King of Iraq, who was asthmatic. – Tr.
2 Ibrahim Saleem Najjar (Op. Cit.), p. 79.

him. When he knew that they came to welcome him militarily, worry abandoned him."[1]

Faisal settled at the house of Ms. Newton, a British lady known for sympathizing with the Arabs. He sent his father in Mecca a telegram asking him for money so he would be able to travel to Europe; therefore, al-Husain sent him a money order drawn on the Ottoman Bank in the sum of twenty-five thousand pounds.

On august 9, Faisal wrote from Haifa a letter to his father in his own handwriting explaining to him the reasons for the catastrophe that befell him and justifying his action in separating Syria from Hijaz. He said, "I used to believe that my duty dictated that we must be lenient with the states due to their ambitions and our weakness, but what prevented that was your principle which is based on the independence of the Arab lands without any term or condition and the opposition of Arab youths to any leniency. It was possible to discipline the opposition parties, but I did not do that for fear history would blame me for it. What has worsened the situation is that the parties did not realize the truth of the country's vulnerability and the enemies' strength. Then the situation worsened, and the enemy amassed his forces as the nation stood looking at it with its eyes in a frozen way as if it had nothing to do with what was going on. What is regretful is that the nation talks but does not act: The residents of the land did not stand positively for the conscription, so the number of those who dodged the conscription was more than that of the volunteers. The residents refused to pay money to the government fund so we would be able to work. The acceptance of paying money and the conscription was nil. We, therefore, accepted Gouraud's terms, but some delirious parties instigated the public to revolt when the enemy was lying in ambush for us..."[2]

---

[1] Herbert Samuel, *Memoirs*, London: 1945, pp. 158-159.
[2] Sulayman Mousa (Op. Cit.), pp. 567-568.

Chapter Three: Sharifi Rule In Syria

Samuel visited Faisal at the house of Ms. Newton and notified him that a telegram had reached him from the British foreign minister, Lord Curzon, saying, "Britain hopes there will be an opportunity in the future to express to him that his friendly stance towards it will not be met with oblivion."

Samuel had suggested to Faisal to return to Hijaz, but Faisal insisted on travelling to Switzerland to meet with the directors of the League of Nations. In the morning of August 18, he left Haifa by train for Egypt. When he reached the Qunaitara station on the bank of the Suez Canal, he found none there to welcome him sent by General Allenby or by the British government, so he had to sit on his luggage waiting to change trains as any ordinary traveler would do.[1] There, Abdul-Malik al-Khateeb, attaché of his father, al-Husain, in Egypt, notified him of his father's instructions and recommendations. He also notified him of his father's reprimanding for what he had done in Syria, i.e. separating it from Hijaz. Faisal, therefore, responded to him saying that he still hoped he would arrive at some arrangement with the French.[2]

Faisal left Port Said on August 20 on board a commercial ship for Italy accompanied by Nouri al-Sa`eed, Sati` al-Husari, Ihsan al-Jabiri, Tahsin Qadri and Prince Zaid. He reached Naples on the 25th. From there he travelled up north in order to go to Switzerland. When he reached the borders of Switzerland, Haddad Pasha, his father's attaché in London, went to him to notify him of an oral message from Lloyd George saying to him, "I am now in Switzerland busy with important meetings, and your presence confuses me, so pelase stay in Italy." Faisal, therefore, had to stay in north Italy in a hotel near Lake Como.

Faisal stayed in Italy for almost three months. There, he was joined by Adil Arsalan and Riyadh al-Sulh. He and his entourage kept exerting efforts and spending money in order to present the

---

1 Storrs, Orientations, London: 1939, p. 448.
2 Sulayman Mousa (Op. Cit.), p. 571.

Syrian issue to the European public opinion. It is said that they paid one hundred gold liras to [Benito] Mussolini to support the Syrian issue, and Mussolini was at the time a journalist issuing a newspaper which he called "The People of Italy" [in Italian, *Il Popolo*, the people].[1]

Faisal kept trying to contact the Turks in order to cooperate with them, sending Sati` al-Husari to Istanbul secretly for this purpose. Al-Husari exerted many attempts to come to an understanding with the Kamalis [followers of Kamal Ataturk] but to no avail.[2]

As Faisal and his entourage were exerting efforts in every aspect, perhaps they could find a way out of their miserable situation, a telegram reached Faisal on the 11th of November from Lord Curzon inviting him to visit London. This invitation was akin to an ease after hardship. An agreement was reached with Faisal to install him as King of Iraq, as we mentioned in Volume Six of this book series. Philby, who relies on some documents, claims that Iraq's throne was given to Faisal as part of the reward for agreeing to establish a nationl homeland for the Jews in Palestine.[3] We do not know the extent of the truth of this claim.

Strange Opinion

Iskiandar al-Riyashi, an Egyptian journalist, has a strange opinion regarding Syria's events that preceded the Battle of Maysalun. It is an opinion which we find hard to believe. It is, however, worthy of the reader's review.

Al-Riyashi was at the time working in the French intelligence, as he himself admitted. He says about those events that they were a French plot arranged with French money in order to oust

---

1 Andrew (Op. Cit.), p. 20. – Ed.
2 Sati` al-Husari (Op. Cit.), pp. 178-194.
3 *Al-Ahram* Egyptian newspaper of June 1968.

Chapter Three: Sharifi Rule In Syria

Faisal. Al-Riyashi states that the French had in the beginning offered a huge bribe, half a million gold liras, and they offered his fellow, Nouri al-Sa`eed, one hundred thousand liras, but they both refused to accept it. The French had to find in Damascus individuals who were ready to accept the bribe from among the men who had the leadership on the street and were fueling the masses' enthusiasm. These folks rushed to call for war, sparking in the man of the street his patriotism and dignity, so the winds of martyrdom and sacrifice blew on Syria as a result of their influence. Enthusiasm prevailed over all considerations, so much so that the most reasonable people kept calling for war, ignoring their knowledge that such a war would end with a catastrophe, and that those who advocated it would let the French achieve what they aspired. Al-Riyashi also says that Faisal and his aides were trying up to the last hour to avoid the war with the French, knowing fully well that if it took place, they would lose it due to the imbalance in the scales of power between both sides to a degree which could not be ignored, but the French plot scored against them.

Al-Riyashi says, "We were in the second office of the French commander monitoring the success of this plot against the Sharif and his throne and against the independence of Syria. We knew that he would be forced to mobilize his armies and volunteers, so he would be the one to start the aggression, and the French would then be in a status of self-defense assisted by those politicians who filled their pockets with that gold which General La Motte had prepared."

Al-Riyashi classifies the leaders who stirred the masses in Damascus into two types: a sincere group which called for war and encouraged amazing martyrdom for the sake of the homeland, such as Yousuf al-Azmah, but they were few compared to the second group which worked in collaboration with the French.[1]

---

1 Iskandar al-Riyashi, *Ru'sa' Lubnan kama Araftuhum* (Heads of Lebanon as I knew

The Gap Between People and Government

The gap between the people and the government in Syria during the Ottoman era was very big as it was in all Eastern lands. But this gap disappeared suddenly at the beginning of the rule of the Sharifs during which popular enthusiasm intensified and the rulers, in the vanguard of whom Faisal stood, were trying to be close to the people, mingling with them and listening to their voice.

We must not forget that that period could not last long and that the gap had to reappear sooner or later. The social phase during which the Syrian people were living did not permit that era to linger for long. There were many factors that caused grumbling in the public circles towards the government. Following, we state the most important of those factors:

FIRST: The conscription, which the government imposed on the citizens, was of course the most important factor in the grumbling. People during the Ottoman era used to feel avert to forced army enlistment to a degree that had no limit and tried to flee from it through all means at their disposal. The main reason for their elation, when the Ottoman rule was no more, was due to their getting rid of the affliction of military enlistment. But they found out, after a short period, that the affliction returned to them anew. It was not easy for people to shift from holding conscription in contempt to loving it by merely hearing martial songs and enthusiastic speeches.

It is narrated that a demonstration went to King Faisal's mansion shouting "To war! To war!", so the king ordered his bodyguard to take the demonstrators to the barracks to enlist them in the army and train them on fighting. But as soon as they heard it on their way to the barracks, they kept stealthily going home. When the bodyguard reached the barracks, he found very few of them with him.

---

them), pp. 272-276.

Chapter Three: Sharifi Rule In Syria

SECOND: Hardly a short period passed since the inception of the Sharifs' rule when favoritism and intervention started playing their role in choosing the government officials just as people were used to witnessing during the Ottoman era. This is normal in a society over which values of tribalism, kinship, neighborliness, manliness and the like prevailed. Sheikh Rasheed Ridha, head of the Syrian Congress, says, "... I do not regard the government as being innocent of the faults of courting men of high status and accepting their intercession when government jobs were sought, from the start and up to the promotion. The most serious weakness was in the ministers and heads close to King Faisal and his tribe as well as those who were close to him. These were used, during the time of absolute military power, to fare with the businesses and funds as they pleased, however they pleased, so it was difficult for them, after the declaration of the independence, to adhere to law and order. The ministers did not have the moral courage and the solidarity to restrict them or get them accustomed to standing at the limits of their official authority since they themselves had become accustomed, during the Turks' time, to inclining to the whims of the heads (bosses) and prominent persons. Despite all of this, the independence government was able to restrict the king to a limited salary which did not please him although it was a lot. He used to spend every month's salary at its start or even before its crescent shone, then he would ask the ministry of finance for one loan after another, but he did not easily get all what he wanted or more. His clout in some ministries was stronger than that in others..."[1]

THIRD: Prior to King Faisal's coronation, the nobles and dignitaries used to meet him and talk to him whenever and however they pleased, and he used to visit them at their homes and talk to them as anyone would talk to his friends. After his coronation, he appointed Ihsan al-Jabiri as head of the royal *diwan* bearing the title "head of the king's trustees". This man

---

1 Yusuf Ibish (Op. Cit.), p. 298.

was in the past an official in the Ottoman court, so he started implementing the rules of the sultan's protocols to the court of King Faisal, putting restrictions on his meetings according to the constitutional principle that placed the executive power in the hands of the government. This caused a great deal of hearsay.[1] It is human that every individual among them regarded himself to be more worthy of being honored than his peers, and his viewpoint was the best. Had he permitted all people to meet the king without restrictions, the king would have had a nervous breakdown because of the crowds and screams around him. But when they were prevented from meeting the king, they would fret, and this applied to junior officials just as it applied to the king.

FOURTH: The appointing of Sati` al-Husari as the minister of education was one of the causes of grumbling in the public circles and among the theologians, for these used to quite often accuse al-Husari of desiring to weaken religion in the schools and of getting the girls used to immodesty. Sheikh Rasheed Ridha says that the theologians kept for so long, before and after the independence announcement, pleading to him to work with them to intercede with Faisal to fire al-Husari, and that he advised them to be patient because he did not want to accustom the public, especially those who coveted positions, to tell the government what to do.[2]

FIFTH: Faisal used to have a special affection towards the Iraqis because many of them had fought under his flag in the Arab Revolution; therefore, he appointed them in various state jobs and high positions. It is said that the total number of Iraqis who were in the government's service at the time reached four hundred officials and army officers. This had to lead to grumbling among the Syrians, especially those who did not get the jobs they hoped they would, and they kept advocating the principle

---

1 Ahmed Qadri (Op. Cit.), p. 188.
2 Yusuf Ibish (Op. Cit), p. 301.

of 'Syria is for the Syrians'." Muhammed Kurd Ali says the following in his book titled خُطَطُ الشام *Khutat al-Sham* (Plans of the Levant): "People in the Levant complained about the policy which Faisal followed in relying on the foreigners—meaning Iraqis—and his lack of trust in the country's notables and thinkers, and they kept advising him secretly to abandon such a policy."[1]

This statement is supported by an Iraqis who was in Syria at the time. He says the following *verbatim*: "What is worth mentioning is that some Syrians were spreading in Syria the attitude of indignation towards the Iraqis because some men from Iraq occupied high positions in the Syrian government. The rudeness of these mischief mongers reached the extent of openly advocating the ousting of the Iraqis from government jobs in Syria, something which created some hatred and coolness between the Syrians and the Iraqis."[2]

Evaluating Faisal

The policy which Faisal followed while ruling Syria received sharp criticism from some men who socialized with him and came to know him. Following, we review statements of four of them: Muhammed Kurd Ali, Jameel Bayham, Abdul-Rahman al-Shahbandar and Ibrahim Saleem Najjar:

1. Muhammed Kurd Ali says the following about Faisal: "Had he demonstrated strictness in dealing with the rioters, the Maysalun [battle] would not have taken place."[3]
2. Jameel Bayham says, "He [Faisal] had little political experience; he was hesitant, not influenced by his entourage, tolerates parties even when they become extremist and avoids public opinion; therefore, he went along with the

---

[1] Muhammed Kurd Ali, *Khutat al-Sham* (Plans of the Levant), Damascus: 1925, Vol. 3, p. 170.
[2] Muhammed Tahir al-Omari (Op. Cit.), Vol. 3, pp. 274-275.
[3] Khayriyya Qasmiyya (Op. Cit.), p. 264.

current instead of facing it, as is the [latter] case with the strong ruler." Then Jameel Bayham compares Faisal's policy in Syria with that in Iraq saying, "As for Iraq, where time had already taught him what he did not know, he was to the contrary: He was a firm and directing king. If he had to cope with the public opinion, he used to take to calm when the storm intensified, then he would advance after its calm paying no attention, nor is he hesitant. There, he enjoyed a strong awe and carried out word despite the toughness of the Iraqis and the strength of their nature, and although they easily become emotional, not accepting what is available. When they are angry, they rise, and they would incline to revolt whenever they could."[1]

3. Abdul-Rahman al-Shahbandar says, "But a horrible rumor was disseminated about Faisal when he returned from Paris, so he retreated disorderly because he was new to political affairs and to plots. Had he stood firmly and defended his views in the same skillful managing way which he later did in Iraq, he would have found moderate supporters who would support him and stand in the face of his opponents."[2]

4. Ibrahim Saleem al-Najjar says, "Interest-seekers filled the country with rumors before his [Faisal's] arrival that due to coveting the throne, Faisal sold Syria to the French (just like that). The Syrian extremists, especially from among the people of the Levant, were the ones who spread those rumors. So, the man's mission was not facilitated, one of a man who was still new to politics. Apparently, he feared lest those rumors would tarnish his reputation. So, instead of throwing them on the wall or denying them firmly and forcefully, or convincing the Syrians that what he achieved was more than what could be achieved, and that nobody could have achieved more, he kept in his speeches declaring his patriotism and exaggerating the independence which is "taken and not

---

1 Muhammed Jameel Bayham (Op. Cit.), p. 181.
2 *Al-Muqtataf* Magazine of October 1933.

given." He coped with the extremists, thinking that he could please them with such coping, letting some of them join the government in order to silence them although such joining was against his will. Then those folks thought that they could put France and the [other] countries before the reality, so they decided to declare his monarchy on May 9 of that year without events having necessitated or encouraged the announcement of this monarchy, or that one of the two states, the British or the French, should be consulted in its regard."

Ibrahim Saleem al-Najjar also says, "Prince Faisal had at the beginning of the year 1920 to know very well what he wanted. If he wanted the war for independence, he should have prepared himself for it realistically. But if he wanted peaceful work in agreement with the mandated government, he should have resorted to firmness with the extremists and appeared as the ruler who knew what he wanted and also knew the way to undertake in order to reach it."

Al-Najjar compares between what the extremists in Syria had done and what they wanted to do in the Trans-Jordan when they resorted to it after the Battle of Maysalun. He says that they tried to push Prince Abdullah to the same position to which they had pushed his brother, Faisal, before. But he stood firmly in their face, and this was the major cause of his staying in Amman.[1]

***

When we examine these statements in the light of our knowledge of the nature of man and of the human society, we find out that they looked at one aspect of the truth while neglecting the other. Had Faisal been strict and tough in Syria towards the masses, shooting them with bullets and putting them under the sword of terrorism, as tyrannical politicians do, he would have been cursed and people would have accused him

---

1 Ibrahim Saleem al-Najjar (Op. Cit.), pp. 73-75.

of being an agent of the colonialists and charged him with high treason. And we would have seen those who criticized his leniency criticizing him for his toughness and cursing him. Faisal was aware of this when he said in a letter to his father, "I could have violently hit the opposition parties, but I did not do it for fear history would condemn me."

Faisal failed in his policy, but he succeeded from another aspect: The two years during which he ruled Syria was a shining period in the history of modern Syria of which the Syrians are proud, signing its praise. Sa`eed al-Afghani, while discussing that period which he lived during his youth, says the following:

"As for counting the years, they were like a swift dream which did not last but only two years during which the country enjoyed sovereignty and happiness, living it one hour at a time, rather one moment at a time. It is the era of revival and resurrection. During it, individuals and groups were in solidarity, building life, promoting language and establishing entity. As in the calculating of the results and outcomes, what was founded then remained working through the strength of motivation and continuation up to our times. We remain enjoying the goodness of that thrust of renaissance, advancing despite stopping once and having a setback another. As a sign of that thrust is that it defied iron and fire and all the outcomes of vile French colonialism: deceiving plans that looked beautiful in appearance but were lethal in outcome for twenty-five years of [French] military occupation..."[1]

We do not deny that Faisal committed a horrible mistake when he tried to surrender to the French after the Battle of Maysalun, for that was a black spot in his history, and he should have avoided falling into that mistake so he would get out of Syria raising his head high as valiant heroes do. Yousuf al-Azmah was better than him: He preferred to die a martyr rather than

---

1 Sa`eed al-Afghani, *Hadir al-Lugha al-Arabiyya fil Sham* (Status of Arabic Language in the Levant), CairoL 1961, p. 57.

Introduction

bear the insult, thus providing a high moral example which coming generations will always remember.

History is not mobilized by only bloodthirsty tyrants; rather, it is mobilized by martyrs, too, each of them having his own role in the march of history.

Chapter Four
Al-Husain as King

Al-Husain as King

We discussed in the second part the biography of al-Husain ibn Ali from the beginning of his life up to declaring the revolution on the Turks in 1916, and we will discuss in this part al-Husain's biography in the last period of his rule, the period during which he was a king ruling Hijaz with his orders, nobody disputing his authority.

Al-Husain's Character

We have in the beginning to paint a brief picture of al-Husain's character, since it sheds light on the nature of the actions which he did and the events in which he participated.

It is known about al-Husain that he was religiously minded, pious and distant from doubts, respecting himself and rising above worldly desires. He is not known as one who immersed himself in pleasures as it is often known about kings. Whenever he was overcome by distress, he would resort to a lizard which he would put under his outer cloak. Then he would summon a man from among his ministers who is known for his acute fear of the lizard. Once the man comes and sits, al-Husain would surprise him by throwing the lizard in his lap, so the man would scream and run to the door in panic. It is then that al-Husain would laugh until falling on his back.[1]

Al-Husain wanted his subjects to emulate him in avoiding distractions and prohibited pleasures. It is narrated that Jidda was during the Ottoman period like other ports with many prostitution and drinking places. When al-Husain was the sole ruler, that era was no more. He took to purging the town, so he ordered anyone who was involved in prostitution to be arrested,

---

1   Ameen al-Rayhani, Mulook al-Arab (Arabs' Kings), Beirut: 1951, Vol. 1, pp. 35-37.

and that wine and its containers be thrown into the sea.¹ Ameen al-Rayhani, who visited Jidda in 1922, says that he found some of its residents drinking wine secretly and also indulging in singing, entertainment and gambling, but they would stop all of this whenever al-Husain visited Jidda, then they would return to their habit upon his departure. In this regard, al-Rayhani quotes a statement made by one of the residents of Jidda:

"It is amazing, Professor, how people in this country are! Let not my statement come as a surprise to you: There is fear in Jidda which overtakes people due to merely mentioning His Majesty's name, the supreme savior—meaning al-Husain—when he honors the town with his presence, as if they are in a mourning. When he returns to Mecca, they return, getting out of the boxes the cups and the pitchers, and you will see even the man of the highest status reciting the *tahleel*²..."

Al-Rayhani also quotes another statement said to him in Jidda: "Al-Husain is frightening, monstrous, during the hours of anger. So, if he summoned someone from among them [the people of Jidda and perhaps elsewhere as well] to Mecca, be he innocent or guilty, the man would write down his will before going out of his house."³

It is worth mentioning that there is an aspect in al-Husain's character whereby he became famous: He was always very proud of his own opinion, not surrendering it easily, and often he did not surrender it at all. He used to imagine the world as he desired, not as it is in reality. Fuad al-Khateeb, who was al-Husain's foreign minister, says that he did not have any power in his position as a foreign minister, nor did he ever do anything that fell within the circle of his specialization. Rather, he was with regard to al-Husain like the angels with regard to the

---

1   Husain Muhammed Naseef, Tarikh al-Hijaz (History of Hijaz), Cairo: 1349 A.H./1930 A.D., Vol. 1, pp. 115-117.

2   The *tahleel* is the pronouncement of *La ilaha illa Allāh* (there is no god save Allāh). – Tr.

3   Ameen al-Rayhani (Op. Cit.), Vol. 1, pp. 55, 57.

Chapter Four: Al-Husain as King

Almighty: praising and sanctifying. Quite often, memoranda would be issued bearing his signature without his being familiar with them or knowing anything about them. If he accidentally came to examine a memorandum and made some grammatical or linguistic corrections, al-Husain would order it re-written as it used to be before.[1]

Describing al-Husain from this aspect, Ameen al-Rayhani says the following:

"Sharif al-Husain was all in all, even in editing the *Qibla* newspaper. He thought that his editorials were translated into European languages, so ministers would read and express interest in them, and that his views in the world politics and in the politics of life, from the tiniest particularities to the greatest theories, were like a revealed inspiration. He believed that his interpretation of some verses of the Qur'an were more accurate than that of senior imams, and that in oratory and logic, as in knowledge, he was the prince of his peers and unique in his time, that if he sought help of the Arabs, they would go to him from the furthermost part of the Peninsula to listen and to obey, that he could, even if he was in his own private office, save the land and establish the Arab state. Actually, he thought the Islamic world, in its entirety, smiled when he smiled and became angry because he became angry, that those who served him actually served the Arabs and Islam without seeking a reward other than his pleasure."[2]

Al-Husain believed that all Arabs loved him and would sacrifice their lives for him. It is believed that this notion grew in him as a result of what was being said by the flatterers from among the pilgrims every year and the resonant poems recited by poets before him. He thought that the Arabs would all rise

---

[1] Ameen Sa'eed, *Tarikh al-Dawla al-Saudiyya* (History of the Saudi State), Beirut, Vol. 2, p. 151.
[2] Ameen al-Rayhani, *Tarikh Najd al-Hadith* (the modern history of Najd) and supplements, Beirut: 1954, p. 344.

together as soon as they came to know that he forfeited his authority. He, therefore, used to always threaten the British that he was determined to abdicate. Once it so happened that when Churchill was the minister of colonies, he lost his patience towards al-Husain's threat, so he wanted to write him a letter saying that the British government wanted him to mention the name of the individual who would succeed him on the throne in case he abdicated. Churchill thought that such a letter would cause al-Husain to stop threatening to abdicate.[1]

From the Family's Heritage

Al-Husain used to carry in his subconscious mind a remnant of his family's ancient heritage, a family called by Muhammed Hasanain Haikal, the famous Egyptian journalist, "the persecution complex." Al-Husain used to always mention the tragedies and pains his Alawid ancestors had suffered, and he used to repeat this statement: "We, the Aal al-Bayt, have our written destiny," and his sons, too, used to also repeat it, especially Abdullah.[2]

This complex had its effective impact on al-Husain's conduct and thinking: He used to look into the conditions of the present through the same glasses whereby he looked into those of the past. For example, he used to look at the people of Iraq in his time as he looked at them in the century when the Kerbala tragedy took place.

Ali al-Bazargan narrates saying that he was once a guest of al-Husain in Mecca in 1921 when a telegram reached al-Husain from one of Iraq's chiefs asking him to let his son, Faisal, be the king over them. Al-Husain, therefore, said [to al-Bazargan], "But I fear, Sheikh, lest the people of Iraq should treat Faisal just as they had treated his grandfather, al-Husain, before." Al-Bazargan

---

1 Sulayman Mousa, *Safahat Matwiyya* (folded pages), Amman: 1977, p. 93.
2 Muhammed Hasanain Haikal, *Al-Uqad al-Nafsiyya allati Tahkum al-Sharq al-Awst* (the psychological complexes that rule the Middle East), Cairo: 1958, p. 101.

Chapter Four: Al-Husain as King

responded to him saying, "Sir! Times have changed, and the people of Iraq now are not the same like their ancestors during the time of al-Husain ibn Ali ibn Abu Talib A. They are generous to the guest and to serving their king." It was then that al-Husain hit one palm with the other and shouted in his Hijazi accent يا عيال! نادوا فيصل "Boys! Call Faisal!"[1]

Ahmed al-Rawi narrates to me a similar incident. It is summed up thus: In 1923, he was al-Muntafiq's police commissioner, so King Faisal sent him to Mecca to bring his family and son, Ghazi. But on his arrival at Mecca, al-Husain did not permit him to take the family. Al-Rawi says that he kept repeating the request to al-Husain time and over again, but al-Husain would every time promise to honor his request, then he would change his mind shortly thereafter. Al-Rawi finally lost patience and had to face al-Husain with some honesty. The gist of what he said to him was, "Preventing the wife from rejoining her husband contradicts the command of Allāh and His Messenger." Al-Husain responded saying, "I am apprehensive of you, people of Iraq [which he pronounced "Irag" in the Hijazi dialect], that you would do to al-Husain's family [his own] what you did to the family of [Imam] al-Husain before." Al-Husain kept insisting on his stance, forcing al-Rawi to return to Iraq disappointed.

When al-Husain visited Amman in January of 1924, King Faisal made another bid to bring his family from Mecca, so he sent a delegation to Amman headed by Nouri al-Sa`eed. The delegation left Baghdad on February 7 and met al-Husain, requesting him to permit the royal family to go to Iraq. Al-Husain expressed his preliminary agreement to honor the request and said that he would send the family on his return to Mecca. But when he returned, he changed his mind just as he had done before with Ahmed al-Rawi.

---

1 Ali al-Bazargan, *Al-Waqai` al-Haqeeqiyya* (the true events), Baghdad: 1954, p. 230.

On August 20, a telegram reached King Faisal informing him of his father permitting Prince Ghazi to leave Mecca to Amman. Ms. [Gertrude] Bell says in a letter dated August 20 the following: "The King is much excited because King Husain [his father] has at last released his only son, Ghazi, who has been kept at Mecca till now. The boy—he is twelve—is now at Amman and H.M. is sending Muhsin Beg across to fetch him."[1] The prince finally reached Baghdad on October 5, 1924.[2]

When al-Husain released Prince Ghazi, he did not do the same to his mother and sisters. Apparently, he was afraid they might be taken captive as took place to the women from among Ahl al-Bayt [Prophet's immediate family members] in Kerbala. The mother and sisters remained in Mecca until October of 1924 when they left Hijaz to al-Aqaba with al-Husain following his abdication, as we will discuss in the next chapter. They moved after that to Amman and from there to Baghdad. Their reached Baghdad on December 16, 1924.[3]

Bedouins' Mutiny

During the last years of his rule, al-Husain went through very tough times financially: Britain kept lowering its monthly financial aid to him starting from the end of the war, then it terminated it for good in April of 1920. Al-Husain, therefore, had to get funds through various ways, including imposing loans on merchants without reimbursements.[4] Another was participation in cattle trade, and in the wages of those who helped pilgrims perform the *tawaf* (circumambulation) of the Ka`ba, those of bakers, cameleers and others.[5] Al-Husain was also forced to cut

---

1 [Elizabeth] Burgoyne, *Gertude Bell: From her Personal Papers 1914-1926* (London: Ernest Benn Limited, 1961), p. 351. [I have relied on this reference a great deal in translating this Volume of al-Wardi's book and also in translating Volume Six of it. – Tr.]
2 *Al-Iraq* newspaper of October 6, 1924.
3 Burgoyne (Op. Cit.), Vol. 2, p. 359.
4 Talib Muhammed Waheem, *Mamlakat al-Hijaz* (the Kingdom of Hijaz), an unpublished Masters thesis, p. 201.
5 Ameen al-Rayhani, *Tarikh Najd al-Hadith* (Modern History of Najd) and Supplements,

Chapter Four: Al-Husain as King

off the grants which Bedouin tribes used to get from him. This led to the spread of public grumbling in Hijaz and among pilgrims' circles. It also led to the mutiny of the Bedouin tribes which started intercepting the pilgrimage routes, especially the main one connecting Medina with Mecca.

The Bedouins have since ancient times been accustomed to intercepting routes and imposing royalties on travelers, and they regard it as their legitimate way of making a living and do not abandon it except if they get annual compensations for it from the government. So, if the government refused to pay, they would go back to being highway robbers. This is what took place in Hijaz following al-Husain stopping his payment of aid money to the Bedouin tribes.

Sayyid Muhsin Abu Tibeekh tells us in the transcript of his *Memoirs* that when he resorted to Hijaz in the company of his fellows from among the men of the 1920 Revolution, following the collapse of the Revolution, the Harb tribe went out to them near Medina and surrounded them in a narrow valley, intercepting their path. When they told the tribesmen that they were guests of King Husain, the tribesmen's answer was: "We want to kill you *because* you are guests of King Husain." They found no way out except to pay a royalty of five hundred gold liras.[1]

In the summer of 1921, Sheikh Ali al-Sharqi went to perform the pilgrimage accompanied by Sheikh Khayyun al-Ubaid. He tells us in his book titled *Al-Ahlam* (the Dreams) in detail about what his caravan had gone through during its trip in the area between Mecca and Medina, the losses of lives and funds. Here is a summary of it:

"Al-Husain had sent with the caravan guards comprised of five hundred men a commander over them. But this did not benefit the caravan; rather, it proved to be detrimental to it. In

---

p. 347.
1 This is quoted from the handwritten manuscript of Sayyid Muhsin Abu Tibeekh's *Memoirs*.

the first night of its trip, it lost two persons who were killed as they were in their loader. In the next night, the caravan lost sixteen men who were found in the morning killed in their loaders. It was then that the caravan decided to return to Mecca without visiting Medina. But the commander asked for a secluded meeting with Sheikh Ali al-Sharqi to whom he said, 'I am going to reveal a secret to you the penalty for its revelation is shedding my blood: These tribes have nothing against you. They have issues against the king who has fallen short of paying them their dues and who has no power to deter them. The calamities that have afflicted you are only due to the flag which accompanies you. If this flag is folded, you can easily come to an understanding with them, so you can go peacefully and comfortably.' The commander asked al-Sharqi to write a letter to the king to thank him so the commander could carry it and return to Mecca with his flag."

Al-Sharqi says, "They did what the commander had advised them to do, collecting an amount of money which they paid to the Harb tribe. Then they resumed their trip towards Medina. But they were hardly close to it, witnessing the lighting in the Prophet's Mausoleum, when they were taken by surprise by the Banu Sulaym, a branch of the Harb tribe who lived near Medina and who showered them with bullets from their rifles, killing forty persons, including four Iraqi women, not counting the wounded, then they looted the caravan."

When the caravan reached Medina, its men submitted their complaint to the government. Al-Sharqi went as the spokesman of the caravan to the Sarai to meet the political ruler, Sharif Shahath. When he met him, there were present with him heads of Banu Sulaym, and each of those men reclined on his rifle with ammunition lined up on his chest. The ruler kept addressing the chiefs, remonstrating and reprimanding them for what they had done to a delegation seeking to please Allāh and His Prophet, meaning the caravan. Then he asked them to lead him to the doer, so a handsome young man named Muhammed ibn Nahar emerged and said, "I am the doer." It became quite obvious that he was the chief of Banu Sulaym, so a dialogue went on between him and the ruler as follows:

RULER: Why (did you do that)?

CHIEF: I did it in order to let Sharif Husain know that there is gunpowder with the Banu Sulaym, and that gunpowder is available not just with others [meaning the king and his men].

RULER: This is a matter between you and the king; what do these guests have to do with it? Suffices you what has happened, and let me get them out in peace, son of Nahar.

CHIEF: Do not get them out, and they shall not get out, unless the Sharif settles our issue.

RULER (angrily): Son of Nahar! I shall get them out with this (pointing at the ammunition on his chest).

CHIEF: Fie on you, donkey, wine-drinker! I swear by the bread eaten by the Messenger of Allāh, if you get them out, I shall slaughter you and slaughter them with you; come along, Banu Harb (and they all left).

The caravan's men finally decided to collect the usual royalty for Banu Sulaym in the amount of six thousand [gold] liras so they would be able to return to Mecca safely. Al-Husain came to know about all of this, and he decided to buy back the reputation of his rule by paying the amount from his own money. He, therefore, instructed his representative in Medina, Sayyid Omran al-Habboobi, to pay the amount to Banu Sulaym and to record it as a loan against his [king's] account. Sayyid Omran did so, and the caravan returned to Mecca safely.[1]

Al-Husain was used to announcing a statement to the pilgrims that the government was obligated to pay compensations for all what the tribes had looted from them, so anyone whose

---

1 Ali al-Sharqi, *Al-Ahlam* (the Dreams), Baghdad: 1963, pp. 129-131.

money was looted should submit a petition to the government stating the amount of what was looted from him and swearing by the Ka`ba on it. Al-Sharqi, quoting the mayor of Jidda, Hajj Muhammed Ali Namazi, says, "Some pilgrims who believed this statement submitted their petitions to the government and stayed in Hijaz waiting for the payment of the compensation up to the time the last pilgrim ship left, thus leaving them stranded to die of starvation."[1]

The Turba Incident

Turba and al-Kharma are two Hijazi oases located to the east of Taif which was ruled by Sharif Khalid ibn Luay, a relative of al-Husain. In 1918, Khalid was angry with al-Husain and his son, Abdullah. It is said that a violent altercation took place between him and Abdullah, so Abdullah hit him on his face with a sandal. Khalid went angrily to Ibn Saud in Riyadh where he declared his "acceptance of the faith," i.e. the Wahhabi sect, thus winning a promise from Ibn Saud to help him. Then he returned to his area declaring his mutiny against al-Husain, challenging him.

Al-Husain sent a force to fight Khalid and subject him to his authority, but Khalid defeated it. Al-Husain sent a second then a third force, and their fate was similar to that of the first. Al-Husain was finally determined to send Khalid a large force that would defeat him, then he would go to Riyadh to discipline Ibn Saud himself.

Al-Husain found his chance in January of 1919 when Fakhri Pasha and his forces surrendered to him in Medina, so al-Husain seized the cannons, machineguns and a great deal of ammunition which Fakhri Pasha used to have. He thought that he would be able, with those war equipment and with the regular army he had, to deal a crushing blow to Khalid ibn Luay.

---

1 *Ibid.*, p. 132.

Chapter Four: Al-Husain as King

Al-Husain instructed his son, Abdullah, to move with his forces towards Khalid. Abdullah says in his *Memoirs* that he objected to his father regarding this order and explained to him the status of his soldiers who were fed-up with fighting during that lengthy period which they spent when the city was under siege. He mentioned to him that they wished to return to their homelands after having become rich and their pockets filled with money, but al-Husain insisted on his order carried out, so Abdullah had no choice except to comply.[1]

Abdullah's campaign was comprised of 850 regular troops and about 1,500 irregulars, and they had with them ten cannons, about twenty heavy machineguns and twenty light ones. It is worth mentioning that most campaign officers were Iraqis, such as Muhammed Hilmi al-Hajj Dhiyab, Sabri al-Azzawi, Ibrahim al-Rawi, Hamid al-Wadi, Abbas al-Ani, Sami Sabri, Rasheed Khammas, Jamal Ali and Khdhayyir Mukhlis.

When the campaign reached a place called Ashira, thirty kilometers from eastern Taif, al-Husain came to it in person to review it. When a parade for it went on, al-Husain was elated and imagined that it would be able to conquer all of the Arabian Peninsula. Abdullah tried to convince him to wait, but al-Husain was determined to continue the march and said to him, "You must go to al-Kharma to crush this corrupt movement, and you have with you a force which, if it fights, will defeat all Arabs."[2]

Husain Rawhi Afandi, who was then working as a secretary to the British consul in Jidda, reached Ashira to meet al-Husain. He was carrying a letter to al-Husain from the consul advising him to be moderate and to resolve his dispute with Ibn Saud peacefully. When al-Husain read the letter, he said in a loud voice addressing Husain Rawhi so others would hear him, too,

---

1   Abdullah ibn al-Husain, *Muthakkarati* مذكراتي (My Memoirs), Jerusalem: 1945, p. 154.
2   *Ibid.*, p. 156.

"Go and tell them that they have no right to interfere in the domestic affairs, for we are free and we do whatever we want."[1]

Al-Husain returned to Mecca, and the campaign continued its march towards Turba, seventy kilometers to the east of Taif, occupying it easily. Ibn Saud had sent a warning to Abdullah against attacking Turba and al-Kharma, so Abdullah responded to him by a warning of his own and a threat. Ibn Saud had ordered a general mobilization in Najd marked as head of an army estimated to number twelve thousand men heading towards Hijaz. He sent before him commando vanguards, men who were known by the name "ikhwan", brothers, estimated to number one thousand and five hundred under the command of Khalid ibn Luay and Sultan ibn Bajad.

The *ikhwan* arrived at al-Kharma and bypassed it heading towards Turba. In the afternoon of May 24, 1919, a Bedouin man reached Turba and said this to Prince Abdullah: "Sharif, beware! Those who accepted the faith—meaning the *ikhwan*—in the Kharma are attacking you." The prince was angry with him and ordered him beheaded. It is said in another narrative that the prince ordered his chief slave to hit the man, so the slave hit him till he died.[2] In order to justify his action, the prince said to those present, "They intended by sending him to us to weaken our resolve."[3]

The *ikhwan* moved towards Turba in the eve of May 24 shouting

هَبَّتْ هُبوبُ الجَنَّة، وين انتَ يا باغيها!؟

"The winds of Paradise have blown; where are you, O one who seeks it?!" They became close to Turba in the dawn of the next day, then they carried out a sudden lightning assault on it.

---

1 Ameen Sa'eed (Op. Cit.), Vol. 2, p. 84.
2 Ameen al-Rayhani (Op. Cit.), p. 254.
3 Ameen Sa'eed (Op. Cit.), Vol. 2, p. 90.

Chapter Four: Al-Husain as King

The battle went on between both parties for about two hours in which the *ikhwan* scored a crushing victory.

Ibrahim al-Rawi was one of the participants in the battle, and he provided us with a description of it in his *Memoirs* saying, "... They attacked us at the time for the call to the dawn prayers. Although we knew that we would be attacked that night, and although we had prepared ourselves for it, the severity of the attack stemmed from a sincere desire and an invincible resolve... Under my command, there was a swift 5.7 cm German mountain battery and another swift Czech battery in addition to two mortar cannons. When I heard about the attack, I got ready to go to the battery of which Sayyid Abbas was the commander. Between myself and the location of the battery was about one hundred meters. I was sleeping in my military outfit. As I was going there, the cannons and machineguns started directing their fires at us and the infantry was shooting its rifles and hand grenades the sound of which was heard in all directions. Despite all of this, some *ikhwan* had infiltrated inside the camp, and there was an engagement with pistols and daggers. Allāh, through His bliss, was kind to me, so I reached the cannons safely and saw their commander, Sayyid Abbas, directing his cannons towards the *ikhwan*, burning them with a fierce fire. Few minutes later, Lt. Khidhir said while weeping, "The *ikhwan* have seized our machineguns." Few minutes later, the *ikhwan* reached the cannons where we were and started seizing them, killing all their cadres. I stayed away from them in order to ride my horse and go to the other battery which was in another location, so I went to the person who was holding my horse and was about to ride. But when my foot was inside the stirrup, four *ikhwan* targeted us. I could not ride the horse because the *ikhwan* killed the soldier and took the horse, so I went to the stable of a mountain battery near me and took a mule from it then distanced myself. I found another horse belonging to me, so I rode it. Before putting the reins in my hand, I found the *ikhwan* near me. They eyed me and one of them shot at me when the distance between myself and himself was only one meter, so I distanced myself after they [*ikhwan*] had fiished all those who were with me with the exception of two cavaliers... At that time, the sun was about to shine, and the battle had reached its end, so I distanced myself from the village as my arm kept bleeding..."[1]

The campaign lost all the cannons, weapons and luggage it had had as well as most of its officers and soldiers, and nobody from among its regular forces survived except seven officers and one hundred and fifty soldiers. Ibrahim al-Rawi says that he had in his possession one thousand gold liras, a valuable gilt sword, two horses, one beast of burden and some furniture, and he lost them all in the battle, yet he praised Allāh for his survival at any rate.[2]

The survival of Abdullah from the battle was miraculous. His cousin, Sharif Shakir ibn Zaid, was able to let him ride behind him on his mare and run away with him in a hurry. Later, Abdullah talked about this incident saying, "The noise of the raiders in the eve of Turba keeps ringing in my ears: *Al-Janna!* (Paradise) *Al-Janna! Al-Janna!*..."[3]

Ibn Saud reached the battlefield after it had ended. There, he received a warning from the British government saying, "The government of His Majesty requests you to return to Najd when this letter reaches your hands and to leave Turba and al-Kharma as a free zone and no man's land until the reconciliation is signed and the borders are determined. And if you do not return, the government of Britain considers the agreement between yourself and it as being terminated, and it will undertake the necessary measures against your hostile movements. It is very sorry for what happened among its friends, and it had hoped they would never happen."[4]

---

[1] Ibrahim al-Rawi, *Thikrayat* (Memories), Beirut: 1969, pp. 134-138.
[2] *Ibid.*, pp. 140-143.
[3] Khair ad-Din al-Zurakli, *Shibh al-Jazeera fi 'Ahd al-Malik Abdul-Aziz* (the Peninsula during the time of Abdul-Aziz), Beirut: 1977, Vol. 1, p. 322.
[4] Ameen Sa'eed (Op. Cit.), Vol. 2, p. 93.

Chapter Four: Al-Husain as King

When this warning reached Ibn Saud, the *ikhwan* were demanding to march on Taif. They kept shouting, "To Taif! Permit Taif to be ours!" Ibn Saud prevented them and said, "The wrongdoer has paid sufficiently for his wrong deeds."[1]

A Crisis In London

The Turba incident led to a sharp crisis in the British foreign ministry. Britain at the time was standing beside al-Husain and supporting him from every aspect. It was also fully confident of his strength and that he was able to defeat Ibn Saud. The British experts were of the opinion that "those extremist Wahhabi scums of the earth" could not seriously withstand facing Hijaz's regular troops which Britain trained and equipped with weapons and supplies.

Philby at the time was in London, so he was summoned to attend the meeting held by British foreign minister Lord Curzon to study this subject. Philby's opinion was the opposite of that of the experts who attended the conference. But the experts slighted and ridiculed his opinion. Philby says in his *Memoirs* that when the Turba incident took place, and when Ibn Saud won it, Lord Curzon held a second conference. When the experts attended, Philby saw them lowering their heads. One of them said, "It seems that we placed our bet on the wrong horse."[2]

Lord Curzon had received a telegram from the British consul in Jidda saying that Jidda was over-crowded with the refugees who fled from Taif and Mecca for fear of the Wahhabis, including eleven thousand Indians from among the subjects of Britain. Pandemics were expected to spread among them. In his telegram, the consul requested a number of ships to transport the refugees.

When the conference discussed this telegram, it became clear that the British Navy was unable to provide any ship to transport

---

1 Ameen al-Rayhani (Op. Cit.), p. 257.
2 Khairi Hammad, *Abdullah Philby*, Beirut: 1911, pp. 74-81.

the refugees. Curzon, therefore, turned to the military commanders who were present during the meeting and said, "What can the ministry of war do? We cannot leave these people slaughtered like goats at the hands of the Wahhabis." A commander answered him saying, "Sir, I am afraid we cannot do anything. The war ministry is determined not to get involved in any military adventure in the Arabian desert; we have had enough up to now."

Philby expressed his opinion saying, "Had Britain agreed that Ibn Saud would keep the Turba and Kharma oases, he would have been pleased and would have stopped his advance." Philby promised to go to Ibn Saud in person to convince him. The meeting endorsed his opinion, and a special plane was prepared to transport him to Hijaz in a hurry. Philby left London by plane, but when he reached Cairo, he came to know that Ibn Saud had stopped the advance and returned to Riyadh and that there was no danger facing the refugees in Jidda.

Britain had sent to Jidda six planes shipped in boxes in order to defend Hijaz against the Wahhabis' assault. The High Commissioner in Cairo, Gen. Allenby, was actually determined to use those planes, but Philby advised him not to do that saying, "If the planes sent to Jidda are used, and if one of them landed in a Wahhabi land, the Wahhabis will cut off the necks of its pilots." The general, therefore, issued his orders to keep the planes in their boxes.[1]

Al-Husain's Complex

The Turba incident had a great deal of impact on al-Husain psychologically and health-wise. Abdullah says the following in his *Memoirs*: "I found him after my return to the center, that is, after the Turba incident and the conquest of Medina, looking different from what I had come to know His Majesty, and he was

---

1 *Ibid.*, p. 81.

Chapter Four: Al-Husain as King

suffering from his ailment because of which Allāh caused him to die—meaning atherosclerosis—starting from then. He was too often boastful, forgetful, hesitant, little relying on those on whom he used to rely..., and this matter is quite serious."[1]

The Turba incident became akin to a psychological complex for al-Husain. It was not easy for him that a man whom he used to consider as a fifth degree prince would score a victory over him. He kept blaming his son, Abdullah, whom he regarded as the first person responsible for the Turba defeat. This means that he let Abdullah be the scapegoat. Al-Husain kept thinking of seeking revenge against Ibn Saud and recovering control over Turba and al-Kharma from him.

Al-Husain, like others suffering from a psychological complex, kept feeling comfortable with those who shared his belief and looked after it. For this reason, he was surrounded by some flatterers who kept painting a life image for him to his own liking. Ameen al-Rayhani narrates the incident of one of those flatterers: He was artistic in creating bad reports about Najd and Ibn Saud, and al-Husain used to bring that man close to him and feel comfortable talking to him. The man came one day and a dialogue went on between both men thus:

MAN: "This is a drought year in Najd. The wells are dry, and thousands of camels have died."

AL-Husain: "Really?! Praise to Allāh...! You, son, know best of all people about the conditions of Najd."

MAN: "Ibn Saud, Master, has the fever, having been hit in the lung. They say it is the TB, and one who has this ailment does not live."

AL-Husain: "Really?! Really?! Praise to Allāh! Nobody tells me true reports other than you."

---

[1] Abdullah ibn al-Husain (Op. Cit.), p. 163.

MAN: "And the Hasa (Ahsa) tribes have revolted against him, and they say that they wanted only King Husain."

AL-Husain: "This is what I always say, son, that the tribes, all of them, would rebel against him, and they will all come to us, by the will of Allāh."[1]

Lawrence's Negotiations

In the summer of 1921, the British government decided to sign a treaty with al-Husain thinking that the latter appreciated what it had done, i.e. appointing one of his sons as King over Iraq and the other as Prince over Trans-Jordan, in addition to himself becoming King of Hijaz. It, therefore, sent his friend, Lawrence, to be its representative in negotiating with him to sign the treaty.

Lawrence reached Jidda on July 29 accompanied by Gabriel Haddad Pasha. On the next day, he held his first meeting with al-Husain who had in his company both his sons, Ali and Zaid, in addition to his foreign minister, Fuad al-Khateeb. Lawrence started the talk saying, "There is a debt that needs to be paid off, and its payment cannot all be paid now, but a small installment of it is paid provided paying the rest will be looked into in the future." Then Lawrence submitted the draft agreement which had been prepared beforehand in London. Al-Husain, therefore, addressed Lawrence thus: "You have honored us [with your visit], and there must be a research and a discussion, so welcome!"[2]

The negotiations lasted five weeks. Al-Husain followed in them the method of procrastination and evasion: He would be courteous to Lawrence during the negotiations, praising Great Britain, but in the end he would not agree on anything. Lawrence sent a telegram on August 2 to the British foreign minister, Lord

---

1 Ameen al-Rayhani (Op. Cit.), p. 346.
2 Ameen Sa'eed, *Al-Thawra al-Arabiyya al-Kubra* (the Great Arab Revolution), Cairo, Vol. 3, p. 158.

Chapter Four: Al-Husain as King

Curzon, saying, "I met with the king several times, and he told me of his abandonment of his stance which is based on McMahon's letters, but he every day stirs new deep ideas. He is a foolish old man with no limits to his conceit and ambitions, but he demonstrates a great deal of love and stresses that he is our sincere friend."[1]

The situation between Lawrence and al-Husain became tense as a result, for Lawrence asked al-Husain to say frankly what he wanted, so al-Husain submitted to him four demands:

1. a recognition that Iraq and Palestine should be under his [al-Husain's] power,
2. Aseer and al-Hudaida must be annexed to Hijaz,
3. he should be advanced over all Arab rulers, and
4. Arab rulers must return to their ancient borders, that is, Ibn Saud should withdraw from Turba and al-Kharma.

These demands caused Lawrence to be angry, so he responded to al-Husain with toughness, accusing him of greed and explaining to him the extent of his potentials, acquainting him with the matters as they were. He meant by that to point out to his weakness, and that Ibn Saud could have reached Mecca within three days. The signs of a strong effect showed on al-Husain as a result of this statement and he left the meeting angry without bidding one word of farewell. Lawrence sent Lord Curzon a telegram describing in it what went on and concluded it by saying, "The king is weaker than I used to think, and I see that he can be pressured until he fully and lastly surrenders. If we can overcome him now, negotiating with him will be easier the next time."[2]

The pilgrimage season started in mid-August, so al-Husain had to return to Mecca in order to participate in and to oversee

---

1 Phillip Knightley and Colin Simpson, *The Secret Lives of Lawrence of Arabia*, New York: McGraw-Hill, 1970, translated into Arabic as المخفي من حياة لورنس العرب by Lawand and al-Abid, Beirut: 1971, p. 153.
2 Sulayman Mousa (Op. Cit.), pp. 69-70.

it. Lawrence, in turn, went to Aden where he stayed for two weeks then returned to Jidda on August 29. Al-Husain, too, returned to it on September 2, so the negotiations were resumed anew.

Al-Husain tried this time to lower the ceiling of his past demands. He asked that all Arab emirates must return to the borders which used to be prior to the end of the war, that he should have the right to appoint all men of the judiciary and of issuing *fatwas* (religious edicts) in the Arabian Peninsula, Iraq and Palestine, and that his sovereignty must be recognized over all Arab rulers and governors of all countries. Lawrence responded to these demands in a way which was tougher than he had done before. Lawrence said the following in a telegram to Lord Curzon: "When al-Husain heard this [my] response, he asked for a dagger and swore that he would either abdicate or kill himself, whereupon I said to him that the British government would resume the negotiations with the man who would succeed him."[1]

Lawrence did not lose hope of succeeding in signing the treaty, and he kept trying repeatedly in his negotiations whenever he failed in them. On September 22, he sent a telegram to his government saying that al-Husain accepted all items of the treaty and declared before witnesses that he would sign it shortly. But when Prince Ali presented to him the text of the treaty to sign, he screamed in his face and threw it on him. Lawrence says in his telegram, "Prince Ali describes his father as being insane, saying that he agreed with his brother, Prince Zaid, to work to oust him." Lawrence expressed his optimism towards the cooperation of Ali and Zaid with him in the negotiation and said this about them: "They both behave in an amazing way, and they may change the matters in the next few weeks."[2]

---

1   *Ibid.*, p. 73.
2   Talib Muhammed Waheem (Op. Cit.), p. 221.

Chapter Four: Al-Husain as King

Lawrence agreed to add another article to the treaty stating that the treaty did not nullify any pledge or promise made to the Arabs during the war. Lawrence expected this article to please al-Husain, but al-Husain was not pleased with anything. His family members and entourage kept insisting on his endorsing the treaty but to no avail. It is said that his wife, Umm [mother of] Zaid, participated in urging him to do so. When he felt that their insistence bothered him, he ascended to the house's rooftop and directed his face towards the Ka`ba to swear by it that he would not sign any treaty which did not achieve the promises made in the past. Then he went down and took to seclusion, not talking to anyone. When his family members saw his conduct, they stopped speaking to him about the treaty, then they agreed with Lawrence that he should visit Prince Abdullah in Amman so the Prince could sign the treaty on behalf of his father, then he would send it to him to ratify it.[1]

Lawrence left Jidda on September 22 heading to Amman. When he reached it, he and Prince Abdullah focused on examining the treaty in order to arrive at a formula that would win the acceptance of both parties. On November 29, Lawrence sent a telegram to Lord Curzon saying that he reached an amended text of the treaty that won the consent of Prince Abdullah, and that the Prince was confident that his father would endorse the new text. The signing of the treaty took place in Amman on December 18 by Lawrence and Prince Abdullah.

On the 27th of the month, the new form of the treaty reached al-Husain. But instead of ratifying it, he sent Lloyd George, head of the British cabinet, a telegram suggesting to send his son, Abdullah, to London to take a second look at the treaty's formula and to edit it. The answer from Lloyd George came through the British consul in Jidda as follows: The consul says, "The British government of His Majesty commissioned me, in lieu of your Majesty's telegram dated December 28, 1921 sent to Mr. Lloyd

---

1   Ameen Sa'eed (Op. Cit.), Vol. 3, p. 158.

George, to indicate to Your Majesty that the issue of editing the treaty is outside the subject, and that it must either be accepted or rejected as is. It adds saying that the visit by His Highness Prince Abdullah to England must be regarded as having been postponed for now. If Your Majesty wishes, after endorsing the treaty, the door will be open to discuss other topics and to commission Prince Abdullah for this purpose, the visit of His Highness to England will then be an opportunity to submit such proposals to the British government of His Majesty the King."

This answer caused a great deal of pain to al-Husain who wrote to the British consul in Jidda to explain the reasons that prompted him to suggest sending Abdullah as an envoy to London. Then he said that he did not understand the reasons behind the defiance and injustice in the answer, and he only wanted a "Yes" or a "No" to his deliberations, and that he would find himself forced to adopt a stance if he did not get from Britain either a "Yes" or a "No."

The next day, al-Husain wrote the consul another letter carrying the same meaning. In it, he said, "The rejection of the British government of Abdullah's visit to London supports the rumor that says that Britain wanted to clear itself of me, and all this prompts me to say that if there is neither a Yes or a No answer reaching me by the end of this month—meaning February 27—I will be forced to announce my forfeiting [the throne]."

Two days later, al-Husain wrote a third letter to the consul stating in it that the articles of the treaty, which he was required to ratify, were based on "what has no root or existence". He hinted, by saying so, to a text in the treaty regarding respect for the ties and borders agreed on among the Arabian Peninsula countries, for he regarded those borders, especially between Hijaz and Najd, as having had no agreement about them, and he wanted to restore the borders to the way they used to be prior to the end of the war.

Chapter Four: Al-Husain as King

Tension in the relationship between al-Husain and Britain reached its peak on February 14, 1922. The British consul in Jidda wrote a letter to al-Husain which was not without an insult. He stated to him that the British government took note of his resolve to abdicate on February 27, that while it remembered his sincere cooperation and friendly ties with it in the past, it regretted that he had to abdicate but it realized that it had nothing to do with this issue, since it is an issue of interest to his citizens, and he has to settle it with them. Al-Husain answered the consul with a letter in which he expressed his disappointment and said that he had to tolerate risks relying on the promises of Britain without going back to the people; therefore, the people have nothing to do with the issue of his abdication.[1]

Dr. Naji Al-Aseel

Naji al-Aseel is a Baghdadi youth who studied medicine at the American University in Beirut. Upon his graduation, he joined the Arab army as a physician bearing the rank of captain. When the war came to an end, he was able to get a job in a company called "The British-French Company for Middle East Reconstruction". This company sent him to Hijaz in June 1922 to set up some projects. There, he found an opportunity to meet and talk to al-Husain.

Some evidences point out to Naji al-Aseel having been able to have a psychological impact on al-Husain and to win his trust. Al-Aseel told him that he knew some personalities who were influential in the British politics and that he, therefore, was able to make a treaty that would please al-Husain. The extent of al-Aseel's impact on al-Husain reached the degree that al-Husain appointed him as his representative in London, authorizing him to negotiate with the British government on his behalf.

---

1 Sulayman Mousa (Op. Cit.), p. 96.

Al-Aseel left for London carrying an amended wording for the treaty. He also carried with him a letter from al-Husain to Lloyd George saying in it that his refusal to accept the treaty in the past stemmed from the absence of an improvement in an understanding with him. Late in September of 1922, al-Aseel reached London where he submitted the text of the amended treaty to the foreign ministry. When the ministry experts studied it, they found the amendments al-Husain introduced into the treaty were acceptable with the exception of his dropping one item: the 17th article which indicated recognition of the special center for Britain in Palestine.

The negotiations between the foreign ministry and Naji al-Aseel were resumed anew. On April 16, 1923, a new formula for the treaty was put. Lord Curzon and Dr. al-Aseel put their initials on it. On the next day, al-Aseel left London for Jidda feeling confident that al-Husain would accept the new form.

Al-Aseel reached Jidda on April 30. When al-Husain studied the new draft treaty, he made some adjustments to it. The British consul sent those adjustments to London to be endorsed. On May 10, the answer came from the British foreign ministry containing some reservations and suggestions. The British consul contacted al-Aseel to notify him of the answer, so al-Aseel thought that the British government had accepted the new amendments, and he went to al-Husain to tell him the news. Al-Husain was elated to an unlimited extent, not knowing that the news was baseless and that it was only a misconception by Naji al-Aseel.

When Eidul-Fitr (fast breaking feast) coincided on May 17, al-Husain told the delegates who went to greet him on the occasion that Britain had accepted the Arabs' demands to recognize their independence. He said, "There is no doubt that two Eids are combined: Happy Eidul-Fitr and عيد الاعتراف باستقلال العرب و وحدتهم the Eid of recognizing the Arabs' independence and unity. And I announce this to the Arab nation, to those who live

Chapter Four: Al-Husain as King

in the cities and those in the deserts." Then the head of the Hashemite Diwan delivered a statement in which he said, "The British government recognizes the Arabs' independence and pledges to actually support the establishment of the comprehensive general unity for all Arab lands with the exception of Aden." Then the statement was concluded by saying: "We, therefore, order that this day must be declared as the Eid of the Recognition of the Independence of the Arab Nation, and surely Allāh is the One Who grants success." After that, al-Aseel delivered a speech in which he pointed out to the start of the great coup in the life of the Arab nation which was undertaken by al-Husain who smashed by it the series of old chains, and now independence and unity had come. So, the Arab nation is indebted to you, Master." Then al-Aseel pointed to himself and how he carried out the duty of the homeland when he responded to the call, leaving the Turkish army and joining the Arab army in order to take part in defending "the independence of my Arab lands in the great battle...", according to him.

Only few days passed since then when it became clear to people that that elation was based on a whim. On June 5, the government of Palestine published in the Jerusalem newspapers a summary of the treaty, and it was clear from what was published that Britain did not abandon the policy of setting up a national homeland for the Jews in Palestine. This caused the Arabs in it to explode in outrage. Mousa Kadhim al-Husaini sent a telegram to al-Husain drawing his attention to the above. Al-Husain answered him saying, "Master, I assure you that our basic resolve, which we hope Allāh's power will support, that we do not lag behind our obligation the distance of one hair. Be informed that it is a movement on which we live and for which we die. The facts, as I have stated, will reach you later. So, rest assured that neither relaxation nor laziness will affect us along the path of achieving this honorable goal whereby we want to serve our countries, sons and brothers."[1]

On September 27, the *Qibla* newspaper [in Jerusalem] published a report in which it said, "His Majesty King al-Husain has refused to ratify the treaty despite threats, and despite all the obstacles and blocks placed in his way. Also, His Majesty is keen about the rights of the Arabs and the safeguarding of their homelands."

Naji al-Aseel returned to London and kept trying to get a treaty that would please al-Husain and Britain at the same time. It was like seeking the impossible. The British consul in Jidda wrote a secret report to his government in which he said, "I do not think that Dr. Naji can be proven innocent of being a very bad servant of the government of Hijaz. It seems he has exerted a great effort for the growth of al-Husain's greatness complex in the beginning... Naji urged al-Husain not to sign the treaty, and to remain firm in his position until he won what he wanted and that he would be ruling all Arab lands and everything. These assurances by Naji may have resulted from his conceit, but cunning alone is what made him tell al-Husain that the British foreign ministry emphasized to him that the Balfour Declaration did not mean a thing and that it would soon be cancelled. This is what led to the famous announcement in Mecca in the spring of 1923. Since then, Naji has kept trying to maintain his post by holding on to hopes from time to time about the treaty being signed."[2]

Meanwhile, Ja`far al-`Askari reached London coming from Iraq on an official mission accompanied by Tawfiq al-Suweedi. They both met Aseel and an argument between al-Suweedi and al-Aseel spurred a personal altercation. Al-Suweedi says in his *Memoirs*, "Al-Aseel used to enjoy in London a position that ensured for him everything anyone of means would spend, for

---

1 Ameen Sa`eed (Op. Cit.), Vol. 3, p. 170.
2 Public Records Office in London No. FO 371/10808.

he was receiving no less than six hundred pounds per month, and he used to demonstrate towards us an attitude of superimposition and affectation in his dealings and movements. He demonstrated arrogance even in his treatment of Ja`far al-`Askari who was his commander in the Arab Revolution's army, for he used to be introduced in the protocols as having a status higher than that of Ja`far al-`Askari in his capacity as representing King Husain, while al-`Askari represented his [King Husain's] son, Faisal." Al-Suweedi stated that al-Aseel was prompted by a feeling that made him believe that he could achieve the objectives of the Arab cause. He used to fully represent the enthusiasm of King Husain in the extra efforts he exerted to get the British government to carry out its usual promises. Al-Suweedi narrates that he was talking once at the table in the presence of al-Aseel and Ja`far al-`Askari, so he mentioned King Husain to whom he referred as "Sharif Husain," whereupon al-Aseel was angry because of this label and kept reprimanding al-Suweedi for it. Al-Suweedi, therefore, responded by saying something the gist of which is that the title "Sharif" is greater and a better source of pride than that of "king". Then al-Suweedi seized the opportunity to criticize al-Aseel for his arrogance saying to him, "I fear for Dr. al-Aseel slipping, and I do not feel comfortable about his future because I know that King Husain has for so long been enthusiastic in his demands, for he sends him as his deputy to facilitate his objective. But this objective, unfortunately, is difficult to achieve, and King Husain will feel tired of demanding just as he will feel fed-up of paying the continuous huge expenses to the doctor at present and will cut them off. The doctor will remain spending what he has until he is afflicted by want, so he will be forced to sever the relationship with King Husain and return to Iraq. And when he reaches it, he will ask for a government job the salary of which will not exceed 25 dinars; thus the doctor's mission will end, and there will be no trace for this arrogance."[1]

---

[1] Tawfiq al-Suweedi, *Muthakkarati* (my Memoirs), Beirut: 1969, pp. 87-89.

Al-Husain and Sons

Al-Husain's sons differed from their father in opinion and political conduct, and they were becoming fed-up with him, but they had to show obedience and respect to him. On his part, he [their father] used to grumble about them and complain about their disobedience time and over again.

Faisal differed from his father more than his brothers. He believed that politics is the art of what is possible; therefore, the British followed in Iraq the principle of "take and demand," whereas his father was the opposite, following the principle of "everything or nothing!" For this reason, he used to demand the British carry out all their promises to him and declared that he would not forfeit them in as much as one hair.

Al-Husain was angry with Faisal when he received the oath of fealty as King in Syria in 1920. Al-Husain regarded that as a betrayal and disobedience by Faisal because Syria is an indivisible part of the Great Arab Kingdom whose king is al-Husain and nobody else. When Faisal was kicked out of Syria, al-Husain said, "This is the reward of one who does not listen to me. Had Syria remained part of Hijaz, the French would not have dared to occupy it." It is worth mentioning that al-Husain did the same to his other son, Abdullah, when this rule of Trans-Jordan was subjected to the British mandate and it was separated administratively from Hijaz.

Muhammed Naseef, senior noblemen of Jidda, narrates saying that he was among those who bade Faisal farewell when the latter boarded the ship heading to Iraq in 1921. He said to Faisal, "We hope to see you close to us in the next pilgrimage season." Faisal responded, "No, I shall not return to Hijaz as long as my father is there." Then Faisal retracted saying, "He has wronged us and made our position critical, becoming the enemy of our friends, leaving us no friend. Even you yourself—meaning Muhammed Naseef—who used to be our sincerest friend, and you supported us and stood by our side in all situations, he was hostile to you and he fought you. No, No, I will not return to Hijaz as long as he is alive."

Muhammed Naseef also narrates saying that Prince Zaid agreed with both his brothers, Faisal and Abdullah, to depose their father and to seat his oldest son, Prince Ali, in his place, but Prince Ali did not agree with them. Ali said, "People do not know the facts; so, if we revolt against him and remove him from the throne, they will tell us that we plotted against him and deposed him so we would replace him before our time comes. We have to respect his old age and status and not mistreat him in his last days. We must be patient with him and bear the results of his actions no matter what they may be, for this is more suitable for us in the public's eyes."[1]

Sulayman Mousa narrates saying that he met Prince Zaid in London in 1968. Many talks went on between them, including what Zaid had said about his father, al-Husain. Describing his father, Zaid said, "Al-Husain is very rigid in his opinions. He is never an easy, lenient man. But he was, without doubt, a man of principle and faith. It is not true that I urged al-Husain to accept the treaty which Britain offered through Lawrence because al-Husain never listened to anyone, nor did he hear anyone, nor did he prefer anyone over himself."[2]

Al-Husain In Trans-Jordan

In early December of 1923, al-Husain announced his intention to visit Trans-Jordan without mentioning the reason. Rumors spread in Trans-Jordan that al-Husain was determined to unseat Abdullah from his post as the emir and install his oldest son, Ali, as his successor.[3]

---

1 Ameen Sa'eed, *Tarikh al-Dawla al-Saudia* (History of the Saudi State), Vol. 2, pp. 149-150.
2 Sulayman Mousa, *Muthakkarat al-Ameer Zaid* (Memoirs of Prince Zaid), Amman: 1976, p. 201.
3 Khairi Hammad (Op. Cit.), p. 139.

Story of the Sharifs and Ibn Saud

On January 9, 1924, al-Husain reached Aqaba, and there were no cannons in it to salute him, so he instructed the ship that carried him to fire its cannons to salute him. British author Jarvis comments about that saying, "Al-Husain followed the Japanese principle which makes man shake hands with his own self."[1]

A large crowd of the country's notables was at Aqaba to welcome al-Husain. Several cars were prepared for him and for his entourage to transport them to the Maan railroad station, but al-Husain refused to ride in cars. Rather, he rode a mule which he had brought with him on board the ship.[2] Those who welcomed him and all the entourage had to emulate him, whereupon animals of all types that could be found in Aqaba were brought to them: camels, horses and mules. It was noticed that some people were not used to riding animals, so they became as a result in a pathetic condition. As for al-Husain, despite his age, which exceeded seventy, was firm and strong on the back of the mule. He crossed the distance between the Aqaba and al-Quwayra—more than thirty-five miles—without turning right or left or showing any sign of exhaustion.[3]

Philby was then Britain's attaché in Trans-Jordan, and he was among those who welcomed al-Husain. He says in his *Memoirs* that when he arrived with the welcoming party to al-Quwayra, al-Husain summoned him to his tent and kept talking to him with full sweetness and gentleness. Then he said to him, "Listen! There is no dispute between me and Ibn Saud. Are we not Arabs? I consider him as one of my sons, and you are his friend and mine. You can be my messenger to him. I accept any settlement that pleases you." Philby comments on this statement expressing his amazement at the new attitude which he noticed in al-Husain compared to what it used to be before. Philby rendered this change to al-Husain perhaps shifting his grudge

---

1 Jarvis, *Arab Command*, London: 1942, p. 110.
2 Khairi Hammad (Op. Cit.), p. 140.
3 Jarvis (Op. Cit.), p. 110.

Chapter Four: Al-Husain as King

from Ibn Saud to his own sons who betrayed him and his cause, especially Faisal[1]. I think that Philby erred in his rendering. What is believed is that al-Husain did not direct his grudge towards his sons as much as he directed it towards the British who, according to his belief, did not fulfill their promises to him.

The welcome al-Husain received in Amman was great and magnificent. Delegations from Syria, Palestine and various Bedouin tribes participated in it. It was also attended by journalists from Egypt, Jerusalem, Beirut and Damascus. When al-Husain looked at them from the train's window, shouts rose saying, "Long live the King of the Arabs! Long live the Greatest Savior!" Bedouin horsemen kept making rounds on their steed and singing martial chants. School children shouted slogans and chants. The British planes were then clouding the sky, participating in the welcome.

A house was prepared for al-Husain facing the Roman Stadium, so al-Husain looked at the crowds welcoming him from the house's balcony. Speakers and poets kept reciting their poems, greeting the supreme savior and champion of the Arab renaissance, cursing colonialism and colonialists, threatening Britain and France. Delegates came after that to shake hands with al-Husain. He, therefore, spoke to them saying that he did not give up a single principle of those that are the corners of the renaissance. "I do not forfeit a single right of the land. I do not accept anything other than Palestine always remaining for its Arab people. I say: 'for its Arab people'. If the British government refuses to amend [the teaty] as I demand, I shall reject it in its entirety. I say: full independence for all Arab countries. There is no difference to me if the center of the Arab government is in Hijaz, Syria, Iraq or Najd."[2]

Al-Husain stayed in Trans-Jordan for about two months and a half. It was noticed that during that period, he was behaving as

---

1 Khairi Hammad (Op. Cit.), p. 140.
2 Ameen al-Rayhani (Op. Cit.), pp. 324-325.

if he was the king of the land. Jarvis says, "Al-Husain was during his stay in Trans-Jordan behaving as if he was the one to issue orders in the land, while Prince Abdullah was occupying the back seat. This caused embarrassment to the British officials who expected Prince Abdullah to be the actual ruler of the land, not to be the deputy of his father in ruling it. They also expected al-Husain to be a guest of honor in the land, not one who issued orders in it. These officials could not bring this to al-Husain's attention but put up with it grudgingly..."[1]

The general secretary of Palestine's government, Sir Gilbert Clayton, came to visit al-Husain in Amman. After his return to Jerusalem, he wrote a report to his government in London saying, "Al-Husain repeated his usual statements about the tough situation in which he finds himself before the Muslims in general, first because of his alliance with Britain and, second, due to Britain not fulfilling its promises to him." Then Clayton added saying that he understood from his talks with al-Husain that the difficulty he was complaining about was relevant to Palestine. Al-Husain assured him that he was fully ready to assist the British government in any possible way, but he could not place himself in a situation that would expose him to the Muslims' criticism. Clayton concluded his report suggesting the dropping of one article from the treaty: the article relevant to Britain's policy in Palestine because al-Husain's acceptance of this policy would subject him to sharp criticism and destroy his influence among the Arabs of Palestine who would immediately abandon him and declare that he abandoned their cause.[2]

Al-Husain As Caliph

On May 1, Mustafa Kamal Pasha announced the abolishing of caliphate in Turkey when al-Husain was still residing in Amman, so his son, Abdullah, kept urging his father to seize the

---

1 Jarvis (Op. Cit.), p. 111.
2 Sulayman Mousa, *Safahat Matwiyya* (Folded Pages), pp. 171-172.

Chapter Four: Al-Husain as King

opportunity and declare the caliphate for himself. German historian [Hans] von Mikosch says, "When Ankara announced its renouncement of the [Ottoman] caliphate, Prince Abdullah was overwhelmed by the thought of seizing that event to gain glory for the Hashemite family and to raise its status. He is the one who is carried out with his ambition much further than the borders of the small emirate of Trans-Jordan where he has no say, and aims at ascending the peak of glory one step after another. He kept trying to convince his father to seize the opportunity, using the means of enticement which he had used to convince him to declare the revolution against the Ottomans, urging al-Husain to declare himself caliph of the Muslims."

Von Mikosch says, "Al-Husain hesitated to accept the view of his son, Abdullah, because the repeated disappointments with which he was afflicted at the hands of the British made him confused, having weak self-confidence, and an unknown feeling might have controlled him that a step of this sort could lead to a catastrophe. But Abdullah kept insisting on him, reminding him that the British, during his first negotiations with them shortly before the declaration of the revolution, demonstrated evidence that they welcomed his being a caliph over the Muslims."[1]

Al-Husain finally accepted Abdullah's view, so it was decided that the oath of allegiance for the caliphate should take place on May 5 in the Shona village near Amman which was used by Prince Abdullah as his winter resort. Delegations from Syria, Lebanon, Palestine and Trans-Jordan went to that village in order to swear the oath of allegiance. Also, some Egyptians came. Prince Abdullah stood to swear the oath of allegiance to his father followed by Ameen al-Husaini in the name of Palestine then the other delegates. After completing the fealty ceremony, al-Husain delivered a lengthy speech in which he said that before the fealty for the caliphate, he was keen about upholding the

---

1   Salah ad-Din al-Mukhtar, *Tarikh al-Arabiyya al-Saudia* (History of Saudi Arabia), Beirut, Vol. 2, pp. 268-269.

religious rituals, safeguarding the clear Shari`a according to those who tie and untie from among the theologians in both sacred Harams and the Aqsa Mosque as well as in countries that neighbor them."[1]

Telegrams kept reaching al-Husain from various Islamic countries to congratulate him and to swear the oath of allegiance to him. We do not need to say that Iraq was a country which was one of the most, if not the very most, interested in al-Husain's caliphate and in swearing the oath of allegiance to him. Iraqi newspapers kept publishing the telegrams that kept reaching them from various cities of Iraq and the tribes unanimously declaring their allegiance to al-Husain. Members of the founding council met at the royal mansion and submitted their allegiance to al-Husain ibn Ali before King Faisal. Ahmed al-Sheikh Dawud rose and delivered a speech which contained a supplication for "our *mawla* [master] the greatest caliph". On Friday, May 14, 1924, King Faisal performed the Friday prayer service at the Sarai Mosque. The sermon in it was recited in the name of "caliph al-Husain ibn Ali". The *Al-Iraq* newspaper published a report under the heading "The caliphate of King Husain: Ja`faris swear the oath of allegiance to His Majesty". It said in it, "Ja`fari ulema (theologians) rushed to swear the oath of allegiance to al-Husain although they had in the past refused to swear it to the sultan from among the Al Othman because they found the required conditions for caliphate present in him, for he is an Arab from Quraish, an Imamite Alawide." The newspaper also published a telegram it received from Abdul-Razzaq al-Wahhab in Kerbala saying, "Three hundred thousand pilgrims at the Shrine of [Imam] al-Husain who came to perform the *ziyara* on the occasion of the Middle of Sha`ban swear the oath of allegiance to al-Husain as the caliph." The newspaper also published a telegram sent to al-Husain by Sayyid Hibat ad-Din al-Shahristani, head of the Ja`fari Appeals Council. This is its text: "To the

---

[1] Ameen Sa`eed, *Asrar al-thawra al-Arabiyya al-Kubra* (Secrets of the Great Arab Revolution), Beirut, pp. 358-359.

thresholds of His Hashemite Majesty, King Husain, the greatest savior, may our souls be sacrificed for him. I am honored to kiss his pure hand, recognizing the greatest Islamic caliphate for that Hashemite Fatimide imam in his good resolve to unite those who believe that Allāh is One, and the magnification of the religious rituals and the protection of the Muslims' *hawza* (religious seminary), may Allāh Almighty grant them victory under his flag, Aameen."[1]

Al-Husain returned to Mecca which he reached on May 30. Decorations had already been put in place for him everywhere. The *Qibla* newspaper kept publishing the telegrams which reached it from various world areas congratulating al-Husain for the caliphate. British author Howarth comments saying, "We do not know which of those telegrams was genuine because al-Husain himself edited the newspaper."[2]

---

1 Refer to *Al-Iraq* newspaper of 10, 12, 15, 18 and 20 May of 1924.
2 David Howarth, *The Desert King: A Life of Ibn Saud*, London: 1964, p. 141.

Chapter Five
Abdul-Aziz ibn Saud

Abdul-Aziz ibn Saud

Unluckily for al-Husain and his family, a man from among his opponents rose to be regarded as one of the most shrewd and tyrannical men in history, namely Abdul-Aziz ibn Saud. Had this man never risen [to power], the contemporary history of the Arabian Peninsula would have been different from what we know it, and al-Husain and his family could have kept ruling Hijaz until our time.

We will try in this chapter to study the biography of this man since the start of his life up to his conquest of Mecca, and we will continue studying his life's story in another chapter.

Early Life

He is Abdul-Aziz ibn Abdul-Rahman ibn Faisal ibn Turki from the famous Al Saud family. He was born in Riyadh in early 1877[1]. When he was a lad, he resorted with his father and younger brother, Muhammed, as well as cousin, Jalwi, to the Banu Murra tribe, a Bedouin tribe deeply rooted in the Bedouin traditions and living on the edge of the Empty Quarter. Ibn Saud grew up in that rough Bedouin environment and learned its values and social culture.[2]

Abdul-Rahman, Ibn Saud's father, was a very religious man, and life among the Banu Murrah did not appeal to him because he found them lenient in their religion and impure, so he left them and resorted to Kuwait with his family. This took place late

---

1 Khair ad-Din al-Zurakli, *Shibh al-Jazera fi Ahd al-Malik Abdul-Aziz* (the Peninsula during the time of Abdul-Aziz), Beirut: 1977, p. 58.
2 H.C. Armstrong, *Lord of Arabia: A Biography of Abdul-Aziz ibn Saud*, London: 1938, pp. 32-33.

in 1892. They lived in a small house in the vicinity of the sea port comprised of one story and having three rooms.

The Ottoman government had set aside for Abdul-Rahman a monthly salary of sixty liras because it hoped to benefit from him one day. This amount had a good purchasing power, but the problem is that it was not paid regularly, as was the habit of the Ottoman state. Abdul-Rahman suffered as a result a great deal of hardship and had sometimes to borrow from friends and shop owners.

The child, Abdul-Aziz ibn Abdul-Rahman, used to play in his early life in Kuwait with his peers in the alleys, as is the case with children in poor quarters. He was noticed during that period that he distinguished himself from his peers through a strong personality and a tendency to lead. Hafiz Wahba quotes some elderly folks from among the people of Kuwait, who were companions of Abdul-Aziz during his childhood, as saying that he surpassed his fellow children in energy and intelligence. He used to be their leader in games. He was also noticed to enjoy listening to what the elderly used to talk about: the glory of his grandfather, Faisal ibn Turki, and his adventures in order to restore the glory of his family.[1]

Armstrong narrates saying that when Ibn Saud was young, he used to brag before his peers that he was the heir to the state of Riyadh and Najd, and that one day he would kick Ibn Rasheed out of it and restore the glory of his ancestors. His peers used to laugh at him and make fun of him, and he used to feel angry with them. Despite that, he never lost his self-confidence.[2]

Late in 1901, Ibn Saud decided to undertake a dangerous adventure in the hope he would thereby restore the glory of his family or die trying. He came out of Kuwait accompanied by forty horsemen from among his relatives and supporters and

---

1 Hafiz Wahba, *Khamsoon Aman fi Jazeerat al-Arab* (Fifty Years in the Arabian Peninsula), Cairo: 1960, p. 27.
2 H.C. Armstrong (Op. Cit.), p. 40.

Chapter Five: Abdul-Aziz ibn Saud

about twenty followers. He took them towards Riyadh in order to extract it from the rule of Ibn Rasheed, the prince of Hail. On January 15, 1902, he was able in a skillful blow to occupy Riyadh. This was the start of the rise of the star of this ambitious youth.

British researcher [Gary] Troeller says, "The story of Ibn Saud occupying Riyadh became a myth in the Bedouin popular heritage, for Ibn Saud proved through it that he had the characteristics that qualified him to be the sheikh [tribal chief] which were: courage, leadership and luck. We must indicate that the daring expressed by Ibn Saud in that adventure appealed to the imagination of the residents of the central region of the Arabian Peninsula..."[1]

Ibn Saud's victories followed one another after that adventure, and so did his defeats. But the defeats did not weaken his resolve, and perhaps they increased his determination and will whenever a defeat afflicted him, and this merit is owned by only very few humans.

Success Factors

There are factors that helped Ibn Saud succeed. We would like to mention the most important of them as follows:

FIRST: He had an instinctive shrewdness that realized that politics is the art of what is possible. It is said that he received practical lessons in politics from Mubarak Al Sabah, the famous sheikh of Kuwait. It is known that Mubarak used to love Ibn Saud and to let him attend his meetings and conferences. Armstrong says that Mubarak taught Ibn Saud a great deal about the art of government, and Ibn Saud learned from him quickly and readily. Whenever he attended Mubarak's meetings and conferences, he used to sit in a corner, folding his legs and

---

1 [Gary] Troeller, *The Birth of Saudi Arabia: Britain and the Rise of the House of Sa'ud*, London: 1976, p. 21.

carrying in his hand an amber rosary beads, listening to what was said and learning from it.[1]

SECOND: Ibn Saud attracted to himself some advisors from various Arab countries in order to become acquainted with their method in the complexities of international politics. But he did not accept everything the advisors said. Rather, he would listen to each of them and compare their statements, then he would issue his final judgment after some contemplation. It was noticed that he did not like his advisors to support everything he said; rather, he wanted them to be honest in expressing their opinions.[2] Ibn Saud differs in this regard from some rulers who are accustomed to bringing flatterers and interest seekers closer to them, so the fact of life are lost to them.

THIRD: Ibn Saud was quite generous, spending the money at his disposal on aides and those whose hearts he wanted to attract. He followed in this regard the Bedouin principle that says, "Spend of what is in the hand, what is in the morrow will come to you." In this regard, he was the opposite of his opponent, al-Husain, who followed the urban principle that says, "The white money benefits on the black day." Al-Husain's motto was that money corrupts men,[3] whereas Ibn Saud's motto was, "Money brings men." Actually, the second motto brings more success in this life than the first.

FOUR: Ibn Saud used to have a psychological gift that enabled him to bear an impact on whoever met him and on attracting him. It is the gift that is called by the science of sociology "charisma". Describing Ibn Saud, Troeller says, "Most historians have agreed that he has charisma: He is tall, broad of shoulder, handsome, representing the Arab manliness, and he has magnetism which many of those who met him noticed..."[4]

---

1 Armstrong (Op. Cit.), pp. 40-41.
2 Hafiz Wahba (Op. Cit.), p. 48.
3 Ameen al-Rayhani (Op. Cit.), p. 48.
4 Troeller (Op. Cit.), p. 21.

Chapter Five: Abdul-Aziz ibn Saud

FIFTH: It can be said that Ibn Saud had what the commoners call "luck". It is worth mentioning that the subject of "luck" is an intricate topic; there is no room to talk about it here. Suffices to say that modern para-psychological researches have started discovering the existence of other hidden forces within some individuals with which they can control opportunities and direct them towards their interests a little or a lot. Science does not know the essence of these forces, but it has discovered some of their manifestations and effects. Who knows, perhaps science will in the future discover their essence.[1]

Whatever the case may be, we can place Ibn Saud on the list of those who have a good measure of those forces. Khair ad-Din al-Zurakli sets aside a chapter in his book about Ibn Saud in which he mentions the events that prove the existence of the "luck" gift in him, and he calls it "fitting success (granted by the Almighty)".[2]

The Rise of the *Ikhwan*

Ibn Saud's army was first comprised of mostly Bedouins, and he knew that the Bedouins did not have a sizeable military value because they like to invade and loot, and they, therefore, would join any new movement when they expect it to have booty. They would soon abandon it when they saw a glimpse of its breakup. Hafiz Wahba says, "If a Bedouin does not find an authority that deters or disciplines him, he justifies looting anyone who goes or comes; right to him is might: He submits to it and brings others to submission through it..."[3]

---

1 Look into the subject of the science of para-psychology in Volume 5, Ch. 2, footote 4 of the author's book لمحات اجتماعية من تاريخ العراق الحديث (*Social Glimpses of Iraq's Modern History*). [The translation of this title, as published by Alwarrak Publishing, Ltd., has been provided as "Social Aspects of Iraqi Modern History" which I, as a translator, think is imprecise. – Tr.]
2 Khair ad-Din al-Zurakli (Op. Cit.), Vol. 2, pp. 581-585.
3 Hafiz Wahba, *Jazeerat al-Arab fil Qarn al-Ishreen* (The Arabian Peninsula in the Twentieth Century), Cairo: 1967, p. 10.

Ibn Saud pondered for a good while on finding a solution for this problem. He wanted soldiers who would obey him during good and bad times so that he could build his anticipated state and restore the glory of his ancestry. His mind finally produced a solution derived from the history of Islam which used to be called *hijra*, migration. During the time of the Prophet, the Muslims were two groups: Bedouins (desert Arabs) and migrants. What was meant by the Bedouins are the ones the Qur'an holds in contempt and describes as **"the worst in unbelief and hypocrisy and the most fitted to be in ignorance of the command which Allāh has sent down to His Messenger"** (Qur'an, 9:97). **Therefore, if one wanted to be a true Muslim, he had to abandon living as a Bedouin and join the group of the migrants in Medina. The Muslims were used to look askance at the Muslim individual who returned to the desert after having accepted Islam, a look having a great deal of denunciation.** They would describe him as having تَعَرَّبَ i.e. becoming a Bedouin and going back on his heels. Actually, the *hijra* had its impact in changing the personality of a Bedouin a little or a lot: When a Bedouin joined the new environment which Islam created in Medina, he found himself obligated to abandon his old values and adopt the new ones which Islam brought.

Ibn Saud encouraged the establishment of fixed villages in Najd so the Bedouins would "migrate" to them and settle. He labeled those villages الهَجَرْ *al-hajar*. The first such *hajar* that came into existence was in 1911 in an area called Artawiyya أرطاوية located mid-way on the highway between Kuwait and Qaseem. This was followed by the gradual appearance of other *hajars* until their number became, eighteen years later, 122 and the number of their men reached 76,500.

Ibn Saud sent to the *hajars* the مُطَوَّعِين *mutawwa'een*, preachers, supplying them with the materials and funds they needed so their villages would have successful agriculture. A new life prevailed on the *hajars* which the Bedouins never had before, for they sold their camels and used agriculture and trade as their professions. They also abandoned living in tents and resided in houses built of clay. They put on the white turban instead of the *iqal* headband and called themselves the *ikhwan*, brethren, since the believers are brethren, dedicating their time to prayer, worship and the study of the biography of the Prophet. Each *hajar* had a mosque in its midst, and the mosque was crowded with worshippers and students most of the time.

The *ikhwan* wanted to be like the early Muslims in everything, and this had to lead them to extremism in the absence of a wise leader among them like [Prophet] Muhammed 7 to bring them back to the moderation track. Hafiz Wahba provides us with an image of some manifestations of extremism which spread among them saying, "These folks have become immersed to a great deal in deficient principles and teachings, so much so that they believe they know the true religion while anything else is misguidance... Many of them believed that anyone who did not live in the *hajars* was not a Muslim no matter what kind of Islam he knew and practiced, how he abandoned the ills and habits of the desert. They do not start others with the peace greeting, nor do they respond to the greeting, nor do they eat the meat of these "others". The fault of these latter folks is that they do not live in the *hajars*. One of the customs of the *ikhwan*, when visitors went to meet with them, is that they would stand in the mosque and say: '*Assalamo Alaikom*, brothers. Our brothers, the *ikhwan*, send you their greeting. They used to believe that city dwellers are misguided, that invading neighbors is obligatory, that it was mandated on them by Allāh, and they do not listen to anyone who prevents them from invading...' up to such types of ignorance. They kept labeling as *haram* (prohibitive) anything which did not agree with their likes. The flow of this rebellious spirit is due to these semi-educated ignorant folks spreading it throughout the *ikhwan* villages in the name of knowledge, dictating these teachings to them and making contemptible fanaticism look good to them."[1]

The *ikhwan* became used to regarding life in the desert as being that of *jahiliyya* [pre-Islamic period of ignorance] itself, believing that true Islam meant getting rid of anyone who had in him the smell of the *jahiliyya* and holding on to the Sunnah of the Prophet and his companions. The *iqal*, for example, became in their view one of the contemptible innovations بِدَع. Some of them went to extremes, in its regard, such as the clothes of the "unbelievers," and this necessitated boycotting whoever put them on. They regarded the Sunnah to be wearing the white turban instead of the *iqal*. They used to address the man who maintained his Bedouin appearances thus: "You are a polytheist Bedouin… You, the one who wears the *iqal*, is one of the unbelievers, and I am the brother of whoever obeys Allāh, while you are the brother of whoever obeys Satan."[2] They regarded the long moustache and the long robe as being contrary to the Sunnah, and some of them carried the scissors with them; so, if they found a man whose moustache or robe was long, they would cut it with the scissors.[3]

We must not forget that this extremism that accompanied the movement of the *ikhwan*, despite its negative aspects, had one positive thing: It created of the *ikhwan* commando soldiers who would throw themselves at death feeling confident that they were going to Paradise. Hafiz Wahba says, "The *ikhwan* became fearless of death and would dart towards it seeking martyrdom and the reunion with Allāh. When a mother bade her son farewell, she would do so using these words, 'May Allāh bring us all together in Paradise.' The call that encouraged people to go to war became: هَبَّت هُبوب الجَنَّة، وين انتَ يا باغيها!؟ "The winds of Paradise have blown; where are you, O one who seeks it?!" And

---

1 Hafiz Wahba (Op. Cit.), p. 290.
2 Ameen al-Rayhani (Op. Cit.), p. 265.
3 Hafiz Wahba (Op. Cit.), pp. 292-293.

their words when they attacked became: إِيَّاكَ نَعْبُدُ وَإِيَّاكَ نَسْتَعِينُ "**You do we worship, and Your aid do we seek**" (Qur'an, 1:5). I saw some of their military battlefields and found them throwing themselves at death and advancing towards their enemies in one row, none of them thinking of anything other than defeating the enemy and killing him. The *ikhwan*, generally speaking, have hearts that do not know mercy towards the enemies, nor does anyone escape their grip, for they are the messengers of death wherever they go."[1]

Hafiz Wahba narrates the story of a man from the *ikhwan* who went to a sheikh, theologian, to ask him about hypocrisy and fear during wartime. He kept complaining to him that there was hypocrisy in his heart. He said to him, "When I attack, I find some hesitation inside me because of the sound of bullets, so hypocrisy has to be within me. Please get hypocrisy out of me with your stick, brother." The sheikh said to him, "This is not due to hypocrisy or to flight from the assault, and I understand it. If you do not turn your back to the enemy [retreat], this is not called hypocrisy or flight." The man said, "No, by the will of Allāh, I shall never turn my back to the enemy; doing so would be apostasy, sheikh!"

Hafiz Wahba narrates another story: A man from among the *ikhwan* found a bundle of gold money after a military war which the *ikhwan* fought, so he brought it to a religious sheikh and asked him if it was permissible for him to keep it. The sheikh said, "It is from the booty, and nothing is permissible for you of it except whatever you get after the distribution is made." The man, therefore, rushed to the person in charge of the booty. He delivered it to him saying, "No, by Allāh, I do not deserve it!"[2]

This sacrificial spirit which seized the *ikhwan* turned them into a major military force in the hands of Ibn Saud who started threatening the neighboring countries with it. Starting from the

---

1 *Ibid.*, p. 291.
2 *Ibid.*, p. 292.

year 1919, the *ikhwan* kept raiding Kuwait, Iraq, Jordan and Hijaz, causing terror in these countries. We have already witnessed an example of their deeds in the Turba incident.

Conducive Opportunity

After the strength of the *ikhwan*'s force had grown, Ibn Saud became ambitious to invade Hijaz, for the Al Saud had conquered Hijaz in their first movement, and he wanted to follow in their footsteps, but he feared the British might prevent him from doing so, and he did not like to collide with the British at any rate.

Ibn Saud kept waiting for the opportunity to make his move towards Hijaz. The opportunity finally came on May 5, 1924 when al-Husain declared himself caliph in Amman. This declaration caused some Islamic circles in India, Egypt and elsewhere to be angry. Moreover, on the 30th of the month, the British cut off the financial aid which they used to pay Ibn Saud, so this was an additional factor that made Ibn Saud determined to invade Hijaz. Researcher Troeller says, "Two incidents took place in the month of May of 1924 that had undoubtedly had their strong impact on prompting Ibn Saud to attack Hijaz: The first was al-Husain assuming the caliphate on the 5th of the month, and the second was Britain cutting off on the 30th of the same month the financial aid it used to pay Ibn Saud. Ibn Saud felt, as a result, that he would not lose much if Britain was angry with him, and he had no strong deterrent to release his enthused followers on Hijaz."[1]

Hafiz Wahba has pointed out to the same in his *Memoirs*. He says, "The circumstances were at the time suitable to release the swords of Islam—meaning the *ikhwan*—on Hijaz: Al-Husain's declaration of the caliphate angered most of the Islamic world. Also, al-Husain's stance vis-à-vis Palestine angered the British,

---

1 Troeller (Op. Cit.), p. 216.

so al-Husain had nobody to rely on except dreams which the days did not help materialize." Hafiz Wahba adds, "Ibn Saud was apprehensive about invading al-Hijaz because he did not forget Britain's warning to him in 1919 following the Turba incident." But Hafiz explained to him that the circumstances differed from those during the days of Turba, mentioning to him how al-Husain was during the Turba days an obedient ally of Britain, as for now, he became an opponent of it. He kept stressing to him that it was a precious opportunity which should be seized, saying that an opportunity was not gifted by time save once.[1]

Invasion Postponed

At the time when Ibn Saud decided to invade Hijaz, he was afflicted by a strange ailment that caused him to delay the invasion for some time.

The ailment started with a swelling in the face after a night which Ibn Saud spent with one of his [many] wives. She was a woman from Shammar tribe, from the Al al-Rasheed. The swelling kept intensifying, poisoning his body and raising his body temperature to a dangerous level.[2] Rumors spread that he died, but the sickness gradually disappeared as time passed by.

It is worth mentioning in this regard that Abdul-Rahman, father of Ibn Saud, believed that that ailment resulted from the incense used by his son that night, accusing the Shammari wife of having mixed poison with the incense in order to seek revenge for her people. He ordered his son to divorce her, so Ibn Saud divorced her instantly in obedience to his father's order despite his belief that she was innocent. It is narrated about Ibn Saud that he said the following about divorcing that wife: "I divorced her as she was crying and I, too, was crying because I was sure the swelling resulted accidentally and that she was innocent of

---

1 Hafiz Wahba, *Khamssona Aman fi Jazeerat al-Arab* (Fifty Years in the Arabian Peninsula), pp. 55-56.
2 Armstrong (Op. Cit.), p. 159.

any ill intention or purpose. But in order to obey my father did I divorce her." Ibn Saud kept visiting that woman because he used to love and respect her a great deal.[1]

What is strange is that four months after that sickness, signs of conjunctivitis started appearing on his left eye. It is believed that it was conjunctivitis pus, so witch doctors were brought but could not do anything for him, and conjunctivitis started intensifying. A white spot appeared on his eye which caused him to lose vision in it, so a Syrian doctor was brought who was able to lighten the eye inflammation, but the white spot remained there. In January of 1936, when the conquest of Hijaz was completed for Ibn Saud, some well known eye doctors were brought for him from Egypt, including Salim al-Hindawi and Jalal Abu al-Saud. They conducted a surgery through which they were able to restore some vision to his affected eye by making a small opening in the cornea through which light could penetrate. As for the spot, they could not remove it.

The Riyadh Conference

When Ibn Saud felt that his health enabled him to invade Hijaz, he issued instructions to hold a conference in Riyadh to be attended by theologians and leaders of the *ikhwan* for deliberations in this regard. The conference was held on June 4, 1924 headed by Abdul-Rahman, father of Ibn Saud.

Abdul-Rahman inaugurated the conference, stating how al-Husain prevented the *ikhwan* from performing the pilgrimage, that he received many letters from the *ikhwan* who wanted to perform the pilgrimage, and that he sent those letters to his son, Abdul-Aziz, and "here is Abdul-Aziz before you, so ask him about what you want," he added. It was then that Ibn Saud stood up and said to those present that their letters reached him and that the matters were pawned by their timings, that everything

---

[1] Ameen al-Mumayyaz, *Al-Mamlaka al-Arabiyya al-Saudia Kama Araftuha* (the Kingdom of Saudi Arabia as I Knew it), Beirut: 1963, pp. 338-339.

had an end. Sultan Ibn Bajad, one of the strong leaders of the *ikhwan*, stood up and said in his Najdi accent, "O imam! We want to perform the pilgrimage and we do not want to be patient any more regarding abandoning one of the pillars of Islam while we are able to perform it. Mecca is not the property of anyone, and nobody has the right to prevent the Muslims or to keep the faithful from performing the pilgrimage obligation. We want to perform the pilgrimage, Abdul-Aziz, so if Sharif Husain prevents us, we will enter Mecca by force. And if you are of the view that our interest lies in postponing the pilgrimage this year, we have to invade Hijaz in order to rid the Haram House of the hands of the oppressors and mischief-makers."

Ibn Saud commented on this statement saying that the pilgrimage issue was to be settled by the scholars of religion, and "here are the scholars present, so let them speak," he added. One of them, Sheikh Saad ibn Ateeq, said that one of the origins of the Shari`a is looking at what benefits and what does not. If the pilgrimage leads to harm or wrongdoing, it must be postponed, and this matter is settled by those in charge of politics. And we want to ask them about it." It was then that Ibn Saud said the following:

"We do not wish to fight those who seek peace with us, nor do we hesitate from being the friends of those who befriend us. But the Sharif of Mecca has always, as you know, been planting the seeds of disunity among our tribes, and he is the one who inherited from his forefathers hatred towards us. Despite that, I have exerted what I could to solve the problems between us and Hijaz through good means. Whenever I drew closer to al-Husain, he distanced himself. And whenever I was lenient to him, he gave me the cold shoulder. Yes, by the Lord of the Ka`ba! I do not see in the development of matters anything that would nourish the hopes. Rather, I see the matters becoming harder and more confusing. It is not good to continue a plan that does not secure our rights and interests."

Abdul-Aziz hardly stopped speaking when everyone shouted, توكلنا على الله! الى الحجاز! الى الحجاز! "We rely on Allāh! To Hijaz! To Hijaz!"[1]

The Jordan Raid

Ibn Saud prepared two military columns: One of them, the main one, was directed to Hijaz and the other to Trans-Jordan. Apparently, the second column was intended to distract people from the movement of the first column.

The second column reached near Amman on August 14, 1924. In the morning of that day, as Colonel Beck, commander of the Jordanian forces, was making rounds on his horse near Amman, he was suddenly faced by a group of women coming towards him screaming: اخوان! اخوان! *Ikhwan! Ikhwan!* When he asked them about it, they told them that the *ikhwan* attacked Tanb village and slaughtered most of its residents and they were now heading towards Amman. The colonel rushed to the soldiers' barracks and ordered them to get into their armored vehicles in order to fight the *ikhwan*. He also went to the headquarters of the air force to request preparing the planes to strafe them. Then Beck flew in a reconnaissance plane in order to oversee the battle from the air.

The *ikhwan* were taken by surprise as fires poured on them from the armored vehicles and planes at the same time, so they suffered very heavy losses and fled away randomly, leaving behind them five hundred killed and about six hundred captives many of whom were wounded.

Actually, it was not a battle but akin to a massacre. Some writers in Britain criticized this "excessive cruelty" in facing the *ikhwan*, describing it as having been more than it should. Maj. Jarvis responded to them saying, "This 'cruelty' was necessary to save the residents of Jordan from the fear which controlled

---

[1] Ameen al-Rayhani (Op. Cit.), pp. 326-327.

Chapter Five: Abdul-Aziz ibn Saud

them because in their raids, the *ikhwan* do not have mercy on even the women and children." Jarvis says, "When one faces a hostile bloodthirsty enemy, he must take into consideration how the enemy will treat him if it won victory over him."[1]

Prince Abdullah was meanwhile in Hijaz. He returned to Amman on August 19, that is, five days after the said massacre, so Col. Beck gave him four of the five flags which he had seized from the *ikhwan*, so the prince asked him about the fifth. Beck answered him that he took it to himself, being his share of the booty, thereupon the prince laughed and said, "Keep it! You deserve it!"[2]

Ibn Saud sent to Britain a protest against what its forces had done to the *ikhwan*. His pretext was that the Jordanian tribes were the ones who started the aggression. Britain responded to him with a telegram, which it sent through its consul in Bushahr [Iran], saying the following to the consul:

"You must tell Ibn Saud that the British government received his protest with full amazement. It regards itself as having the right to protest against what went on during the past month of August when a group of Wahhabi tribes carried out an armed raid on an area that falls under the British mandate. The British government is committed to repelling such an attack with all means at its disposal. Ibn Saud can be assured that the British government will face another similar raid in the same way it faced the first... He must clearly understand that the British government will not tolerate any attack on an area that falls under its responsibility. As regarding his complaint about the party that started the aggression, you must remind him of the letter sent in our telegram dated the first of this past month of August. Instead of demanding an investigation about the raid, which they claimed was launched against them from Trans-Jordan, the Wahhabis chose to take the law into their own hands.

---

1 C.S. Jarvis, *Arab Command*, London: 1924, pp. 115-118.
2 *Ibid*, p. 118.

They must blame only their own selves for an act of aggression which was ill directed and which led them to collide with the British forces..."[1]

The Taif Incident

When al-Husain came to know about the massacre that afflicted the *ikhwan* in Trans-Jordan, he saw it as a good omen. He did not know that Ibn Saud was making preparations for him and was about to attack him. Al-Husain was confident that if the *ikhwan* attacked him, they would suffer the same as they did in Trans-Jordan. Ameen al-Rayhani says, "Al-Husain was at the time in his mansion reclining on the caliphate pillow, feeling comfortable, confident of what the days were hiding for him, fabricating articles for his newspaper, *Al-Qibla*. He [al-Husain] says, 'We appreciate the good deeds of the government of Great Britain for the zeal it demonstrated in the Arab East—meaning Trans-Jordan—but we, nevertheless, do not forfeit any of our rights. Syria is part of the Arab lands, and Palestine belongs to the Arabs. We do not sign any treaty in this regard which contradicts this statement, rather, this right... Who is more knowledgeable of the Bedouins and of those who claim to follow the creed—meaning the *ikhwan*—that one bomb from a cannon would wipe them out and one plane would disperse them, and the evidence is in the Arab East?!"[2]

The *ikhwan* assembled in Turba, and their number reached three thousand. They were headed by Sharif Khalid ibn Luay and Sultan ibn Bajad. Late in August of 1924, they marched towards Taif, crossing the borders of Hijaz. On the first day of September, their vanguards reached the Hoya village, few miles from Taif. There, they were met by a regular force sent from Taif. A battle started between both groups which lasted several hours; the *ikhwan* won it.

---

1   Public Records Office in London No. FO 371/10013.
2   Ameen al-Rayhani (Op. Cit.), p. 330.

Chapter Five: Abdul-Aziz ibn Saud

The regular force withdrew towards Taif and camped on its western plateaus. A number of Bedouins joined it. On the eve of September 5, Prince Ali arrived at Taif with a cavalry brigade and another brigade of cameleers. But he did not stay there for long. Rather, he went out of it the next day in the afternoon and camped at a nearby place called al-Hada.

In the afternoon of September 7, the *ikhwan* drew close to Taif, and their bullets started falling inside the fence, so terror prevailed throughout the town, and some of its residents and those who were vacationing in it started running away. Also, minister of war Sabri Pasha withdrew from it with his soldiers and joined Ali in al-Hada. Taif's governor, Sharif Sharaf, withdrew with his government officials.

After that, the *ikhwan* entered the town like a sweeping torrent shouting "Allāhu Akbar!" and firing from their rifles in the air. Then they started roaming the town's markets and alleys, firing on anything they saw on their way. The situation developed after that whereupon the *ikhwan* started breaking house doors and entering by force, looting and killing. They regarded all people other than their own selves as unbelievers whose blood and wealth were free games. Among those they killed was Sheikh Zawawi, the *mufti* of the Shafi`ites, and the sons of Sheikh Abdul-Qadir al-Sheebi, caretaker of the Ka`ba. Ameen al-Rayhani narrates saying that they caught al-Sheebi himself and wanted to kill him, but he saved his skin with a trick. When he fell in their hands and one of them pulled his sword to kill him, he started weeping. The *ikhwan* man asked him, "Why are you crying, unbeliever?" The Sheikh answered, "I, by Allāh, am crying out of joy. I, brothers (*ikhwan*), cry because I spent all my life in polytheism and apostasy, but Allāh did not want me to die except as a believer in His unity. *Allāhu Akbar! La Ilaha illa Allāh!*" This statement impressed the *ikhwan* who all wept in response to the sheikh's tears and kept kissing him and congratulating him for having accepted Islam [at their hands].[1]

Prince Ali and those with him had all withdrawn to Arafa, and when al-Husain came to know about it, he was very angry with the prince and ordered him to return to retake Taif. On September 26, both parties met at al-Hada and a fierce battle took place which went on for several hours; the *ikhwan* won it.

Al-Husain Abdicates

When the news of the defeat that befell al-Husain's army in al-Hada reached Mecca, fear and panic spread among the residents who feared a massacre would happen to them as it did in Taif, and they kept running away to Jidda. Many of them went on foot because of so many runaways but not enough means of transportation, so Jidda became crowded with them.

Al-Husain used to think that the British would intervene to save him as they had done last month in Trans-Jordan. He, therefore, sent a telegram on September 26 to Mr. Bullard, the British consul in Jidda. In it, he stated that the situation was critical, that his relationship with the British government made him ask it to be interested in repelling Ibn Saud in order to avoid a repetition of what had taken place in Taif, that he hoped it would look into his request as soon as possible. The consul sent this request to his government in London. The answer came on the 28th of the month indicating that the British government upheld its traditional policy of not interfering in religious affairs. It, therefore, did not want to interfere in any dispute relevant to the ownership of sacred places in Islam.[2]

At the same time, Dr. Naji al-Aseel, representative of al-Husain in London, wrote the British foreign ministry saying, "His Hashemite Majesty pleads to the British government, in the

---

1 *Ibid.*, p. 333.
2 Public Records Office in London, No. FO 371/10014.

Chapter Five: Abdul-Aziz ibn Saud

spirit of the treaty being negotiated, to intervene to put an end to the brutal aggression of the Wahhabis against the sacred places and to get them out of Taif." The British foreign ministry answered him saying, "The British government does not want to get involved in the standing dispute among independent Arab rulers about the ownership of the sacred places in Islam, and the head of the British administration delivered a statement in this meaning in the British House of Commons."

Al-Aseel responded to the answer of the foreign ministry on October 2 in which he pointed out to the great risk the people of Hijaz undertook in supporting Britain in the general [world] war. Hijaz, therefore, expected Britain to help it save Mecca from the woes of the war." Al-Aseel also stated that the Islamic world did not accept the holy places to fall, not even for a very short period of time, in sectarian hands such those of the Wahhabis, and it looked with apprehension at the possibility of Mecca being invaded by the sultan of Najd and his followers.[1]

What is strange is that when al-Husain was in Britain pleading to be saved from the Wahhabis, some residents in Jidda were pleading to Britain to save them from al-Husain himself. The British consul in Jidda said in his secret report to his government that two senior Jidda businessmen went to him demanding al-Hijaz be placed under Britain's protection or mandate. The consul rejected this request. Then the consul said that the prevalent public opinion among the people of Jidda was that they were during the Turkish era comfortable despite the Turks' oppression. They had some freedom in practicing their professions so the pilgrims could benefit from them, and they did not have any interest in issues of defending the country. Then Britain finally came and kicked the Turks out of the country and set up in it a government which was more oppressive than the Turks. It also placed the responsibility of defending it on its people. The residents wanted now Britain to defend them after

---

1 *Ibid.*

having crushed their means of defense and to save them from the rule of al-Husain who was the direct cause of the Wahhabis' attack.[1]

On October 3, Prince Ali reached Jidda sent by his father. He summoned the dignitaries of Jidda, as well as those of Mecca who had sought shelter in Jidda. He said to them, "The situation calls for despair. My father is ready to abdicate if this does not lead to improving the situation." The dignitaries asked for one hour to deliberate on the issue. After the deliberation, they decided to accept al-Husain's abdication and that his son, Ali, would take his place. Prince Ali refused to accept the throne, so they insisted on him and immediately sent a telegram to al-Husain asking him to surrender the throne to his son, Ali, in order to save both Sacred Harams from the catastrophe and the people from chaos. Al-Husain answered them with this telegram: "With pleasure and appreciation; this is the basis of our desire which I have been declaring since the start of the Renaissance and up to this date. I announced it minutes ago saying that I am ready to do so with ease of mind if you appoint someone else other than Ali. I am comfortably awaiting your speedy response. Husain."

The dignitaries were still assembling when this telegram reached them, so they decided to contact him directly by telephone. One of them took the telephone receiver and tried to speak to al-Husain, but al-Husain refused to speak to him saying, "You are one of the men of my government; so, let someone else speak to me." When another man held the receiver, al-Husain refused to speak to him, too. It was then that Tahir al-Dabbagh took the receiver, and the following dialogue went on between them:

AL-DABBAGH: "Master, based on the critical situation the country has reached, the nation decided that Your Majesty should surrender the throne to His Highness Prince Ali..."

---

[1] Public Records Office in London, No. FO 371/10015.

AL-Husain (interrupting): "Both I and my son are one and the same; therefore, if I now, according to you, have become useless, that is alright. But I do not understand what it means. I do not care about the matter of authority, whoever the one in power may be. But I do not surrender to my son, Ali, at all because if I am useless, so is my son."

AL-DABBAGH: "No, master, we do not attribute to Your Majesty anything like that. Rather, we want to follow a policy different from the one you have followed, perhaps we may be able to rid the country of its critical plight. The nation is now unanimous regarding asking Your Majesty to do it, and we hope you will respond to its wish."

AL-Husain: "Son! You may do whatever you please. As for me, I do not surrender to my son at all. You have Sharif Ali, formerly the emir of Mecca, and my brother Nasir. And you have the Khedive of Egypt, Abbas Hilmi, and you have many Sharifs. Choose whomsoever you want, and I am ready to surrender to him. As for my son, this is not possible because I and he are one and the same: His goodness or evilness belongs to me."

AL-DABBAGH: "The nation is unanimous, master, about choosing Prince Ali and does not wish..."

AL-Husain: (interrupting): "There can be no surrendering to my son! I say this can never be at all."

AL-DABBAGH: "I shall inform the board then we notify Your Majesty."[1]

Prince Ali, meanwhile, visited the British consul and asked him if he could depend on the help of the British government in case he accepted the throne. The consul's answer was negative. Prince Ali returned to the board of notables and announced to them that he would not accept the throne because the situation was hopeless and he did not wish to be a king for two or three

---

1 Ameen al-Rayhani (Op. Cit.), pp. 337-338.

days. It was then that the notables decided to send four board members to meet the British consul, and the time then was late at night. The four deputies went to the consulate as a large crowd of people trailed them. When they met the consul, they told him that Prince Ali refused to accept the throne and they, therefore, had no way other than pleading to Britain for mercy. They offered the consul either Britain placing Hijaz under its protection or mandate, or it would interfere to prevent Ibn Saud from occupying Mecca, or it would support the notables in their negotiations with the Wahhabis so the latter might not commit massacres, or it would undertake any other action that would save them "in the name of humanity." The consul answered them that he was not authorized by the government to do any of what they had stated.[1]

The four delegates returned from the consulate disappointed and had to insist anew on Prince Ali accepting the throne. Prince Ali finally accepted. They sent al-Husain in Mecca a telegram containing something like a warning to him; here is its text: "The situation is very critical, and there is no time for negotiations. If you do not surrender [the throne] to Ali, we plead in the name of humanity that Your Majesty should abdicate so the nation would be able to form an interim government. If you are late to respond to this request, the blood of the Muslims will be on your shoulders."

The notables remained vigilant that night waiting for the answer. At four o'clock in the morning of October 4, the answer arrived. In it, al-Husain said that he agreed to abdicate with pleasure, and if Prince Ali accepted, "you must appoint him as the chief, for the situation requires speed, and if you are late, you will be responsible."[2]

---

1   Public Records Office in London No. FO 371/10015.
2   Ameen al-Rayhani (Op. Cit.), p. 339.

Chapter Five: Abdul-Aziz ibn Saud

The Fall of Mecca

A celebration was held in Jidda on the occasion of swearing the oath of allegiance to Prince Ali as the King of Hijaz. The celebration was quite simple. It was decided during it that Ali would be a constitutional king who would follow the nation's view in achieving its hopes and wishes, and that the country would have a parliamentary council whose members are elected from all parts of Hijaz according to a basic law put together by a founding assembly similarly to what takes place in civilized countries.

King Ali issued instructions to put a cabinet together according to the constitutional way. It was comprised thus: Abdullah Sarraj as its head, Tahsin al-Faqir as minister of war, Tahir al-Dabbagh as minister of finance, Khalid al-Khateeb as minister of health, Muhammed Taweel as minister of taxes (treasury), Abdul-Qadir Ghazawi as minister of transportations, Arif al-Adlabi as minister of the navy, Muhammed ibn Mansour as minister of the interior and Fuad al-Khateeb as foreign minister.[1]

King Ali left for Mecca following the forming of the administration in order to prepare his forces to defend the city. As for his father, al-Husain, he had decided to leave the country; therefore, he sent in advance a caravan of camels carrying his luggage and money under the guard of his loyal slaves. It is said that it carried one hundred and sixty thousand gold liras placed in forty oil tin cans.[2] When the caravan came out of Mecca, some mobsters bade it farewell with foul words.[3]

On October 9, al-Husain left with his women and slaves for Jidda where he stayed alone for six days, not meeting anybody. At the end of the six days, he sent the head of the new

---

1 Salah ad-Din al-Mukhtar, *Tarikh al-Mamlaka al-Arabiyya al-Saudia* (History of the Kingdom of Saudi Arabia), Beirut, Vol. 2, p. 304.
2 Ameen al-Rayhani (Op. Cit.), p. 340.
3 Salah ad-Din al-Mukhtar (Op. Cit.), Vol. 2, p. 306.

administration a notification protesting the constitutional government saying, "As for the constitutional government, especially in both Sacred Harams, acting according to it contradicts the rulings of the Book of Allāh and the Sunnah of His Messenger. Work in the holy land according to human laws is renounced by the rites of Islam, religious obligations and honorable ethics in matter and in essence."

On the eve of the 15th of the month, al-Husain left Jidda on board his ship "Al-Raqmatain". It was a small ship similar to a yacht, and he had bought it from Greece not long ago. It is narrated that when he saw it for the first time after his purchase, he liked it and said, "One day, we will travel in it a distant trip."[1] His prediction came true.

The king stayed in Mecca for only one week. He realized that the forces he had in Mecca would not be enough to defend it, so he decided to withdraw and go to Jidda. On the eve of October 14, he left Mecca with his forces, which were no more than two hundred soldiers and a like number of policemen.

The commander of the Hashemite army was an Iraqi man: Sabri Pasha al-Azzawi. Reports have varied about his fate. Some say that he withdrew with al-Husain, but Philby opposes this view saying, "King Husain's army evaporated in the air since the first battle, and its former commander, Sabri Pasha, who originally was from Baghdad, was the first to flee from the battlefield."[2]

In his report, the British consul says, "Sabri Pasha was tasked with idling the cannons in Mecca so the enemy could not benefit from them, but he left them without idling them and ran away. The cannons fell after that as a cold booty in the hands of the *ikhwan* who benefitted from them a great deal."[3]

---

1 Ameen al-Rayhani (Op. Cit.), pp. 340-341.
2 Khairi Hammad, *Abdullah Philby*, Beirut: 1961, p. 160.
3 Public Records Office in London No. FO 371/10807.

Chapter Five: Abdul-Aziz ibn Saud

When the *ikhwan* came to know about the withdrawal of King Ali from Mecca, they sent four unarmed men. When these men reached Mecca, they found its streets empty, its entrances blocked with barricades and shops closed, so they kept roaming throughout the town on horseback shouting, "Security! Security!" On October 16, the *ikhwan* entered Mecca wearing the *ihram* (white pilgrims' shrouds) garbs, so they circumambulated the House and made the rounds between the Safa and the Marwa, whereupon the people of Mecca welcomed them warmly.[1]

Khalid ibn Luay was appointed as governor of Mecca, and the *ikhwan* set out to the homes of government officials and of the Sharifs to loot them, then they offered them for sale. Some people of Mecca went to them to lead them to other homes whose owners had fled Mecca, so the *ikhwan* kept looting them and also offering them for sale.[2]

The *ikhwan* then set out to the sacred domes to demolish them, such as the dome over the grave of Khadija and those of the Prophet's household. They imposed on the residents the attendance of the Friday prayer services five times a day. They also banned smoking, the recitation of chants on the Birth of the Prophet and the visiting of the graves. Anyone whom they saw doing any of these things, they would taunt and beat him and may lead him to jail or impose a fine. When the Jawis set up pavilions to recite the Prophet's Birthday chants, as customary every year, the *ikhwan* went to them to expel them, calling them "polytheists". They demolished the pavilion. When two Indians went to visit Khadija's grave, they were arrested and jailed and were not released except after al-Munshi Ihsan-Allāh, scribe at the British consulate in Jidda, went and paid a fine of five dollars on behalf of each of them, thus getting them released.[3]

---

1 Salah ad-Din al-Mukhtar (Op. Cit.), Vol. 2, p. 310.
2 Ameen al-Rayhani (Op. Cit.), p. 370.
3 Public Records Office in London No. FO 371/10808.

Ibn Saud Hesitates

Ibn Saud was in Riyadh when reports reached him about al-Taif falling in the hands of the *ikhwan*. On November 11, 1924, he left Riyadh for Hijaz leading an army of five thousand men, but he was upset and hesitated. He feared a warning might reach him from Britain as took place in 1919 following the Turba incident. He did not wish to fight the British anyway because they had planes and armored vehicles, whereas he did not have them, and he might suffer in Hijaz what the *ikhwan* had suffered in Trans-Jordan.

As Ibn Saud was on his way to Hijaz, newspapers reports reached him from Iraq about the fall of the Laborers administration in England and the forming of a new Conservatives cabinet. One of his advisors, who is believed to be Yousuf Yasin, took him aside and told him that the new Conservatives administration would follow a new policy towards the Arab issues that would be different from that of the previous Laborers administration, and that the first of its actions would be to maintain the rule of the Sharifs in Hijaz.

Ibn Saud was disturbed at hearing this report and summoned the other two advisors who were in his company for the campaign, namely Hafiz Wahba the Egyptian and Abdullah al-Damalooji, an Iraqi. When both men were in his presence, they found him grim, distressed, so he asked them what news they had. Then he said, "Do the Conservatives have any impact on our situation? Do they support the Sharifs?" Hafiz Wahba answered him, "The British foreign policy is almost the same because those who make it are permanent government officials. The British parties, despite their differences, implement what those officials decide, and seldom is there a total change." Ibn Saud was not satisfied with this statement, and signs of skepticism and hesitation appeared on him. He asked Hafiz Wahba, "Are

Chapter Five: Abdul-Aziz ibn Saud

you sure of what you say." Hafiz answered him that he was completely sure.

Hafiz kept trying to convince Ibn Saud that he should not hesitate in his resolve and to continue to march towards Hijaz. He said to him, "If you have doubts, it is better you return home. And if you are confident that Allāh is the One Who promises the faithful to achieve victory and His support, continue along your path and do not hesitate. Do not worry, master, about these doubts. Britain is not concerned except about safeguarding its subjects and interests, it is the same for it: Sharif Husain or Ibn Saud. It had great hopes on King Husain, and I warned you in 1919, but now the situation has changed, and all its hopes on him have been dashed; so, march relying on Allāh and do not hesitate. Allāh is the One Who supports those who fear Him and who do goodness." Ibn Saud said, "We have relied on Allāh, and the curse of Allāh be on so-and-so," meaning the first advisor, "who confused my thoughts and let me surrender to doubt and hesitation."

Four days later, mail reached Ibn Saud from Hijaz carrying letters from all country consulates in Jidda declaring the neutrality of their countries regarding the standing war in Hijaz and holding both parties accountable for any harm or assault that would happen to their subjects. Those letters had a good impression on Ibn Saud who regarded them as a good omen for the future.[1]

Mecca's Scholars Consent

Ibn Saud and his army reached Mecca on December 4, 1924. On the next day, he reviewed his troops. Then the *ikhwan* came to greet him, kissing his nose and forehead according to their tradition. After them, Mecca's notables and businessmen came and wanted to kiss his hand, according to their habit, but he

---

1 Hafiz Wahba (Op. Cit.), pp. 61-63.

prevented them saying, "Hand shaking is one of the customs of the Arabs. As the habit of kissing, it reached us from the foreigners, and we do not accept it."[1]

After Ibn Saud had finished looking into his coming problems, he summoned Sheikh Abdul-Qadir al-Sheebi and asked him to invite Mecca's scholars to meet with him. The scholars met the next day, and Ibn Saud delivered a statement to them at the conclusion of which he said, "And now I am entrusted to you and you to me. Religion is advising. I am of you and you are of me. Such is our faith in the books in your possession. If they contain what opposes the Book of Allāh, keep it away from us and ask us about what confuses you in its regard. The judge between us and your own selves is the Book of Allāh and what the books of *hadith* and Sunnah contain... We did not obey the son [Muhammed] of Abdul-Wahhab and others except in what they expressed as being a statement in the Book of Allāh and the Sunnah of His Messenger. As regarding our rulings, they agree with the *ijtihad* of imam Ahmed ibn Hanbal. If this is agreeable to you, come and let us continue to work according to the Book of Allāh and the Sunnah of His Messenger and that of the righteous caliphs after him."

When Ibn Saud finished his statement, some of those present shouted, "We all swear the oath of allegiance," whereupon Ibn Saud responded saying, "Tell us honesty what you have to say." They said, "We have nothing else to say." Ibn Saud then said, "I seek refuge with Allāh against the *taqiyya*; so, do not hide from us anything." One of those present said, "Let us, imam, get together with the scholars of Najd so we may discuss with them the roots and branches [of our religion] then decide what we agree on by the will of Allāh." Ibn Saud accepted this viewpoint and said, "Good, you will soon meet [with them]."

On December 8, fifteen scholars from Mecca and seven from Najd met. After having discussed and debated among themselves,

---

[1] Ameen al-Rayhani (Op. Cit.), p. 373.

Chapter Five: Abdul-Aziz ibn Saud

they agreed on the soundness of the Wahhabi sect. Then Mecca's scholars issued a statement the text of which was as follows:

"An agreement has taken place between us and the scholars of Najd regarding *usool*-related [principles of the religion] matters including the following: Anyone who takes mediators between himself and Allāh from among His creation to call on and to plead to, for bringing a benefit or repelling harm, is a *kafir* (unbeliever) who is required to seek repentance three times. If he repents, so be it; otherwise, he is to be killed. Another is: Anyone who pleads to Allāh through the status of one of His creation with Him, commits a *bid`a* (innovation) and a prohibitive act. These matters we discussed and accepted. Thus, our doctrine has established an agreement among us, we scholars of the Sacred Haram, and our brethren the scholars of Najd."[1]

This agreement, which took place in Mecca, is in some aspects similar to that which took place between the scholars of the Shi`ites and Sunnis at the Najaf Conference of 1743. Both took place according to the desire of an oppressive ruler. Had it not been the desire of that ruler, the scholars would have differed among themselves and disputed, and each of us would have called the other an apostate. One must not give up any opinion or belief under the influence of argument and logical evidence alone. The logical evidence does not convince anyone other than its advocate. As in the eyes of his opponent, it is a trivial and silly "evidence".[2]

---

1 *Ibid.*, pp. 372-374.
2 Refer to pp. 134-137 of the first Volume of this book published in Baghdad on 1969.

Chapter Six
Ali's Days as King

Ali's Days as King

Ali ruled Hijaz as king about fifteen months which represent an amazing period of time full of morals and social lessons, and we will try in this part to briefly mention some of these lessons.

The Defense Line

Military experts say that had the *ikhwan* marched on Jidda after their occupation of Mecca, they would have easily seized it, King Ali's government would have fallen and the matter would have been settled for Ibn Saud in the entire Hijaz. Ibn Saud feared a massacre in Jidda, like the one that took place in Taif, would take place, and it might lead to the interference of foreign countries and to a setback. Hafiz Wahba says in his Memoirs, "When reports about the *ikhwan* entering Mecca reached us, whereas entering Mecca was outside the plan drawn for them, I told King Abdul-Aziz that the duty necessitated on him to first prevent the *ikhwan* from attacking Jidda for fear what had happened in Taif would also happen there and the outcome would be dire, and that duty obligated him, secondly, to travel immediately to Hijaz to oversee in person the situation there and to get to know people personally, to assure the Hijazis and remove from their hearts the bad effect that resulted from the Taif tragedy."[1]

The *ikhwan* stopping short of invading Jidda was a precious opportunity for King Ali to fortify Jidda and strengthen its means of defense. Actually, King Ali exerted his utmost effort to utilize this opportunity. He was assisted in doing so by two men: One

---

[1] Hafiz Wahba, *Khamsson Aman fi Jazeerat al-Arab* (Fifty Years in the Arabian Peninsula), Cairo: 1960, p. 60.

of them was Tahsin Pasha al-Faqir, the minister of war, a Syrian officer sent by Prince Abdullah to help his brother and one of the Ottoman army officers who fought on the Shatalja [an area in Istanbul] line to protect Istanbul in the Balkan war. As for the second man, he was Nawras Beg, a Turkish military engineer who demonstrated skill, focusing on setting up the defense line, and he was regarded at the time as "the army's thinking brain".

The defense line was prepared in the shape of an arch that started from the sea coastline in north Jidda and ended with it in its south. Its length reached six miles. It was guarded by twenty cannons and more than thirty machineguns. Barbed wires were installed before it in short poles surrounded by buried land mines. Also, floodlights were installed on them.

The Hashemite army in Jidda was a mixture of various groups. In it, there were Hijazis from the Bedouins and some villages, and there were Yemenis who resided in Hijaz but descended from Yemeni origins. Prince Abdullah kept sending the volunteers whom he gathered in Trans-Jordan to Jidda. They arrived in batches. Most of them were Palestinians, Syrians and Jordanians, and few of them were Egyptians who were remnants of the work division that served in the British army during the war and remained in Palestine thereafter. These were joined by a number of paupers who resided in Jidda and who were Sudanese, Somalis and Negroes. The total number of Hashemite troops in Jidda—according to the estimate of Khair ad-Din al-Zurakli—was about 1,650.[1]

The *ikhwan* surrounded Jidda from its three land directions. They numbered between five to six thousand men. Ibn Saud went to personally oversee how the fighting was going on. He camped north of the Rughama, twenty-five minutes from Jidda.

Ibn Saud did not bring his cannons from Riyadh, but he made use of the ones which he [his men] seized in Mecca, and they

---

[1] Khair ad-Din al-Zurakli, *Shibh al-Jazeera fi Ahd al-Malik Abdul-Aziz* (the Peninsula during the time of Abdul-Aziz), Beirut: 1977, Vol. 1, p. 345.

Chapter Six: Ali's Days as King

were twenty cannons with a range longer than that of Jidda's cannons. He used the officers who had served in the past in the Hashemite army to operate them.[1] He directed the men to aim at Jidda and to keep bombing it and bombing the ditches around it. A bomb fell on the house of the British consul, piercing his bedroom's wall, and another entered his office as a third hit the house of the Soviet consul, breaking the flag hoisted on it.[2]

The *ikhwan* were accustomed to attacking the defense line during dark nights for two reasons: so they would cast fear and terror in the hearts of the residents in order to firstly stir them against the government, and secondly to let the soldiers use plenty of ammunition. Some *ikhwan* would address the [Jidda] line's guards, as they got close in their attack, saying, "Brothers! People of the Levant! Shammar! Harb! Uqaylat! Get out of the line and you are in the face of Allāh and in that of Ibn Saud! Do not be afraid! By Allāh! We want nothing but goodness for you. Come to us, we are your brothers, by Allāh, by Allāh!"[3]

King Ali was in the beginning optimistic and confident that due to the planes and armored vehicles in his possession, he would be able to defeat the *ikhwan* and expel them from Hijaz. His war minister, Tahsin Pasha, was more optimistic and confident. Ameen al-Rayhani narrates a story which he personally witnessed in early January of 1925 when the vanguards of the *ikhwan* started getting close to Jidda: Tahsin Pasha and his fellow, minister of navy Arif Pasha al-Adlabi, met King Ali as the signs of anger and confusion appeared on their faces. One of them said, "We knew that the *ikhwan* marched from Bahra and will soon reach Rughama." Another said, "We must send the planes against them, the curse of Allāh on them and on their ancestors!" Then they said together, "Tomorrow morning, we will send all the planes to them to let fire and bullets

---

[1] Public Records Office in London No. FO 371/10807.
[2] Ameen al-Rayhani, *Tarikh Najd al-Hadith wa Mulhaqatih* (Najd's Modern History and Supplements), Beirut: 1954, p. 409.
[3] *Ibid.*, p. 407.

rain on them by the will of Allāh." Both ministers kept strongly criticizing the reconciliation attempts which al-Rayhani and others were carrying out. Tahsin Pasha said, "These peaceful efforts prevent us from carrying out our military plan." Addressing the king, Arif Pasha said, "They actually foiled our plan and harmed the interest of Your Majesty and those of the country."[1]

In the company of the king there was a senior Iraqi officer, namely Jameel Pasha al-Rawi, a cousin of Ibrahim al-Rawi about whom we talked while narrating the Turba incident. This officer is known to be different from and more realistic than Tahsin Pasha al-Faqir. He used to advise King Ali differently from Tahsin Pasha. In his secret report to his government about this subject, the British consul said, "The Hijazi military command is comprised mainly of three persons: Tahsin Pasha the Syrian, the minister of war and commander of the army, Jameel Pasha, the Baghdadi commander who was linked to King Ali, and the king himself. Apparently, none from Baghdad agreed with anyone from Syria. The king used to shift from one line to the other at the same speed and regularity whereby the clock pendulum moved; therefore, there was weakness in harmony and objective in the command."[2]

A newspaper called *Umm al-Qura* [the mother town, i.e. Mecca] started publication in Mecca to replace *Al-Qibla* newspaper which used to be issued during al-Husain's time. It was edited by Yousuf Yasin. Its purpose was to propagate for Ibn Saud and besmear the reputation of the Sharifs, mentioning their faults, particularly those of al-Husain. In December of 1924, the Hashemite government in Jidda issued a newspaper in the name of *Bareed Al-Hijaz* [Hijaz Post] in order to respond to *Umm al-Qura* newspaper and to rebut it in a similar way. On January 18, 1925, the Hijazi *Bareed al-Hijaz* newspaper published a lengthy

---

1 *Ibid.*, p. 393.
2 Public Records Office in London FO 371/10807.

statement by King Ali saying that he was about to march on Mecca to liberate it, asking the people of Mecca to be patient for a short while and to bear the hardship of the siege which the Hashemite government would impose on them.[1]

Persistent Al-Aseel

Dr. Naji al-Aseel kept representing Hijaz in London during King Ali's era, and he continued his efforts to sign the treaty with Britain and to ask the latter to help the Hashemite government against Ibn Saud. The British consul in Jidda sent his government a letter saying, "King Ali did not have a good impression about Naji al-Aseel, and he used to think that he was useless in London, but there was no harm in his staying in it until the money he had taken from al-Husain ran out."[2] The consul says, "The total of what al-Aseel took from al-Husain reached fifteen thousand pounds, a huge amount that would be sufficient for about three years."[3]

On October 13, 1924, the British foreign ministry wrote Naji al-Aseel a letter in which it said, "The British government is not ready to enter into new negotiations with the Hashemite government about amending the draft treaty." Al-Aseel answered it in a letter in which he said that he was granted full power to sign the treaty which the previous king wanted to amend. Al-Aseel stated that the amendments of the previous king were now irrelevant and that King Ali did not have any obligation towards them; therefore, he requested the British government to intervene to end the presently standing vacuum between Hijaz and Najd, and that he wished to receive the answer as soon as possible.[4]

---

1 *Ibid.*
2 Public Records Office in London FO 371/10808.
3 Public Records Office in London FO 371/10807.
4 Public Records Office in London FO 371/10014.

Five days after the writing of this letter, al-Aseel wrote another longer letter to the British foreign ministry in which he stated that King Ali had authorized him to request the British government to intervene to repel the Wahhabis according to the spirit of the treaty. Al-Aseel pointed out that the negotiated treaty had now become incumbent even though it was yet to be signed. He also pointed out to the alliance which was in the past standing between Britain and the founder of the Hashemite House and how Britain pledged in it to respect and support the Arabs' independence. Al-Aseel mentioned how Britain declared the war on Germany in 1914 because of Germany merely having violated a treaty which Britain had signed with it; so, it did this great work for the sake of honor and justice. Then al-Aseel discussed the pretext which Britain used for not entering the standing dispute in Hijaz as being about religious issues. He said that the dispute is in fact not religious, for there is no religion on the face of earth that permits the shedding of innocent blood, blocking routes and carrying out massacres. Wahhabism is a political movement and not a religious one. It is Bolshevic in its ugliest form and has nothing to do with Islam in any aspect. Then al-Aseel stated that King Ali had withdrawn from Mecca not because of his army having suffered a defeat, but because he wanted to avoid shedding blood in that sacred town. He, therefore, pleads to the British government, through the rights of the treaty between himself and Britain and the past promises which were given to His Hashemite Majesty, to undertake the swift measures to save the lives of thousands of innocent souls and to ensure the withdrawal of the Wahhabis from Mecca and Taif.[1]

These efforts which Naji al-Aseel exerted produced nothing, and the British government kept sticking to its neutral position vis-à-vis the standing dispute in Hijaz; it did not flinch from it. Al-Aseel's position became quite critical, for he, on the one hand,

---

[1] Public Records Office in London FO 371/10015.

Chapter Six: Ali's Days as King

could not bear an impact on the British government; on the other hand, he did not receive from King Ali any amount of money. In the month of April of 1925, he sent King Ali a telegram in which he said, "I plead to Your Majesty to send me whatever money you can. The country's political fate is in the hands of Your Majesty."[1] The king did not send him anything. Actually, he did not have extra money to send him. In the month of May, al-Aseel announced in London that he would seek the arbitration of the League of Nations in order to end the standing dispute in Hijaz. He also announced that he would go to Jidda in person to use his personal influence in this regard. The Hashemite government in Jidda was taken by surprise with this announcement which was broadcast by Reuters, so the said government made a statement in which it mentioned that it did not instruct al-Aseel to undertake this step and that al-Aseel did so on his own. At this juncture, al-Aseel sent a telegram to Jidda submitting his resignation which the Hashemite government readily accepted.

In the month of July of 1925, King Ali wanted to appoint an Egyptian man, namely attorney Hassan Sabri, to represent him in London instead of al-Aseel. But when he inquired from the British government about this matter, it answered him saying that it was not ready under the present circumstances to accept anyone to represent him in London, whether such representation was official or personal.[2]

As for Naji al-Aseel, he stayed in London until his money ran out and became in a miserable condition.[3] He had to return to Baghdad in 1928. Tawfiq al-Suweedi was at the time in charge of the ministry of education. He points out in his *Memoirs* that his 1922 prediction about Naji al-Aseel came true: Al-Aseel went to him asking him for a job, so he placed him in a job the salary of which was no more than twenty-five dinars. Al-Suweedi

---

1 Public Records Office in London FO 371/10807.
2 Public Records Office in London FO 371/10809.
3 *Al-Iraq* newspaper of May 10, 1925.

comments on this saying, "So, how amazing chances and fates are!"[1]

Philby Mediates

Three men went to Jidda to mediate a peace agreement in their capacity as friends of both parties. They were: Philby, Ameen al-Rayhani and Sayyid Talib al-Naqeeb. Each of these individuals has regarding his mediation effort a story worth narrating here:

Philby was the first to reach Jidda. He went in his personal capacity and did not have any official attribute. King Ali was notified of his coming prior to his arrival, so this created elation among the people of Jidda who thought that he was commissioned by his government to negotiate peace between the two warring factions. The British consul went to King Ali to inform him that Philby did not have any official capacity that qualified him to mediate or negotiate on behalf of the British government, but the residents kept, despite that, resting their hopes on Philby's presence in Jidda and on the results of his peace efforts.

Philby reached Jidda on October 28, 1924. His method of arrival was odd, strengthening the rumor that spread about him among the residents, i.e. that he had come on an official business. When he was in Suez, he missed the post ship, so he had to ride in a cargo boat in order to expedite his arrival. When he reached the waters of Jidda, King Ali sent him a steam boat to transport him to the shore.[2] The king met him immediately after his arrival, welcoming him cordially and warmly.

Philby says this in his *Memoirs*: "I was expected to play a major role, but my troubles soon started few hours after my arrival. I received from Mr. Bullard, the consul of the British government of His Majesty and its representative, the following

---

1 Tawfiq al-Suweedi, *Muthakkarati* (My Memoirs), Beirut: 1969, pp. 89-90.
2 Public Records Office in London FO 371/10015.

Chapter Six: Ali's Days as King

letter: 'I would like to notify you, Sir, that when the government of His Majesty came to know about your going to Jidda, it ordered me to notify you that with regard to the turbulent conditions in the centers of the Arabian Peninsula, it does not permit you to go inside the Peninsula. I will be grateful if you notify me of the arrival of this letter at your end."[1]

It is worth mentioning that the newspapers in some Islamic countries kept attacking Philby for going to Jidda, accusing him of being an undercover British agent. At the same time, some British newspapers kept describing Philby as an opportunist who tried to enter the stage from which Britain came out in despair and hopelessness.[2]

Philby sent two letters: One was directed to Khalid ibn Luay, governor of Mecca, and the other to Ibn Saud who was at the time in Riyadh. He received the answer from Khalid the context of which is that he wanted to remove Ali ibn al-Husain from Jidda. Then after that Ibn Saud's answer arrived saying, "The subject, from its beginning to end, hinges on the opinion of the Islamic world which stands, all of it, strongly opposing the sons of al-Husain... We, by the will of Allāh, will soon reach Mecca, and we will surely meet with you by the will of Allāh in order to exchange views. We wish you good health, *Wassalam*."[3]

Philby waited for Ibn Saud to reach Mecca. Meanwhile, Philby was afflicted with dysentery just as was the case with his two other fellows. When Ibn Saud reached Mecca on December 5, Philby and both of his fellows wrote him requesting to meet him. On the 22nd of the month, the answer reached each of them separately. Ibn Saud's answer to Philby was as follows:

"To the dear friend, Mr. Philby. If you have come to meet us to discuss some private matters, you are quite welcome, and we will facilitate the route to meet with you outside the Haram. But

---

1 Khairi Hammad, *Abdullah Philby*, Beirut: 1961, p. 157.
2 *Ibid.*, p. 158.
3 *Ibid.*, p. 174.

if you intend to interfere in the matters of Hijaz, I do not see that the discussion will have any benefit... It is not in my personal interest or in yours, our friend, to make you a mediator in this purely Islamic matter."[1]

It became obvious to Philby during his stay in Jidda that Ibn Saud's victory was imminent. He says in his *Memoirs* that the subject of the peace, or of any peaceful settlement, became impossible, for the fate of the Hashemites' throne in Hijaz had been determined, and no human power would be able to save it. But minister of war Tahsin Pasha al-Faqir, despite that, imagined that he was able to save his master's throne. Philby describes Tahsin Pasha saying, "This military commander was conceited about the role he played in the Shatalja battle in the Balkans... He imagined that he was able to remain firm before the poorly armed Wahhabi armies, according to his expression, so he took me for a tour of the defense centers which he had set up with participation from his chief engineer, Nawras Beg, a Turk, around the city."[2]

Philby had intended to leave Jidda late in December of 1924, but King Ali insisted on his staying. The British consul says this in his report to his government: "The reason for this insistence by the king is that the military command was afraid that Philby would go to Ibn Saud after his departure from Jidda and acquaint him with the secrets of its defense plans, keeping in mind that Philby had personally helped the Turkish officer put the plan for the ditches."[3]

Philby finally left Jidda on January 3, 1925 for Aden. He was still sick with the dysentery, and he hoped he would be treated by doctors there.

---

1 Ameen al-Rayhani (Op. Cit.), p. 381.
2 Khairi Hammad (Op. Cit.), p. 159.
3 Public Records Office in London FO 371/10807.

Chapter Six: Ali's Days as King

Sayyid Talib's Mediation

Sayyid Talib al-Naqeeb was in Alexandria when Philby reached Jidda, so King Ali sent him a telegram about Philby's presence in Jidda and invited him to go there. When Sayyid Talib received King Ali's telegram, he sent a telegram to Mr. Bullard, the British consul in Jidda, seeking his suggestion. The consul sent him the answer via post saying that he could not express any opinion, and that Philby was not officially authorized to negotiate a peace agreement.[1]

Sayyid Talib decided to go to Jidda anyway which he reached on November 25, 1924. Apparently, he was not interested in the matter of mediation as much as he was interested in [promoting] himself. He, as we have already come to know him, is a man of great ambitions who wanted to reach the peak via any means and through any route.

Ibn Saud knew Sayyid Talib personally very well. When Sayyid Talib wrote him asking to meet him to mediate in the reconciliation, he answered him saying, "There is no benefit in the mediation, and if Sharif Ali wants to avoid bloodshed, he has to relinquish Jidda. But if the Islamic world accepts him and chooses him as ruler of Hijaz, his place is not unknown."[2]

Sayyid Talib spent thirty-seven days in Jidda during which he used to meet with both his fellows, Philby and Ameen al-Rayhani, and he used to quite often spend the evening once with Philby and once with al-Rayhani. It is known that he was fond of drinking whisky; so, if he drank too much of it, he would set out to reveal what was hidden of his inner self. Al-Rayhani describes his meeting with Sayyid Talib in Jidda and points out to glimpses of his character saying the following:

"It is only for the sake of glory that I do what I do and for the sake of the homeland. Sayyid Talib was conceited in his

---

1 Public Records Office in London FO 371/10015.
2 Ameen al-Rayhani (Op. Cit.), pp. 381-382.

patriotism, tyrannical in his actions, flying in his opinions and believing strongly, even when he is drunk, in what is inside that head that stood between his shoulders like an ivory tower, in what he believed. I remember our meeting in Jidda in the fall of 1924, and I remember a talk about Iraq. He narrated to us some incidents of his time then, as we were drinking whisy and soda, he put the cup on the table and raised his hand to that shiny Sharif head to rub and pet saying, 'There is here, right here, something which is invincible, invincible.' He was thinking of returning to Iraq and to politics. He was still entertaining golden dreams. He resumed his talk to say, 'Matters are pawned by their timings, and you will hear, when I return, what will surprise and please you by the will of Allāh, and I will then summon you, Professor, and appoint you minister of education...'"[1]

Philby talked in his *Memoirs* about Sayyid Talib in the same manner. He says that Sayyid Talib confided in him about why he had gone to Jidda: He did not actually go for the sake of mediating a reconciliation but for contacting Ibn Saud so the latter would help him become the ruler of Trans-Jordan, and that Sayyid Talib had come to know before reaching Jidda that the British were not pleased with Prince Abdullah and wanted to replace him with someone else. Sayyid Talib stated to Philby that Ibn Saud could not tolerate his enemy, Abdullah, being present in Trans-Jordan, and he asked Philby to meet Ibn Saud in order to convince him of his [Tālib] being the best for ruling Trans-Jordan. Sayyid Talib pledged that if he won that position, he would forfeit for Ibn Saud Wadi al-Sarhan and Qaryat al-Milh. Then he said to Philby that in case he became the ruler, he would ask him to be the representative of Britain in it...[2]

On December 31, 1924, Sayyid Talib left Jidda for Egypt empty-handed of attaining the heights, quite regrettably!

---

1 Ameen al-Rayhani, *Faisal al-Awwal* (Faisal I), Beirut: 1958, p. 84.
2 Khairi Hammad (Op. Cit.), p. 173.

Chapter Six: Ali's Days as King

Al-Rayhani's Mediation

Ameen al-Rayhani reached Jidda on November 5, 1924 according to an invitation he had received from foreign minister Fuad al-Khateeb. When he wrote Ibn Saud asking to meet him for the sake of the reconciliation, Ibn Saud's answer to him was different from that he had given both fellows: He did not shut in his face the venues of hope; rather, he left one door open for him through which he could enter the negotiation. Al-Rayhani relied on that answer for sending Ibn Saud a messenger carrying his letter. The messenger left Jidda on the eve of December 22nd, and on the 25th of the same month, the messenger returned carrying Ibn Saud's answer.

Al-Rayhani was meeting with King Ali when the messenger returned carrying Ibn Saud's answer. When the king read the answer, signs of happiness showed on his face. He said, "The matter is settled, and only secondary things remain. Allāh bless you, Husain—the messenger—and Allāh bless you, Ameen." The king kissed Ameen al-Rayhani and also kissed the messenger due to his extreme pleasure. Then he took off the *iqal* and *kafiyyeh* from his head and demanded tea brought to him. He said, "Allāh testifies that I do not like a drop of Arab blood to be spilled..."[1]

This excitement did not last long. A Hashemite plane flew over Mecca at the same time when the messenger was leaving it carrying Ibn Saud's answer. It dropped leaflets assuring the people of Mecca that there was readiness to hit the usurping enemy and to purge the land of him, pledging that the planes would soon start strafing the enemy. The leaflets asked them to prevent the enemy from fleeing. It is worth mentioning that those leaflets had already been prepared, and the king had instructed to delay dropping them on Mecca until the result of

---

1 Ameen al-Rayhani, *Tarikh Najd al-Hadith wa Mulhaqatih* (Najd's Modern History and Supplements), p. 387.

the mediation appeared, but some military men who did not desire the mediation sent the plane without the king's knowledge.

Al-Rayhani was upset because of what happened, so he went to the king to ask for an explanation. He was surprised when he found out that the king and his ministers did not have any knowledge of the matter. When al-Rayhani told the king about what took place, the king rang the bell before him on the table and asked for the immediate presence of Tahsin Pasha, the minister of war. When the minister of war was present, and when the king faced him with the news, Tahsin kept seeking excuses, whereupon al-Rayhani said to him, as he was suppressing his anger, "I do not think, Pasha, that this excuse is sufficient to justify the infringement. You know the result of violating the high orders during war times." The war minister asked, "It is not important." Al-Rayhani responded to him saying, "Every royal order is important, Pasha." It was then that the king started speaking with the war minister in Turkish, explaining to him those leaflets' impact on Ibn Saud. The king said to him, "I incline to think well of people, and I do not entertain bad thoughts except after persistence and investigation. Some things have been confirmed; I have become certain of them, Ameen, so-and-so, so-and-so and so-and-so will travel on the next ship. And I will rebuke Tahsin Pasha, but I prefer to do that in a meeting especially set up for him."[1]

Activity of the Soviet Union's Consul

The diplomatic ties between the Soviet Union and the Hashemite government started late in al-Husain's time. An agreement was reached between them in April of 1924 that the Soviet Union would have a representative and a general consulate in Hijaz, and that Hijaz would likewise have an official delegation in the Soviet Union.

---

1 *Ibid.*, p. 390.

Chapter Six: Ali's Days as King

Al-Husain appointed Habib Lutf-Allāh as his delegate to Moscow, and this man reached it early in October. As for the Soviet Union, it appointed a Muslim man to represent it in Hijaz named Kareem Abdul Ghafour Hakimov. This man reached Jidda in August of 1924 accompanied by fourteen men who were Muslims with the exception of one. He rented a house in Jidda to be his and his officials' headquarters, and it is said that he started, as soon as he reached Jidda, a noticeable activity in propagating for Communism, and al-Husain used to overlook such an activity out of vendetta towards the British.

When King Ali ascended the throne following his father's abdication, he adopted a stance towards Communism that was different from his father's, and he might have done so in order to seek nearness to the British. The *Al-Mufid* Baghdadi newspaper published on June 17, 1925 a photo of King Ali under which it wrote this statement: "His Majesty King Ali, we publish his photograph on the occasion of his statement against Communism which has been said that it spread throughout Hijaz."

When the month of Ramadhan started on May 26, 1925, the Soviet consul, Kareem Hakimov, decided to go to Mecca to perform the rites of the `umra (minor pilgrimage). He was accompanied by the vice Iranian consul, Ahmed Lari, and the Dutch vice consul Sheikh Pravira of Java. It is worth mentioning that these three consuls formed the first group of foreigners to enter Mecca after the *ikhwan* had overrun it, so the *ikhwan* started looking at them with suspicion, regarding them as apostates who went to defile the sacred land. Hafiz Wahba says that the *ikhwan* tried to kill them although they were carrying a permit from Ibn Saud, but Allāh's care saved them from sure death.[1]

The Soviet consul's trip to Mecca stirred the interest of the British consul; therefore, we find him writing the following in

---

[1] Hafiz Wahba, *Jazeerat al-Arab fil Qarn al-Ishreen* (The Arabian Peninsula During the 20th Century), Cairo: 1967, p. 283.

his confidential report to his government: "Hakimov, the Soviet deputy in Jidda, is visiting Mecca in his capacity as a Muslim desiring to perform the minor pilgrimage. He is openly ridiculing the Islamic faith; therefore, we suppose his visit to Mecca was not prompted by piety. He took an Iranian youth with him, the son of a merchant who is presently looking after the Iranian interests. This youth is in the pocket of Hakimov and he repeats the Bolshevik statements, that is, Iran was saved by the noble Soviet government from the claws of British imperialism."[1]

In another report, the British consul says, "Hakimov was welcomed by Ibn Saud in his personal capacity, and Ibn Saud called him 'Sheikh Kareem'. He did not earn there a great deal of respect, for Abdullah al-Damalooji, one of Ibn Saud's main men, asked Sheikh Bravira, as people overheard him, how he allowed himself to accompany a minor, claiming to be a general consul. Al-Damalooji was speaking in a loud voice which Hakimov could hear. From the political standpoint, Ibn Saud threw a banquet for the three consuls and talked during it in an emphatic way about himself that he had no feud with the European countries, that he was considering learning a great deal from them."

The British consul also says this in the report: "There is strong evidence that Hakimov was in Mecca busy publicly promoting propaganda against the imperialist governments, especially the British government." The consul also states that Hakimov spent five or six days in Mecca. When he returned to Jidda, he remained busy drinking wine for twenty-four hours as a strong reaction to the artificial piety which he showed in Mecca, and he remained for forty-eight hours after that with little or much sobriety.

The British consul was unable to go to Mecca because he was non-Muslim, and he might have felt that it was necessary to send someone who would represent him in Mecca in order to

---

[1] Public Records Office in London FO 371/10807.

remove the effect which Hakimov might have left behind. The British consul chose his Indian scribe, Ihsanullah, to undertake this mission. The consul describes this scribe as a man who used to be a merchant in the city prior to the [first] World War and enjoyed a good reputation, but the war crushed his trade and he became since then an employee of the British consulate. The consul says this about him: "He is an expert on pilgrimage rituals, and he is reliable as an intelligence informer, for he is in contact with various classes of people and knew the important persons in Mecca. Moreover, he combines his strong Islamic faith with his loyalty to the British government whom he considers to be the best guard over the Muslims' rights and interests in India."

The Indian man went to Mecca and carried out the task which the consul had commissioned him to do. The consul says this in his report to his government: "Ihsanullah met Ibn Saud, and Ibn Saud kept talking to him about his ties with the British government. He talked about the relationship between Britain and al-Husain during the World War and kept complaining about the reliance Britain placed on al-Husain which was, in his opinion, unjustified. Then Ibn Saud said that he was able to do much more than al-Husain in exchange for half the sums Britain had paid al-Husain."[1]

Story of the Planes

We have already indicated that the Hashemite government in Jidda was proud of having planes and armored vehicles, and it was confident of defeating the *ikhwan* and expelling them from the land. Actually, those planes and armored vehicles were not in a condition to rely on in any serious fighting. It can be said that the Hashemite government fell from this aspect in the same dilemma in which growing nations fall when buying modern technological machinery believing that they can rise through

---

1 Public Records Office in London FO 371/10807.

them to the level of advanced nations. They forget that these machines have no significance by themselves but in the technical hands that move and oversee them.

Al-Husain used before the fighting in Hijaz to have six Italian planes of which only two could fly. And he had two Russian pilots from the remnant of the Czarist period. One of the good planes fell among the *ikhwan* during the Taif battle, so the *ikhwan* beheaded its pilot, and al-Husain had only one pilot named Shirkov. This pilot left al-Hijaz as soon as al-Husain abdicated and went to Egypt.

In November of 1924, King Ali's deputy in Egypt was able to convince Shirkov to return to Hijaz, so he returned accompanied by four Russian mechanics. Shirkov preconditioned, in exchange for his return, that he should be given a bottle of whiskey every day and a monthly salary of sixty gold liras; they accepted his condition.

On the 22nd of the month, the ship Noor arrived at Jidda carrying on board [boxes containing parts of] three planes purchased from England. They were old planes from the remnants of the war. On December 2, Shirkov tried one of them. While landing it, its wing hit a tree, putting it out of commission. Later on, it was discovered that another plane from those three could not fly. As for the third, it was good to fly to a certain extent.

Shirkov kept making reconnaissance flights on enemy positions every morning and evening. The British consul says in his report to his government, "The results of Shirkov's reconnaissance were not of a great value because he refused to fly at a height less than nine thousand feet. Also, the observer who accompanied him on the plane was one-eyed and always put on dark glasses."[1]

---

[1] Public Records Office in London FO 371/10807.

Chapter Six: Ali's Days as King

War minister Tahsin Pasha used to insist on Shirkov hurling bombs at enemy concentrations, but Shirkov used to refuse for a good reason: They did not have air bombs. Tahsin Pasha, therefore, asked him to use hand grenades in the strafing, so Shirkov explained to him that those bombs could explode before reaching the ground, and they could blowup the plane and everyone in it. Tahsin Pasha suggested the use of artillery shells. The pilot tried them twice, but the experiments failed.[1]

A military workshop was set up in Jidda to repair weapons. This workshop, according to instructions from Tahsin Pasha, kept working on transforming cannon bombs into air bombs, making a sort of bombs lit by a match. Tahsin Pasha was of the view to bomb enemy concentrations near Mecca with those bombs. But Shirkov proved to King Ali the error of this viewpoint because shelling Mecca with bombs at the hands of a *kafir*, an apostate, pilot would bring a strong propaganda to Ibn Saud throughout the Islamic world against the Hashemite family. Apparently, King Ali was hesitated, not knowing to what side he should incline: to that of Tahsin Pasha or to that of Shirkov.

Early in December of 1924, two new pilots arrived at Jidda and two mechanics, all Russians. The Hashemite government now had three pilots and six mechanics plus two good planes. The planes started flying from time to time, dropping bombs on enemy concentrations near Jidda and midway between Jidda and Mecca.

On January 18, 1925, a regrettable incident took place in which one plane exploded and Shirkov was killed. This is the summary of the incident: A Syrian youth named Omar Shakir was a refugee in Hijaz since al-Husain's time. When the war around Jidda intensified, this youth became enthusiastic in his contempt towards Ibn Saud and the *ikhwan* and wished to throw at them from the air at least one bomb. That day, an order was issued to Shirkov to fly to strafe the *ikhwan* concentrations in

---

1   Ibid.

Rughama. Omar seized the opportunity and inserted himself in the plane with the observer, and he was carrying two bombs that could be lit with a match. Someone present heard him say that he would drop them on Abdul-Aziz's head. When the plane was over Rughama, and it was two thousand feet high, Omar saw from it the *ikhwan*'s camp which included the tent where Ibn Saud was sitting. It was easy to throw both bombs at Ibn Saud and to kill him, but Omar hardly lit the match, in order to explode one of the two bombs, when it exploded in his hand and the plane blew up in the air then fell to the ground in flames before Ibn Saud's tent. Khair ad-Din al-Zurakli regards this incident as one of those proving that Ibn Saud had the "luck" gift.[1]

In July of 1925, four German pilots reached Jidda from Egypt.[2] After that, six German planes arrived. They were new planes equipped with machineguns and had their own bombs. It was possible for those planes to have a decisive impact in the war, but they faced two problems: One of them was that the Hashemite government did not have enough fuel.[3] The other was that the pilots refused to fly them because they did not receive their salaries, so they left Jidda. The planes remained idle until Jidda fell in December of 1925, so Ibn Saud seized them as a cold booty.[4]

Story of the Armored Vehicles

The condition of the armored vehicles was not any better than that of the planes. On January 31, 1925, five trucks (lorries) arrived from Germany, but they were old and in a bad shape, and one of the Russian mechanics described them as probably being

---

1 Khair ad-Din al-Zurakli (Op. Cit.), Vol. 2, pp. 584-585.
2 Public Records Office in London FO 371/10809.
3 Ameen al-Rayhani (Op. Cit.), pp. 401-402.
4 Husain Muhammed Naseef, *Tarikh al-Hijaz* (History of Hijaz), Cairo: 1349 A.H./1930 A.D., Vol. 1, p. 198.

Chapter Six: Ali's Days as King

remnants of the American army sold in Germany as scrap metal for five pounds each.[1]

With the trucks, fourteen boxes arrived containing iron plates, the workshop workers kept plating the trucks with them, continuing their work for a month. When the trucks were armored, it became clear that they needed a lot of water, for they hardly drove for two hours when signs of thirst appeared on them.[2] Moreover, the truck engines were unable to go for a distance because of the weight of their iron plates. One of them was tested on the Jidda highway, so it was driven at eight to ten miles per hour.[3] One truck was discovered to be out of commission, so camels had to tow it.[4]

On December 25, six Germans specialized in driving armored vehicles arrived; they were sent by Prince Abdullah. But they did not stay in Jidda for long. Apparently, Abdullah had promised them huge salaries more than the government of Jidda could provide; therefore, they left Jidda on January 9, 1925.[5]

On March 8, 1925, excitement and optimism overwhelmed Jidda when an Italian ship reached it carrying two armored vehicles, one thousand rifles and about seven hundred boxes of ammunition. The British consul says in his report to his government, "This shipment added a great strength to the Hashemite army, and the armored vehicles had their own significance: They were not fake as were the five trucks that arrived from Germany before. They were small but fast and light, and each was equipped with three machineguns, two in the rear and one in the front. Three drivers came from Egypt to drive these armored vehicles, and it is thought they (drivers) were Syrian."[6]

---

1 Public Records Office in London FO 371/10807.
2 Ameen al-Rayhani (Op. Cit.), p. 402.
3 Public Records Office in London FO 371/10807.
4 Husain Muhammed Naseef (Op. Cit.), Vol. 1, footnote on p. 198.
5 Public Records Office in London FO 371/10807.
6 *Ibid.*

Both of those armored vehicles had a significant role to play in the battle that erupted around Jidda on March 14, but they, despite that, did not have a decisive role in it.

The March 14 Battle

The March 14, 1925 battle was the largest scale battle fought by the Hashemite army around Jidda. The Hashemite government made many preparations for it, and it was optimistic regarding its outcomes, thinking that it would deal a crushing blow to the *ikhwan* and would soon reverse the occupation of Mecca and Taif.

Four large cannons reached Jidda from Media via Maan and Aqaba routes and kept bombing sites of the *ikhwan* during the day that preceded the battle. At ten o'clock in the morning of the battle day, four convoys of soldiers came out in a front that was two miles wide. They were accompanied by five armored vehicles, including the two new ones.[1] Fighting erupted between them and the forces of the *ikhwan* for about five hours.

The *ikhwan* were fighting in the commando spirit whereby they are known, and some of them kept circling the armored vehicles firing their rifles, paying no heed to the bullets of the machineguns raining on them. One of them, a Negro slave, was seen climbing on one of the armored vehicles as he kept shooting with his pistol, so a bullet caused him to drop dead on the ground.[2]

The battle was witnessed from rooftops in Jidda, and among those who witnessed it was the British consul and Ameen al-Rayhani as well as King Ali who was watching it with his binoculars. The battle came to an end at three o'clock in the afternoon after about three hundred men had been killed from both sides. The armored vehicles withdrew inside the barbed

---

1 *Ibid.*
2 Ameen al-Rayhani (Op. Cit.), p. 411.

Chapter Six: Ali's Days as King

wires. They were torn and the sides of some of them were hit. Two of their drivers were seriously wounded.[1]

Describing the battle, the British consul wrote his government saying that the Wahhabis fought fully fiercely. As for the soldiers of the Hashemite government, they were not participating in the battle with all their hearts. This is indicated by the high percentage of their wounds being in their backs and buttocks. Most losses have been among the Hijazi and Yemeni soldiers who are remnants of al-Husain's old army. As for the Palestinians, who are new volunteers and were supported by armored vehicles, they fought with a great deal of caution. About the overall outcome of the battle, the consul said that it weakened the resolve of the Hashemite command while strengthening that of the Saudi command. It was a heavy blow to the Hashemite leadership. Apparently, this leadership realized that it needed larger and better forces in order to be able to kick the Wahhabis out of the land.[2]

The intensity of the fighting died down after the May 14 battle. When the month of Ramadhan came on the 26th of the month, something like a truce took place. It was rumored in Jidda that the decisive battle would be in Shawwal [April/May of that year], but when Shawwal came, nothing took place.[3] When the pilgrimage season approached late in the month of June, the *ikhwan* who were laying a siege to Jidda started leaving their positions in order to go to perform the pilgrimage, so the Hashemite government thought that the *ikhwan* withdrew from the fighting for good. King Ali sent his brother [King] Faisal in Baghdad a telegram dated the 21st of June saying, "Ibn Saud has been forced to vacate his positions around Jidda and to withdraw to the outskirts of Mecca." This telegram had a pleasant impact on King Faisal, and the Iraqi government issued an official

---

1 *Ibid.*, p. 411.
2 Public Records Office in London FO 371/10807.
3 Ameen al-Rayhani (Op. Cit.), pp. 410-412.

statement congratulating the nation for this "victory". *Al-Iraq* newspaper commented on this statement saying, "Iraq congratulates the Arab nation for this clear victory and pleads to Allāh to crown this victory by getting the enemy out of all lands of Hijaz and to grant victory to the Hashemite army against the opponents and enemies of the Arab unity."[1]

It finally became clear that the glad tiding of victory was based on whim, for the *ikhwan* returned to their former positions after the end of the [ten-day] pilgrimage season.

Residents' Condition

Jidda's residents suffered hardship, stringency and harm during the war's months. The share of the poor was quite significant compared to that of others, as is always the case. Food prices rose in the town, especially those of vegetables and fruits, and malaria, dysentery and thiamine deficiency diseases, such as scurvy beriberi, spread among the population. The number of the dead in the town kept rising day after day.

Jidda depends for drinking water on a desalination machine which they call "condenser". This machine kept working during the war more than its capacity, and most of its production was set aside for the army's needs. Malfunction started afflicting it from time to time, and people started suffering from thirst just as they suffered from hunger. One water tin sold for ten pennies, a price which the poor could not bear.[2] Commenting on this, Philby says, "The absolute neutrality policy which Britain followed cost the city of Jidda dearly. More than twenty-thousand persons died as victims of disease, hunger and suffering in a full year of siege. It came to an end, and the city's residents succumbed pleading for water, looking for barley and animal feed to eat instead of human food."[3]

---

1 *Al-Iraq* newspaper of June 23, 1925.
2 Public Records Office in London FO 371/10809.
3 Khairi Hammad (Op. Cit.), p. 158.

Chapter Six: Ali's Days as King

Another problem appeared in Jidda in addition to that of hunger and thirst. It was the slave problem. There were in Jidda, as was the case with other cities of the Arabian Peninsula, many slaves, and some of those slaves used in past days to run away from their masters and seek shelter at British consulates so they would repatriate them in Africa. When famine intensified in Jidda, the number of those who sought refuge at the Jidda consulate increased. In the month of July, the consulate repatriated twenty slaves most of whom were Sudanese, and there were among them some Ethiopians. The residents of Jidda became angry because of that, and a delegation from among them went to the Hashemite minister of foreign affairs, namely Fuad al-Khateeb, protesting against what the said consulate had done. Their excuse was that the fleeting slaves were thieves and the rule of the Shari`a must be carried out against them. King Ali had to interfere in the matter, so he asked the consulate to stop sending the slaves away. His excuse was the public resentment against it in Jidda, for such an action increased the frustration of the residents, and it could lead to their revolution. The consul responded to the king's request temporarily.[1]

Jidda's Notables

During the war, the notables of Jidda split into two groups: One of them inclined towards the Hashemites and the other towards the Saudis, and there was an undeclared feud between them.

The head of the Hashemite group was a man named Muhammed Taweel who, in fact, was quite loyal to King Ali and to the Hashemite House. He spent most of his wealth assisting King Ali during the war. His opponents explain this loyalty by saying that the Hashemite House was behind his wealth in the first place.[2] No matter what the reason was, this man's firmness

---

1 Public Records Office in London FO 371/10809.
2 Husain Muhammed Naseef (Op. Cit.), Vol. 1, p. 163.

in his loyalty indicated his sincerity, and it is rare for one to be loyal under such circumstances.

As for the group that inclined towards the Saudis, it was headed by Qasim Zeenal. This man used to repeatedly declare that Jidda's interest necessitated its surrender to Ibn Saud and that King Ali had to leave it. King Ali came to know that this man and his supporters were communicating with Ibn Saud and providing the latter with intelligence, so the king instructed the war minister to refer them to a military court which gave them a prison sentence. On November 7, 1924, the court re-tried them, sentencing them this time to death. The war minister insisted on carrying the sentence out, but the king invited them to his mansion on the 14th of the month and announced his amnesty towards them after advising them not to oppose the government or talk about politics.[1] Philby says, "The defendants paid King Ali a price for the amnesty: Each of them donated two thousand pounds to the Jidda defense plan."[2]

Only a month or less later, Qasim Zeenal started again publicly declaring his opinion which opposed the Hashemite government, advocating the need to get King Ali out of Jidda. Apparently, this man trusted the good-heartedness of King Ali, so he started to defy him. Describing King Ali, Philby says, "He was good-hearted to the extent that gets him to reach the degree of naïvety."[3]

Humans' problem is that they dare to confront good persons while tolerating bad ones. But when they meet a strong and firm person, they immediately humble themselves before him, and we have noticed this matter clearly in the students towards their teachers, and it is more clear in the general public towards their rulers.

---

1   *Ibid.*, p. 167.
2   Khairi Hammad (Op. Cit.), p. 163.
3   *Ibid.*, p. 162.

Chapter Six: Ali's Days as King

The Soldiers' Story

When we compare Ibn Saud's soldiers with those of King Ali, we find an obvious difference. The first defied death as they fought—as we have already stated—believing that if they were killed, they would enter Paradise, whereas the others were reluctant mercenaries. In his confidential report, the British consul described the latter party saying that, with the exception of a small number of them, they were nothing but a gang of bloodthirsty mercenaries, each group fearing the hegemony of that of the other. They, generally speaking, are united in rioting, but when it comes to doing something of benefit, they disperse."[1]

The most rioting of soldier groups and the most troublesome were the Palestinians followed by the Syrians who were mostly Druze. The Palestinians started declaring their frustration a short period after their arrival at Jidda and kept going to the British consul complaining to him about their bad condition, shabby clothes and bad food. They claimed that they did not volunteer to fight but to work in Maan's railroad, but they were moved to Jidda against their will. Their grumbling started increasing when the Hashemite government was unable to pay their salaries starting from late 1924. On February 15, a group of Palestinians of about one hundred and fifty persons declared a strike, refusing to obey orders unless the government paid their late salaries. Some of their officers went to them to talk, but they refused to speak to them and directed the fires of their rifles above the officers' heads. Then King Ali went to them and promised to pay their salaries in five or six days, so they returned to obedience. The salaries were paid by the promised deadline.[2]

The problem was aggravated anew in the month of April of 1925 when the Palestinians and Egyptians declared their grumbling due to their salaries being late and demanded to be

---

1   Public Records Office in London FO 371/11432.
2   Public Records Office in London FO 371/10807.

repatriated. The government had to send thirty-five men from among them home. This deportation encouraged others to declare their grumbling and to demand deportation, and some of them went to the British consulate requesting its intervention. The government now was alarmed and feared its army system would collapse, so it arrested some soldiers who had gone to the consulate, whipped them then expelled them to Yanbu` and al-Wajh. The consul protested to the king for so doing, whereupon the king assured him that the whipping had taken place without his knowledge and that he had issued strict orders not to whip the soldiers in the future.[1]

The condition improved in the month of May following the arrival of twenty thousand [gold] liras from al-Husain at al-Aqaba. Also, the sum of twenty-five thousand rupees arrived from Iraq sent by King Faisal from the revenues of the Prophet's Endowments. The king was able to use both amounts to pay soldiers' one month's salaries, so they calmed down in the hope of getting all their unpaid salaries later.

Late in July, the mayor of Jidda summoned the senior merchants to a meeting and asked them for a loan to the government in the sum of twenty thousand liars, but they refused. After attempts with them, the sum was brought down to only four thousand liars, so they paid it. In the month of August, King Ali sold some of the shops that belonged to him in Jidda for five thousand liras. They were bought by Sulayman Qabeel, a wealthy Jidda merchant.[2] The king had finally to pawn his personal properties in Egypt in lieu of a loan in the sum of fifteen thousand pounds[3], and it is said that he also had to sell some personal artifacts his family had, including the clothes and jewelry of his wife.[4]

---

1 *Ibid.*
2 Public Records Office in London FO 371/10909.
3 Ameen al-Rayhani (Op. Cit.), p. 401.
4 Ameen Sa`eed, *Tarikh al-Dawla al-Saudia* (History of the Saudi State), Beirur, Vol. 2, p. 177.

Chapter Six: Ali's Days as King

These amounts, which the government obtained, were not sufficient to meet the soldiers' increasing needs, so the government was forced on August 12 to deport 475 soldiers from among the Palestinians, sending them to Aqaba on board the ship Taweel.[1] The remaining soldiers kept getting money through various means. Husain Muhammed Naseef, a resident of Jidda, says, "Some soldiers started looting whatever they could find before them, and some others broke into empty homes which they demolished, pulled their wooden items to sell. The value of what they destroyed through this method amounted to twenty thousand pounds. Some soldiers had to go begging on the streets."[2]

The crisis intensified in the afternoon of November 28 when the soldiers assembled and decided to loot the town the next day. The king knew about it at midnight, so he summoned the sheikhs of the Hijazi and Yemeni tribes to whom a group of the soldiers belonged and requested them to prevent their folks from participating in the mutiny. The sheikhs responded to him and prevented them. As for the Palestinians and Syrians, they insisted on their stance.[3] In the morning of the next day, about 220 men from among them demonstrated and went out walking in the markets shooting their bullets until they reached the Grand Mosque which they entered, fortifying themselves inside it. They took their rifles' nozzles out through its windows, threatening to kill anyone who approached them. The war minister went to them, so they threatened to kill him, whereupon he went back to wherever he had come from.[4]

The king's guards and armed slaves surrounded the mosque, and the British consul intervened in the matter supported by the Italian consul who was then deputy of the French consul. Both men asked that the Palestinians and Syrians be left alone in the

---

1 Public Records Office in London FO 371/10809.
2 Husain Muhammed Naseef (Op. Cit.), Vol. 1, p. 199.
3 Public Records Office in London FO 371/11442.
4 Husain Muhammed Naseeb (Op. Cit.), Vol. 1, p. 199.

pretext they were subjects of countries under the mandate of both their governments, so the guards and slaves withdrew from around the mosque.

An agreement was reached with the rebelling soldiers to be deported ten days later, that each of them should be fined one lira, and they would be provided with fifteen days' rations. On December 12, they were deported on the small ship Rushdi to Aqaba.[1] But the problem did not end there. The remaining soldiers felt that they were deprived of being paid due to remaining silent and obedient, and grumbling started spreading among them, and there was fear the town would be looted.[2]

The situation in Jidda became very dangerous, and King Ali realized that he was in a hopeless miserable situation. What increased his misery was the arrival of a report about the fall of the Enlightened Medina at the hands of the Saudi forces on December 6. It became clear to him that perhaps Ibn Saud would be able to move his cannons from Medina to around Jidda in a short while. It was then that King Ali decided to surrender to Ibn Saud and to leave the country so he would relieve others and be himself relieved!

How the Surrender Took Place

In his confidential report to his government, the British consul says, "King Ali visited me accompanied by his foreign minister, Fuad, on the eve of December 9, days after a report reached him that Medina had fallen, and he kept talking about various matters. Before leaving the consulate, he sought my advice about what he should do in the coming days. I, therefore, told him that I could not give him any advice due to the very neutral stance which the government of His Majesty had undertaken, so the king left the consulate. In the morning of the next day, he asked me to meet him, so I went to him. He asked

---

[1] Public Records Office in London FO 371/11443.
[2] Public Records Office in London FO 371/11442.

Chapter Six: Ali's Days as King

me the same question and I repeated the same answer. On the eve of the 13th of the month, when the situation became more tense, King Ali asked me orally to mediate for the surrender of the town. I told him that I would contact my government in this regard and would notify him of the outcome as soon as I received its answer. He also asked me to permit him to reside in Palestine, Trans-Jordan or Iraq, saying that he was an Arab and wished to live in an Arab country if possible near one of his brothers, Faisal or Abdullah. In the morning of the next day, King Ali emphasized to me his previous oral request with a written one, providing me with the list of terms which could be the basis for the mediation..."[1]

The British consul sent a telegram to his government asking it for permission to mediate. The answer reached him in the morning of Wednesday, the 16th of the month, permitting him to do so; therefore, the consul quickly wrote a letter to Ibn Saud asking him to meet him in Rughama in the late morning of the next day. He sent his letter with his Indian scribe, Ihsanullah. The consulate's car left Jidda carrying the Indian scribe with a white flag fluttering on it. The car met Ibn Saud's convoy near Bahra, and the scribe submitted the letter to the consul. When Ibn Saud read it, he said to the scribe, "You have come at the right moment because had you been late one day, it would have been too late." Ibn Saud told him that he was going to Rughama to steer the attack on Jidda based on the request of the residents of Jidda who had promised to assist him if he attacked.

Khair ad-Din al-Zurakli narrates saying that when the consul's scribe met Ibn Saud, the latter was at one of the most critical hours of his life: Heads of the *ikhwan* had by then become fed-up with their siege of Jidda and kept arguing with Ibn Saud violently, pressing him to choose one of two options: He should either permit them to open Jidda by force, or they would leave and go home in Najd. Ibn Saud answered them saying, "I will not

---

[1] Public Records Office in London FO 371/11432.

enter Jidda fighting, and I shall remain at its gates, and it is up to you to stay or to leave." As the *ikhwan* were getting ready to leave, news reached Ibn Saud that King Ali had decided to surrender. According to al-Zurakli, this event is another evidence for the existence of the "luck" gift which Ibn Saud had.[1]

Ibn Saud agreed to meet the British consul the following day, Thursday. At ten o'clock in the morning of Thursday, the consul met Ibn Saud at the Rughama, and that was the first time he met him. The consul wrote in his report to his government expressing his admiration of the attraction he found in Ibn Saud in ethics and generous tolerance at the time of victory. The consul stated that Ibn Saud accepted most of the terms which King Ali wanted, and this was generous of him.[2]

The terms [of the surrender] were comprised of seventeen articles the summary of which is that Ibn Saud must issue amnesty for all those who had helped King Ali, i.e. the officials, officers and notables, to ensure their safety and that of their families and wealth, to distribute to the officers and soldiers the sum of five thousand pounds, to pledge to deport anyone who wished to go back to his homeland while keeping those whom he saw to be qualified as government officials, to grant the family of al-Husain all their personal possessions which they had inherited from their forefathers, to grant King Ali the right to take with him upon his departure all his personal luggage, including his private car, prayer rugs and horses. On his part, King Ali pledged to hand over all the weapons, machineguns, planes, cannons and armored vehicles in good condition and without tampering with them and also hand over the four Hijazi ships: Taweel, Rushdi, Raqmatain and Radhawi, permitting King Ali to use Raqmatain ship to transport his personal luggage, then it would return.[3]

---

1 Khair ad-Din al-Zurakli (Op. Cit.), Vol. 2, p. 585.
2 Public Records Office in London FO 371/11432.
3 Ameen Sa'eed, *Al-Thawra al-Arabiyya al-Kubra* (The Great Arab Revolution), Cairo, Vol. 3, pp. 218-219.

Chapter Six: Ali's Days as King

The consul returned to Jidda after sunset of the same day and met King Ali after supper. The king bitterly protested the amendments which Ibn Saud made to his terms, but he finally agreed to them and signed them. King Ali started after that getting ready to leave Jidda as soon as possible.

In the morning of the 22nd of the month, King Ali left Jidda on board the British barge Cornflower. Before his departure, he emancipated twenty of his slaves whom he handed over to the British consulate to repatriate to their homelands in Africa.[1] It is said that he took with him upon his departure from Jidda all the postal stamps the offices used to have.[2]

The barge sailed with King Ali and his entourage on board heading to Aden. Upon their arrival, they remained in it.

The British attaché in Aden tried to get a ship to transport them to Basra but could not, so he had to reserve places for them on a ship sailing to Bombay. They left Aden on the 27th of the month. When they reached Bombay, they could not get down from it because they had no passports, so they were transported to another ship that carried them to Basra.[3] From there, they took the train to Baghdad which they reached on January 8, 1926. At the train station, King Faisal and his son, Ghazi, welcomed them.[4]

Ibn Saud Enters Jidda

In Jidda, an interim government was formed in order to maintain security between both governments during the period. Following King Ali's departure from Jidda, the British consul went to Rughama accompanied by the head of the interim government whom he introduced to Ibn Saud. Then the consul

---

[1] Public Records Office in London FO 371/11442.
[2] Anees Saigh, *Al-Hashimiyyoon wal Thawra al-Arabiyya al-Kubra* (The Hashemites and the Great Arab Revolution), Beirut: 1966, p. 246.
[3] Public Records Office in London FO 371/11433.
[4] *Al-Iraq* newspaper of January 9, 1926.

thanked Ibn Saud for accepting his peace mediation, mentioning to him that his government permitted him to mediate only for the sake of avoiding bloodshed in the holy land and to bring peace and prosperity to it as well as to ensure the safety of millions of pilgrims who were subjects of His esteemed British Majesty. Ibn Saud answered him saying, before all those present, that he warmly thanked the British government for all of that on his behalf and on behalf of his people and the entire Islamic world. He said that he regarded Britain as his only sincere friend in the world, and that he had no relationship, small or big, with any other country. In his confidential report to his government, the British consul says, "Ibn Saud repeated this statement several times and with enthusiasm and sincerity, using his hand to support his statement, for he was moving his fist with every word he pronounced. Ibn Saud continued his talk with the [British] consul saying that based on the sanctity of the word and the commands of his religion and belief, he was obligated, as the executor of the treaty signed between him and Great Britain, to be in full harmony with his friend and ally, the British nation, whose policy is his policy so long as it did not tamper with two matters that were dearer to him than his life, and that he was ready to spill the last drop of his blood for their sake: his religion and honor. "I strengthen the ties of friendship that are always in existence between my people and Great Britain by the will of Allāh!," Ibn Saud said.[1]

Ibn Saud moved in the morning of the next day from Rughama in a large convoy for Jidda. When he reached Kindara, he settled at the guest house in it. He hoisted the Najdi flag over the house, and the cannons fired one hundred and one shot. The consul, notables and officers went to greet Ibn Saud. The Italian consul advanced towards him and spoke in Arabic saying, "Due to being the oldest consul, I offer, on behalf of myself and on behalf of my fellows, our congratulations to your greatness on entering Jidda

---

[1] Public Records Office in London FO 371/11432.

in this peaceful way which prevented bloodshed. We wish your greatness continuous success and happiness." Ibn Saud answered him saying that he did not slow down the military operations except to reach those peaceful results. Then Ibn Saud expressed his thanks to the British attaché for his effort. He also thanked all other consuls.[1]

Ibn Saud stayed at Kindara for one day. In the morning of the next day, he moved inside Jidda and stayed at the house of Sheikh Muhammed Afandi Naseef. People of various classes went to greet him, and poets delivered their resonant poems as is their custom on such occasions!

---

[1] Ameen al-Rayhani (Op. Cit.), pp. 425-426.

Chapter Seven
Al-Husain's Last Years

Al-Husain's Last Years

Following his departure from Jidda on October 15, 1924, al-Husain went to Aqaba where he spent eight months, then he was forced by the British to leave it for Cyprus. Al-Husain remained in Cyprus up to June 4, 1931. We will try in this chapter to indicate what happened to him during that period in as much information as we have been able to obtain.

Where He Stayed

As soon as al-Husain left Jidda for Aqaba, telegrams kept going on in London, Baghdad and Jerusalem looking for a suitable place where al-Husain should stay. Ms. Bell says the following in her letter of October 15, "There is fierce rivalry between us and Palestine as to who is *not* to have King Husain. No doubts he will be rather a bore in Palestine but he can't do much harm where he hasn't a son on the throne. I console myself with the reflection that in whatever way King Husain may continue to add his quota of irritation to the general burden of the universe, it will not, at my rate, be in the capacity of King of the Hejaz and Khalif of Islam."[1]

Al-Husain reached Aqaba on the 18th of the month. One day before his arrival, the British attaché in Amman, Mr. [Alec] Kirkbride, went to meet Prince Abdullah to tell him that the British government decided to permit his father, al-Husain, to stay in Aqaba temporarily until it found another place for him to settle. When al-Husain reached Aqaba, Mr. Kirkbride went to him and told him about the decision of the British government just as his son, Abdullah, was notified yesterday. Then Kirkbride

---

[1] Elizabeth Burgoyne, *Gertrude Bell: From Her Personal Papers 1914-1926*, London: Ernest Benn Limited, 1961, p. 281.

wrote a confidential report to his government in London about having met al-Husain and his son of which we would like to quote the most important text:

"I talked with His Highness Prince Abdullah at two o'clock in the afternoon of October 17 and told him of the British government's decision, so the Prince was very much touched. Apparently, he desired his father to go to Amman before the British government made its decision. The Prince kept speaking bitterly about the British government and how it betrayed its Arab friends, expressing his regret (perhaps in an unofficial way) because they [Arabs] did not keep their loyalty to the Turks. I, therefore, asked the Prince to immediately notify his father, al-Husain, in Aqaba of the British government's decision. The Prince, therefore, sent a telegram in the evening of that day notifying him of the decision and also telling him that he was going to Aqaba.

"I went to Aqaba at 10:25 am on the 18th of the month, arriving there the next day at 12:55 pm... Al-Husain got down the ship at 3:30 pm. I immediately informed him of the British government's decision..., so al-Husain said that his son, Abdullah, had already informed him of it yesterday and that he regretted the British government had only very little faith in him, so it is concerned he might stay in a country for which the Arabs spilled their blood for the common issue between them and Britain. I explained to him that everyone's interest dictated that he should not be hasty in what he did and that the British government was busy trying to find a place for him to settle in the future, and that it certainly would work hard to resolve the issue as soon as possible.

"Formerly King Husain spoke in detail about his relationship with Britain since the start of the Arab Revolution against the Turks. He pointed out to the old agreements and promises, to the reasons that made him reject the treaty which Britain offered. He also pointed out with some emphasis to the plots which the

Chapter Seven: Al-Husain's Last Years

present British consul schemed against him in Jidda, accusing him of trying deliberately to oust him. Husain stated specifically that the only reason that made him leave his kingdom was his realization that the British government was not pleased with him, and it became clear to him that it would be glad to get rid of him. He believes that the British government turned against him in order to please the Turks, Indians and Egyptians. Since his friendly sentiments towards Britain did not change, he saw that it would be best to withdraw.

"Prince Abdullah reached Aqaba in the early morning of the next day. I told him that the former king [Husain] agreed to the British government's wish, and I expressed to him my hope that he would not say anything to him that would make him change his mind. The Prince expressed coolness towards this entire issue, and I think that he felt that his dignity was wounded because he could not invite his father to stay in his country.

"At 7:30 that morning, I escorted the Prince when he boarded the ship Al-Raqmatain, so the former King met us on board, and the king kept once more talking in detail about his past, supporting his statements with documents signed by McMahon and others. Apparently, he carries with him many official documents. Perhaps it will be boring to write in my report in detail about all what the former King had said, for most of his pretexts are old, and they must be well known to the government of His Majesty. But I can submit a detailed report about them if needed. The former King said at the conclusion of his talk that he desired to meet Sir Gilbert Clayton and to discuss the matters with him..."[1]

An agreement was finally reached between Iraq and Britain to let al-Husain settle in Basra. Britain preconditioned that he should not interfere during his stay in political matters. Ms. Bell wrote a letter on October 22 saying, "We are going to be saddled

---

1 Public Records Office in London FO 371/10016.

with King Husain. He is to live at Basrah and sit still, taking no part in politics. You might as well expect a flea to stay still."[1]

King Faisal sent his father a telegram inviting him to reside in Iraq in the name of the people and the government. On November 10, Mr. Kirkbride reached Aqaba and met al-Husain then wrote his government the following report:

"On the tenth of this month, I met former King Husain in Aqaba and told him that the British government had no objection to his acceptance of Iraq's invitation provided he accepted the terms put by the Iraqi government with regard to his place of residence and that he would not interfere in politics. I also informed him that the British government desired that he should go by sea to Basra. Then I asked him if he had received the invitation with the details of the terms which the Iraqi government had put.

"The former King answered that he received King Faisal's letter telling him that Iraq's government and people would be glad if he settled there, but the letter did not contain any of the terms to which I referred, but that he heard from other sources that the Iraqi government feared his interference in the political and religious matters and it, therefore, desired that he should provide a specific pledge not to interfere in these matters. He emphasized to me that he would not accept the invitation anyhow at the present time because he was comfortable in Aqaba and had no desire to undertake an unnecessary trip that could lead to exhausting his family, that even if he had accepted the invitation, the Iraqi government's mistrust had hurt his pride, making him refuse to go there. He realizes that it is not appropriate for him to interfere in politics while residing in Iraq as a guest of its government, and if they could not trust him without an advance pledge, he preferred not to go.

---

1   Burgoyne, p. 357.

Chapter Seven: Al-Husain's Last Years

"Husain invited me to meet him the next morning, but he did not have anything to say other than repeating what he had said before. He expressed his opinion that the time was opportune for the British government to intervene to stop bloodshed in the Arab lands..."[1]

Aid Sent

The war around Jidda had just started when al-Husain reached Aqaba, so he sent a letter to his son, Ali, in Jidda urging him to remain steadfast and pledging to send aid to him in the form of cash and military supplies. Husain fulfilled his promise to his son. He opened the cash coffers which he had carried with him from Mecca and kept sending sums of money from them to Jidda in installments. He also sent amounts from them to Abdullah to purchase planes and armored vehicles and to hire volunteers.

Abdullah exerted efforts to gather volunteers and buy supplies and weapons. But what is regretful is that many of those who were commissioned to do so grew up during the Ottoman period and were immersed in its values and traditions; therefore, we found them seizing the opportunity for getting rich quickly. Because of that, most of the money Husain sent was wasted. Salah ad-Din al-Mukhtar, who was an eyewitness of what happened, says the following:

"Prince Abdullah son of al-Husain received from his father in Aqaba forty thousand gold liras for sending volunteers and buying some mechanical weapons and planes for the purpose of expelling Ibn Saud from Hijaz... But I determine here that most of this sum found its way to the pockets of hypocrites, interest-seekers, thieves and men having no conscience. I determine this fact arbitrarily, for I moved from Amman to Maan as the head of 145 soldiers without receiving one penny with the exception of

---

[1] Public Records Office in London FO 371/10807.

some bread and other food rations which were a must so we would not starve on the distance between Amman and Maan!"[1]

Salah ad-Din al-Mukhtar also says, "The military warehouses in Maan were full of weapons and ammunition, and they had three cannons. Prince Abdullah came in person to Maan and ordered the cannons and weapons to be transported to Jidda, and it was decided to pay ten Majidi riyals as the fare for [the owner of] each camel working in transporting the weapons to Aqaba. It became obvious later that a large portion of the weapons was sold to nearby tribes." Al-Mukhtar personally saw one of the three cannons, their largest, thrown at the bottom of an alley between Maan and Aqaba.[2]

It is worth mentioning in this regard that al-Husain did not abandon his old habit of bringing close to him flatterers and sweet talkers, believing what they said. In Aqaba, he was surrounded by some of them[3] who were similar to those who used to surround him in Mecca. They kept fabricating for him reports which he desired to hear, and he, on his part, would give them huge sums of money in order to get volunteers and purchase weapons, so they would keep most or all of the money in their pockets.

Ameen al-Rayhani narrates the following: "Al-Husain gave, before getting out of Mecca, one of those flatterers ten thousand liras to buy planes and armored vehicles from Europe, but the man went to Egypt and bought in the amount real estate for himself." Al-Rayhani also narrates saying, "Three old planes were bought from England for seven thousand pounds and sent to Jidda. It was found out that they were not worth more than one thousand and five hundred pounds. As for the rest, it went to the pockets of dealers and agents."[4]

---

1 Salah ad-Din al-Mukhtar, *Tarikh al-Mamlaka al-arabiyya al-Saudia* (History of the Kingdom of Saudi Arabia), Beirut, Vol. 2, p. 313.
2 *Ibid.*, Vol. 2, p. 318.
3 Storrs, *Orientations*, London: 1939, p. 518.
4 Ameen al-Rayhani, *Tariksh Najd al-Hadith wa Mulhaqatih* (Modern History of Najd

Chapter Seven: Al-Husain's Last Years

The Aqaba Problem

Prior to the war, the Aqaba and Maan area used to be within the Sham (Levant) governorate, but al-Husain annexed it to Hijaz thereafter. When the war in Hijaz erupted, the British felt the need to get this area out of the borders of Hijaz and to annex it to Trans-Jordan. The British used to regard it as having an important strategic location; therefore, they wanted to attach it to Trans-Jordan so it would be under their mandate and not fall in the hands of Ibn Saud.[1]

In mid-May of 1925, Ibn Saud sent a letter to the British government informing it of his sending a force to attack Aqaba due to his belief that al-Husain's stay in it was the main reason for prolonging the war in Hijaz, since al-Husain is supplying Jidda with funds, weapons and soldiers.[2] This letter caused on arrival a crisis in the British administration. Minister of colonies, Mr. [A.M.] Amery, was of the opinion that a warning should be sent to Ibn Saud not to attack Aqaba. But the foreign minister, Mr. [Sir Joseph Austen] Chamberlain, differed from him in his opinion and defended Ibn Saud saying that his attack on Aqaba had its justifications due to the presence of Husain in it; therefore, Husain had to be taken out of it through nice ways or by force, and as soon as possible. Chamberlain was of the opinion that Husain did not deserve Britain entering into a war with Ibn Saud for his sake.[3]

The British government finally decided to settle the problem by annexing Aqaba and Maan to Trans-Jordan and to move al-Husain to Cyprus. It notified Ibn Saud of it via its consul in Jidda,

---

and its Supplements), Beirut: 1954, pp. 246, 401.
1   Jarvis, *Arab Command*, London: 1942, p. 119.
2   Public Records Office in London FO 371/10809.
3   Gary Troeller, *The Birth of Saudi Arabia: Britain and the Rise of the House of Saʾud*, London: Routledge, 1976, p. 225. [The name of the author of this book, as it appears in the footnote on p. 287 of the original Arabic work which I have translated, is indicated as "Troeder", and this is one of many errors which I have luckily detected and corrected. – Tr.]

alerting him that the Aqaba became under its responsibility. On May 28, the British barge Cornflower reached the Aqaba waters, and its captain presented to al-Husain a warning from the British government asking him to leave Aqaba in three weeks. When al-Husain received this warning, he addressed the captain saying, "I do not go away from here even if I and my family perish in the bombs of what used to be, only yesterday, my ally." The captain responded to him saying something like he was only a messenger commissioned to convey a message and that he would return the next morning to receive the answer, then he left without sitting. When the captain returned at the set time, al-Husain handed him a lengthy letter which contained his rejection of the warning. Here below we quote a good portion of it:

"Since the beginning of the Arab Renaissance and up to this hour, I have been sincere in my loyalty to the government of His Majesty the King of Britain, remaining firm on my principle relying on its honor and based on its promises and official covenants... I have sacrificed everything, giving up authority and leaving my homeland out of my love for peace and in order to avoid bloodshed. I came to Aqaba to prove to the whole world that I have no ambition except to keep my people happy and to liberate my homeland, having performed my obligation... Now here I am residing in one of the villages of Hijaz isolated from the world and keeping a distance from anything that may cause disturbance and misunderstanding. Since this isolation and distance did not rid me of such plots, there is no doubt that wherever I go, the matter will not be without something taking place as in the recent notifications. And these maybe more horrific than my present situation, for I cannot ensure the eruption of the Arab people at that time and that things could happen towards the ally and others which do not carry good implications. I, therefore, find no option other than staying in my present place, and if the government of His Majesty the King wishes to send me to Mars, I am ready to carry out its opinion in this mission the first minute of the notification. Or if its greatness appointed and decided to send one of its military means to annihilate me together with my family so everyone else will be saved from these perils, let her do so because I have promised myself not to stop assisting my citizens and countrymen. I brag before you of having assisted and continue to assist the Hijazi government with my private money which I saved for my unknown future because if anyone is not good to his homeland, he cannot be expected to be of any goodness to his allies and friends. I am also honored for having remained firm to my principle and sincere in my actions, and I have carried out my obligations, so I am not responsible for others who do not fulfill their promise or carry out their pledge, those who use the force of their armored vehicles and the heads of their lances to achieve their ambitions. It is there that judgment will be for those who win... Besides, if I did not recognize the mandate over the Arab lands from its basics, and I still protest against the British government which turned Palestine into a national home for the Jews and northern Syria having been placed under the mandate and turned into a safe haven for the Armenians... I am surprised to see how the British government ignores what has happened to Hijaz, even to Mecca, i.e. the crushing and the looting of wealth and the destruction which cannot be avoided except after tens of years... Yet it now expresses an interest in Maan and Aqaba, the matter that leaves no room to extend the research in it because this suffices one who contemplates the least on it... I will not leave Aqaba no matter what the result may be, even if the matter leads to my annihilation and the obliteration of my family from existence. I do not mean by being so adamant to be hostile to Britain or to anyone else; rather, it is for the cause of saving my homeland and the sons of my nation. Anything [wrong] which the British government does to me only increases my honor and pride among my people and nation. History records the actions of each one of us, and there is wisdom in this."¹

It seems that this strongly worded reply by al-Husain put the British government in a delicate situation: It was difficult for it to carry out its warning to al-Husain by force because this would tarnish its image before the [Islamic] world's public opinion; so, what should it do?

The British government resorted to Prince Abdullah to ask him to convince his father to leave Aqaba for Cyprus. The Prince went to Aqaba, met his father, kissed his hands and said, "O master of blessings! The policy of violence and toughness is of no avail towards force. Now, since you have carried out your obligations towards your nation and fulfilled your message, the Arab nation must carry out its obligations."² It is said that Abdullah mentioned to his father that his throne in the Trans-Jordan and that of Faisal in Iraq were threatened with disappearance if he himself remained insisting on his refusal.³ Facing Abdullah's pleas, al-Husain had to succumb to the British warning.

Another barge reached the waters of Aqaba called Dalhi and joined the first. At five o'clock in the afternoon of Thursday, June 18, al-Husain, accompanied by his family and slaves, boarded the boat of Barge Dalhi. One of those who saw him boarding it narrates saying that al-Husain was muttering, "May Allāh never grant you success, O Abdullah!"⁴ It is also narrated that during the entire period, which he spent on the barge between Aqaba and Cyprus, he used to repeat to himself this line of poetry:

---

1 Ameen Sa'eed, *Al-Thawra al-Arabiyya al-Kubra* (The Great Arab Revolution), Cairo, Vol. 3, pp. 209-211.
2 Sulayman Mousa, *Safahat Matwiyya* (Folded Pages), Amman: 1977, p. 193.
3 Salah ad-Din al-Mukhtar (Op. Cit.), Vol. 2, p. 315.
4 *Ibid.*, Vol. 2, p. 315.

Chapter Seven: Al-Husain's Last Years

وَمَـنْ كُتِبَتْ عَلَيْـهِ خُطىً مَشاها   مَشَيناهـا خُطىً كُتِبَتْ عَلينــا

We walked steps destined for us,
Whoever is destined to walk steps does walk.[1]

On June 24, that is, one week after al-Husain's departure from Aqaba, Prince Abdullah issued an official statement announcing the annexation of Aqaba and Maan to Trans-Jordan and their cessation from Hijaz. The statement said that this took place "for the appointing of His Hashemite Majesty great Ali as King of the Hijazi land, may Allāh support him and sustain his victory."[2] On the next day, a fabulous official celebration took place in Maan to hoist the emirate flag attended by Prince Abdullah accompanied by his prime minister, Ridha Pasha al-Rikabi.[3]

The annexation of Aqaba and Maan to Trans-Jordan had a bad impact on the government of Jidda because it led to cutting off the supplies going to the Enlightened Medina and it could ultimately result in its falling in the hands of the Saudi forces. As for King Ali, the impact of the news on him was two-folded. The British consul in Jidda says the following in his report to his government: "King Ali expressed his pleasure with his father getting out of his own way, but his pleasure was mixed because his father distancing himself would lead to stopping the financial aid from reaching Jidda. He, of course, loves his father's money separately from his father, but he surely prefers his father staying with the money over losing the money."[4]

---

1 Ameen Sa'eed, *Asrar Al-Thawra al-Arabiyya al-Kubra* (Secrets of the Great Arab Revolution), Beirut, p. 385.
2 Abdullah ibn al-Husain, *Muthakkarati* (My Memoirs), Jerusalem: 1945, p. 205.
3 Husain Muhammed Naseef, *Tarikh al-Hijaz* (History of Hijaz), Cairo: 1349 A.H./1930 A.D., p. 205.
4 Public Records Office in London FO 371/10809.

Al-Husain In Cyprus

At seven o'clock in the morning of Monday, June 22, 1925, Dalhi arrived at Larnaca Port in Cyprus carrying al-Husain and those in his company, and police commissioner Maj. [Cecil Stephen] Northcote received him. Al-Husain stepped down to the port pier at 11:00 am. With him, there were 192 large bales and large Fiat limousines. He was also accompanied by his wife, Queen Adila Hanum, both his daughters, his private confidant, Salih, his military escort, Kamil Pasha, and about 25 slaves and bondmaids.[1]

Al-Husain first stayed at a Nicosia hotel called [Ledra] Palace Hotel, then he rented a house in Nicosia where he lived. The house was comprised of two buildings separated by a garden. He set aside one of them for the *haram* and the other for those who worked for him and for guests. In 1928, he was joined by his younger son, Prince Zaid, who wanted to look after his father in his old age. In fact, Zaid exerted an appreciated effort serving his father, remaining with him until his last Cyprus days. His mother, Adila, died in Cyprus and was buried there.

When al-Husain was in Aqaba, prior to being transported to Cyprus, he had some hope left on Britain going to save him and to expel Ibn Saud from Hijaz. He did not imagine that Britain would turn its back to its friendship with him that easily. He did not discover how mistaken he was except when Britain forced him to leave Aqaba and to go to Cyprus. It is narrated about him that he said to one of those who accompanied him on board the barge after leaving Aqaba that he was wrong and did not know the manners and nature of the Europeans.[2]

Two incidents took place to al-Husain in Cyprus that made him lose hope on Britain for good and bear a great deal of grudge

---

1 *Ibid.*
2 Ameen Sa'eed, *Al-Thawra al-Arabiyya al-Kubra* (the Great Arab Revolution), Cairo, Vol. 3, p. 211.

Chapter Seven: Al-Husain's Last Years

against it. The first took place when British newspapers kept taking him lightly and describing him using reprehensible remarks. Al-Husain became very angry when he discovered that The Times newspaper, which is known for being balanced, followed in the footsteps of the other newspapers and criticized him in a scathing way and made fun of him. On August 24, 1926, he wrote a letter to the British foreign minister complaining about the criticism of the newspapers and saying that they insulted his honor, dignity and self-respect. Al-Husain mentioned in his letter how he relied on Britain and tried to safeguard its honor and progress, risking his life when he joined the [first] World War for its sake at the time when Britain was threatened with dangers in Kut [I believe it should be Kuwait], the Dardanelles and Paris. Then he said, "This attack by the British newspapers will be regarded by everyone as evidence that Britain now turned against him and is assisting his opponents." Al-Husain pointed out, at the conclusion of his letter, to what is recorded in a historic British reference about the Zionist movement, that McMahon's promise to al-Husain was erroneously interpreted, and that al-Husain responded to that by asking the foreign minister to refer to McMahon's letter dated august 15, 1915.[1]

The second incident that brought about al-Husain's grudge towards Britain took place to the house in which he lived in Nicosia. After having lived in it for eight months, he wanted to move out of it to another house, but the owner of the house tried to extort him, suing him at the court and presenting a contract which al-Husain had supposedly written pledging in it to pay nine thousand pounds in case he left the house. When the case was submitted to the court, he was asked to bring his wife to testify, so al-Husain became very angry and did not permit his wife to attend the trial.

---

1   Public Records Office in London FO 371/11450.

Al-Husain wrote on September 27, 1926 a letter to the British prime minister complaining about the court mistreating him, indicating that he regarded himself as a guest of King George V and expected a treatment that suited the honor and prestige of His Majesty. The prime minister did not answer him. Late in October, a letter reached the governor of Cyprus from the British foreign minister. Its gist is that al-Husain did not have any rights or legal privileges that distinguished him from other foreigners in Cyprus, and that he had only been granted asylum in Cyprus in order to protect him from his enemies, that the foreign minister, nevertheless, commended the governor saying that, in agreement with the minister of colonies, the requirements of courtesy and humanitarianism mandated on him to treat al-Husain with some flexibility as much as possible with regard to his religious concerns or other matters relevant to attending the trial.[1]

The Complaint to the League of Nations

Al-Husain's hatred towards Britain reached its peak in November of 1926. It prompted him to write to the head of the League of Nations in Geneva to seek for his help and to complain about Britain. The letter is lengthy, below is a summary of it:

Mr. President,

I, the undersigned, King Husain ibn Ali, King of Hijaz, a founding member of the Nations' Assembly and an ally of the coalition in the [first] World War, would like to explain to Your Excellency the following:

FIRST: The Nations' Assembly [perhaps he meant the League of Nations] was not created except for one purpose: to prevent any independent country from being aggressive towards another. What is odd and amazing is that this basic law was not applied to my issue with the Wahhabis who swept my homeland and that of my fathers and forefathers up to the Hashemite Arab

---

1 *Ibid.*

Prophet Muhammed 7. I, therefore, strongly protest first against this action by the leader of the Wahhabis and, second, against the Assembly for not treating me according to its basic law [charter]. I request persistently the respectful Assembly to get the Wahhabis out of my homeland through the force of the members of the Nations' Assembly.

SECOND: The Nations' Assembly remembers that the leaders of the Wahhabis had before that entered the emirate of Kuwait, prompting the British State to send British soldiers stationed in Iraq with its planes, tanks and armed vehicles to Kuwait and to foil the Wahhabis' attempt.

THIRD: Wahhabi gangs stormed, after that, the Trans-Jordan Kingdom, so my son, Prince Abdullah, stood in their face with all the military forces and tough men he had, and he was joined by divisions of British soldiers with their planes, tanks and armed vehicles. Thus, he was able to conquer those gangs and push them back. Some senior people saw it with their own eyes, and they are fair witnesses. Now, whenever the Wahhabis, after their flight, found a wounded person, they would alight from their horses and pierce his heart with their daggers.

FOURTH: As for me, the undersigned, the King of Hijaz and a member of the Nations' Assembly as well as an ally of the victor of the [first] World War, I did not concern myself about these gangs as one who feared their transgression on my domain. This is so because I knew that we nowadays are not living in the Middle Ages, and because I was fully convinced that they would not dare to attack a land which three hundred million Muslims who believe in the Unity of God regard as being sacred, a land the independence of which is guaranteed by the Nations' Assembly, one the independence of which is protected and respected by all allied countries. I did not think that one of these great countries—meaning Britain—would urge the men of these gangs, through some of its stupid politicians, to enter the holy lands and destroy the mausoleums, places of worship and ban religious rituals. Yes, I could not imagine that this great ally would come behind the greatest of its allies in the East, the one who helped it in the great war the most, to stab him in the back without having a conscience that rebukes it or any manliness or loyalty that prevents it from this horrible unfair action. As regarding this great ally, it felt how horrible its action was especially when it saw the revulsion of the noble British people towards the stumbling, shaky, actually sick and stupid politicians, who deprived the British people of an honest ally and of a King who is deeply rooted in lineage and progeny, a man of peace who never at all thought of harming others. Yes, the men of the British government who committed this horrible mistake, this blatant error, now fall with their heads down, lowering their gaze before the public opinion of the noble British nation which will hold them to account severely when the British Parliament resumes its sessions.

FIFTH: I request the honored Nations' Assembly[1] to vacate the holy land from the Wahhabis and to hold a referendum for its residents so it may see that more than ninety percent of the residents will vote against them. I request giving me the freedom to work to restore my usurped authority and that of my fathers and forefathers and lift the unfair ruling against me [imposed] by men of the British government. I request to let my complaining voice be conveyed from my exile in the island of Cyprus to all men of the states, particularly to the noble British people in order to let them understand the truth in all honesty and frankness, i.e. that the dishonest policy of their government does not produce anything but grudges and hatred between the Britons and the true Muslims—I say the true Muslims, that is, the majority of the Muslims who are concerned about their religion, Prophet and his Progeny. There is no moral lesson to be derived from individuals who are regarded as being few in number

---

1 In the original Arabic text, the king here uses the term جمعية الأمم which means "Nations' Assembly" rather than the term عصبة الأمم which means "League of Nations" which is most likely what he meant. – Tr.

among the Muslims, those few who are ignorant, stupid and duped by the deceivers and evildoers who do not teach them a thing of their creed, nor do they follow the path commended to them by the Great Book (Qur'an). So, they are Muslims only in name. Had their Islam been sound, they would have respected the Progeny of their Prophet 7 who commended them to be good to his Progeny, and they would have all stood in one stance like a hero and a true Muslim who is forgiven, who resides in Paradise, the senior of the honored Alawi family in Egypt and in the rest of the Egyptian state's corners, when he sent his sons then went in person to Hijaz to fight the Wahhabis and to get out of the sacred Hijazi lands those who introduced innovations into the creed.

"I write this strong protest to the Presidency of your Assembly so all countries in general may get to know, and so the noble British people in particular may get to know, that the unfair and unjust actions of men of its government in Hijaz are lowering its status and that of His [Majesty's] status in the eyes of the true Muslims in general and in India in particular, actually in all British and international colonies. This is so because they, in all their power, want to safeguard their religious rituals in their holy lands. Yes, let the noble British nation know these facts and let it move out of its stagnation and stand like one who is a fair and honest savior in order to put a separating line between the oppressor and the oppressed, lifting the oppression which its government has caused from the oppressed. It is only then that we can say that the British nation is noble, fair and loves justice and what is right, and that the superpowers respect their Muslim subjects and their religious rituals.

"I would like to take this opportunity, Mr. President, to express my extreme respect for the efforts of your respectful self, and may you live in peace."

Al-Husain ibn Ali[1]

---

[1] Ameen al-Rayhani (Op. Cit.), Vol. 3, pp. 213-217.

What Storrs Says

Few days only passed since al-Husain wrote the above letter to the League of Nations when the British government appointed Mr. Ronald Storrs as governor of Cyprus. We do not know if this was accidental or intentional. No matter what the case may have been, it was noticed that Storrs started treating al-Husain in a way which was not free of meanness. Prince Zaid says, "... In Cyprus, Storrs demonstrated much disloyalty after we used to think that he was our friend and the friend of my master, Abdullah, in particular."[1]

In his *Memoirs*, Storrs talked about al-Husain's life in Cyprus and tried to be objective in writing about him, but we sense from what he wrote that his heart did not incline to al-Husain. He says about him the following: "He was not known—in Cyprus— by anyone, nor did anyone know him. He was, in as far as senior officials in the island, like a prisoner and to the junior officials like a nobody. I found him living in a small house surrounded by his youngest son, Zaid, in paternal sincerity. It was a moving sight to see this young prince who had led battalions in the war and spent a year at Balliol College [one of Oxford University's schools] reading for his father in a loud voice the boring comments on the Qur'an by al-Bukhari's *Sahih* (Storrs described the book as "Salih al-Bukhari"), serving him day and night."

Storrs also says, "The only source of happiness that lingered with al-Husain in Cyprus was limited to three genuine Arabian mares, and the most beautiful of them and the nicest is called Zahra. She ascends with agility the steps connecting the garden and the guest hall. Al-Husain used to shout to her, 'Ahla! [Welcome!] Masha-Allāh! [The will of Allāh be done!] Allāhu Akbar! [God is Great!], قَرِّبي يا بِنتَ العَمّ 'Come close, cousin!'... Al-Husain used to call this mare قُرَّة العَيْن the apple of the eye, and

---

1 Sulayman Mousa, *Muthakkarat al-Ameer Zaid* (Memoirs of Prince Zaid), Amman: 1976, p. 201.

used to give her dates, so she would eat them slowly then throw the stones in a bowl... But this source of happiness for al-Husain ended in a sad conclusion: The groom of those mares was expelled by al-Husain from his service, so he sought revenge against him by piercing their bellies." Storrs says, "When I was one morning at my official quarters, al-Husain came requesting permission to see me immediately. When he entered, he threw himself between my arms as his tears heavily rained."

Storrs says that when al-Husain was its ally in the war, the British government gave him the Great Cross Medal with a sash, but the medal arrived late when al-Husain was banished to Cyprus, so Storrs gave it to him at the inauguration of the Cyprus Public Library. Storrs comments about that saying, "I saw and came to know many changes of time, but I never knew the like of this event which is filled with irony when I presented him with the medal which is coveted by ambassadors, great army commanders and kings of Europe. Al-Husain was then an old expelled man, but his awe was still there!"

Storrs points out to the rumors circulated among the public about the hundreds of thousands of gold pounds placed in oil tins, the pounds which Britain had given him when he revolted against the Turks. He says that what remained of them was less than what the rumors stated, rumors that exaggerate such matters. Storrs states that the Palestinians who surrounded al-Husain in Aqaba were able to extract a good portion of those pounds because they are skilled experts in so doing, and this was done to him by some cunning merchants in Cyprus as well. Al-Husain, therefore, used to go to him (to Storrs) to ask him to intervene at courts on his side as is done in Mecca. Storrs also says that al-Husain's sons used to go to al-Husain to ask for money, but he used to disappoint them even before they asked by asking them for a loan. Storrs says that King Faisal complained to him [once] about it when he was playing with him the roulette on the Troodos Mountain [in Cyprus].¹

It is worth mentioning that what Storrs states about al-Husain's money is not supported by Prince Zaid. Zaid says, "When al-Husain arrived at Cyprus, we used to think that he had a lot of money, but it became clear that he did not have more than four thousand liras. After that, my master, Abdullah, and my master, Faisal, started sending him limited sums, but even these did not reach him regularly..."²

His Last Days

Al-Husain was sick with arteriosclerosis (the hardening of the blood veins) which started in 1919 following the Turba incident, as we pointed out then. In November of 1930, he had a light bleeding in the brain that caused him to have hemiplegia. This bleeding happened to him following the insult which Storrs directed at him. Following I would like to mention a summary of that incident as narrated to me by a man whom I trust and who was quoting Prince Zaid:

"In his last days, al-Husain ran out of money; therefore, his son, King Faisal, used to send him from Iraq a money order in the amount of one hundred pounds every month. For an unknown reason, the money order was late to arrive in August of 1930. The delay went on for more than two months, so they sent a telegram to Baghdad asking for the reason behind the delay, but they did not receive any answer from Baghdad. Prince Zaid renders this to British schemes, to the Britons' desire to harm his father. The delay of the money order led to the shopkeeper in their neighborhood refusing to provide them with the living materials with which he used to provide them before. Al-Husain had to go in the company of his son, Zaid, to Storrs in the hope he would find a solution for the problem.

---

1 Storrs (Op. Cit.), pp. 518-519.
2 Sulayman Mousa (Op. Cit.), p. 201.

Chapter Seven: Al-Husain's Last Years

Zaid says that when they both met Storrs at his office, he [Storrs] did not offer them any courtesy and did not even ask them to sit, so al-Husain sat on a chair without permission followed by Zaid. Al-Husain kept talking to Storrs about his problem then asked him for a loan until the money order arrived from Baghdad, but Storrs rudely said to him, "What is the warranty for this loan?" Al-Husain, thereupon, gave Storrs his gilt dagger and said, "This is the warranty". Storrs was holding a pencil in his hand, so he moved the dagger away with his pencil, taking the warranty lightly as if he was saying that it was not good enough. Then he summoned his scribe and ordered him to give al-Husain the loan he had asked for. But al-Husain could not tolerate that insult, and his hand kept shivering due to the impact, then he immediately left Storrs' office. He hardly reached his house when he suffered a bleeding in the brain.

On November 21, 1930, King Faisal left Baghdad for Cyprus on board a plane and was able to get the British government's agreement to move his father to Amman. Having moved him there, Faisal returned to Baghdad. In Amman, a medical team of five doctors was formed to examine al-Husain. Those doctors were: Jameel al-Totonji, Husam ad-Din Abu al-Saud, Tawfiq Ken`an and [famous Protestant Palestinian doctor] Izzat Tannoos Woolkh. After the examination, the team wrote the following report:

"We have been honored to examine His Hashemite Majesty King Husain ibn Ali at the Raghdan Mansion in Amman, and we found out that His Majesty, due to his advanced age, is sick with arteriosclerosis. About a month ago, light bleeding in the brain took place to him, but his general health improved due to the health measures which were undertaken for him, and the improvement continues. What increases our contentment is that we found all bodily systems to be in a good condition."[1]

---

[1] This is quoted from the handwritten manuscript of Sayyid Hibat ad-Din al-Shahristani.

On November 15, the Iraqi parliament agreed to send a delegation to Amman on behalf of the Iraqi government to greet al-Husain and to invite him to reside in Baghdad. The delegation was comprised of Sayyid Muhammed al-Sadr as the head, Ali al-Imam and Rauf al-Loos as members. The delegation travelled to Amman on the 29th of the month. Al-Husain thanked them for their invitation and promised to accept it when his health improved. But his health did not improve. On June 4, he breathed his last. His body was transported to Jerusalem where it was buried in the courtyard of the Sacred Haram near the Aqsa Mosque.

Actually, al-Husain failed in many matters, but he succeeded in one: He turned his life into a screaming publicity against Britain. Britain could have looked after al-Husain in his last years, considering his old age, at least for the sake of publicity, but it did not. Thus, it proved that it often does not know anything other than its own interest.

Poets Wander

A memorial was held for al-Husain in two large gatherings. One of them took place in Jerusalem on July 12, 1931 and the other in al-Adhamiyya [Baghdad] on August 14. In both of these gatherings, many poets and speakers participated. In the first, among the participants were: Ahmed Shawqi, Khalil Matran, Shibli Malat, Abdul-Hameed al-Rafi`i, Shafeeq Jabri, Fuad al-Khateeb, Muhammed Ali al-Homani, Mustafa al-Ghalayeeni, Sulayman al-Zahir and others. In the second, these poets were among the participants: Ma`ruf al-Rusafi, Ridha al-Shibeebi, Habeeb al-`Ubaidi, Abdul-Husain al-Azri, Kazim al-Dujaili and others. We do not need to say that these poets did not abandon, in their poems, the traditional mourning clichés since the world—according to their statements—sank into pitch darkness, the Arabs were lost, the corner of Islam collapsed, and the like,

Chapter Seven: Al-Husain's Last Years

and there was no difference among them except in coining the expressions and being artistic in imagination.

Al-Rusafi's poem drew attention because it was the contrary of his famous poem which he composed as a satire against al-Husain in 1916 following al-Husain's declaration of a revolution against the Turks. Here below we quote from his eulogy poem the following verse lines:

غَداةَ قضى الحُسينُ أبو المُلوكِ   بَدا وجهُ العروبةِ في حُلوكِ
كَذاكَ الشَّمسِ تَجْنَحُ للدُّلوكِ   قضى مُتنازلاً بعد اعتلاءٍ
وفي العَزَماتِ ليسَ بِذي شَريكِ   قضى في المَجدِ ليسَ بذي نَظيرٍ
الى أن ماتَ محمودَ السُّلوكِ   وقد سَلَكَ الطريقَ الى المعالي
قديمٍ كانَ كالعِذنقِ التَريكِ   وجَدَّدَ للعروبةِ عُرسَ مَجدِ
جَنوبَ الأرضِ كالريحِ السَّهوكِ   وأحدثَ نَهضةً في العُربِ هَزَّت
مؤيدةً بكلِّ دَمٍ سَفيكِ   وأثبتَ بالسيوفِ لهم حُقوقاً
وما بالدمعِ من طَرَفٍ مَسيكِ   قرينُ القِبلتَينِ عليكَ تَبكي
وخَيرَ نضيجِ تَجربةٍ حَنيكِ   فقدنا منكَ خيرَ زَعيمِ قومٍ
وضَجَّ من الخَليجِ الى دَموكِ   فقد ناحَ العِراقُ عليكَ حُزناً
الى أرضِ الشآمِ الى تَبوكِ   وناحَ المسجدُ الأقصى جميعاً
كما نُزِّهتُ من شِعرٍ رَكيكِ   لقد نُزِّهتَ من غَمزٍ ولَمزِ

Story of the Sharifs and Ibn Saud

Here is the gist of these lines:

Darkness overshadows the face of the Arab world:
Al-Husain, the father of kings, has passed away,
He passed away in surrender after ascending,
Like the sun descending into the darkness.
He passed away unparalleled in glory,
And in hardship having no partner.
He took the path to lofty things,
Till he died praised in his conduct.
He rejuvenated for the Arabs a glorious plant
As old as the old date cluster.
He created a renaissance in the west that shook
The south of the earth like a cyclone.
He proved with the swords rights for them
Supported by every spilled blood drop.
O consort of the two Qiblas that mourn you,
Tears have no way to be controlled.
In you, we lost the best leader of a people
And the best skilled man of mature experience.
Iraq has mourned you out of grief,
And from the Gulf to Damuk there is an uproar.
The Aqsa Mosque mourns with them,
Up to the Levant, to Tabuk.
You are cleared of every insinuation,
As I am cleared of any poor rhyme.

Chapter Seven: Al-Husain's Last Years

As for the satirical poem which al-Rusafi composed in 1916, it included the following lines:

قد كنتُ أحسبُ أنَّ اللؤمَ أجمعَه	على الحُسَينينِ في مصرَ قد انقَسَما
حتى بدت مُخزيات اللومِ مُشركةً	من الحجازِ حُسَيناً ثالثاً بهما
لكنما ذاك قد أربت جريمتُه	عليهما، فهو أخزى جارمٍ جرما
فذانَ أخزى الأهرامَ بغَيِّها	وبغي هذاك أبكى البيتَ والحَرَما
هذا الذي منه تنشقُ السماءُ أسىً	والأرضُ ترتَجُّ حتى تقذِفُ الحُمَما
فأنتِ يا قُدرةَ اللهِ التي عَظُمَت	خذي حُسَيناً بذنبٍ منه قد عَظُما

وأنتِ يا أرضُ مجّي نحوَهُ ضَرَما	ويا سماءُ عليه أمطري نِقَما
بغى فَفَرَّقَ شَمْلاً كان مُجتَمعاً	للمسلمينَ وشِعباً كان مُلتَئِما
قالوا: الشريفُ، ولو صَحَّت شرافتُه	لم ينقُضِ العهدَ أو لم يخفُرِ الذِّمَما
وكيف لا وهو الذي بانت خيانتُه	فَصَرَّحَت عن طباعٍ تُخجِلُ الكُرَما؟
لم تَكفِهِ في مجالِ البغي فِتنتُه	حتى غَدا بعدوِّ اللهِ مُعتَصِما
اذ راحَ بالانكليزِ اليومَ مُمتَنِعاً	فضاعَفَ الشرَّ فيما جَرَّ واجتَرَما[1]

---

1   Mustafa Ali (Op. Cit.), Baghdad: 1975, Vol. 3, pp. 50-52.

Story of the Sharifs and Ibn Saud

Here below is the gist of these lines:

I used to think that blame, all of it,
Has been divided in Egypt for both Husains,
Until blameworthy acts of shame did add,
From Hijaz, to them a third!
But the crime of this one has exceeded
Theirs, for he is a most shameful criminal.
Those men shamed the pyramids with misguidance
While this one caused both Harams to cry.
Of this one, the sky splits in grief,
And the earth shakes and hurls lava!
O you, Might of Allāh, the great,
Punish Husain for a crime so great,
And you, O earth, burn under him the ground,
And you, O heavens, pour on him wrath upon wrath,
He oppressed, dividing assemblies that used to be intact,
For the Muslims, and a crack that used to be intact.
They said "Sharif" (honest)! Had he been honest,
He would not have violated the promise, betrayed the trust.
Why not, he is the one whose treachery appeared,
Revealing habits that embarrass men of nobility?
He was not satisfied, in the field of oppression, with sedition
Until he sought strength from the enemy of Allāh,
Now he is emboldened by the Britons,
Doubling the evil of what he caused and committed.

Chapter Seven: Al-Husain's Last Years

Chapter Eight
Ibn Saud Suffers From Problems

Ibn Saud Suffers From Problems

At the time when al-Husain was bringing to memory his woes in Cyprus, his opponent, Ibn Saud, was suffering from the problems of ruling which robbed him of sleep and caused him to suffer a great deal.

It is the human nature that one prefers to suffer problems as he ascends over being free of them while being at a halt or descending. This also proves that the human nature is mobile, tending to rise, and that comfortable stillness does not suit it.

We will try in this chapter to review some of the problems which Ibn Saud faced in his new situation following his occupation of Hijaz. They are problems in which the reader may find a good number of social lessons.

Allegiance For Ibn Saud

Since the beginning of the war in Hijaz, Ibn Saud had repeatedly declared that he did not covet the domain of Hijaz but would let its matters be consulted by the Muslims, and that he would side with whatever the conferees decided.[1]

When Ibn Saud completed the occupation of all of Hijaz, he found himself obligated to carry out his promises. Some Islamic delegations had started reaching Hijaz in order to honor the invitation sent to them before. Among them was a delegation representing the Islamic Caliphate Society in India and delegates representing Syria, Lebanon, North Africa, Java and Sumatra [Indonesia]. It was noticed that the Islamic Caliphate delegation was enthusiastic about setting up a republican government in

---

1 Hafiz Wahba, *Al-Arab fil Qarn al-'Ishrin* (Arabs in the Twentieth Century), Cairo: 1967, pp. 268-275.

Hijaz in which all Muslims would participate. This was based on Hijaz being a country in which all Muslims are interested and no party should solely rule it rather than another. This delegation started advocating this opinion and trying to realize it.

Ibn Saud felt that he was in a dilemma and did not know how to get out of it. His men started being active in finding a solution for it. They finally found it when a committee of the notables of Mecca and Jidda was formed. This committee decided to swear the oath of allegiance to Ibn Saud as King of Hijaz. They submitted the matter before Ibn Saud who agreed to it, and he published a statement in which he announced the cancellation of the Islamic conference which he had promised, stating that he responded to the request of the people of Hijaz in granting the freedom which they were promised to determine their destiny.

An allegiance celebration was held at the Safa gate in the Haram Mosque following the Friday prayer service on January 7, 1926. Abdullah al-Damalooji advanced and recited the formula of the allegiance. Its gist was: They were swearing the oath of allegiance to the great sultan, Abdul-Aziz Al Saud, as King of Hijaz according to the Book of Allāh and the Sunnah of His Messenger and to the way followed by the *sahaba* (Prophet's companions), the righteous ancestors and the four [Sunni] imams [Abu Haneefa, Ibn Malik, Ahmed ibn Hanbal and al-Shafi`i], and that its people are the ones who manage its affairs. Those present advanced to swear allegiance to Ibn Saud one class after another, and the cannons were firing the usual greeting shots.

After the allegiance ceremony had been completed, Ibn Saud walked towards the Ka`ba which he circumambulated seven times, prayed at the Maqam [of Abraham] then moved to a large pavilion to receive well-wishers. Speakers stood to praise Ibn Saud. One of them said, "Allāh did not grant you all of this, O Abdul-Aziz, except because you are treading the path that pleases Him." Another delivered a speech. Then Ibn Saud spoke

Chapter Eight: Ibn Saud Suffers From Problems

saying, "I hear your speakers say: This is a just imam, this is such-and-such... Be informed that there is no man, no matter how high his station may be, who can have an impact and can do a good deed if he does not fear Allāh. I warn you against following the lusts in which there is the destruction of both religion and this short life, and I urge you to be honest and truthful when you speak, to abandon pretension and flattery when you talk. Nothing corrupted domains save kings, their grandsons, servants, flattering scholars and their helpers... I admonish you just as I admonish myself and my sons." It was then that those present shouted, جزاك الله خيراً!جزاك الله خيراً "May Allāh reward you well! May Allāh reward you well!"[1]

Ibn Saud's allegiance ceremony stirred resentment in Egypt, India and some other Islamic countries which regarded it as Ibn Saud's violation of his many past promises regarding the Islamic conference and his acceptance of its decisions. Hafiz Wahba says in his *Memoirs* that he was in Egypt when Ibn Saud received the news and felt a great deal of embarrassment when he heard it. Hafiz Wahba sent a telegram to Ibn Saud asking him for details. He also wrote him a letter in which he said, "... Reuter published today a report that you called yourself King of Hijaz. If this is true, whoever suggested this to you has surely cheated you because this matter has stirred the public opinion abroad against you. This is on the one hand. On the other hand, it does not agree with the promises which you made before the Islamic world and Muslim kings in forming the government of Hijaz. Had you waited a little bit until the holding of the Islamic Conference and its decision regarding the fate of the land, it would have been better and more sustaining. And the result would have been in your favor anyway. It seems there are sinful hands that made this matter look good in your eyes so they may eradicate the Islamic Conference idea and, at the same time, crush your reputation abroad..." Ibn Saud wrote Hafiz Wahba an

---

[1] Ameen al-Rayhani, *Tarikh Najd al-Hadith wa Mulhaqatih* (Najd's Modern History and Supplements), Beirut: 1954, pp. 427-430.

answer in which he said something like he accepted the allegiance so quickly "because I had to, since the people of Hijaz stood up like one man to commit themselves to it, while the people of Najd rioted: Whenever they were asked to wait, they refused," he said. Ibn Saud concluded his answer saying, "Facing this critical situation on which the security of Hijaz at present and the settlement of the matter, I did not find a choice other than accepting the allegiance, relying on Allāh. I still keep my pledge to safeguard the Muslims' legitimate rights in these holy areas."[1]

In Abha [capital of the Aseer Province south of Saudi Arabia], some Islamic societies declared their denunciation of Ibn Saud's allegiance. The most outspoken of those societies in its denunciation was the Society of Servants of the Harams followed by the Islamic Caliphate Society. Shawkat Ali, president of the Islamic Caliphate Society, announced his denunciation of the allegiance and said, "Few Hijazis from among the enemies of Sharif Husain are not entitled to determine the fate of Hijaz which must be determined by the entire Islamic world."[2]

Each of the Islamic Caliphate Society and that of the Servants of the Harams decided to send a delegation to Hijaz on a fact finding mission about the rumor that the sacred graves there were demolished. Both delegations reached Jidda on January 22, 1926 and were given the cold shoulder upon their arrival. The delegation of the Society of the Servants of the Harams in particular adopted a stiff critical stance towards Ibn Saud and the *ikhwan*. Ibn Saud tried to be courteous and nice to its delegates but to no avail. They presented to Ibn Saud questions about some political matters, and his answers were acceptable or convincing to them, and they asked him to let a man debate with him and also someone who prays before them and who follows

---

[1] Hafiz Wahba, Khamsoon Aman fi Jazeerat al-Arab (Fifty Years in the Arabs' Peninsula), Cairo: 1960, pp. 134-135.
[2] *Al-Iraq* newspaper of February 17, 1926.

Chapter Eight: Ibn Saud Suffers From Problems

an imam from among the four [Sunni] sects so their doubts might be dispelled, but Ibn Saud did not honor this request.[1]

Ibn Saud's patience finally ran out with this very critical stance which the delegation adopted, so he ordered to get them out of Hijaz in the pretext they were advocates of sedition. On March 3, 1926, the delegation left Jidda for Egypt.[2]

In November of 1926, the Islamic Conference was held in Lucknow, India, under the auspices of the Society of Servants of the Harams, and decisions against Ibn Saud were made. It also recommended not to encourage the performing of the pilgrimage so long as the Wahhabi rule was standing in Hijaz. *Umm al-Qura* newspaper attacked this conference and its resolutions, describing the Society of Servants of the Harams as being hostile to the Harams.[3]

The New Society

The new era in Hijaz is distinguished from the extinct Hashemite era in many ways, and we would like to mention the most important of these distinctions:

FIRST: The lowering of the status of Sharifdom; Sharifs now did not have any distinction over others in anything, and some commoners were led even to insult them in order to avenge what they had done. Hafiz Wahba narrates a story that has its connotations in this regard. It is summed up thus: One Sharif gave a pair of binoculars to a watch repairman in Mecca to repair it, then he claimed later that the watch repairman did not repair the binoculars according to the term, suing him in court before Mecca's judge. When the trial went on, the governor of Mecca, Khalid ibn Luay, was present. The Sharif wanted to sit next to him [next to Khalid], whereupon the judge rebuked him and

---

1 *Ibid.*
2 *Ibid.*
3 Public Records Office, London, FO 371/11442.

ordered him to stand before his opponent. The watch repairman addressed his opponent thus: "My standing with you side by side before the judge is worth the whole world and everything in it. The time of oppression is gone. They used to require us to do things but did not pay us any wages; rather, they did not even speak to us but would sometimes beat us. Praise belongs to Allāh." The judge commented on this statement saying, "People before the court are all equal, and the Sharifs are more apt from among all people to follow their grandfather, the Master of Prophets, Muhammed 7, who says, 'O Fatima daughter of Muhammed! I cannot do anything for you against the will of Allāh.' And Allāh says إِنَّ أَكْرَمَكُمْ عِندَ اللَّهِ أَتْقَاكُمْ '**Truly the most honored of you in God's sight is the most righteous (one) among you**' (Qur'an, 49:13) and also فَإِذَا نُفِخَ فِي الصُّورِ فَلَا أَنسَابَ بَيْنَهُمْ يَوْمَئِذٍ وَلَا يَتَسَاءَلُونَ '**So when the trumpet is blown, there will be no more ties of kinship among them that Day, nor will one ask about another**' (Qur'an, 23:101)." While the judge was speaking, the *ikhwan* men who stood near him were repeating "Amen" to his statements. Meanwhile, the Sharif was made to hear scathing whispers to his disliking.[1]

SECOND: the disappearance of the habit of theft and of highway robbery which used to be common in the old era. Late in April of 1926, a thief was arrested in Jidda, so one of his hands was cut off according to the ruling of the Shari'a, then it was dipped in boiling oil fat. He was taken for a tour after that in the markets in order his sight would provide a moral lesson for others.[2] One day, a Bedouin tribe intercepted a caravan of pilgrims, looting it and killing some of its members. Ibn Saud sent it a force that surrounded the tribe's quarters and killed every man in it. A [foreign] consul found that cruelty strange and expressed his amazement to Ibn Saud. Ibn Saud said to him, "This is not cruelty; rather, it is mercy; it is the only way to deal

---

1 Hafiz Wahba, *Jazeerat al-Arab fil Qarn al-Ishreen* (The Arabian Peninsula in the Twentieth Century), pp. 105-106.
2 Public Records Office, London, FO 371/11442.

Chapter Eight: Ibn Saud Suffers From Problems

with the Bedouins. Its news will spread among the Bedouin tribes and they will desist from looting the caravans after that."[1]

THIRD: the *ikhwan*'s strictness towards anyone who in their view violated the Sunnah, such as by smoking or visiting the graves and sacred places. In the month of February of 1926, four Afghans went to see the Hira Cave. As they were praying near it, some *ikhwan* saw them and shot them, wounding two of them lightly. In the same month of February, another interesting incident took place. Its summary is that an Egyptian driver was sitting at a café near the Ka`ba smoking, so one of the *ikhwan* approached him and snatched the cigarette from his mouth then beat him with his stick. The driver became angry, stood up and kept hitting that man; one hit hurt his eye. It became clear after that that the *ikhwan* man belonged to the Al al-Sheikh, that is, the lineage of the founder of the Wahhabit sect. The driver, therefore, was taken to the judge who ordered him whipped. The driver died as a result of the whipping.[2]

In April of 1926, when the *ikhwan* intensified their activity against anyone who violated the Sunnah, as they understood it, Ibn Saud was forced to issue instructions to define violations and to set a penalty for each. *Umm al-Qura* newspaper published those instructions; they were as follows:

1. Anyone who deliberately does not attend congregational prayers must be punished with imprisonment from one to ten days in addition to the payment of a fine.
2. Anyone who drinks wine is to be penalized according to the rulings of the Shari`a then jailed from one to six months in addition to paying a fine, and if he does it again, he is to be banished from the Haram land from two to three years.
3. Anyone who makes or sells wine or prepares a place for drinking it is to be jailed from six months to two years and

---

[1] David Howarth, *The Desert King: A Life of Ibn Saud*, London: 1964, p. 148.
[2] Public Records Office, London, FO 371/11442.

his place must be confiscated. If he does it again, he is to be expelled from the Haram land from two to three years.
4. Smoking is bad; it harms the body, the wealth and the mind, and some scholars have prohibited it; therefore, the sacred places must be purged of this evil. Anyone who smokes publicly must be imprisoned from one to three days in addition to being fined.
5. Anyone who participates in a meeting for the purpose of disseminating false rumors, or to plot against the policy of the government, must be jailed from two to five years or banished from Hijaz.
6. Anyone who helps shelter criminals mentioned in the previous article is to be regarded as their equal and must receive a penalty similar to theirs.
7. Anyone who participates in a meeting that violates the Shari`a is to be jailed from three to six months and to be fined.
8. The government must be notified of any meeting intended for some benefit and must be informed of its location in order to obtain a permit for it.
9. The concerned officials must carry out these articles with extreme care, and any of them who is negligent must be severely punished.[1]

Al-Baqee` Graves Demolished

---

[1] Public Records Office, London, FO 371/11442.

Chapter Eight: Ibn Saud Suffers From Problems

Al-Baqee` used to be Medina's cemetery during the time of the Prophet and thereafter; therefore, al-Abbas, uncle of the Prophet, caliph Othman, the Prophet's wives and many *sahaba* and *tabi`een* were all buried in it and so were four of the Imams of Ahlul-Bayt: al-Hassan ibn Ali, Ali ibn al-Husain, Muhammed ibn Ali and Ja`far ibn Muhammed G. The Shi`as built for the last four Imams a magnificent shrine similar to the ones known in Iraq and Iran, but on a smaller scale. The Shi`as were used to visit this shrine, kissing it, seeking blessings at it and praying there just as they do at shrines in Iraq and Iran.

These graves remained safe during the Saudi era for more than four months without anyone harming them. Grumbling started spreading among the *ikhwan* as a result, and they started criticizing Ibn Saud and accusing him of leniency in carrying out the "Commandments" of Allāh.[1] Ibn Saud, therefore, had in mid-April of 1926 to send the senior theologian of Najd, namely Sheikh Abdullah bin Blaihid[2], to Medina for the purpose of demolishing the graves. When bin Blaihid reached Medina, he met with its scholars and asked them this question:

"What do Medina's scholars, may Allāh increase their understanding and knowledge, say about building on graves and using them as mosques, is it permissible or not? If it is not permissible, perhaps even prohibitive and strongly banned, should they be demolished and prayer banned there? If the

---

1 *Ibid*.
2 I searched for any information in English about this sheikh on the Internet but could not find anything, not even in the Internet's Wikipedia, but I found a good deal of information about him on an Internet site; therefore, I decided to briefly state a word about him, perhaps his name will one day enter future encyclopedias. His full name is Abdullah ibn عبدالله بن سليمان بن سعود بن سليمان بن سالم بن محمد بن بليهد الخالدي Sulayman ibn Saud ibn Sulayman ibn Salim ibn Muhammed ibn Blaihid al-Khalidi, the first chief judge رئيس القضاة (justice or chief judge) in Mecca whom King Abdul-Aziz (Ibn Saud) placed in charge of religious and some political affairs. A detailed biography of him is included in a book titled من أعلام القُضاة *Among Famous Judges* by Muhammed ibn Abdullah al-Muqrin محمد بن عبد الله المُقرن who tells us that this sheikh was born in al-Qar`a north of the Qaseem area. His exact date of birth is unknown but must be placed around the year 1277 A.H./1860 A.D. based on his age, which is said to be over 80, at the time of his death in 1359 A.H./1940 A.D. – Tr.

building is on a pedestrians' path, as is the Baqee`, which prevents using the area according to what is built on it, is it usurpation which must be lifted because it oppresses those who have a right to it, preventing them from the use of what belongs to them? What about what is done by the ignorant folks at these shrines, i.e. rubbing them and pleading to Allāh and seeking nearness to Him through offerings and pledges, lighting lanterns on them, is it permissible or not? What is being done at the chamber of the Prophet 7, i.e. directing the faces towards it when pleading to Allāh and doing other things, circling it, kissing and rubbing it, and the same is done at the Mosque, seeking blessings and reciting *thikr* between the *athan* and the *iqama*, before dawn and on Fridays, is it legitimate or not? Issue your *fatwa* (verdict), may you be rewarded, and explain to us the evidences on which you rely, may you remain the refuge of those who seek benefits."

Seventeen men from among those who were present there and then agreed that it was obligatory to demolish the graves and wrote their *fatwa* in this regard then signed it. This is the text of their *fatwa*:

"As regarding building on the graves, it is unanimously prohibited due to authentic *ahadith* (traditions) regarding its prohibition; therefore, many scholars have issued their verdicts that they must be demolished, relying on one *hadith* by Ali who said to Abu al-Hiyaj, ألا أبعثُكَ على ما بعثني عليه رسول الله (ص)؟ أن لا تدع تمثالاً الا طمسته و لا قبراً الا سَوَّيتَه "Shall I send you to what the Messenger of Allāh 7 had sent me [to do]? You should not let any statue without burying it or a grave high in structure without leveling it with the ground." This is narrated by Muslim. As for using graves as mosques to pray and lighting lanterns on them, it is prohibitive based on one *hadith* by [Abdullah] Ibn Abbas: لعن الله زائرات القبور و المتخذين عليها المساجد و السرج "The curse of Allāh be on those [females] who visit the graves, who use them as mosques and place lanterns on them." The author of *sunan* books have narrated it. As regarding what is done by ignorant folks at the shrines, i.e. rubbing them, seeking nearness to them by slaughtering animals, making pledges and pleading to those in them as they plead to Allāh, it is prohibitive and banned by the Shari`a, it must not be done at all. As regarding the chamber of the Prophet 7 and praying there, it is better to ban it as it is known to be advocated in the sect's books, and because the best directions is that of the *qibla*. As regarding circling, rubbing and kissing it, it is absolutely prohibitive. As regarding making *thikr*, seeking Allāh's mercy and peace during the said times, it is an innovation; such is concluded according to our knowledge."[1]

Following the issuing of this *fatwa*, the Baqee` graves were quickly demolished. Reports of this act sent tremors throughout the Islamic world, and the outrage in Shi`ite countries was, of course, the most intense.

Incident's Echo In Iraq

A letter was received by one of the Shi`a `*ulema* (theologians) sent by a Shi`i man who was in Medina when the graves were demolished. It was dated Shawwal 8, 1344 A.H./April 21, 1926; here below is its text:

"I submit to you the fact that all Hijazi lands are oppressed under the control of Ibn Saud and his absolute rule in them. Nobody in these lands, from their furthermost point to their

---

1 Muhsin al-Ameen, *Kashf al-Irtiyab* (Unveiling the Doubt), 3rd ed., pp. 359-360. [Shi`ites, by the way, reject the *ahadith*, Prophet's statements, cited in this "fatwa" and say that they are fabricated. Most importantly, they are not supported at all by a single verse of the Holy Qur'an. Shi`ites also ask the Wahhabis: The domes and other structures over the graves of the Prophet's wives, *sahaba* and *tabi`een* remained intact during the entire period of the "righteous caliphs" whose era is described as the golden period of Islam. This period extended from 632 to 661 A.D., that is, for 29 years. Why neither those caliphs nor those who succeeded them up to the time of Muhammed ibn Abdul-Wahhab, founder of Wahhabism, that is, from 632 to 1926, i.e. one thousand and two hundred and ninety-four years, ever ordered their demolition? Were they waiting all those years for the Wahhabis to do it? Why did none of the four main founders of the Sunni sects, i.e. Abu Hanifah, Malik, Ibn Hanbal and al-Shafi`i, ever issue a *fatwa* to demolish those graves? Were those mjor Sunni imams, Founders of the Sunni sects, waiting for the Wahhabis to do it? Do the Wahhabis know better than those major Sunni imams, their mentors...?! – Tr.]

nearest, one individual, be he a resident of the cities or of the deserts, who can oppose his orders and commands. Few days ago, the chief judge of the Wahhabis—meaning Sheikh Abdullah ibn Blaihid—came to Medina. As his meeting place was crowded with theologians, he declared to the latter the prohibition of visiting the graves, that doing so was an innovation in the creed and an association with Allāh, that an agreement must be obtained from all scholars of the four [Sunni] sects to completely destroy them and obliterate the last of their traces from the face of earth. Because of that, visiting all sacred resting places was banned and their [cemeteries'] gates were closed. For the past twenty days, we do not dare to go, see and visit these honored sites since the Wahhabis' soldiers (the *ikhwan*) monitor the Prophet's Purified Haram and prevent any pilgrim from being honored by visiting the Chief Lady of the Women of the World[1] G or get close to the shrine of the Messenger of Allāh 7. The Wahhabis' chief judge could not get the desired consensus he wanted from Medina's theologians except after days, having used measures such as pressuring, intimidating and coercing them. Some others readily agreed. So, they ruled according to his desire, absolutely prohibiting the visiting of graves, the pleading to Allāh near them and the seeking of their intercession with Allāh or even reciting the *ziyara* there. An order was issued to demolish and efface the sacred shrines, so the soldiers started first to loot all the contents of those sacred buildings in the Baqee' from the flooring, draperies, hung items, lanterns and other items. Then they started demolishing those sacred sites, forcing all the builders of Medina to participate in the demolishing and effacing. The objective [behind this letter] now is that all the believers who rest their hopes on the intercession of these pure Imams to bring them closer to Allāh Almighty, and they are all in this matter, be they Arabs, Persians, Indians, Turks, etc., each

---

1 This is a reference to Khadija daughter of Khuwaylid, first wife of the Prophet of Islam 7. But this title is usually used for the Prophet's daughter, Fatima, for whom there is no known grave at all. Shortly before her death, she willed that she must be buried at night and her grave be obliterated... – Tr.

Chapter Eight: Ibn Saud Suffers From Problems

and every one of them must plead to his government to interfere to lift this momentous injustice and to rectify what has taken place. Today, the eighth of the month of Shawwal, the demolishing and effacing of the sacred dome in the Baqee` started, so there is neither will nor strength except in Allāh, the most Exalted One, the most Great. You must inform all scholars of Iraq about this painful incident."[1]

At the same time, telegrams started coming one after the other to Shi`a `ulema in Iraq. We quote here the one sent to Sayyid Hassan al-Sadr in al-Kadhimiyya: عَظَّمَ اللهُ أُجوركم في مصيبة الرسول و أهل بيته الوهابيون خَرَّبوا القبور المقَدَّسة "May Allāh magnify your divine rewards on the [occasion of the] calamity of the Prophet and his Ahlul-Bayt. The Wahhabis have demolished the sacred graves."

Having received these reports, the Shi`a `ulema decided to declare a period of grief, demonstrate the signs of sadness, suspend classes and hold a congregational prayer service. In the courtyard of the Kadhimiyya Grand Shrine, a meeting was held and attended by a large crowd of people. Incoming telegrams and letters on this occasion were read. Telegrams were composed to send to the kings and scholars of the Islamic world in their various countries. The same took place in Kerbala and Najaf. We would like here to quote the text of the telegram which Najaf's `ulema sent to [then emperor] Ridha Shah in Tehran:

"According to authentic reports, after having looted the sacred area of the Baqee` Imams, the Wahhabis' chief judge ordered the demolition and effacing of the sacred Baqee`, including the domes and sacred shrines. This action started on the eighth of Shawwal. It is certain that the safeguarding of the canons of the Islamic faith in general and those of the Ja`fari sect in particular is entrusted to the Ja`fari King. The public's hopes hinge and rely on the zeal and ardor of Your Majesty. We are

---

1 *Al-Iraq* newspaper of May 25, 1926.

Story of the Sharifs and Ibn Saud

patiently waiting for your undertaking the most important obligation at the fastest by the will of Allāh."[1]

Iraqi newspapers kept publishing essays denouncing Ibn Saud and protesting his actions. *Al-Iraq* newspaper wrote an editorial in which it said, "The matter is settled, Ibn Blaihid issued the well known *fatwa*, thus affording his master, Ibn Saud, the greatest service without knowing that his effort was like an arrow that rested in the heart of the Islamic world, causing it pain the like of which there is non other."[2] It published another article by Isma`eel Al Yasin from al-Kadhimiyya titled "The greatest tyrant and the holy places in Hijaz" in which this statement existed: "O Muslims! What is this hibernation, and what is this stagnation that led you to remain silent rather than pay attention to this painful issue and shameful roles of that tyrant [Ibn Saud] in the holy lands...?"[3]

On June 4, 1926, *Al-Iraq* newspaper published an interview between one of its editors and Sayyid Mahmoud al-Gailani, chief Sharifs of Baghdad, in which the latter announced his criticism of what the Wahhabis had done, i.e. the demolition of the Baqee` graves. He stated that building domes over graves did not violate the Prophet's Sunnah because the Prophet himself was buried in the chamber of Aisha, and it is a chamber having walls and a roof built like a dome. He also stated that kissing the shrines is akin to kissing a loved person, which is not prohibited by Islam.

Al-Iraq published after that three verses of poetry, asking the poets to add a fourth and a fifth line to it; they were:

يَشيبُ لهولِها لعمري ان فاجعةَ البقيعِ
اذا لم نَصْحُ من هذا الهُجوعِ و سوفَ تكونُ فاتحةَ الرزايا
حُقوقَ نَبيِّهِ الهادي الشفيعِ؟ فَهَل من مسلمٍ للهِ يرعى

---

1 *Al-Murshid* magazine of June 1926.
2 *Al-Iraq* newspaper of May 27, 1926.
3 *Ibid.*

Chapter Eight: Ibn Saud Suffers From Problems

Here is a rough translation of these lines:

By my life! The Baqee` calamity
Causes an infant's hair to turn grey,
And it will be the start of shameful deeds
Unless we wake up from this slumber.
So, is there any Muslim at all who safeguards
The rights of his Prophet who guides and intercedes?

A number of poets took part in adding a fourth and a fifth line to the lines above, including Mustafa Jawad, Isma`eel Al Yasin, Kamal Nasrat, Abdul-Mahdi al-Azri and "a Muslim from al-Kadhimiyya in pain".[1]

The month of Muharram that year started on July 12, so the speeches of mourning gatherings and chants of grief of the Husaini processions mostly centered round the "Baqee` Calamity", appealing to the Occult Imam [al-Mahdi, the Awaited One] to reappear to seek revenge against Ibn Saud.

It is worth mentioning that the 8th of Shawwal—the day when the Baqee` graves were demolished—became an anniversary for mourning in the next years in Najaf and Kerbala when all markets shut down and chest beating processions come out as they are accustomed to doing on anniversaries of the death of the Imams. It is said that the people of Kerbala continued to do that for several years, calling the 8th of Shawwal "the death of al-Baqee`".

Shi`ites still hope that they will have the opportunity to rebuild the Baqee` graves. Had they been granted such an opportunity, they would have built them many times better than they used to be. A trusted friend told me once that Bohra Shi`ites in India collected plenty of money and put the designs for rebuilding the graves. I remember during my 1958 visit of the Twelver (Ithna-`Asheri) Shi`ite mosque in Karachi, I saw in it a

---

[1] *Al-Iraq* newspaper of September 2, 1926 and of September 16, 1926.

precious gold shrine. When I asked about it, I was told that it was the Baqee` graves shrine, and it was made possible through the donations of the Shi`ites in Pakistan and India and was waiting permission to be moved to Medina when the opportunity comes, and I wonder if such an opportunity will ever come.

During the Pilgrimage Season

In the month of June of 1926, the first pilgrimage season under the Saudi era started. Many pilgrims went to Hijaz. Their number was more than those who had performed the pilgrimage the year before. This led to many clashes and altercations between the pilgrims and the *ikhwan*. The pilgrims wanted to perform their rituals as they had always been doing, but the *ikhwan* regarded those rituals as violating the Sunnah, so they prevented them.

Ibn Saud had appointed Hafiz Wahba as his deputy in administering the affairs of Mecca in order to tamper the zeal of the *ikhwan*. Hafiz Wahba says the following in his book: "The *ikhwan* were cruel in their treatment of anyone who in their view committed a transgression or violated one of Allāh's commandments, for each of them regards himself as the judge of it. The stick was doing its job in the name of enjoining what is right and forbidding what is wrong." Hafiz Wahba narrates that late in the month of Thul-Qa`dah of 1926, while he was at the government house in Mecca, Egypt's consul, the deputy consul of India and Holland's deputy consul accompanied by about ten pilgrims came with blood dripping from them. The *ikhwan* had assaulted those pilgrims, so Hafiz promised to deal with the matter, stressing that such matters happened everywhere in the world. But they protested saying that such assaults were in the name of religion and with support from the government, that they happened as the policemen looked on. Hafiz assured them that the government had no knowledge of such incidents and did not endorse this transgression. Hafiz Wahba further says

Chapter Eight: Ibn Saud Suffers From Problems

that he went to Ibn Saud to explain to him the seriousness of the matter and the chaotic repercussions of the *ikhwans'* actions, but Ibn Saud did not pay attention to what he said, so he had to resign from his post. Ibn Saud later realized the extent of the extremism of the *ikhwan*, so he instructed his guards to discipline the *ikhwan* and to appoint a judge to look into the problems they were causing.[1]

The Egyptian loader incident was the most serious incident that season which caused a friction between the *ikhwan* and the pilgrims. It almost led to a general massacre. This is the summary of it: The Egyptian government was accustomed for a long time to send every [pilgrimage] season a loader [carrier, sedan] called the Prophet's loader accompanied by soldiers, cannons, a military music band and a commander called the emir of the pilgrimage. All those were matters which the *ikhwan* very strongly denounced, for they regarded the loader as being "pagan" and "worshipped" instead of Allāh, and they called the trumpet that went ahead of it as the "voice of Satan".

When the season of pilgrimage drew nigh in 1926, the Saudi government wrote the Egyptian government asking it to commit itself to three terms at the time when the said loader and the pilgrims were in Hijaz: 1) Music must not accompany the loader after leaving Jidda, 2) There must be no smoking, and 3) There must be no visits to the graves or circling them. The Egyptian government wrote the Sheikh of the Azhar and the *mufti* of the Egyptian lands asking for their opinion in this regard. Both men issued their verdict that the three things which the Saudi government mentioned as being prohibitive did not violate the Book (Holy Qur'an) or the Sunnah, stating the evidences which they derived from the Shari`a [Islam's legislative system] to support their *fatwas*.[2]

---

1   Hafiz Wahba (Op. Cit.), pp. 306-308.
2   Public Records Office, London, FO 371/11442.

Story of the Sharifs and Ibn Saud

Early signs of the crisis appeared when the loader arrived at the Haram's courtyard in Mecca. The loader was taken down on the yard, and some pilgrims came seeking its blessings, so the *ikhwan* were outraged. Ibn Saud sent a message to the [Egyptian] emir of the pilgrimage requesting him to let the loader be put at a covered place in order to avoid sedition, so the Pasha responded after repeated intense pleas by some intercessors.

In the afternoon of Thul-Hijjah 8, 1344 A.H./June 19, 1926 A.D., the loader left Mecca heading towards the Arafa Mountain. At 7:30 in the evening of that day, when the loader was stopped near Mina, a group of the *ikhwan* came close to it and kept cursing it as they screamed هُبَل! هُبَل! *Hubal! Hubal!* [chief pagan deity during the pre-Islamic period], throwing rocks and stones at it, so Mahmoud Azmi Pasha ordered his soldiers to line up in a military formation then asked the *ikhwan* to disperse, but they did not pay him any attention. The Pasha, therefore, ordered his soldiers to shoot in the air in order to scare the *ikhwan*, but it had no effect on them. It is said that the *ikhwan* fired at his soldiers[1]. It was then that the Pasha ordered to use bombs and bullets to shoot at the *ikhwan* directly. Twenty-five of them were killed and a larger number were wounded[2].

That year, about sixty thousand persons from Najd performed the pilgrimage, setting up their tents in Mina. When these men heard about what had happened to their brothers, they rushed to the site of the incident carrying their rifles. Ibn Saud heard about it, and he was camping near the site, so he went running then stopped between both groups calling at them "I am Abdul-Aziz! I am Abdul-Aziz!" The shooting stopped. Ibn Saud ordered his soldiers to hide and protect the loader, then he sent it to Jidda under the heavy guard of Saudi soldiers commanded by Prince Mishari ibn Saud [ibn Abdul-Aziz] ibn Jilwi[3].

---

1   *Ibid.*
2   Armstrong, *Lord of Arabia*, London: 1938, p. 193.
3   Khair ad-Din al-Zurakli, *Shibh al-Jazeera fi Ahd al-Malik Abdul-Aziz* (The Peninsula During the Time of King Abdul-Aziz), Beirut: 1977, Vol. 2, p. 663.

Chapter Eight: Ibn Saud Suffers From Problems

Armstrong narrates the following: "Ibn Saud came close after the incident from the Egyptian emir of the pilgrimage, Mahmoud Azmi Pasha, and started rebuking him for what he had done, so the Pasha responded to him saying, with some pride and arrogance, 'With all due respect to Your Majesty, I stopped the shooting; otherwise, I would have wiped out all of those mobsters.' Ibn Saud controlled his nerves and said to him, 'This is not the time for bragging. This is a sacred place which Allāh ordered that nobody is to be killed in it, and you are our guests and under our protection; otherwise, I would have punished you.'"[1]

When the news reached King Fuad of Egypt, he was furious and ordered to stop sending the Ka`ba *kiswa* [drapes] which Egypt was accustomed to sending every year. He also ordered to stop sending funds from Egypt to Hijaz from the share of both Harams. On May 13, 1927, when the second pilgrimage season approached, the *Ahram* newspaper of Egypt published an official notification that said, "The Egyptian government has decided not to send the loader this year, and it announces to the Egyptian pilgrims that they may face some dangers during their travel to Hijaz, and it is not responsible for their protection; so, if they wish to travel, it will be at their own risk."

The Egyptian government kept following this policy towards the pilgrimage up to the last days of King Fuad. It is narrated that when King Fuad was lying on his deathbed in 1930, the head of his *diwan*, Ali Mahir Pasha, entered and said to him, "Are you not going to enter in your Record of Deeds negotiating with the land of the Two Holy Harams?" The King made a sign which meant "There is no harm in doing so."

The friendly ties between Egypt and the kingdom of Saudi Arabia resumed after the death of King Fuad, and the Egyptians were permitted to perform the pilgrimage. The sending of the *kiswa* to the Ka`ba every year was resumed, too. But the loader

---

1 Armstrong (Op. Cit.), p. 193.

remained banned from entering Hijaz. The Egyptians kept celebrating the loader every year, but they do not go with it beyond the Suez city.[1]

Islamic Conference Held

Letters and telegrams kept reaching Ibn Saud from India and other lands demanding the holding of the Islamic Conference which he had promised to do before. Hafiz Wahba, on his part, used to repeat his insistence on Ibn Saud to do it. Ibn Saud finally agreed to hold the conference provided it would not mention anything about the system of government in Hijaz. On March 26, 1926, an invitation was sent to all Islamic boards and governments to attend the Conference which was to be held on the 20th of Thul-Qa`da of 1344 A.H./June 2, 1926.

Representatives from various Islamic countries, with the exception of Iran and Iraq, responded to the invitation. Brothers Muhammed Ali and Shawkat Ali arrived to represent the Islamic Caliphate Society, and Dhia ad-Din ibn Farid ad-Din arrived to represent the Muslims of the Soviet Union. The Saudi side was represented by four men: Hafiz Wahba, Yousuf Yasin, Abdul-Aziz al-Ateeqi and Abdullah bin Blaihid, senior theologian of Najd [see footnote about him above].

The inauguration of the conference took place in Mecca on the 7th of June. Hafiz Wahba delivered the inauguration speech on behalf of Ibn Saud. The speech mentioned the reasons that prompted Ibn Saud to accept the allegiance swearing as King of Hijaz, and they are summed up thus: The people who tie and untie in Hijaz and Najd obligated him to do so, and he in the beginning rejected their request, then he agreed in response to the ruling of the Shari`a "because we, Al Saud, are not despotic kings, nor do we rule in person; rather, we in our land are tied by the rulings of the Shari`a and the viewpoint of those who tie and

---

1   Khair ad-Din al-Zurakli (Op. Cit.), Vol. 2, p. 669.

untie... If we oppose them without a legitimate argument which they accept, they will not obey me, and there will be corruption in that, as is quite obvious. The masses of the cities and the heads of the desert tribes are regarded among those who tie and untie because their tribes follow them during the time of peace or of war." Then Ibn Saud asked those present for the conference to consult regarding the religious and construction interests of Hijaz, purging it of innovations, superstitions, immoralities and abominations which nobody doubted existed. Then he said to them, "You have the absolute freedom in what you discuss except two matters from which you should stay at bay: One of them is to discuss international politics; the other is discussing the dispute between the Islamic nations and their governments, for these concern those nations themselves." Ibn Saud concluded his sermon saying, "The Muslims have been exhausted by differences in sects and tastes, so enjoin each other regarding bringing them closer and cooperate for serving their common public interests and do not let the differences among sects and races be the cause of hostility among them..."[1]

The conference's sessions went on for ten days. On June 17, its sessions were delayed in order to give the delegates the opportunity to perform the pilgrimage rituals. Meanwhile, two delegations from Egypt and Turkey arrived, so the conference's sessions were resumed anew on the 22nd of the month. The last sessions witnessed sharp arguments and altercations in which the Egyptian delegation played the main role.

Egyptian Delegation's Conference Activity

The Egyptian government had in the beginning ignored the invitation to attend the conference. This took place when the cabinet of Zayyur Pasha[2] was ruling. When this administration

---

[1] Hafiz Wahba, *Khamsson Aman fi Jazeerat al-Arab* (Fifty Years in the Arabian Peninsula), pp. 140-144.
[2] I could not trace this name, so it is likely a misprint. – Tr.

fell, and when a new administration was formed headed by Adli Pasha, it was decided to send a delegation representing Egypt at the conference. The delegation was comprised of Sheikh Muhammed al-Zawahiri as its head, Muhammed al-Maseeri Beg and Muhammed Tawfeeq Beg as members. The delegation faced difficulty in reaching Mecca since it was late after all pilgrim ships had already sailed. Adli Pasha, therefore, instructed to prepare Aida, the official Egyptian government ship, to transport the delegation to Hijaz as soon as possible. The delegation was able to reach Mecca and to participate in the last sessions of the conference as stated above.

It seems that Sheikh Muhammed al-Zawahiri, head of the Egyptian delegation, was sent to the conference for a certain purpose: to criticize the extremism of the Wahhabis and to denounce their actions. This is why we saw him going to the conference charged with cited and logical evidences that rebut the Wahhabis' pretexts. The first thing he did in the conference was submitting a written proposal asking the delegates to support it; this is what is said:

"Since the Revered Hijaz is a general religious center for all those who direct their faces towards the *qibla*, one to which the Muslims come from everywhere regardless of the differences of their *fiqhi* and logical sects in order to worship their Lord and perform their rituals, the Conference determines that they all must be enabled to perform their ways of worship and rituals according to their sects, and they must not be prevented from doing anything so long as it does not harm the dignity of anyone, be he alive or dead, nor does it violate the consensus which is agreed on by the scholars of *usool al-fiqh* (principles of jurisprudence). And it must determine that each pilgrim must perform what agrees with the sect to which he belongs, though doing so may disagree with the scholars of other sects."

Sheikh al-Zawahiri delivered an extemporal speech in which he urged the delegates to accept his resolution. He said, "... Let me say it frankly, and I hope nobody will suffer pain. Quite few people have said that the folks of Najd call people *kafir* (apostate) if they do this or that. We have come to ascertain this matter, to get together and to clear the air... I saw with my own eyes something which hurt me. I was inside the Haram passing behind the Maqam [of Ibrahim] after the *tawaf* [circling of the Ka`ba] when I saw a group of men who surrounded an Egyptian man and kept saying this to him with extreme violence and cruelty: أَأَنتَ قُلتَ: يا رسولَ اللهِ؟! 'Did you say: O Messenger of Allāh!'? Here, the man was scared, so he denied saying it, shrunk and was petrified to the degree that brought tears to my eyes. He came to me after that accompanied by many Egyptians and said, 'Did you see how they prevent us?' I calmed those who came to me and said to them, 'Be calm, do not be afraid and be patient until the truth becomes clear; surely the guidance is Allāh's guidance.' This, Gentlemen, is part of what prompts me to endorse this proposal which I hope will be endorsed [by you all]. I plead to you in the Name of Allāh and His Messenger... And if I say "... and His Messenger', I hope nobody objects, for this is my belief which I follow as I worship Allāh. I plead to you in the Name of Allāh and His Messenger to act upon tolerance and patience, perhaps we will eradicate the reasons behind these differences which have harmed the Muslims very seriously."

The conference discussed al-Zawahiri's proposal. After deliberations on it, it was endorsed. This caused Ibn Saud and his protégés to be angry. It prompted Ibn Saud to deliver a speech in which he explained his position thus: "... I do not want to interfere in your actions, nor do I wish to curtail the freedom of the Conference in its research, as I had promised in the inauguration speech. But I wish to direct your attention to some matters in my capacity as one of the leaders of Islam on whom the responsibility of the matters of this land has been placed. I do not aspire to be high in the land or to corrupt, but I want the Muslims to return to their first [Islamic] era, the era of happiness and strength, the era of the *sahaba* and those [*tabi`een*] who followed them in goodness... We do not force anyone to follow a particular sect or take a certain route in the religion, for this is entrusted to the scholars of the religion and to those who bear the Shari`a, but I do not accept under any circumstance the appearance of innovations and superstitions which the Shari`a does not regard and which sound nature rejects. Nobody is asked about his sect or belief, but it is not right that someone openly does what opposes the consensus of the Muslims or stirs a blind sedition among the Muslims. It is better for us to look at righteous Muslims and to leave these secondary matters to the scholars, for they are more keen than we are in their regard..."

Sheikh al-Zawahiri wrote a memorandum in response to Ibn Saud's speech. It is lengthy, so we would like to quote excerpts from it:

1. His Majesty the King expressed his desire to leave the religious matters to the scholars, but this is not possible because the scholars differ among themselves; when they meet, they argue and wake up sectarian fanaticism.
2. His Majesty said he did not accept the appearances of innovations and superstitions, and this is right if it means what is determined [to be as such] by *all* scholars of the Islamic sects, not what is determined by a single group from among them rather than by another.
3. His Majesty said that it is not right for anyone to demonstrate something which opposes the consensus of the Muslims or stirs a blind sedition, but this expression is broad in its scope, unlimited in its meaning, and some people may understand it to mean preventing people from matters that are permissible according to their sect as leading to stirring a blind sedition. Take, for example, smoking. Sheikh Ibn Blaihid says, "We do not ban it because it is *haram* (prohibitive)..., rather, we prevent it because if the people of Najd see someone smoking, they behead him." So, who are those who really cause the

Chapter Eight: Ibn Saud Suffers From Problems

blind sedition? Are they the ones who do what their sect permits or those who behead them?!

4. His Majesty has said, "It is better for us to look into the Muslims' interests and leave these secondary issues to the scholars." We wish this principle had been observed in the beginning so monuments and other things would not have been demolished before the scholars of Islamic sects express their opinion in their regard.

This memorandum gained reputation among the delegates before being submitted to the conference, and they all, with the exception of the Saudi delegate, appreciated it. Members of the latter delegation went to Sheikh al-Zawahiri to request him not to submit the memorandum to the conference. Al-Zawahiri said to them that he would do that on the condition the King withdrew his speech. It was agreed on doing so, and the King did, indeed, withdraw his speech from the conference.

The last day of the conference was charged with intense discussions. On that day, Shawkat Ali submitted a proposal which he had presented before and which contained three matters: (1) the rebuilding of the domes and demolished monuments as soon as possible, (2) the safeguarding and maintaining of the graves that have not been demolished yet, and (3) commissioning the rebuilding of the demolished graves to a Sunni and Shi`ite committee of scholars of the sects, and the opinion of this committee shall be final.

Sheikh Muhammed al-Zawahiri talked about this proposal saying, "This day is the last of the conference days, and we want to leave in peace and tranquility. I see that a movement from the side of our Indian brothers indicates some anger. I also see a movement opposing it from the government's side that indicates some toughness; so, I hope this will not be the case. Let there be looking into the proposal relevant to the graves and monuments." Yousuf Yasin responded to him saying, "If you do not wish there will be a dispute and desire the matter to end peacefully, I hope this proposal will not be looked into because it by itself opens a door for schism and dispute." Al-Zawahiri responded to him saying, "We want to remove the misunderstanding. As regarding keeping silent about what we have, it is harmful. We want tranquility to reach the depths of hearts. What is right is right for everyone. Among what is right is what is bitter and must be allayed. You know best and see best the consequences of angering the hearts. So, I request the submission and recitation of the proposal." Here, the confidant of the conference stood up and recited the text of the proposal. Shawkat Ali stood up to explain it. Then the conference agreed to refer the proposal to the board of `ulema to see what they would decide about it. Sheikh Abdul-Aziz al-Ateeqi then stood up and said, "I would like to draw attention to our disagreement on using the graves as idols, and what took place did not affect a corpse but stones." Al-Zawahiri responded to him saying, "Far it is from Allāh that one can say that the Muslims have undertaken the graves as idols, and we want some people from among ourselves not be extremists and exaggerate in what is useless."

The conference came to an end without the participants in it being able to reach a decisive result. In the evening of the last day of the conference, Ibn Saud threw a banquet for the delegates. Al-Zawahiri took that opportunity to deliver a statement in which he demanded to rebuild the monuments which were demolished due to their having been mosques and are now areas where the dogs urinate." When Ibn Saud heard this statement, he stood up and left...[1]

The British consul says the following in his confidential report to his government: "It is believed that the conference cost Ibn Saud no less than twenty thousand pounds some of which were fuel expenses and the others were bribes to the conferees." The consul also stated that the members of the delegations, with

---

1 Fakhr ad-Din al-Zawahiri, *Al-Siyasa wal Azhar* السياسة و الأزهر (Politics and al-Azhar), Cairo: 1945, pp. 240-250.

the exception of few, received bribes from Ibn Saud, each according to his importance. Sheikh Rasheed Ridha, for example, received two thousand pounds, Ameen al-Husaini received one thousand, Abu al-`Azaaim received three hundred. Ibn Saud meant by so doing to woo their hearts and ensure good publicity for himself in their countries.[1]

Ibn Saud's Dilemma

We saw how Ibn Saud defended the *ikhwan* during the conference and justified their actions, but deep down, he was not pleased with them. It can be said that Ibn Saud was in a two-fold bewilderment towards the *ikhwan*, which is called scientifically "dilemma", i.e. standing between two options each of which is bad. On the one hand, he was indebted to the *ikhwan* for the sacrifices they had offered for his sake and the wars they waged. But he was, on the other hand, a man of politics who walked according to what was dictated to him to do. He, therefore, saw in the *ikhwan* a fanatical movement stirring problems and placing obstacles in the way of the state's growth. It is right to reword it thus: Ibn Saud was suffering from a psychological struggle towards the *ikhwan*, for he could not tolerate their fanaticism on the one hand, nor could he, on the other, do without them.

We have said that Ibn Saud was deep down displeased with the *ikhwan*, and in fact they, too, were not pleased with him. Since the beginning of their movement, they were critical of Ibn Saud because he was wearing the *iqal* rather than the turban, letting his moustache grow and wearing long outfits. They also criticized the sheikhs—scholars of theology in Najd—whom they accused of falling short of their religion, for flattering Ibn Saud while hiding the truth from him.

---

1 Public Records Office, London, FO 371/11442.

In the beginning, Ibn Saud followed with the *ikhwan* the principle of tolerance and leniency. He used to always say, "The *ikhwan* must be tolerated. No matter what they have done, their condition now is better than in the beginning. As regarding fanaticism and toughness, time ensures to allay its intensity." When some of his friends advised him to control the *ikhwan*'s extremism, he said to them, "These are my sons, and it is my duty to bear with them and overlook their bad actions and mistakes. I must advise them. I do not forget their actions, and I think they have good intentions and what is right will be revealed to them."[1]

Ibn Saud used to think that the *ikhwan*'s extremism would wear out by the passage of time, but he finally found out that their extremism intensified instead of winding down. In 1914, Ibn Saud had to hold a meeting for Najd's 'ulema in order to discuss this matter. The theologians met on September 30. After the discussion, they issued a circular advising the *ikhwan* to be moderate. The circular included the matters that were discussed and which the *ikhwan* were accustomed to accuse people, because of them, of being *kafir*, apostate. They were five matters as follows:

FIRST: Does the term "kafir" apply to Muslim Bedouins who are firm on their religion and follow Allāh's commandments and prohibitions?

SECOND: Is there a difference between one who wears the *iqal* and that who wears the turban as long as their belief is the same?

THIRD: Is there a difference between the first urban dwellers and the later immigrants?

FOURTH: Is there a difference between the sacrificial animal (*zabiha*) of the Bedouin who lives as a Muslim subject, whose

---

1 Hafiz Wahba, *Jazeerat al-Arab fil Qarn al-Ishreen* (The Arabian Peninsula in the Twentieth Century), pp. 293-294.

Chapter Eight: Ibn Saud Suffers From Problems

route is theirs, whose belief is their belief, and that of the early urban dwellers or of the immigrants in as far as *halal* and *haram* issues are concerned?

FIFTH: Do the immigrants have an order or a permit to attack those who did not migrate, so they would beat, discipline, intimidate or force them to migrate? Does anyone have the right to displace anyone, be he a Bedouin or a city dweller, without a clear matter or obvious apostasy or one of the actions because of which he must be expelled, without the permission of *wali al-amr* (person in charge) or the Shari`a-appointed judge?

At the conclusion of the circular, it was stated that the scholars had issued their *fatwa* as follows: "All these matters violate the Shari`a and its commandments. The individual who does them is to be forbidden and rebuked. If he repents and admits his error, he is to be forgiven, but if he continues to do what he was ordered not to do and resorts to stubbornness, he must be disciplined before the Muslims; he is neither to be treated as an enemy nor befriended except as ordered by the said *wali* or ruled by the Shari`a-appointed judge. Anyone who does the opposite, his route is not that of the Muslims. This is what we believe and invoke Allāh to testify to it. We hope He will enable us and your own selves to goodness; Allāh blesses Muhammed, his Progeny and companions and sends him salutations." Signed in the year 1337[1]. Signatures and Seals.[2]

This circular was distributed in the *ikhwan*'s villages and another circular was also distributed with it signed by Ibn Saud advising them to follow the verdicts of the scholars of religion since the latter know the Shari`a better. Apparently, both circulars did not have any serious impact on the *ikhwan*. Anyhow, the *ikhwan* intensified their extremism when Hijaz was

---

1 This is what the Arabic text reads, but this date does not seem to me to be right. The Hijri year 1337 is the equivalent of the Anno Domini year 1918. The text suggests a continuation of the events that took place in 1926, so why do we go back so many years? Most likely, there is a mistake here. – Tr.
2 Ameen al-Rayhani (Op. Cit.), pp. 433-434.

conquered. Hafiz Wahba says, "The extremism of the *ikhwan* increased after the fall of Jidda and the surrender of all of Hijaz. Many times did Ibn Saud become strict with them and clear himself of their extremism, but their transgression never stopped while their cruelty continued."[1]

Actually, the *ikhwan* did not stop at interfering in people's affairs but started interfering in Ibn Saud's affairs himself. In the month of October of 1925, when Sir Gilbert Clayton was negotiating with Ibn Saud at Bahira near Jidda, his [Ibn Saud's] aides went for a walk outside the camp, and there was a group of the *ikhwan* praying. Their imam started threatening them and saying that they defiled the land on which they were praying. When Ibn Saud heard about it, he summoned the chief of the group and kept rebuking him saying, "According to what right do you speak to my guests like that? And according to what right do you monopolize the sacred land to yourself and your fellows? You, dog, must know that the land, all of it, belongs to Allāh, and it is all a place for prayers." Then he ordered that man whipped so he would serve as a lesson to others.[2]

When Ibn Saud started using some modern inventions in Mecca, such as the telephone and bicycle, the *ikhwan* denounced it. The bicycle in their view moves by the force of magic and is an act of Satan by the token if the rider gets down off it, it does not stop, and they call it "Satan's carriage" or "the carriage of Eblis". It happened once that a servant of Ibn Saud was riding his bicycle and going on an errand when one of the *ikhwan* intercepted and beat him.

When Ibn Saud ordered to stretch telephone cables between Mecca and his camp outside it, the *ikhwan* kept cutting the cables in the pretext the telephone was an abomination.[3] Ibn Saud was forced to postpone the stretching of the cable for several weeks,

---

1 Hafiz Wahba (Op. Cit.), pp. 307-308.
2 Armstrong (Op. Cit.), pp. 199-200.
3 Hafiz Wahba (Op. Cit.), p. 293.

and he kept trying to convince them that the telephone was not made by Satan by the token it transfers verses of the Holy Qur'an when it receives them, knowing that Satan flees from the recitation of the Qur'an, according to their belief. They were finally convinced of the soundness of his statement, and the cables were stretched.[1]

Faisal Al-Duweesh:

Faisal al-Duweesh, head of the Muteer tribe, was the most extremist and fanatical of the *ikhwan*, and he was the first to publicly grumble about Ibn Saud whom he regarded as being not strict in his religion, lenient with the *kafirs*, apostates. The first signs of his grumbling appeared during Eidul-Fitr of the year 1343 A.H. which coincided on April 25, 1925. Hafiz Wahba says that he and Abdullah al-Damalooji went to greet Khalid ibn Luay, governor of Mecca, and found Faisal al-Duweesh and a group of the *ikhwan* there. Faisal started saying things which implied a threat. He said, "Praise to Allāh, Khalid and *ikhwan*, for His blessing, for we have entered Allāh's Sacred Haram and expelled the Sharif from it. We are the hosts of Allāh and the servants of His religion. We want only the word of Allāh to be the uppermost and His religion is the most dominant. We want only to lift the injustices and remove the innovations and abominations. This sword and these hosts will do their job against anyone who treads the path of the Sharif and does what he used to do." The *ikhwan* said, "Aameen" to his statement.[2]

Faisal al-Duweesh was put in charge of laying a siege around Medina, so he attacked the Awali village near Medina and kept killing its residents and looting as was his habit in every town he overran. It is said that he was determined to demolish the dome over the Prophet's grave in Medina when he directed his cannons at it, believing that that dome was not different from other sacred

---

[1] Khair ad-Din al-Zurakli (Op. Cit.), Vol. 2, p. 742.
[2] Hafiz Wahba (Op. Cit.), pp. 294-295.

domes and must be demolished. He almost did it, had Ibn Saud not dealt with him, ordering him to leave Medina and to go back to his Artawiyya village. Then Ibn Saud placed the responsibility of besieging Medina to his own son, Muhammed.

Faisal returned to Artawiyya full of anger and grudge against Ibn Saud and kept spreading rumors in the villages of the *ikhwan* charging Ibn Saud of having sold himself to the *kafir* Britons. Many *ikhwan* who were grumbling like him started rallying round him. In the fall of 1926, the grumbling *ikhwan* in Artawiyya held a meeting in which they pledged to support the religion of Allāh and to declare *jihad* in His cause. They publicly declared their denunciation of the actions which Ibn Saud had undertaken and which, in their eyes, opposed the religion of Allāh, and they were as follows:

1. sending his son, Saud, to Egypt,
2. sending his other son, Faisal, to London, the land of polytheism,
3. the use of cars, telegraphs and telephones,
4. the imposition of taxes in Najd and Hijaz,
5. his permission to the tribes of Iraq and Trans-Jordan to let their animals graze in the lands of the Muslims,
6. preventing trade with Kuwait; so, if the people of Kuwait are apostates, they are to be fought, but if they are Muslims, why boycott them?
7. Leniency towards the Rafidhis[1] of al-Ahsa and Qateef and not forcing them to accept the religion of the people of the Sunnah and *jama`a* (group).

Ibn Saud was in Mecca when reports of the Artawiyya meeting reached him, so he hurriedly returned to Riyadh and summoned the chiefs of the *ikhwan* to a conference in which they would meet with the scholars of theology. The conference

---

1 This term, "Rafidhi", means literally "rejectionist", and it is a misnomer used to refer to Shi'ite Muslims who, according to the Wahhabis, rejected allegiance to the first three caliphs. This misnomer continues to be used by the Wahhabis and Salafis up to our time. – Tr.

Chapter Eight: Ibn Saud Suffers From Problems

was held on January 7, 1927 and was attended by Faisal al-Duweesh and all grumbling folks with the exception of one: Sultan ibn Najad, head of the Utaiba tribe. Ibn Saud spoke and said about himself that he was still a servant of the Shari`a, safeguarding it fully, and that he never changed from the way he used to be as some people erroneously think. The conference was concluded with a *fatwa* issued by the scholars in which they answered all the issues which the *ikhwan* had raised. Here below we cite the most important portion of the said *fatwa*:

"As regarding the issue of the telegraph, it is something that has recently taken place and we do not know its truth, nor have we come to know anything said about it by the people of knowledge, so we halted in its regard, and we do not say anything about Allāh and His Messenger without knowledge, while stating absolute permission or prohibition needs getting to know its reality. As regarding the mosques of Hamzah and Abu Rasheed, we sought the *fatwa* of the imam, may Allāh grant him success, to demolish them immediately. As regarding the graves, if there are any of them in Hijaz, it must immediately be removed, and only the purified Shari`a rules... As regarding the Rafidhis, the imam has issued his *fatwa* to us that they are obligated to swear allegiance to Islam and are prevented from demonstrating the rituals of their false religion. The imam must also obligate his deputy over the Ahsa to bring them to Sheikh Ibn Bishr so they may swear the oath of allegiance according to the religion of Allāh and His Messenger and to leave alone making pleas to the righteous ones from among Ahlul-Bayt and others, and that they must abandon all innovations, such as their assembling to commemorate them and other things their false religion does, and they must be prohibited from visiting the Haram and also obligated to assemble for the five daily prayers together with others at the mosques. Imams and *muathins* (callers to prayers) from the Ahl al-Sunnah must organize them, and they must be obligated to learn the three principles. Also, if they have built places for the purpose of upholding innovations, they must be demolished, and they must be prevented from upholding innovations at mosques and elsewhere. If anyone refuses what has been stated, he is to be banished from the land of the Muslims... As regarding the Rafidhis of Iraq who have spread and mingled in the Muslims' desert, we sought the imam's *fatwa* to prevent them from entering the Muslims' pasture lands and areas. As regarding the tariffs, we have been informed by the *fatwa* that they are apparently among the prohibitions. If he leaves them, it is only his obligation, and if he refuses, there must be no dissension among the Muslims or the abandoning of obedience to him on their account. As regarding the *jihad*, it is directed to the attention of the imam who has to take into consideration what is best for Islam and Muslims according to the dictates of the Shari`a. We plead to Allāh for ourselves, for him and for all Muslims to grant us success and guidance; surely Allāh blesses and salutes our Prophet Muhammed, his Ahlul-Bayt and companions." Written on Sha`ban 8, 1345 A.H. (1926 A.D.).[1]

Ibn Saud tried to implement this *fatwa* in order to please the *ikhwan*, and among what he did in this regard was his demolition of the Hamzah Mosque at Ohud Mountain near Medina, and it was erected on the grave of Hamzah, uncle of the Prophet 7. He also ordered to tighten the rope round the necks of the Shi`ites of al-Ahsa and Qateef. Before then, they used to carry out their Husaini rituals at homes and Husainiyyas, now they were banned from doing so, and their Husainiyas were shut down. This prohibition included also the Shi`ites who reside in the Nakhawla quarter of Medina.

The *Ikhwan* Attack Iraq

In 1927, the Iraqi government, having reached an understanding with the British government, decided to set up police stations equipped with wireless equipment and armored

---

1 *Ibid.*, pp. 296-297.

Chapter Eight: Ibn Saud Suffers From Problems

vehicles near the Najdi borders in order to oversee the movements of the Bedouins and to prevent raids. In October, the building of the first police station started at a place called al-Basiyya 125 kilometers from the borders with Najd. When Ibn Saud heard about it, he was concerned and thought that King Faisal was building those police stations, in an understanding with the British, in order to make them formidable frontier fortresses in the desert in preparation to invade his land in the future.

On the eve of November 5, a group of the *ikhwan* attacked the Basiyya police station which was still being built, killing a number of workers and the policemen who were in it, then they returned to where they had been. British references estimate the number of those killed at twenty among whom there was one woman.[1]

The Iraqi public opinion was outraged because of this aggression, and the Iraqi government was upset. The High Commissioner, Sir Henry Dobbs, sent a protest to Ibn Saud. Ibn Saud answered saying that the raid of the *ikhwan* was due to the "ominous castle", meaning the Basiyya police station, for it was not erected except to spark sedition and create evils, and its building led to stirring the *ikhwan*, so it became difficult to control them and curb their reins. Ibn Saud expressed his regret for what had happened and promised to prevent the invasion through all means available to him, but he demanded the police station demolished and said, "The people of Najd prefer to be invaded by the people of Iraq every morning and evening but do not accept the building of one fortress."[2]

The *ikhwan* kept launching their raids on Iraqi tribes, looting and killing them. Sir Henry Dobbs became angry, and he was known for quickly getting angry, so he sent a telegram to his

---

1 Report on Iraq Administration, 1927, London: 1928, p. 57.
2 Sadiq Hassan al-Soodani, *Al-'Alaqat al-Iraqiyya-al-Saudia 1920 – 1931: Dirasa fil 'Alaqat al-Siyasiyya* (Iraqi-Saudi Relations 1920 – 1931: A Study in Political Ties), Baghdad: 1975, p. 271.

government in London asking it to impose a siege on Ibn Saud so he might discipline the aggressors and pay compensations for those killed. But the British government did not agree to this suggestion, so Dobbs submitted to it another suggestion: The planes must drop leaflets on the desert warning the *ikhwan* to keep their distance of four hundred [Arabian] miles away from the Iraqi borders. If they refuse to obey this demand, the planes will bomb them. The British government accepted this suggestion.

In mid-January of 1928, the British planes started dropping leaflets on the desert, but the *ikhwan* did not pay them heed, or perhaps they did not understand them. In the month of February, the planes started strafing concentrations and villages of the *ikhwan*. This strafing created arguments in the British House of Commons where questions were directed at the minister of colonies about the reasons that promoted the planes to bomb the Saudi lands. The minister answered saying that Ibn Saud announced that he could no longer control his subjects.[1]

Hafiz Wahba says that he was at the time in Egypt, so Ibn Saud sent him a telegram on February 24, 1928 saying, "The condition in Najd is unstable because the pledges have been broken by Iraq. Planes have hit the borders in the east and in the west. Humanity has not been respected. The situation is very dangerous, efforts are exerted to calm the situation, yet the result is unknown."[2]

We notice here Ibn Saud saying, "Humanity has not been respected." He apparently forgets what the *ikhwan* did, their killing and looting, while remembering what the planes did to them, strafing them. Such is the human nature when people dispute. They forget the aggression which they commit while exaggerating the assault on them.

---

1 Abdullah Philby, *History of Najd* (translated as) تاريخ نجد و دعوة الشيخ محمد بن عبد الوهاب, translated by Omar al-Dirawi, Beirut, p. 359.
2 Hafiz Wahba, *Khamsoona Aman fi Jazeerat al-Arab*, p. 91.

Chapter Eight: Ibn Saud Suffers From Problems

The Riyadh Conference

The strafing of the planes put Ibn Saud between two fires: the fire of the British and the fire of the *ikhwan*. Those folks ask him to curb the *ikhwan* and prevent them from raiding, and these folks demand him to declare "jihad" on the "kafirs", apostates. Ibn Saud finally found out that it would be better for him to negotiate with the British instead of fighting them. After communications with them, an agreement was made to negotiate in Jidda in May of 1928.

Ibn Saud was of the opinion that he should meet with the chiefs of the *ikhwan* before negotiating with Britain in order to assure and calm them. He met them in April in the town of Buraida and let them understand that he shared their anger about the building of police stations on the borders, but he preferred to solve the problem through negotiations. He informed them that he would be going to Jidda to meet the British negotiator, and he promised to meet with them again in Riyadh after his return from Jidda in order to familiarize them with the outcome of the negotiations.[1]

The negotiations went on in Jidda twice. The first was in May and the second was in August. The British side was represented by Sir Gilbert Clayton. In the second, Tawfiq al-Suweedi and Bahaa ad-Din Nouri participated in them together with Ahmed Hamid al-Sarraf in his capacity as the scribe [for writing the minutes]. The fate of the negotiations both times was a failure.

Ibn Saud left Jidda after that for Riyadh in order to meet with the *ikhwan* as he had promised. When he reached it, he summoned the *ikhwan* to a conference which they would attend with the *sheikhs*, i.e. scholars of religion. The conference convened on October 25, 1928 and was attended by about eight hundred persons. But three chiefs of the *ikhwan* did not attend

---

1 Hafiz Wahba, *Jazeerat al-arab fil Qarn al-Ishreen*, p. 297.

it; they were: Faisal al-Duweesh, Sultan ibn Bajad and Dhaidan ibn Huthailin, but they sent some of their sons and relatives to attend on their behalf.

Ibn Saud inaugurated the conference saying, "Nobody among you should entertain the thought that fear of you is what prompted me to hold this meeting. Listen, I have built my domain with help from Allāh and the strength of my arms. He, the One with the Great Might, granted me victory. Only my fear of Him is what prompted me to gather you here in order to be enlightened by your ideas so we may carry out His command among us through consultation. So, I am not overcome by conceit or stubbornness which usually overcome humans." Then Ibn Saud kept talking about his favor on them: They used to be divided, killing each other, looting each other, so he united them and made them a great and strong nation. Then he said that many people are not pleased with him, that he came to know about their many complaints, but he is not one of those who forfeit their authority under pressure and coercion. He also did not desire to rule subjects who are not pleased with him. He, therefore, offered them the option to choose any member of his family to be King over them, and he pledged before Allāh to carry that man to the throne and to sincerely and faithfully serve him. It was then that voices rose from those present saying, "No, No, we do not want any King other than you, O Abdul-Aziz!"[1]

After that, he offered to speak frankly about their complaints against him and pledged to them that he would not blame or punish anyone for what he had said. They started presenting their complaints, stating his relationship with the *kafirs* and friendship with the Britons, his use of their Satanic inventions, such as the cars, telephones and telegraph, his leniency towards the police stations built by the *kafirs* on the borders and his

---

[1] Salah ad-Din al-Mukhtar, *Tarikh al-Mamlaka al-Araibyya al-Saudia* (History of the Kingdom of Saudi Arabia), Beirut, Vol. 2, p. 442.

Chapter Eight: Ibn Saud Suffers From Problems

preventing the Muslims from the *jihad* in order to raise the word of Allāh high and support His religion.

Ibn Saud responded to their complaints with patience, according to their measure of comprehension. He mentioned to them that he did not love the *kafirs* or the Christians or the Britons, but he found in their friendship a benefit for the Muslims, and his policy with them is to get from them everything that is of benefit to true Muslims. He used with them the policy of "give and take", but that Faisal al-Duweesh was the one who steered the situation against him.[1]

Then Ibn Saud talked about the telephones saying that the Islamic Shari`a had nothing that prohibits their use. They are not the products of sorcery or the doing of Satan. He turned to the present sheikhs and asked them, "Do you find in the statements of the Prophet anything that opposes seeking benefit from these modern inventions?" The *sheikhs* answered, "No."[2]

When the discussion revolved round the police stations, Ibn Saud said that they were built to prevent the aggressions carried out by Faisal al-Duweesh on Iraq. Faisal, then, is the cause, and he bears the responsibility for them. Those present declared their dissociation from Faisal al-Duweesh and stated that they severed their ties with him, but they kept insisting that those stations had to be demolished. The *sheikhs* supported them in this regard and issued their verdict that the stations harmed the Muslims and the Arabs, especially the residents of Najd, and that demolishing them was akin to a Muslim defending his wealth and religion. Ibn Saud said that the *fatwas* of the *sheikhs* were right, and that he himself believed that the stations posed a danger to the Muslims, but he desired to let the discussion of this subject and that about the *jihad* be done in a special meeting. He asked them to choose fifty men from among them so he could

---

[1] Public Records Office in London FO 371/13713.
[2] Omar Abul-Nasr, *Ibn Saud*, Beirut: 1935, p. 105.

explain to them all the matters. The attendants, whereupon, agreed and renewed their allegiance to him.[1]

Following the commencement of the conference, a special meeting was held in the evening after the night prayers ritual which was attended by the fifty men who were chosen to deliberate with Ibn Saud, and the deliberation went on from 2:00 after sunset [Arab time] until 6:00. We do not know what went on during it, but it is believed that Ibn Saud was able to convince them that the *jihad* against the *kafirs* must not be absolute but must be within the limits of the ability of the Muslims; otherwise, catastrophe would happen, so they felt pleased upon leaving.

The Revolt of the *Ikhwan*

The result reached by the Riyadh conference was not accepted by the three chiefs of the *ikhwan*: Faisal al-Duweesh, Sultan ibn Bajad and Dhaidan ibn Hithilin, so they kept spreading bad rumors in the villages of the *ikhwan* against Ibn Saud, accusing him of destroying the religion, accepting the *kafirs* as his masters and seeking power. They kept intercepting the routes of the caravans and imposing fines on the villages and also attacking the tribes of Iraq and Najd.

The number of the *ikhwan* who revolted was about five thousand men, so Ibn Saud prepared a large army numbering fifteen thousand men to fight them. Both groups fought at a place called al-Sabla near al-Zulfa to the north of Buraida. Before fighting between them started, the *ikhwan* sent Ibn Saud a messenger named Majid ibn Khatheela accompanied by a letter. When the messenger met Ibn Saud, he did not greet him, so Ibn Saud was angry on account of this insult and rebuked the messenger saying, "Who are you? Are you not Majid ibn Khatheela...?" Then he started narrating the man's biography while reprimanding him. Then he said to him, "Do you meet me

---

[1] Public Records Office in London FO 371/13713.

Chapter Eight: Ibn Saud Suffers From Problems

without greeting me?! Go right now to whoever sent you and tell him that we are coming to attack you tomorrow. If they want to prevent bloodshed, let them surrender without any term or condition, and the Shari`a is the judge between myself and themselves. These scholars are present. Go to your fellows."

The messenger returned to the *ikhwan* to advise them to surrender to Ibn Saud before it would be too late. Faisal al-Duweesh was of the opinion that he would go in person to Ibn Saud to see the extent of his strength. When Faisal met Ibn Saud, he started flattering him, pretending that he was ready to surrender and that he would spend that night at his place, but Ibn Saud said to him, "Stand up, go and spend the night with your folks; your date is tomorrow after sunrise..." Faisal returned to his fellows. When some of them asked him about the strength of Ibn Saud, he answered them saying, "Whom did I see?! I saw an urban dweller whose limbs shiver of fear, and those around him are only cooks who know nothing but to sleep on mattresses. Receive the glad tidings, *ikhwan*, I found out that they have a large number of domesticated animals and huge sums of money; so, receive the glad tiding of winning and gaining. We will subdue this tyrant tomorrow and seize his wealth."[1]

The battle between both parties took place in the morning of the next day, March 30, 1929 and went on for several hours, ending with the defeat of the *ikhwan*. It seems that one of the factors of their defeat was the presence of scholars of religion on the side of Ibn Saud, for this must have led to weakening the resolve of the *ikhwan* and minimizing their spirit of sacrifice and religious fervor.

Faisal al-Duweesh was seriously wounded in the battle, so he was brought to Ibn Saud on a carrier made of palm leaves surrounded by his wife and daughters who all were weeping and interceding for him with Ibn Saud. Ibn Saud was moved by this sight, so he forgave him and issued orders to move him to his

---
[1] Hafiz Wahba (Op. Cit.), pp. 299-300.

house in Artawiyya. He also sent his private doctor, Madhat Sheikh al-Ardh, to treat him.

Three days later, Sultan ibn Bajad surrendered to Ibn Saud, so Ibn Saud ordered him tried by judges of the Shari`a. The court sentenced him to life in prison at the Riyadh Fortress. As for Dhaidan, he was able to flee to Kuwait.

The *Ikhwan* Crushed

Ibn Saud went to Hijaz to attend the season of pilgrimage which coincided in the month of May. He did not stay in Hijaz for too long, for he received reports that Faisal al-Duweesh recovered from his wounds and declared the revolution anew. Ibn Saud, therefore, returned quickly to Riyadh in the month of July. There, he prepared his forces which had vehicles equipped with machineguns and led them towards Faisal al-Duweesh.

It is worth mentioning in this regard that Faisal al-Duweesh wrote on December 15, 1929 to King Faisal in Baghdad addressing him as the "sultan of the Muslims" and inviting him to cooperate with him to fight Ibn Saud. He also wrote Captain [John Bagot] Glubb [1897 – 1986], inspector of the southern desert, in Iraq expressing his desire to be one of the subjects of the Iraqi government, placing himself at its disposal.[1]

Early in December of 1930, the decisive battle between Ibn Saud and Faisal al-Duweesh took place at a location near the Kuwaiti-Iraqi borders. Faisal was defeated, so he fled with some of his fellows into the borders of Iraq, surrendering to the British who moved them to al-Sha`sa[2]. Following negotiations between Ibn Saud and the British, the latter decided to hand over Faisal al-Duweesh and his fellows to Ibn Saud provided the latter would

---

1 Sadiq Hassan al-Soodani (Op. Cit.), pp. 308-309.
2 This is what the Arabic text says: الشعسة, but I could not locate this place anywhere in Iraq, my homeland, so it is likely this word is misspelled. The site may be the Iraqi town of Shu`ayba الشعيبة (there is another Shu`ayba in Kuwait) where the British, during Iraq's monarchy, maintained a military base which is still there. – Tr.

Chapter Eight: Ibn Saud Suffers From Problems

keep them alive and pledge to return what they [*ikhwan*] had looted from the people of Kuwait and Iraq.¹

On January 28, Faisal al-Duweesh and his fellows were air lifted to Ibn Saud who was camping at a place called Khabari Wadhha خباري وضحة one hundred miles south of Kuwait. Faisal was brought in a car to Ibn Saud's tent as the curses kept pouring on him from both sides while being transported. Ibn Saud thanked the British officers who brought him and also the British government for its friendship and kindness, saying that every day, it provides a new evidence for its deep friendship.

After the officers had gone, Faisal al-Duweesh advanced towards Ibn Saud in humiliation, so Ibn Saud addressed him saying, "You know, Faisal, what I did to you in the past; I did not fall short of doing anything for you. I was in a continuous war with the people of Najd for your sake. So, is this how you reward me? Do you want to rule? You ruled in the areas where you were. Who among you has done a favor to me? The favor, all of it, belongs to Allāh alone. Which of you I did not take with my sword? There is none of you whose father or brother I spared; and I did not conquer you save through help from Allāh then from the sword. I used to fulfill your wishes, suffer for your sake, work day and night for your convenience and happiness. Did you not fear Allāh when you wrote Glubb—meaning Captain Glubb—that you wanted to migrate to Iraq and liked to be one of its [Brittain's] subjects? Do you think that you will be in a status higher than that which you used to occupy with me?"

Faisal answered him saying, "Allāh knows, O Abdul-Aziz, that you did not fall short in what you did for us. You did everything that grants you a shiny image. We met your goodness with badness. We fled away from you to the *kafirs*, so they transported us in one of their planes. Suffices the humiliation and ignominy from which I suffer before the *ikhwan* after I used to be dignified, respected. May Allāh fight Satan who tempted us

---
1 Hafiz Wahba (Op. Cit.), p. 303.

and made our actions look good in our eyes, getting us to reach our present status."[1]

Faisal was transported to Riyadh in a car and was submitted to a Shar`i court and, as was the case with Sultan ibn Bajad, he was sentenced to life in prison at the Riyadh Fortress.

This augured the end of the *ikhwan*'s movement which stirred amazement among the people for two reasons: the *ikhwan*'s commando spirit during wartime and the excessive extremism during peace time. Philby says, "Ibn Saud's conduct towards the *ikhwan*'s movement was a skilled one, unparalleled in his elimination of this movement after eighteen years [of its establishment] when it was proven to him that it was no longer anything but a stumbling block in the way of stabilizing the conditions which he built with his lengthy patience and efforts. This movement, which Ibn Saud created from nothing, could have destroyed and annihilated him had he himself not destroyed it."[2]

History has shown how most builders of states kill those who help their building. The reason is that those helpers want to share the builder in the fruit of what he built, whereas he does not want to forfeit that fruit to them, so a dispute erupts among them. The dispute may end by the elimination of those helpers. Truthful is the one who has said that [the art of] politics has no heart.

Problem of the Sheikhs

After crushing the movement of the *ikhwan*, Ibn Saud, expressing his elation, said, "From this day, we shall lead a new life." He actually did start a new life, opening modern schools in his homeland, setting up a regular army from the urban dwellers under the supervision of some Arab officers from the remnants

---

1 *Ibid.*, pp. 303-304.
2 Abdullah Philby (Op. Cit.), pp. 367-368.

Chapter Eight: Ibn Saud Suffers From Problems

of the Ottoman army. He also imported cars and wireless sets in order to connect the wide areas of his kingdom. Philby assisted him in so doing a great deal.

This Najdi movement which Ibn Saud underwent was faced with the opposition of the sheikhs, i.e. Najd's theologians. He got rid of the opposition of the *ikhwan* so he would be afflicted anew with that of the sheikhs. But the sheikh's opposition differs from that of the *ikhwan*: It is calm, it does not have violence, and it does not interfere in people's affairs.

The first sign of the sheikhs' opposition surfaced in June of 1928 when Ibn Saud opened some elementary schools in Hijaz. An uproar started among the sheikhs because of that, and they held a meeting in Mecca in which they issued a resolution protesting the opening of those schools because, first, they teach painting and, second, foreign languages and, third, geography.

Ibn Saud sent them Hafiz Wahba to discuss the matter. When Hafiz Wahba held a meeting with them, they kept mentioning to him the reasons that prompted them to prohibit painting, foreign languages and geography. They said, "We explained to imam Abdul-Aziz the evidences and abominations that result from these sciences. As for painting (or drawing), it is imaging, and it is absolutely prohibitive. As for the languages, they form a pretext to get to know the beliefs and corrupt branches of knowledge of the *kafirs*. This poses a danger to our beliefs and to the manners of our children. As regarding geography, it says that the earth is similar to a ball, that it turns, that there is talk about the stars, planets, etc., according to the knowledge of the Greeks and which scholars from among our ancestors reject."

Hafiz Wahba kept arguing with them in this topic and mentioning to them the evidences that permit teaching painting, languages and geography. When the sheikhs saw that the debate took too long, they said, "We have decided what we believe, and we have submitted it to the imam, and we do not need to argue since the Shari`a bans arguing. If the imam accepts our opinion, praise is due to Allāh, and if he opposes us, it will not be the first time he opposes us."[1]

Once the school problem had ended, the wireless problem started. The sheikhs protested against this invention out of their belief that it had to be the product of sorcery and the doing of Satan. Their evidence is that the wireless transmits the news between Mecca and Riyadh in one moment while knowing that the camels cross the distance between them in twenty days. This cannot be done by a human except with help from Satan, so they have to offer a sacrifice for Satan in exchange for the service he renders them.

When the first wireless station was established in Riyadh, some sheikhs kept going to the station and asking its operator about when the Satans would be visiting, and whether the greatest Satan is in Mecca or in Riyadh, how many of his sons aid him in the mission of transmitting reports... Some sheikhs would tempt the operator with cash while pledging to keep the matter confidential if he told them about it.

Hafiz Wahba tells us about a dialogue that went on between him and a sheikh in Medina about the wireless. The sheikh said, "Undoubtedly, these things result from the use of the jinns. Some trusted friends have told me that the wireless telegraph does not move except after an animal has been sacrificed on which the name of Satan is mentioned. Then the sheikh kept mentioning some stories about how humans use Satan [for their own benefit]. Hafiz Wahba tried to convince him that the wireless is a physical invention that haf nothing to do with the jinns or with Satan, but he did not succeed; rather, the sheikh took to silence against his wish.[2]

---

1 Hafiz Wahba (Op. Cit.), pp. 126-127.
2 *Ibid.*, pp. 286-287.

Chapter Eight: Ibn Saud Suffers From Problems

The sheikhs kept denouncing the modern inventions which come to the country. They denounced the record player, the cinema, the flood lights and the planes. They believed that the planes, for example, carry people who defy their Lord when they are inside.[1] When the Americans started exploring for oil in the Dhahran area, the *sheikhs* said to Ibn Saud, "The *kafirs* must not enter the country because they corrupt the men and the women and bring wine, photographs and such Satanic things to the country."[2]

Ibn Saud used to sometimes tolerate them and sometimes interact with them. They opposed him in 1930 because he permitted the celebrations on the occasion of his ascension to the throne of Hijaz, regarding doing so as violating the Sunnah, so Ibn Saud listened to them and cancelled the celebrations.[3] The same happened in 1950 when the Saudi government decided to celebrate the passage of fifty years since the fall of Riyadh. A statement was issued by the Saudi foreign ministry thus: "The government had decided to celebrate the golden anniversary of His Majesty the King entering Riyadh fifty years ago, and the scholars of religion were requested lately to issue their *fatwa* in this regard. They, therefore, decreed that this is not a Sunnah of the Muslims and the Muslims must not take another Eid besides Eidul-Fitr and Eidul-Adha. Obeying the ruling of the Shari`a, His Majesty ordered the cancellation of the ceremonies and preparations."[4]

A sheikh narrates how he once met Ibn Saud at his mansion in Riyadh and saw him walking, wearing a long gown that touched the ground, so he said to him, "[Fear] Allāh! Allāh, O Abdul-Aziz! You are overcome by pride, so now your gown's tail drags behind you!" Ibn Saud turned to the servants and said,

---

1 Abdullah Philby (Op. Cit.), p. 356.
2 Ameen al-Mumayyaz, *Al-Mamlaka al-Arabiyya al-Saudia Kama Araftuha* (The Kingdom of Saudi Arabia as I knew it), Beirut: 1963, p. 229.
3 Hafiz Wahba (Op. Cit.), p. 284.
4 Khair ad-Din al-Zurakli (Op. Cit.), Vol. 2, pp. 742-744.

"Bring me the scissors!" When they brought him the scissors, he [Ibn Saud] gave them to the sheikh saying, "Cut off what you see as opposing the religion."[1] Armstrong narrates a similar story saying that a sheikh confronted Ibn Saud one day in front of people to say to him, "Your moustaches are longer than the Sunnah permits." Ibn Saud accepted it with an open mind and asked for a pair of scissors and immediately trimmed his moustaches.[2]

It seems that Ibn Saud used to put up with the criticisms of the sheikhs when they were simply personal, for he found it politically appropriate to respond to them in order to improve his reputation among the public. But he did not tolerate them when he saw them as harming the interest and future of the State. Hafiz Wahba narrates the following: "One day, senior sheikhs met in 1931 with Ibn Saud and kept blaming him for introducing the wireless into his land. They said to him, 'May your life be long! Cheated you were those who suggested the use of telegraph and getting it to enter our land. Philby will bring us calamities, and we are afraid he will hand over our land to the British.' Ibn Saud answered saying, 'You are wrong. Nobody cheated us. I, praise to Allāh, am neither weak in mind nor short-sighted to be cheated by deceivers. Philby is only a businessman. He was a middleman in this deal, and our land is dear to us and I will never hand it over to anyone except for the price for which we received it. Brother sheikhs, you are now over my head; hold on to each other; do not let me shake my head so some of you or most of you may fall off my head, and you know that anyone who falls on the ground cannot be put over my head again. Two matters I do not permit anyone to talk about because their benefits for myself and my country have already shown, and there is no evidence from the Book of Allāh or the Sunnah of the

---

1 *Ibid.*, Vol. 2, p. 744.
2 Armstrong (Op. Cit.), p. 208.

Chapter Eight: Ibn Saud Suffers From Problems

Messenger of Allāh 7 that prevents the use of the wireless and of cars."[1]

Among interesting incidents narrated in this regard is that a group of Britons visited Ibn Saud in his Riyadh mansion. While they were in the mansion, prayer time approached, so Ibn Saud and his protégés prayed behind an imam. The imam recited in the first *rek`a* this verse: وَلاَ تَرْكَنُواْ إِلَى الَّذِينَ ظَلَمُواْ فَتَمَسَّكُمُ النَّارُ **"Do not incline to those who do wrong or else the Fire will seize you" (Qur'an,** 11:113). He repeated its recitation in the second *rek`a*. When the prayer service ended, Ibn Saud crawled from his place towards the imam and gave him a good beating and kicking, rebuking him and saying, "What do you have to do with politics, you malicious man, and what do you mean by repeating this verse in every *rek`a*? Is there no other verse?"[2]

Lobbin Meeting

Following the crushing of the *ikhwans*' movement, the new High Commissioner in Baghdad, Sir Francis Humphrys, kept trying hard to bring Faisal ibn al-Husain and Ibn Saud together and to bring about harmony between them instead of contention. After many communications, an agreement was reached for both kings to meet on board a British barge in the waters of the Arabian Gulf.

King Faisal left Baghdad on board a special train on February 20, 1930 accompanied by an entourage comprised of Naji al-Suweedi, [Sir Kinahan] Cornwallis, Rustum Haidar, Abdullah al-Mudha'ifi, Khalil Isma`eel, Captain Glubb, Dr. Sanderson together with bodyguards, a scribe and a photographer. Also, there were in his company four journalists: Rafael Batti from *Al-Bilad* newspaper, Mr. Karmi from *Al-Awqaf al-Iraqiyya* (Iraqi Endowments) newspaper, Saleem Hassoun from *Al-Aalam al-*

---

1 Hafiz Wahba (Op. Cit.), p. 287.
2 Ameen al-Mumayyaz (Op. Cit.), p. 609.

Arabi (Arab World) newspaper and Abdul-Razzaq al-Hassani from the Egyptian *Al-Ahram* (Pyramids) newspaper.

British barge Lobbin was docked in the Gulf waters fifteen miles from the Faw. Sir Francis Humphrys and his entourage were on it. Shortly after that, two ships came near it one of which was carrying Faisal and the other was carrying Ibn Saud. Ibn Saud's entourage was comprised of Hafiz Wahba, Yousuf Yasin, Abdul-Aziz al-Qusaibi, Dr. Madhat Sheikh al-Ardh, Capt. Muhammed al-Mani` and Ibrahim al-Mu`ammar. The presence of one hundred and fifty armed men was noticed in the company of Ibn Saud to protect him.[1]

Ibn Saud had presented two conditions for meeting Faisal: The first was: The talk between them must be restricted to clearing the air and expressing affection and friendship without delving into the matters relevant to the dispute between both governments. The second was: The meeting must be without music and smoking. The Saudi government had notified the High Commissioner in Baghdad, Sr. Francis Humphrys, of both of these conditions as well as the head of the Iraqi administration, Naji al-Suweedi. But when Ibn Saud met with Faisal on Barge Lobbin, he found him talking about the issues of the dispute between both governments, so Ibn Saud remained patient until Faisal finished his statement. It was then that Ibn Saud pointed out to an advance condition that he should not discuss such matters, so the High Commissioner said that he was sorry he did not inform King Faisal of this condition. Also, Naji al-Suweedi spoke saying that he saw the interest necessitated both kings to meet, and that there was no objection to discussing the matters relevant to the dispute between both governments. King Faisal then turned to Naji al-Suweedi and rebuked him for what he had done. It was then that Ibn Saud retracted saying, "The matter is left to His Majesty, King Faisal, if he wishes to discuss the contention issues, and if he wishes, he can leave them." Faisal

---

[1] Sadiq Hassan al-Soodani (Op. Cit.), pp. 335-336.

answered that he was of the view that those matters should be referred to the delegates of both govern-ments to discuss. It was then that the delegates withdrew from the ship and started discussing the subject.¹

Both kings returned after that to the talk relevant to both of them, and it was full of courtesy. Each of them kept calling the other أخي Brother or خُوي (also brother in the colloquial). Ibn Saud explained how the hostility between him and al-Husain started, stating that the cause behind it was not due to him. Here, Faisal did not hesitate to direct some blame to his father. He also pointed out to the primary instigator being Khalid ibn Luay.²

Actually, this meeting between both kings heralded a new era in the relations between both States. Nothing took place thereafter that would pollute the air of relations between them. We must also remember in this regard that both men were masters of realistic politics. They both were of the opinion that the common interest dictated to forget the grudges, for a grudge can harm only the one who harbors it.

Yemen's War

There was a dispute between Ibn Saud and Yemen's imam, Yahya Hameed ad-Din, about the Najran area which is located between Yemen and Najd, each claiming that he had a right to it more than the other. Negotiations went on between both parties for a long time but to no avail. In the month of March, Ibn Saud's patience ran out, so he warned imam Yahya. On the 21st of it, Ibn Saud declared war on Yemen, and his forces advanced across the Yemeni borders.

The Saudi forces depended on vehicles (trucks) for moving about, and they were comprised of two convoys: One of them advanced parallel to the coastline carried by about eight hundred

---

1 Khair ad-Din al-Zurakli (Op. Cit.), Vol. 2, pp. 510-512.
2 Khair ad-Din al-Zurakli (Op. Cit.), Vol. 2, p. 513.

vehicles led by Prince Faisal ibn Abdul-Aziz, and the other advanced in the direction of the capital, Sanaa, via Saada route under the command of Prince Saud ibn Abdul-Aziz. The first convoy did not meet any resistance in its advance. Imam Yahya's plan was for his forces to withdraw from the coastline and fortify themselves in the mountains. On May 6, the convoy was able to occupy the Hudaida Port without resistance. As for the other convoy, its march was very slow and it could not achieve its goals due to the rough terrain and to many mountains and valleys.

This war stirred a great deal of interest throughout the Islamic lands and in Europe. The Supreme Islamic Council in Palestine formed a delegation to mediate a peace between both groups. It was comprised of al-Hajj Ameen al-Husaini as its head, Prince Shakeeb Arsalan, Muhammed Ali Ilwiyya Pasha and Hashim Beg al-Atassi as members, and Ali Afandi Rushdi as confidant. The delegation was expected to be joined by Yasin al-Hashimi and Nouri al-Sa`eed, but obstacles prevented it. On April 13, the delegation left Suez for Mecca. When it reached it, it met Ibn Saud, then they all travelled to Taif.

The following telegram reached Ibn Saud from imam Yahya: "What has happened suffices; we seek refuge with Allāh from the evils of those who lie in ambush against Islam in order to achieve their ambitions. Yemen is under your rule, and we ordered the removal of our soldiers from the Najran land. Please accept the request of Sayyid Abdullah ibn al-Wazir as the emissary to Your Excellency to complete the brotherly treaty. May Allāh grant you good health. This telegram has had to be routed via Asmara because the wireless set here is out of order and is being repaired, so please answer through Asmara [Eritrea]."[1]

---

1 Ameen Sa`eed, *Tarikh al-Dawla al-Saudia* (History of the Saudi State), Beirut, Vol. 2, pp. 376-377.

Chapter Eight: Ibn Saud Suffers From Problems

Ibn Saud responded to imam Yahya's telegram expressing the readiness for peace according to certain conditions, so the imam sent a telegram saying he accepted the conditions. On May 1, Abdullah ibn al-Wazir, delegate of imam Yahya, reached Taif. The delegate members of the Islamic Council exerted good efforts to bring both parties together, and on May 21, a peace treaty was signed, and the war ended.

This quick peace stirred the attention and amazement of the world public opinion because Ibn Saud agreed, through this reconciliation, to withdraw his forces from the Yemeni lands for terms which were regarded as being quite simple as follows: (1) the Yemeni forces' withdrawal from Najran, (2) handing over Idrisis refugees in Yemen to Ibn Saud, and (3) the release of the hostages imam Yahya had had.

It is believed there are two main reasons that prompted Ibn Saud to sign the peace agreement; they were:

FIRST: Ibn Saud feared the interference of foreign countries in Yemen. Apparently, he feared Italy in particular, for it is known about that country that it was eying Yemen, coveting it. When the Saudi forces occupied the Hudaida Port on May 6, three Italian war ships arrived at the port in the pretext of protecting Italian nationals. The Italian commander tried to land some of his soldiers, but the Saudi forces prevented him. It is said that the Italian foreign ministry announced at that time that Italy would not accept [control over] Yemen being shifted to a non-Yemeni government.[1]

SECOND: The Saudi forces had no experience fighting in mountainous areas, whereas the Yemeni forces were to the contrary: For a long time, they were used to fighting on mountains. Some news agencies broadcast from Cairo that the convoy under the command of Prince Saud had suffered in its

---

1 Ameen al-Sa'eed (Op. Cit.), pp. 378-379.

mountain battles very serious losses.¹ It can be said that Ibn Saud feared his forces would suffer a crushing defeat in the mountain areas the outcome of which will be known only by Allāh.

It is narrated that Ibn Saud confided to someone he trusted about the reason that prompted him to accept the peace treaty saying, "There are many people in my homeland, in other Arab lands and other Muslims who suggested to me with enthusiasm and conviction to continue the military action in Yemen and to annex it to the kingdom in order to establish the United Arab state in the Arabian Peninsula, but I did not listen to these consultations and pieces of advice because when I looked at the shores of the Peninsula in the Arab south, I saw that Britain could have occupied all those areas militarily and imposed its mandate on them. It is obvious that the British government did not leave Yemen alone because it did not desire it; rather, it did that because it knew the Yemenis as well as itself knew Yemen and its nature. It would have been foolish, therefore, for me to carry out a step from which Britain, which is in the peak of its military, political and financial strength, kept its distance, and to expose myself and my fledgling homeland to an adventure which Britain, a great empire, hesitated to undertake due to its seriousness. Moreover, there is a basic difference between my Islamic Arab goals and the British goals."²

This statement explains Ibn Saud's nature in avoiding adventures. He does not make a step except after discerning and waiting, as if he feared he would face the same fate meted to his ancestors when they ventured and expanded in their invasions without a halt, and their fate was being arrested, killed and their kingdom lost.

---

1 *Al-Iraq* newspaper of May 10, 1934.
2 Ahmed Assah, *Muʾjiza Fawq al-Rimal* (A Miracle over the Sands), Beirut: 1986, p. 123.

Chapter Eight: Ibn Saud Suffers From Problems

War's Echo In Iraq

The Shi`ites in Iraq were the most enthusiastic of all people about the Yemen war and the most interested in it, and they hoped it [Yemen] would conquer Hijaz and rebuild the Baqee` graves. It so happened that the month of Muharram coincided with the same time when the war was going on in Yemen, so the mourning chants of the Husaini processions and calls revolved round support for imam Yahya and supplication for his clear victory.

What is noteworthy is that the Iraqi newspapers kept publishing the exciting reports about the victories of the Saudi forces. Some newspapers, following the occupation of Hudaida on May 6, issued special supplements stating that a revolution erupted in Yemen against imam Yahya, and the masses attacked his mansion in Sanaa, so he was forced to forfeit his throne for his son. The newspapers also stated that the Saudi forces occupied Sanaa and Prince Faisal ibn Abdul-Aziz was declared King of Yemen, etc.

The Shi`ites could not relish such reports, so they kept on their side creating opposite reports. Rumors spread among them about the huge size of the Yemeni armies and how they would soon reach Mecca, crush the Saudi armies and wipe them off the face of earth. Some of them sent telegrams to imam Yahya expressing their support for him, so he responded to them via telegrams expressing his appreciation.

The problem of Yemen's war reports came from almost a single source: the Saudi source. Ibn Saud had agents and supporters who spread throughout the Arab lands and in some other lands as well, and these were spreading exaggerated reports about the victories of the Saudi armies. Add to this, the European newspapers found in those reports material that attracted the readers, especially what was relevant to Ibn Saud and the rise of his star and romantic Bedouin character. As for

Yemen's imam, he had adopted a policy of isolation from the world and did not have any admirers or advocates in the world. News agencies, therefore, undertook a biased stance, inclining to Ibn Saud while neglecting imam Yahya. But after the announcement of the peace agreement, they started denying many of the reports which they themselves had published before.

An Attempt to Assassinate Ibn Saud

Ten months after the signing of the peace treaty, an attempt took place in Mecca to assassinate Ibn Saud. It was carried out by three Yemenis. The summary of the incident is that as Ibn Saud was circling the Ka`ba on the first day of Eidul-Adha of 1353 A.H./May 16, 1935 A.D., a Yemeni man came out of Hajar Isma`eel (Ishmael's Rock) raising his dagger and shouting *"Allāhu Akbar!"* A policeman intercepted him, but the Yemeni subdued him, stabbing him with the dagger and killing him. It was then that one of Ibn Saud's slaves aimed his rifle at him and killed him. At the same time, another Yemeni man came out carrying a dagger and approached Ibn Saud, but Prince Saud, who was circling behind his father, shielded the latter with his body, receiving a stab in his lower shoulder area as a result. One of his slaves rushed to his aid and shot one bullet at the Yemeni man from the back which killed him. A third man was lying in ambush at Hajar Isma`eel, so he ran for safety after having seen the fate of his fellows, wherepon a policeman shot him with his rifle and wounded him. He was arrested as he was trying to draw his last breath, dying on the way before reaching a police station.

Many Yemeni pilgrims were in Mecca that year, and there was concern that the Najdis would seek revenge on them, but Ibn Saud issued an order not to bother any of them, warning that a deterring punishment would be meted to anyone who assaulted them. *Umm al-Qura* newspaper issued a special supplement of

Chapter Eight: Ibn Saud Suffers From Problems

which large numbers were printed and distributed among the pilgrims free of charge in order to calm the public's nerves.[1]

There was also in Mecca an Iraqi scout delegation comprised of teachers and students headed by Yousuf Izz ad-Din al-Nasiri. This delegation went with the other delegations to congratulate Ibn Saud on his safety and to greet him on the occasion of the Eid. Abdul-Hadi al-Shammaa, a member of the delegation, recited a poem greeting Ibn Saud in the name of the Iraqi people. Another member, namely Yahya Qaf, delivered a brief speech.

The Iraqi delegation was included in the invitation of all other delegations and VIPs to attend a review of the Saudi army. An incident took place then which almost killed one of the delegation's members. The summary of the incident is that Abdul-Kareem Aseeran, a member of the delegation, tried to take a photograph of Ibn Saud upon his coming to the review when one of Ibn Saud's slaves who was escorting him thought that the camera was a weapon intended to kill his master. He, hence, aimed his rifle at Abdul-Kareem in order to kill him, but Ibn Saud shouted at the slave, [2]حلي! Leave him! Leave him! Abdul-Kareem's life was thus saved.[3]

The public security commissioner undertook the investigation into the assassination attempt. He was an Iraqi man named Mahdi Beg. After an intensive effort for three days, it became clear that the three Yemenis belonged to the Bayt Hadhir village in Yemen. They were: Ali ibn Ali, his brother Salih, and Mabkhoot ibn Mabkhoot. Imam Yahya sent a telegram to Ibn Saud denouncing the incident and describing it as horrible, clearing himself before Allāh from having anything to do with it.[4]

---

1 Nu'man al-Ameen al-Ani, *Fil Mamlaka al-Arabiyya al-Saudia* (In the Kingdom of Saudi Arabia), Baghdad: 1937, p. 78.
2 This is what the Arabic text reads on p. 354, but I really think the typesetter forgot to use the خ instead of the ح, the difference is only the dot, so the word must have been خَلِّي which means "Leave him alone!" – Tr.
3 مجلة «التربية البدنية و الكشافة» *Athletic Education and Scouts* magazine (Baghdad, Iraq), a special issue dated May 15, 1935.
4 Khair ad-Din al-Zurakli (Op. Cit.), Vol. 2, p. 621.

Whispering among the public in Mecca went on saying that Saif al-Islam Ahmed, elder son of imam Yahya, played a role in staging the plot.[1] And surely Allāh knows best!

From Hardship to Prosperity

The year 1930 and those that followed it brought Ibn Saud and the residents of Hijaz in general bad luck. A major economic crisis took place during them that cast its dark shadow on most world countries, so fewer pilgrims went to Hijaz. After the pilgrims in the past years used to average about one hundred thousand, this figure decreased to forty thousand in 1931, to thirty thousand in 1932 and to twenty thousand in 1933.[2] Misery and deprivation prevailed throughout Hijaz, and many of its residents stood at the verge of famine. Wherever the pilgrims went, they were surrounded from all directions by beggars and children running behind them pleading. If a pilgrim threw some food leftovers or fruit peels, the children would attack it due to their acute hunger.

Revenues of the Saudi government declined in 1930 from five million pounds to only two.[3] Saudi minister of finance, Abdullah al-Sulayman, suffered as a result a great deal. He stood between two fires: Ibn Saud's requests which could not be turned away on the one hand, and, on the other, the scarcity of the resources. It is said that he demonstrated a great deal of skill in bypassing that crisis.

The government employees who were paid a little had to bear a good deal of that burden. It was imposed on them to participate in a large loan to the government. A period passed when the government employees were not paid for eight months. Those employees had to involve shop owners in their plight: They were buying from them the necessities of life on credit,

---

1 Nu'man al-Ameen al-Ani (Op. Cit.), pp. 134-135.
2 Monroe, *Philby of Arabia*, London: 1973, p. 178.
3 Khairi Hammad, *Abdullah Philby*, Beirut: 1961, p. 208.

Chapter Eight: Ibn Saud Suffers From Problems

promising they would pay them when they received their salaries.[1]

Philby at the time maintained a strong tie with Ibn Saud. He tells us in his *Memoirs* about the bad psychological mood that took control of Ibn Saud in 1930. He says, "Worry started controlling King Abdul-Aziz, and I started seeing the signs of despair controlling him, weakening his vitality and optimism. One day I was riding the royal car in his company on an afternoon tour we made when he set out to talk about his country's hopes and conditions. He expressed his worry that the weakness of the pilgrimage season the next year would cause an economic catastrophe in the country due to the absence of other resources for it." Philby says that he took the opportunity and said to Ibn Saud, "There is no need to despair provided you are ready to exert an effort instead of relying on the will of Allāh to save you especially since إِنَّ اللَّهَ لاَ يُغَيِّرُ مَا بِقَوْمٍ حَتَّى يُغَيِّرُواْ مَا بِأَنْفُسِهِمْ *Truly Allāh will never change a people's condition until they change it themselves (with their own souls)* **(Qur'an, 13:11).** You sleep on treasures buried in the ground then complain of poverty without trying to do anything to utilize these treasures." Ibn Saud asked him what he meant, so Philby answered, "I mean your country is full of buried treasures: oil and gold, and you are unable to utilize them in person or, at the same time, allow others to utilize them on your behalf." Ibn Saud, with signs of exhaustion showing on his face, said, "Listen, Philby, if I can find someone who pays me one million pounds right now, I would grant him all the concessions he wants in my country." Philby then said to him, "These concessions are worth a lot more than this amount. If you really mean what you say, I know a man who can help you. He came to visit you several years ago but you refused to meet him. This man is now present in Cairo. If you set the date when you will be in Jidda, I can send him a telegram, and I can

---

1 Abdullah Philby (Op. Cit), p. 369.

guarantee for you that he would come [to meet you]. He is ready to sacrifice one of his eyes for meeting you."[1]

The man to whom Philby referred was the wealthy American, Mr. Crane, who headed the referendum committee in Syria in 1920, as we stated in the third chapter [of this book]. Ibn Saud wrote him inviting him to visit him in Jidda. The man came in May of 1931 and pledged to Ibn Saud that he would invite, at his own expense, the famous geological engineer, Karl Twitchell, to discuss the country's mineral resources.

Mr. Crane fulfilled his promise. Engineer Twitchell reached Jidda in the summer of 1931 and toured throughout the Saudi kingdom in search of riches buried in its land. In the spring of 1932, he submitted to Ibn Saud a report in which he stated that there are signs about the presence of oil in the Dhahran area near the Arab Gulf.

Following the submission of that report, there was a competition over getting the concession for drilling for oil in the Saudi lands between two companies, an American company and a British one. On May 29, 1933, an agreement was signed in Jidda by [attorney] Mr. [Lloyd] Hamilton [on behalf of SOCAL, Standard Oil of California] and Sheikh Abdullah al-Sulayman, representative of the Saudi government.

The American company started exploring for oil in the area which Twitchell determined, but it did not find anything. The company kept searching for four years but to no avail, so much so that it lost hope and almost packed its luggage and returned home empty-handed. On March 3, 1938, as the company engineers were making their last attempt, torn between despair and hope, oil gushed forth before them in a way that stirred their amazement and great elation.[2]

---

1   Khairi Hammad (Op. Cit.), pp. 208-209.
2   Howarth (Op. Cit.), p. 195.

Chapter Eight: Ibn Saud Suffers From Problems

Oil production in Saudi Arabia kept increasing year after year, and this kingdom changed from a poor country to one of the richest in the world. It is now the top exporter of oil in the world and the third producer after the Soviet Union and the United States of America, and it now occupies the first rank in the world in as far as the quantity of its oil reserves which is estimated at about twenty billion tons.

His Wives and Children

Ibn Saud married [and divorced] to a degree the like of which is rare in our time. He used to get married then divorce time and over again, so long as the number of his wives did not exceed four, the maximum allowed by the Islamic Shari`a. He always kept three wives so he would be able to marry a fourth if needed. A Briton asked him in 1917 about the total number of his wives, including those whom he had divorced, so he answered saying that they were one hundred and "I will marry more *Insha-Allāh*", he added.[1] He is known to marry and divorce several times per year, but he decided in 1930 not to marry more than two new wives per year.[2]

Many marriages lead of course to many offspring. Tawfiq al-Suweedi narrates in his *Memoirs* saying that when he met Ibn Saud in Jidda in 1928 accompanied by Sir Gilbert Clayton, the latter asked Ibn Saud about the number of his male offspring, whereupon Ibn Saud said that they were eighteen. Here, his brother, Muhammed, who was with him, objected saying, "O one protected by Allāh, they are more, and there is a blessing in them." Ibn Saud then took his rosary beads and kept counting the number of his sons with it, and it became obvious that they were twenty-one. Those present laughed, and Ibn Saud laughed with them.[3]

---

1 Armstrong (Op. Cit.), p. 137.
2 Monroe (Op. Cit.), p. 171.
3 Tawfiq al-Suweedi, *Muthakkarati* (My Memoirs), Beirut: 1969, p. 127.

Story of the Sharifs and Ibn Saud

The number of his male offspring finally became forty-five. Ten of them died and thirty-five survived. As for his daughters, we do not know anything about their number. The last son of Ibn Saud was born in 1947 when he himself was seventy-one years old. It is said that the number of his sons and grandsons, including the girls, reached at the time of his death more than three hundred.[1]

It is worth mentioning that Ibn Saud was not the only one who loved to have many offspring. Some of his sons, brothers and cousins were like him; therefore, the number of the Saudi family amazingly increased, so much so that it is said that the princes and princesses from the Al Saud reached about five thousand.

This large number of princes became a social phenomenon that had its significant impact on Saudi Arabia. They became a distinctive class living above the law. The members of this class, as a result of the flow of oil, acquired a huge wealth which is almost uncountable. We do not need to say that these two factors—class distinction and plenty of money—had to naturally lead to lavish luxury and the immersing into pleasures without limit.

British author [David Armine] Howarth has given us in his book titled *The Desert King: A Life of Ibn Saud* an amazing portrait which is hard to believe about the luxury and extravagance with which the Saudi princes are afflicted. He states that Ibn Saud knew very little about what his sons were doing. If he heard something about it, he would be angry, and he may hit them with the stick; therefore, in his last day, he used to feel deeply miserable.[2]

Philby says in this regard the following:

---

1 Khair ad-Din al-Zurakli (Op. Cit.), Vol. 3, pp. 957, 1002; Vol. 4, p. 1400.
2 Howarth (Op. Cit.), pp. 212-229.

Chapter Eight: Ibn Saud Suffers From Problems

"The problem which the King—meaning Ibn Saud—faced was this inflation that happened to the royal family, which formed a special class all by itself. Security men had oral orders not to bother the princes or do anything wrong to them for fear reports about them would spread among the public... As for the other problem, the results of which kept increasing as time passed by, was the King immersing himself in his generosity and outgiving. He is generous and is known to be so since his first days... But with the increase in money and resources, and with their expected growth in the future, the King's generosity started exceeding all limits of wisdom and logic, sowing the seeds of corruption in his path. The first to benefit from this generosity were definitely the harem's women and princes followed by the men of the palace, the entourage and government officials. The desire of these folks intensified for getting money whenever the King increased his outpouring of gifts and those gifts reached a limit which no other country has come to know in modern times. But the King himself did not change his simple way of life. His clothes remained as they used to be, and he maintained his love for producing children up to the last moment of his life, and the last of his sons was born in 1947."[1]

The Saudi princes feared their father during his lifetime; therefore, they were discreet in whatever they did as much as they could. So, when their father died in 1953, they set out in pleasures to devour as they desired. With his death, the deterrent which they feared or of which they felt shy was now gone.

People in the kingdom of Saudi Arabia tell each other stunning tales about the extent of immersing in the desires with which the princes were afflicted following their father's death. Perhaps there is in these tales some exaggeration or embellishment, as is the habit of story tellers in such matters, yet they anyhow may not be without the truth, much or little. To be

---

[1] Khairi Hammad (Op. Cit.), p. 237.

immersed in desires is normal in mankind when the deterrent is absent, and very few rare people are the exception to this rule.

Philby

We have, in the conclusion of this chapter, to shed some light on the life of Philby, the man whose life was strongly connected to Ibn Saud. Actually, this man lived as a stranger and died as a stranger, and many individuals have regarded him as a riddle.

Philby was born in the Ceylon Island in 1885 to British parents. In his *Memoirs*, Philby narrates a strange incident which took place in his childhood. Here is its summary: He was lost by his mother when he was an infant. After looking for him, they found a gypsy woman carrying two infants of the same age, and they both were amazingly alike; he was one of them, so they took him from the gypsy. In his *Memoirs*, Philby wonders if they actually took the son of that gypsy woman!

In 1904, Philby [photo to the right→] joined Cambridge University and kept going in his university life in the direction of socialism and intellectual freedom. When he graduated from the university in 1907, he joined the service of the Indian

Chapter Eight: Ibn Saud Suffers From Problems

government. In 1910, he married a British lady named Dora. In 1915, he joined the British campaign in Iraq and worked in Basra, Imara and Baghdad where he learned Arabic.

In 1917, Philby travelled in the company of a political delegation to Riyadh which he reached on November 30 and met Ibn Saud then crossed the desert wearing Arabian clothes for Jidda which he reached on December 31, and it was there that he met [then King] al-Husain. His trip had a strong impact on his life; he felt sympathy towards Ibn Saud and loved the desert and penetrating its mysteries.

Upon Philby's return to Iraq, he was instructed to travel to Riyadh again, so he met Ibn Saud for the second time. Ibn Saud was very glad to see him, or he pretended to be so. Philby seized the opportunity to tour the southern deserts to discover their mysteries accompanied by twenty men as his guards who were provided for him by Ibn Saud. Then Philby returned to Iraq.

Late in 1918, Philby was given a vacation to spend in his homeland, so he reached England after a long absence of more than ten years. After the end of his vacation, he carried out some tasks which his government commissioned him to undertake. In August of 1920, he was ordered to return to Iraq accompanied by High Commissioner Sir Percy Cox, but he could not stay in Iraq for long because he differed with Cox about the policy which the latter followed in Iraq. Philby used to advocate the establishment of a republican system, whereas Cox was ordered to install Faisal as King. Cox had finally to transfer Philby to the Trans-Jordan.[1]

Philby spent two years and a half in his job in Trans-Jordan where he disputed with Sir Herbert Samuel, the High Commissioner in Palestine, just as he had disputed with Sir Percy Cox, so he resigned. He wrote a friend of his stating the reason behind his resignation saying, "I have resigned from this job for many reasons at the top of which is that I cannot continue

---

1   Refer to the details in chapter two, Volume Six of these series.

to work with the present High Commissioner who is a Zionist Jew and who cannot maintain a balance between the Zionist interests and the Arab ones. Moreover, [King] Abdullah betrayed me due to his extravagance to the extent that led to the interference of the British government, and this means the interference of the Zionist influence; therefore, I got out."[1]

In April of 1924, Philby was given a long vacation as a prelude for the resignation, so he left Amman on the 17th of the month. After touring Turkey, he went to England. On October 28, he reached Jidda to mediate the peace between King Ali and Ibn Saud, as we stated in the fifth chapter.

After Ibn Saud's takeover of Jidda, Philby returned to it and opened a commercial shop in it. He obtained a Ford auto agency and imported thousands of surveying and engineering tools in addition to oil-operated fans. At the same time, Philby became an adviser and a friend of Ibn Saud and the latter trusted him and listened to his advice.

The confidential reports written by the British consul in Jidda to his government during that period proves that Philby was demonstrating a noticeable activity in spreading the propaganda against Britain and in hindering its interests. In one of his reports, the consul says, "Philby upholds with complete stubbornness his dualistic faith in which Britain represents the god of darkness."[2] In another report, he says, "I think that the presence of Philby in Jidda will not lead to improving the relations between Britain and Ibn Saud."[3] In a third report, he says, "The activity of Mr. Philby continues. It seems he does not miss a chance to create difficulties for the government of His British Majesty. I do not know what his purpose is: Is it to flatter the officials here in order to get some certain concessions, or is

---

1 Monroe (Op. Cit.), p. 132.
2 Public Records Office, London, FO 371/10807.
3 Public Records Office, London, FO 371/11431.

it due to his being a formerly grumbling government official who wants to seek revenge against his government...?"[1]

In August of 1930, Philby declared his embracing the religion of Islam and called himself "Abdullah". Statements have varied regarding the reason that prompted him to do so. Some say that Jidda's weather did not suit Philby, and he would faint in it during the summer, so he wanted to move from it to other Saudi cities. He also was ambitious to achieve his greatest goal: to be the first man to penetrate the Empty Quarter area, and he found out that his embracing Islam would facilitate that for him.[2] There are those who say that the reason why Philby embraced Islam was his love for women, especially young ones, and he found in Islam an easy way to marry them as he liked.

As for Philby himself, he calls all these statements lies, indicating that he embraced Islam out of conviction and sincerity, and he pointed this out in his *Memoirs* where he says the following:

"Islam attracted me since my early days in India where I was influenced by its simplicity in dealing with the facts and philosophy of the eternal life. I stopped for some time back from being a Christian and became a philosopher looking forward to life in a deeply philosophical outlook without having religious beliefs or sentiments despite my admission that religion makes for most people an indispensable necessity. Despite that, it seemed to me that Islam in India became surrounded with rituals and appearances that are foreign to it, and they are rituals and appearances which no man can accept except after a precise discerning. When I moved to Iraq, I found its Sunni sect clinging too much to formalities and appearances in performing the religious obligations, whereas I found it difficult to believe in the Shi`ite theory which is based on Imams and *walis*. When I went to Saudi Arabia, I came in contact in what seemed to me to be

---

1 Public Records Office, London, FO 371/11442.
2 Howarth (Op. Cit.), p. 179.

the simple idea of Islam deriving its inspiration from the Holy Qur'an and the Sunnah of the greatest Prophet and distances itself from the entangled and complex religious theories and beliefs. It seemed to me that the Wahhabi sect is the exemplary religion, and I did not find in the extremism of its followers what makes me feel bad or turns me off it. I saw that their sect agrees with the needs of the human life and society in their simplest forms. I believed that Islam in such a way is what man can accept well, and I sincerely believe in it as directing life and conduct, and that its religious criteria are in harmony with the basic human needs, more so than any other religion. If there is some roughness in it, it on the other hand rejects any artificiality and deception. It also sees in polygamy the best way to prevent prostitution along the path of the Ten Commandments."[1]

No matter what the case was, Philby became an exciting expert in the Arab and Islamic lands, and most people in the Arab lands thought that his Islam is artificial for the purpose of espionage or insinuation. Sir Percy Cox wrote him saying that he made a bad "move". He was also criticized by Sir Arnold Wilson in the "Baghdad Times" newspaper. As for his wife, Dora, who was then in England, she was disturbed by his acceptance of Islam for fear he would marry another woman besides her, but she pretended before people as having accepted it and said to them, "I think you know that I am now Mrs. Abdullah."[2]

It is worth mentioning that what Dora feared had actually taken place. Shortly after Philby's acceptance of Islam, he was sitting at Ibn Saud's meeting place, so Ibn Saud talked about his resolve not to marry more than two new wives per year. Philby remonstrated with him saying, "Do not forget that I have had only one single wife all my life." Ibn Saud responded to him saying, "Having accepted Islam, you now have a greater freedom in this regard." Following this, Ibn Saud gave Philby a small

---

1 Khairi Hammad (Op. Cit.), pp. 253-254.
2 Monroe (Op. Cit.), p. 169.

Chapter Eight: Ibn Saud Suffers From Problems

concubine named Maryam daughter of Abdullah al-Hassan. Philby wrote his wife Dora describing that concubine saying, "She is not beautiful but she is young and sweet enough."[1]

Philby went during World War II through a very rough period. His government accused him of inclining towards Nazi Germany. When he went to India, it arrested him and transported him to Britain where he stayed during the war. Philby claims that Nouri al-Sa`eed is the one who slandered him to the British government.[2] When Philby returned to the Saudi kingdom after his release, Ibn Saud gifted him a new concubine of a Baluchi [Afghani] or Persian origin named Rosie Al Abdul-Aziz. This sixteen-year old concubine was slim and short, but she was beautiful.[3] As regarding his first concubine, we do not know how fate treated her, and Philby may have freed her or gave her as a gift, and surely Allāh knows best!

Philby had two modest houses given to him as a gift by Ibn Saud. One of them was in Riyadh and the other in Mecca. Philby kept residing once in Riyadh and once in Mecca. His new concubine gave birth to four sons two of whom died and the other two survived; they were Khalid and Faris. Philby was keen about giving those sons an Islamic Arab upbringing.

Ameen al-Mumayyaz tells us that he visited Philby on December 24, 1954 at his Mecca house, and it was in the neighborhood of the Haram. He found the house to be simple, comprised of one story, and its reception room furnished with the simplest furniture. His small sons, Khalid and Faris, came to him, so Philby asked Khalid to go to his mother and ask her to come to greet the guest. Khalid went to his mother then returned disappointed. He said in a Najdi accent, ما تَبغي تَجي *ma tabghi taji* "She does not want to come." Al-Mumayyaz says that he accompanied Philby to pray at the Haram and saw him perform

---

1 *Ibid.*, p. 171.
2 Ameen al-Mumayyaz (Op. Cit.), p. 277.
3 Monroe (Op. Cit.), p. 244.

the prayers with full solemnity and recite supplications and verses of the Qur'an from the depths of his heart. Al-Mumayyaz comments about that saying, "He, and I testify truly, is a believing Muslim in the full sense of the word."[1]

Philby's relationship with Ibn Saud remained good up to the end. When Ibn Saud died, his relationship with his son, later King Saud, started to worsen gradually. The reason is that Philby started criticizing the luxury and moral degradation that prevailed throughout the kingdom in the new era. He wrote some articles about that in foreign newspapers, causing King Saud and his entourage to be angry with him. Late in April of 1955, Philby left the country.

The Saudi government stated to the British attaché in Jidda the reasons that prompted it to get Philby out of the country as follows:

(1) He propagated Communism in the Saudi kingdom; (2) He was an agent of Zionism and an advocate for the Jews; (3) He persisted in writing what demeaned the status of King Saud compared to that of his father; (4) He continued to publish articles in foreign newspapers criticizing the Saudi kingdom and its policy; and (5) He recently delivered a series of lectures to the employees of the Aramco [Arab-American Oil Co.] Company in al-Dhahran which include defaming the kingdom and its personalities.[2]

Following his banishment, Philby lived in a house in the Lebanese village of Ajaltoun and recalled to him from Riyadh his new wife and sons, Khalid and Faris. On September 7, 1955, the wife and both sons reached Beirut Airport. Philby asked her to remove the veil from her face immediately[3], so she obeyed his order against her wish.

---

1 Ameen al-Mumayyaz (Op. Cit.), p. 276.
2 *Ibid.*, pp. 332-333.
3 Monroe (Op. Cit.), p. 284.

Chapter Eight: Ibn Saud Suffers From Problems

Expelling Philby from the Saudi kingdom became an axis for bad publicity against it, and some British newspapers started publishing articles about the immorality and extravagance going on in the Saudi kingdom. The Baghdad Radio station participated in this campaign. This led to a great tension in the relationship between Iraq and the Saudi kingdom. King Saud had finally to reconcile with Philby and to permit him to return to Riyadh.

In the morning of September 30, 1960, when Philby was in Beirut on a casual visit, he had a low heart pressure attack, so he was taken to the American University's Hospital. At sunset that day, Philby breathed his last. The last word he pronounced was أنا سَئِمْت "I am fed-up". In the afternoon of the next day, his body was moved to the Bashura Islamic Cemetery in the Basta quarter. Only ten persons witnessed his funeral, including his oldest son, Kim. Kim ordered this phrase to be engraved on his father's tombstone: "The greatest explorers of the Arabs' Peninsula."[1]

No matter how views about Philby and his goals in life vary, there is a consensus among the researchers that he was honest, rising above loving this world. He could have earned millions from Ibn Saud or from his son, Saud, as many people did, but he died owning nothing of the wares of this life save little. Actually, he is better than those who accumulated millions, for they left them for others to enjoy while they themselves had to bear their burdens.

---

1 *Ibid.*, p. 295.

Conclusion

History Lessons

When the first volumes of this book series was published, some critics started criticizing me for being a historian while neglecting the social aspect of history. The problem of these critics is that they understand the science of sociology in a limited or wrong way from some aspects. The fact, which I would like these critics to know, is that there is no serious separator between history and sociology. Both matters are interrelated; they are two faces of the same coin.

Almost a quarter of a century ago, some sociologists were treading in their studies the path which these critics want: If they wanted to study a society, they would focus on its present without being interested in studying its past. This method became common in the United States to a great extent. The scholars wanted to make sociology a science like any other natural science; therefore, they kept relying in their study on the method of statistics and questionnaires and the like. It became clear to many of them lately that their method is faulty and may not enable them to reach a viable result. Here, I would like to quote a statement in this regard by a famous American scientist of sociology, namely Robert A. Nisbet [1913 – 1996] which he stated in a book[1] by him published in 1970 where he said:

"The gap between the science of sociology and history started in late years to shrink continuously, and it is the gap that used to exist for a long time especially in the United States of America.

---

[1] The title of the book to which the author, al-Wardi, refers here is *The Social Bond: An Introduction to the Study of Society*. A second edition of it was published in New York in 1977 by Alfred A. Knopf, its original Publisher, in 321 pages, and it was reviewed by Jeffers Chertok of the Eastern Washington University. The original form of the book was submitted by the University of Michigan in 1970 in 425 pages. – Tr.

In the last ten or twenty years, historians started gradually to derive benefits from concepts of the science of sociology. Also, sociologists started benefitting from the historic information... The greatest benefit reaped by the sociologists from history is in the subject of social change..."[1]

Between the Past and the Present

Actually, the social researcher who tours the pages of history may derive from them lessons that are no less important than those which he drives from touring the areas of the society. In other words, the action of the researcher who tours time is no less beneficial than that who tours places. Both provide the necessary information for understanding the human society and nature.

Take, for example, the movement of the *ikhwan* which gained momentum in Najd after World War I and which we have studied with some detail in past chapters. This movement may provide us with social lessons that are no less valuable than those which we derive from a study of a contemporary social phenomenon.

When the reader sees the excessive fanaticism of the *ikhwan*, such as their prohibition of the use of telephone, telegraph, the bicycle or the plane, he may be overcome by amazement, for he cannot imagine how the human mind can sink to this amazingly low level. The reader does not know that his mind is not different from the mind of the *ikhwan* in anything, for both are of the same nature, but the circumstances in which the mind emerges are the ones that make it think this way or that. Had the reader been born in such a social environment in which the *ikhwan* emerged, he would have been like them in its thinking and conduct, and we may have seen him carrying the sword to kill the likes of the writer of these lines!

---

[1] Robert Nisbet, *The Social Bond*, New York: 1970, pp. 344-345.

Conclusion: History Lessons

I was contemporary in my youthful age to people in Iraq who used to prohibit reading newspapers, going to school and learning English, wearing a hat, shaving the beard and using a spoon to eat. In 1924, a book was published in Najaf by a theologian, namely Sheikh Abdullah al-Mamqani, titled السَيف البَتّار على مَن يَقول انَّ الغيم من البُخار *The Cutting Sword in Rebutting Whoever Says that Clouds are Made of Vapor*. And I witnessed during that period a man from among the commoners assaulting another because he heard him say that rain resulted from vapor. The reader may be surprised when he comes to know that five books published in Iraq dealt with the subject of prohibiting the shaving of the beard; they were:

1. ارشاد أهل الحِجى في حُرمَة حَلْق اللِحى *Guiding People of Wisdom to the Prohibition of Shaving Beards* by Hibat ad-Din al-Shahristani,
2. تحريم حَلق اللحية *Prohibiting the Shaving of the Beard* by Qasim al-Jaleeli,
3. التفتيش في حَلق الريش *Looking into Shaving the Feathers* by Hassan al-Sadr
4. زِينَة الرجال – رسالة في اثبات حُرمَة حَلْق اللِّحْيَة *The Ornament of Men – a Dissertation in the Prohibition of Beard Shaving* by Muhammed Husain al-Adeeb.

There may be other books which we do not know of that discuss this subject.

We must not blame these men for what they said or did, for they were only the product of their environment and circumstances. Whoever studies the history of the European nations will find out that they did not differ from us when their circumstances were similar to those of ours.

The human brain is subject in its thinking to the clichés which the social environment pours into them. If a man grew up in an environment filled with superstitions and kept living in it, not knowing anything else, we will find him believing emphatically that those superstitions are clearly facts, and he is surprised when he finds us disagreeing with his beliefs, and he may bear grudge against us and harbor ill intentions.

I saw once a man who was zealous a great deal about his faith in which he grew up, so I asked him if he had been raised in the such-and-such town, which varies in its beliefs than his, will he have the same enthusiasm towards those beliefs? He answered: "Yes, certainly, because what is right is as clear as the sun!" He does not know that had he been raised in that other town, he would have found the truth to be clear in the other side.

The Human Nature:

When I study events of history, I feel as if I look at events that take place in our days. I do not deny that there are many differences between the events of the past and those of the present, but we must not forget that these differences are superficial. As for the essence, it is the same, unchangeable, and I mean by "it" this rational animal called "mankind".

Man may change a great deal in his habits and clothes, values and beliefs, according to the change of time and place, but he in the essence of his nature did not change, remaining as he is: the same fanatical animal whom we have come to know since time immemorial. Most likely, he will remain to be so for as long as the Almighty wants.

Philosophers have agreed that the most important difference between man and animal is reason, but they have differed in defining the essence of this reason and in determining its scopes. Ancient philosophers used to believe that the human mind is capable of fully realizing the truth if he gets rid of fanaticism, egotism, emotion and other obstacles that stand in the way of sound thinking. And they used to imagine that getting rid of these obstacles is easy, and it can be done by anyone if he wants.

It was said to those philosophers: If one can get rid of the obstacles in the way of sound thinking, as you claim, why, then, did you yourselves *not* get rid of them?! We see you differing among yourselves and disputing just as the commoners differ and dispute. This means that your minds in the basis of their nature do not differ much from those of the commoners.

Modern scientific studies have proven that the human mind is biased and limited by nature, and that the obstacles in the way of sound thinking, such as fanaticism, egotism and emotion, are not coinci-dental but are innate, motivating him.

Man is capable of being fair and objective in judging a matter, if that matter is outside the scope of his social fanaticism, personal interest or emotion. When the matter hardly enters the scope of these motives, all or some of them, we find fairness and objectivity disappearing from man's mind. It is then that he becomes a human like other humans: unfair while thinking that he is fair.

Modern man has been able to go to the moon. At the same time, it has remained just as his ancestors have for thousands of years been waging wars, committing horrible things, practicing racial and sectarian discrimination. So, while he has scored a great progress from one aspect, he is from the other aspect has remained where he has always been.

We saw the Najdi *ikhwan* committing horrible abominations while they think that they are treading the path of the Sunnah of Allāh and His Messenger, so we regarded that as barbarism contradicting civilization. Then World War II came, and it is then that we saw some civilized people being no less barbaric than the *ikhwan*, and they may have exceeded them from some aspects. What they did at detention camps, gas chambers, mass genocides, suffices to be denounced even by the *ikhwan*. We must not forget that the *ikhwan* were granting an opportunity to those who fall in their hands to repent from their apostasy and seek Allāh's forgiveness for it. They, despite that, forgive him, kiss him and congratulate him for accepting *iman*, conviction.

As for the civilized folks, they never accepted the repentance or the seeking of Allāh's forgiveness!

Man, generally speaking, is good-natured: He smiles at you when you are in harmony with his motives which we indicated. As soon as he sees you opposing him in their regard or competing with them, his smile turns into a show of fangs; so, woe unto you when Allāh grants you power over you!

We notice in this human child, since his early years, how he is very nice with you because he finds himself weak towards you, and he expects from you some benefit and care. But as soon as he notices a child who is weaker than him and who is playing with a toy, he rushes to attack him, slapping him on his face and extracting the toy from him by force, then he leaves him to weep without feeling any pity for him!

***

I apologize to the reader for repeating these statements in my books time and over again, for they, in my viewpoint, contain a major fact which we must absorb in order to understand the events of history and the phenomena of the society.

What I wanted to say in this conclusion is that life has gone, and is still going, according to one pace which never changes. Anyone who wants to succeed in it ought to understand it as it is in reality, not as it should be.

www.ingramcontent.com/pod-product-compliance
Lightning Source LLC
Chambersburg PA
CBHW030252100526
44590CB00012B/372